UNITED STATES DIRECT TAX OF 1798

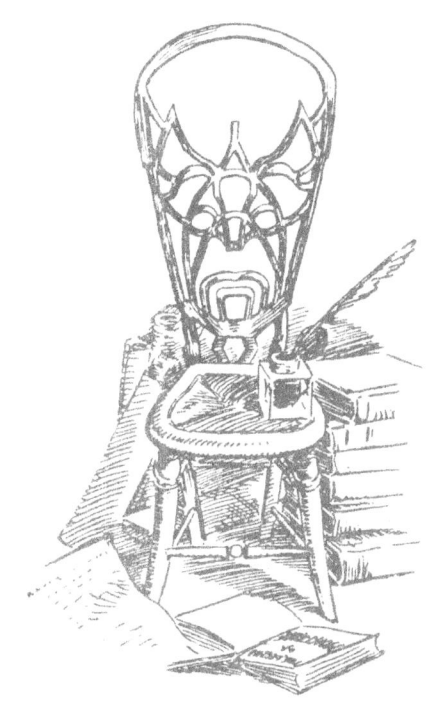

Tax Lists for Cumberland County Pennsylvania

Wilbur J. McElwain

HERITAGE BOOKS
2010

HERITAGE BOOKS
AN IMPRINT OF HERITAGE BOOKS, INC.

Books, CDs, and more—Worldwide

For our listing of thousands of titles see our website
at
www.HeritageBooks.com

Published 2010 by
HERITAGE BOOKS, INC.
Publishing Division
100 Railroad Ave. #104
Westminster, Maryland 21157

Copyright © 1994 Wilbur J. McElwain

Other Heritage Books by the author:
A Documentary and Genealogical History of the Family of Andrew McElwain and Mary Mickey of Cumberland County, Pennsylvania
Cumberland County, Pennsylvania Cemetery Records Collected by Jeremiah Zeamer
Genealogical Data Abstracted from History of Middle Spring Presbyterian Church, Middle Spring, Pennsylvania, 1738–1900
United States Direct Tax of 1798: Tax Lists for Cumberland County, Pennsylvania
United States Direct Tax of 1798: Tax Lists for the City of Philadelphia, Pennsylvania:
United States Direct Tax of 1798: Tax Lists for the City of Philadelphia, Pennsylvania: New Market Ward
United States Direct Tax of 1798: Tax Lists for Washington County, Pennsylvania
Upper Delaware, Lower Delaware, High Street, Chestnut Street, Walnut and Dock Wards

All rights reserved. No part of this book may be reproduced or transmitted in any form or by any means, electronic or mechanical, including photocopying, recording or by any information storage and retrieval system without written permission from the author, except for the inclusion of brief quotations in a review.

International Standard Book Numbers
Paperbound: 978-0-7884-0118-3
Clothbound: 978-0-7884-8437-7

TABLE OF CONTENTS

THE UNITED STATES DIRECT TAX of 1798

TAX LISTS FOR CUMBERLAND COUNTY, PENNSYLVANIA

Introduction v

Chapter 1 Allen Township 1

Chapter 2 Carlisle Borough 18

Chapter 3 Dickinson Township 49

Chapter 4 East Pennsboro Township 63

Chapter 5 Frankford Township 82

Chapter 6 Hopewell Township 95

Chapter 7 Middleton Township 105

Chapter 8 Mifflin Township 131

Chapter 9 Newton Township 145

Chapter 10 Southampton Township & Shippensburg . . . 163

Chapter 11 West Pennsboro Township 189

Appendix 201

    Introduction to the Microfilm Publication

    Circular of the Secretary of the Treasury,
        September 8, 1798

    Sample pages from the Lists

Indexes 214

Introduction

INTRODUCTION

GEOGRAPHICAL AREA COVERED BY THIS VOLUME

The tax rolls summarized in this compilation cover the area of present-day Cumberland County. In 1798 Cumberland County included what is now Perry County; the townships which later became Perry County are omitted.

Apart from the omitted area, Cumberland County, for the purpose of the assessment, was divided into eleven subdivisions--ten townships and one independent borough. Several of the townships have since been divided. The former and present townships are shown in the accompanying table, as are the abbreviations used in this compilation. (The original volume for Southampton was entitled "Southhampton and Shippensburg"; here the name has been shortened to "Southampton".)

In 1798 rolls	Present-day townships	Abbreviation
Allen	Upper Allen, Lower Allen, Monroe	ALLN
Carlisle	Carlisle	CARL
Dickinson	Dickinson, Penn, Cooke	DICK
East Pennsboro	East Pennsboro, Hampden, Silver Spring	EPEN
Frankfort	Upper Frankfort, Lower Frankfort	FRAN
Hopewell	Hopewell	HOPE
Middleton	North Middleton, South Middleton, Middlesex	MIDD
Mifflin	Upper Mifflin, Lower Mifflin	MIFF
Newton	North Newton, South Newton	NEWT
Southhampton	Southhampton	SHTN
West Pennsboro	West Pennsboro	WPEN

The rolls for Cumberland County are fairly complete. Six are entirely and one partially missing, but, fortunately, no more than one is missing from any single subdivision. This means that all the information is present, though some of it is in abbreviated format because it is extant only on List D or List E (Lists 1 or 2 in the original document). The most serious loss of information occurs in East Pennsboro township. For that township List B is missing and List E is extant only for surnames beginning with the letters A through K. Thus, for persons whose surnames occur in the latter part of the alphabet, information is completly lacking on land, houses of value of $100.00 or less, and various other structures.

Introduction

The following table summarizes the present status of the rolls and the number of entries in each roll. The designation outside parenthesis is the original designation; that inside the parenthesis is the designation used in this volume.

Township	A (A)	B (B)	1 (D)	2 (E)
Allen	165	166	194	175
Carlisle	263	111	263	missing
Dickinson	95	missing	95	136
East Pennsboro	250	missing	250	extant only through K
Frankford	82	122	82	122
Hopewell	57	85	57	85
Middleton	281	missing	278	225
Mifflin	101	131	101	131
Newton	115	146	115	146
Southampton	missing	145	199	145
West Pennsboro	112	missing	112	121

HISTORY AND OPERATION OF THE 1798 DIRECT TAX

The Direct Tax of 1798 was a tax on the ownership of dwelling houses, lands, and slaves. It was enacted on July 14, 1798, during the presidential term of John Adams, primarily for the purpose of increasing the armed forces during a time of tension with France over attacks on American shipping.

The Act was intended to raise the sum of $2,000,000. This sum was to be collected primarily from a tax on the assessed value of dwelling houses. To the amount to be collected from that portion of the tax there was to be added the amount collected from a tax of fifty cents upon every slave between the ages of twelve and fifty. The total to be collected from these sources was then to be deducted from the total of $2,000,000, and the balance was to be collected from a tax, at an appropriate rate, on land. Because the Constitution at that time required that taxes be apportioned according to population, an appropriate amount was assigned to be collected from each state. Pennsylvania's share was $237,177.72.

The plan of the tax on dwellings was remarkable for its time in that the rates applied to the assessed value were progressive, in the manner of modern income taxes. The tax was payable only on dwellings of a value greater than $100.00; above that level the rates varied from .002 to .010. Another remarkable characteristic of the tax is that the rate, in contrast to our modern income tax, applieD to the entire assessment, not merely to the marginal amount.

Introduction

The schedule was made up of nine categories, and these rates applied equally to all houses, whether urban or rural. The table is reproduced below.

Lower class limit	Rate on entire value
$ 100.00	.002
500.00	.003
1,000.00	.004
3,000.00	.005
6,000.00	.006
10,000.00	.007
15,000.00	.008
20,000.00	.009
30,000.00	.010

Under this schedule a house assessed at $100 was taxed $.20 (.2%); a house assessed at $1000 was taxed $4.00 (.4%). Thus the house worth ten time the other was taxed twenty times more. The following table illustrates these variations. The Index columns compare relative valuations and taxes for several sample assessments to those for a dwelling assessed at the minimum taxable amount.

Actual			Index	
Valuation	Rate	Tax	Valuation	Tax
100	.002	$ .20	1	1.0
500	.003	1.50	5	7.5
1,000	.004	4.00	10	20.0
10,000	.007	70.00	100	350.0
25,000	.009	225.00	250	1,125.0

The modern progressive income tax pales in comparison with this degree of progression.

ORGANIZATION OF THE TAX LISTS

To put the Direct Tax into operation it was necessary to compile a list of every piece of property within the country. This was done by state and township and the results were recorded in two "Particular Lists" (A and B). These lists, in turn, were used to produce two "General Lists" D and E (so called in the Circular from the Secretary of the Treasury, but designated 1 and 2 in the original Cumberland County lists), which summarize the predecessor tables.

In this volume the lists are called A, B, D, and E, instead of A, B, 1, and 2. The purpose of this change is to make the terminology here agree with that used in the Circular of the Secretary of the Treasury.

Introduction

FORMAT OF THIS VOLUME

It is the intention of this volume to present the information found in the four tables in one comprehensive set. To do so presents some difficulties.

Table A and Table 1 contain the same information, a list of houses of a value greater than $100.00, together with the land appertaining to the house, and certain structures directly related to the dwelling (additions, kitchens, spring houses, etc.). Table B and Table 2 are devoted to land other than the house lot, houses of a value of $100.00 or less, and other structures, usually those not pertaining directly to the dwelling house (particularly barns, but also commercial structures). Tables 1 and 2 are derived, respectively, from Tables A and B and therefore provide no independent authority; they do however provide a great deal of assistance in those instances where Tables A or B are missing, and where individual entries are missing or undecipherable. The use of all four tables also provides some check against copying errors.

To construct a single entry giving a description of an entire property which contains a dwelling valued at more than $100.00 it is necessary to combine the information in Table A with that in Table B. Unfortunately, there is no certain reference to connect the two sets of information. Although the entries are usually numbered, the numbers in Table A are not necessarily related to those in Table B. The obvious connection is the name of the owner, and this makes a definite connection when there is but one person with a particular name within the township, and when that person owns but one piece of property. When these conditions do not obtain, other clues must be used.

It must be remembered that when the same name appears for two entries in the same table, it is not possible to determine, without additional information, whether this is one person with two pieces of property or two different persons. The task is sometimes simplified if one or more of the properties has an occupant other than the owner, since the occupants name will ordinarily appear in both sets of tables. Another possible clue is the sequence of the entries: if, for example, Table A has the same owner for two consecutive entries and the same name appears in two consecutive entries in Table B, it is probable (though by no means certain) that the first entries in each table relate to the same property, and the second to another property.

The reason for presenting such, admittedly tedious, detail, is to alert the user to the fact that it is possible, and even probable, that some entries have been combined incorrectly. Every effort has been made to avoid such misconjunctions by a most careful consideration of each combination. This care has been extended in some cases to keeping entries separate; in these few cases the reader will be obliged to make judgements for himself.

CONTENTS OF THE TABLES

This work is intended to consolidate within a single entry all of the information in the original four lists for each separate piece of property. The headings provided show the nature of the information, some of which is indicated by position, as is shown in the sample below.

Owner, location, occupant, and adjoining landowner appear in the first two columns. The name of the owner is placed on the first line at the margin; if the name of the owner or owners cannot be completed on one line it is continued on the second line adjacent to the margin. Should there be two or more owners these names will also appear on subsequent line adjacent to the margin.

The name of the occupant of the property, if other than the owner, will be found on the second line, or on subsequent lines if the owner's name occupies more than one line, indented two spaces. If the owner is the sole, or the chief occupant, his name is not recorded as an occupant. In a few entries occupants of specific structures on the property or of specific portions of the property appear on the appropriate line, indented two

ix

Introduction

spaces. In most entries occupants of only a part of the property are recorded in the notes.

Abbreviated given names have been expanded to the full form when possible; alternate spellings for surnames are recorded as a "note". All names are given with the surname first.

The the second column of the first line gives the location of the property. This may be a town, a street, a location on a watercourse or a road, a mountain, or some other descriptive word or phrase. A second indicator of the location of the property is the name of owners of adjacent land. Such adjoining owners are listed on the second, or a subsequent line when necessary, indented two spaces from the location entry. Unfortunately, many entries contain neither a location nor the name of an adjoining owner.

The format of the first two columns is diagrammed here.

```
Owner                  Location of property
  Occupant, if other     Adjoining landowners
  than owner
            Ref.
```

The third column lists specific structures and, occasionally, the nature of the land (tract or lot). In this column will be found entries for houses, additions, rooms, kitchens, and a great variety of other structures pertaining to the house or to the use to which the land is put (barn, smith shop, saw mill, and so forth). When there is more than one of a particular type of structure those structures are numbered (house 1, house 2, etc.). This numbering has been adopted to facilitate reference; it does not appear in the original documents. Dwellings of a value greater than $100.00 (from List A) are listed as "house and lot"; those valued at $100.00 or less, as "house".

The next five columns describe the structures, giving the dimensions in feet, a description (usually the material used in construction, but sometimes other information), and the number of stories, windows, and lights (panes of glass).

The last two columns, Area and Value, require some explanation. Houses of a value greater than $100.00 (those from Table A) are listed in column 3 as "house and lot." When such a house is on a town lot, the size of the lot will appear in the Area column; when a house is on a farm the law provided that an area not to exceed 2 acres should be appraised as the house lot and included in the valuation of the house. The area so designated was then deducted from the total area to determine the area to be assessed as land. In most townships the assessor assigned two acres for all house lots; in Hopewell and Southampton townships, however, one acre was assigned. The amount in the Value column is the total value of the house and lot.

The area and valuation of the non-residential portion of rural properties is recorded in the appropriate column in a convenient place, usually opposite one of the secondary structures such as the barn or stable. The placement implies no particular relation to the structure mentioned on the same line. Only when purposes of greater clarity are served, such as when there is no structure on a property, is the land is placed on a separate line and specified as a "lot" or "tract".

The area of lots and tracts is given in acres (A), perches (P), and square feet (F). Since some modern urban dwellers may not be familiar with all of these terms they are here clarified.

        Acre   43,560 square feet, 160 perches, or 1/640 of a square mile

        Perch   272 1/4 square feet or 1/160 of an acre
                  (a perch is also a linear measurement of 16 1/2 feet)

x

Introduction

Most of the town lots were probably laid out, as in modern times, by specifying the frontage and the depth in feet. The typical lot in Carlisle, for example, is 52 perches, 243 square feet, or a total of 14,400 square feet--a lot 144 x 100 or some variation thereon.

The acreage given for most farms must be considered approximate, although most are given in exact acres. A few are given in acres and perches, for example, 371 acres, 120 perches. It seems unlikely that the majority do not vary a few perches from the exactly even number of acres.

The value of the property is given in the last column. For most town properties there is only one value given, that of the house and the appertaining lot; for farms two values are ordinarily given, one for the house and lot and another for the land. The values are placed adjacent to the area.

Values are also usually given for houses appraised at one hundred dollars or less, even though these are not subject to the tax. Values are also frequently given for other structures such as mills, shops, and other structures related to commerce or industry.

Both the Principal Assessor and the Assistant Assessor provide valuations for each property. When these differ, that of the Principal Assesor has been used.

Several kinds of information are provided on the "note" line. Most common are notes on occupants of a portion of the property, variations in surname spelling, and ambiguities in the original text. Other miscellaneous information may also be recorded in the notes, as are a few observations by the compiler (the latter always in brackets).

On the last line of each entry, in a column, headed "Ref.", and beginning in the first and continuing into the second column, a reference to the list and entry number within the list is provided, thus making it possible to refer to the original entries should it be felt desirable to do so. Most of the original lists were numbered, but some were not; in the latter case numbers were assigned by the compiler.

ANOMALIES IN THE ORIGINAL LISTS

The information for each township was collected by a different person or group of persons, and, it seems, there was a minimum of coordination between the assessors. As a result each set of assessments displays idiosyncracies of the particular assessor. A brief discussion of some of these difference seems worthwhile.

In most townships there are a large number of houses which are listed as being of one and one-half stories. That, presumably, means that the second floor was immediately under the roof, with windows only at the gable ends, if anywhere. In Middleton Township, however, there are no 1 1/2 story houses listed. It seems unlikely that the entire township did not contain a house similar to one so common elsewhere. Instead it is reasonable to believe that the assessor for Middleton simply did not treat houses in the same manner, and that there existed in Middleton houses that elsewhere would have been called 1 1/2 story.

Similarly, the rolls for Allen township lists a number of "bank" barns, a structure which is built into a hillside or a mound so that the first floor is accessible from the ground level, and the second floor from the bank. That there is no such designation in other townships leads to the belief that the assessor for Allen township noted such construction while the assessors for the other townships did not, rather than that there are no such structures outside Allen township.

A third such anomaly occurs in the use of the term "squared log" to describe structures in East Pennsboro township. That there were no such log structures elsewhere seems doubtful.

Introduction

Descriptions of buildings as "log" or "frame" are clear enough, but the term "wood" is ambiguous. In some townships, within the a single entry, the terms "wood" and "log" are used; in other townships "wood" and "frame" appear together. Probably "wood", in most instances, means lumber, but the reader will have to decide for himself just what the term means in the description of a particular structure. It is worthwhile to note that "frame" is used comparatively rarely.

The term "cabin" is of course used to name a small, simply constructed dwelling. It is also used, however, as a term to describe the construction of a house, stable, kitchen, or other structure. This usage occurs only in a few of the townships and therefore must be attributed to the habit of the assessor. Both as a structure and as a descriptive term the spelling is usually "cabbin", which has been modernized here to "cabin." Books on domestic architecture of the period mention that the original dwelling of a settler was frequently converted to another use when the owner was able to afford the construction of a more commodious dwelling, an obvious derivation of the adjectival usage.

In Newton township most entries have given a "rate" per acre. This rate when multiplied by the number of whole and partial acres usually produces the amount of the land value, though not always. When the variation is greater than a few cents the amount calculated is entered in parenthesis. The amount entered in the Value column is always that provided by the Assessor. In no other sub-division in the County is a rate given.

THE INDEXES

Two indexes are provided.

1. Index to Land Owners
    All land owners are listed individually in a single index; joint owners are listed separately. The township in which the property lies is included in the listing as an additional assistance.

2. Index to Occupants and Other Persons
    Both occupants listed in Column 1 and those whose names appear in notes are included in this index. In addition, a few persons who are neither owners nor occupants are mentioned in the notes, and these persons are indexed here, with an identifying remark. As with the Owner Index, the township in which the property is located is given.

SELECTED WRITINGS ON THE DIRECT TAX

Both social and economic aspects of the Direct Tax are discussed in "America's First Progressive Tax" by Lee Soltow (Department of Economics, Ohio University), published in Volume XXX of National Tax Journal, pp. 53-59.

A brief account of the political events surrounding the Direct Tax can be found in Sidney Ratner's American Taxation, its History as a Social Force in Democracy, pp. 29-30. (New York, W. W. Norton & Co., [1942]).

Of somewhat broader interest is a discussion in Jack Larkin's The Reshaping of Everyday Life, 1790-1840, pp. 109-115 (New York, Harper & Row, 1988). Beyond the few pages directly concerned with the housing of 1798, persons interested in the history of everyday life will find the entire chapter, " 'Comfortable Habitations', Houses and the Domestic Environment", and for that matter, the entire book, to be a valuable contribution to their understanding of the life of the people of the period.

Mr. Larkin is Chief Historian at Old Sturbridge Village in Sturbridge, Massachusetts, but his book is by no means narrowly concerned with that village or the area in which it lies.

Introduction

FINAL COMMENT OF THE COMPILER

A user of reference books, in his days of innocence, usually wonders why an author invariably mentions that, despite his best efforts, there will remain some errors. The initial effort at compiling a book such as this quickly relieves one of his innocence, and one feels compelled to repeat the warning. The manipulation of large amounts of data has been made immeasurably easier by the development of the personal computer, but that wonderful instrument has no power to detect human errors, apart from the relatively trivial errors of spelling. The text of this work has been reviewed at least a dozen times, and the microfilm has been revisited as many times, but nevertheless it is reasonably certain that some errors remain, (lurking behind an out-house or in a wooded tract--or, perhaps, within a still house.) Therefore I must follow my predecessors and make my apologies, hoping that the errors are few and that the reader will find that, overall, the picture here presented of Cumberland County, of the townships, and of the individual properties is accurate and that it will prove both useful and interesting.

VITA

Wilbur J. McElwain was born at Chicago, Illinois, on February 8, 1923. He completed his elementary and secondary education Chicago, Illinois.

He received the degree of Bachelor of Science, with a major in English Literature, from Northwestern University, Evanston, Illinois in 1950. In 1958 he received the degree of Master of Arts (English) from the University of Miami, Coral Gables, Florida. His thesis was entitled <u>The Development of the Social and Political Thought of James Fenimore Cooper</u>. He received the degree of Doctor of Education from Florida Atlantic University, Boca Raton, Florida in 1976. His dissertation was entitled <u>Academic Achievement of Students Earning Credit through the College Level Examination Program General Examinations</u>.

Mr. McElwain taught in the Dade County Public School Adult Education Division from 1952 to 1960. He joined the faculty of Miami-Dade Community College in 1960 and held the position of Associate Dean in charge of adult, military, and off-campus programs at the South Campus from 1967 to 1986.

He retired in 1986 and moved to his present address, 10122 Northeast 126 Street, Kirkland, Washington, 98034.

Allen Township

CHAPTER I   ALLEN TOWNSHIP

Owner Occupant	Ref.	Location Adjoining Owner	Structure	Dimensions	Descr.	Stories	Lights Windows	Area		Value
Anderson, Benjamin			house 1 & lot	21 x 19	wood	2	6	72	36 P	200.00
			kitchen	20 x 19	wood	1	6	63		
			stable	15 x 12	wood					
			barn	36 x 18	wood, old				88 A	946.00
	A1 B1 D1 D2 E1		house 2 & lot	25 x 20	wood	2	3	27	2 A	110.00
Apley, John		in Lisburn	house 1 & lot	30 x 18	wood	1	10	94	36 P	200.00
			stable 1	15 x 12	wood					
			house 2 & lot	22 x 18	wood	2	7	84	36 P	150.00
			stable 2	14 x 14	log					
	A2 B2 D3 D4 (no E entry)		notes: Young, James, occupant of house 2; house 2 value $110.00 in D							
Beelman, Christopher			house & lot	28 x 24	wood	2	3	33	2 A	400.00
			spring house	18 x 14	stone					
			barn	88 x 30	log bank, unfinished				258 A	4280.00
	A18 B18 D22 E19		note: Bellman ?							
Beelman, Jacob			house 1 & lot	18 x 16	wood	1	1	4	2 A	150.00
			barn	50 x 18	old				200 A	2350.00
			house 2	26 x 20	wood, unfinished					
	A13 B13 D17 E12		note: name also Belman							
Beelman, Peter			house & lot	24 x 20	wood	1	4	36	2 A	200.00
			barn	52 x 20	old				75 A	1000.00
	A14 B14 D18 E13		note: name also Bilman							
Belsover, George			house & lot	22 x 20	wood	1	4	25	2 A	250.00
			barn	48 x 20	log				234 A	2860.00
	A20 B20 D24 E21		notes: name also Bellsoover							
Bishop, Adam			house & lot	25 x 17	wood	2	7	48	2 A	200.00
	A15 B15 D19 E14								2 A	30.00
Bitner, John			house & lot	35 x 15	wood	1	3	24	2 A	150.00
	A30 B30 D34 E32		barn	30 x 20	log				120 A	1500.00
Black, Andrew			house & lot	22 x 18	wood	1	2	24	2 A	210.00
	A24 B24 D28 E25		barn	68 x 25	log bank				115 A	1194.00
Black, John			house & lot	22 x 22	wood	1	4	28	2 A	150.00
	A28 B28 D32 E30		barn	58 x 28	log				100 A	1250.00
Bollinger, Abraham			house 1 & lot	24 x 22	wood	2	8	72	2 A	300.00
			barn	57 x 20	log, old				87 A	2250.00
			house 2 & lot	19 x 16	wood	1	1	6		100.10
	A12 B12 D15 D16 E11		note: Bollinger, John occupant of house 2							

Allen Township

Owner / Occupant	Location Ref. / Adjoining Owner	Structure	Dimensions	Descr.	Stories	Windows Lights	Area	Value
Bowman, Christopher		house & lot	25 x 17	wood	2	4 / 24	2 A	150.00
Sheffer, John		barn	30 x 20	log			87 A	1100.00
	A29 B29 D33 E31							
Brand, Adam		house & lot	38 x 32	stone	2	18 / 240	2 A	1000.00
	A6 B6 D9 E5	barn	71 x 30	log bank			240 A	4140.00
Brand, Jacob		house & lot	22 x 20	wood	1	2 / 18	2 A	200.00
	A9 B9 D12 E8	barn	54 x 23	log			75 A	900.00
Brand, John		house & lot	20 x 18	wood	1	2 / 24	2 A	200.00
		wash house	16 x 14	wood				
	A16 B16 D20 E15	barn	60 x 24	log			198 A	2376.00
Brand, Ludwick		house & lot	18 x 16	wood	1	2 / 18	2 A	100.10
							98 A	1372.00
	A8 B8 D11 E7	tract 2		pine land			100 A	300.00
Brand, Martin		house & lot	45 x 38	brick	2	16 / 216	2 A	1000.00
		barn	70 x 30	stone			228 A	4148.00
	A7 B7 D10 E6	still house	24 x 18	stone				
Bricker, Jacob		house & lot	38 x 32	wood	1	5 / 32	2 A	250.00
							200 A	3350.00
		mill	48 x 45	stone			14 A	2000.00
		tract 3		pine land			100 A	300.00
	A17 B17 D21 E16 E17 E18	note: mill is on 14 acre tract, and is occupied by Crawl, Joseph						
Bricker, Jacob Jr.		house & lot	20 x 20	stone	2	5 / 66	2 A	550.00
		kitchen	20 x 14	wood	1			
		barn	54 x 25				198 A	2970.00
		pine land					100 A	300.00
	A25 B25 D29 E26 E27	note: barn 24 x 25 in D						
Bricker, Peter		house & lot	30 x 26	wood	2	11 / 111	2 A	550.00
		spring house	18 x 15	stone				
		barn	70 x 30	stone bank			298 A	6460.00
	A19 B19 D23 E20	still house	35 x 30	log				
Brindle, George		house & lot	24 x 24	wood	1	4 / 36	2 A	200.00
		out house	15 x 12					
	A10 B10 D13 E9	barn	60 x 28	log bank			200 A	3020.00
Briniser, Adam		house & lot	22 x 20	wood	2	7 / 90	72 P	250.00
Smith, James		stable	18 x 16	wood				
	A11 B11 D14 E10	notes: name also Brinizer						

Allen Township

Owner Occupant	Location Ref. Adjoining Owner	Structure	Dimensions	Descr.	Stories	Lights Windows		Area	Value
Briniser, John & Briniser, Adam		house 1 & lot	20 x 20	wood	2	7	63	2 A	300.00
		barn	60 x 80	log bank				198 A	2076.00
		house 2 & lot	20 x 18	wood	1	3	33		120.00
	A5 B5 D7 D8 E4	note: John occupant of house 1, Adam of house 2							
Brison, James		house & lot	23 x 22	wood	1	4	40	2 A	200.00
		barn	52 x 20	log, old				98 A	728.00
		still house	16 x 14	log					
	A3 B3 D5 E2	note: name appears as Brinizer in D							
Brison, William		house & lot	28 x 26	stone	2	8	96	2 A	800.00
		barn	50 x 20	log				110 A	540.00
	A4 B4 D6 E3	tanyard							
Brooks, Joseph		house & lot	30 x 20	stone	1	5	54	2 A	550.00
	A26 B26 D30 E28	barn	60 x 25	log				158 A	2280.00
Brooks, William		house & lot	20 x 15	wood	1	7	66	2 A	250.00
		stable	20 x 25	wood				18 A	216.00
		grist mill		wood					800.00
	A27 B27 D31 E29	saw mill							100.00
Brown, Ephraim		house & lot	20 x 18	wood	1	2	16	2 A	150.00
	A23 B23 D27 E24	barn	45 x 20	log, old				198 A	1450.00
Brown, James		house & lot	19 x 19	wood	1	1	2	2 A	150.00
	A22 B22 D26 E23							148 A	1100.00
Byremaster, Chri----		house & lot	18 x 15	wood	1	2	10	2 A	170.00
		barn	30 x 12	log				20 A	200.00
	A21 B21 D25 E22	note: name also Biremaster							
Carver, Christopher		house & lot	27 x 21	wood	1	4	31	2 A	320.00
		barn	54 x 24	log				198 A	5940.00
	A47 B47 D51 E49	still house	28 x 16	log					
Carver, John		house & lot	18 x 16	wood	1	1	6	2 A	100.10
	A48 B48 D52 E50							50 A	800.00
Cashler, David		house & lot	28 x 26	wood	1	4	48	2 A	250.00
	A41 B41 D45 E43							2 A	40.00
Clark, James		house & lot	19 x 16	wood	2	2	24	2 A	210.00
		out house	18 x 16						
	A46 B46 D50 E48	barn	40 x 16	log				122 A	1254.00
Clark, John		house & lot							500.00
		spring house		stone					
	A39 B39 D43 E41	barn	70 x 26	log				154 A	3080.00

Allen Township

Owner Occupant	Location Ref. Adjoining Owner	Structure	Dimensions	Descr.	Stories	Windows	Lights	Area	Value
Clark, William		house & lot	17 x 17	brick	1	4	32	2 A	400.00
		stable	18 x 18	wood				133 A	1995.00
	A40 B40 D44 E42	mill	30 x 30	stone					1000.00
Cockley, Jacob		house & lot	30 x 29	stone	2	10	120	2 A	850.00
		barn		old				268 A	4974.00
	A37 B37 D41 E39	still house	20 x 15						
Cockley, John		house & lot	32 x 26	wood	2	6	63	2 A	420.00
	A38 B38 D42 E40	barn	70 x 29	log bank				271 A	4674.00
Coover, Frederick		house & lot	30 x 20	wood	1	7	27	2 A	210.00
		barn	60 x 25	log, old				188 A	2070.00
	A33 B33 D37 E35	smith shop							
Cover, George		house & lot	28 x 24	wood	1	7	57	2 A	270.00
		spring house	14 x 12	wood					
		out house							
		barn	85 x 24	log				178 A	2610.00
	A35 B35 D39 E37	note: name also Coover							
Cover, George		house & lot	24 x 20	wood	2	6	66	2 A	250.00
		barn	45 x 20	log				98 A	1200.00
	A43 B43 D47 E45	note: name also Coover							
Cover, Gideon		house & lot	28 x 23	wood	1	6	63	2 A	310.00
		barn	70 x 21	log				98 A	1372.00
	A34 B34 D38 E36	note: name also Coover							
Cox, William		house & lot	24 x 20	wood	1	5	36	2 A	250.00
		spring house	13 x 11	stone					
	A36 B36 D40 E38	barn	50 x 16	log				50 A	400.00
Crawl, Abraham		house & lot	26 x 24	wood	1	5	48	2 A	270.00
	A32 B32 D36 E34	barn	72 x 14	log				243 A	2916.00
Crawl, Mathias		house 1 & lot	30 x 25	stone	1	5	69	2 A	550.00
		kitchen	20 x 26	stone	1			238 A	2380.00
		house 2 & lot	20 x 18	wood					100.10
		saw mill							
	A49 B49 D53 D54 E51	mill	50 x 48	stone, unfinished					500.00

Allen Township

Owner / Occupant	Location Ref. Adjoining Owner	Structure	Dimensions	Descr.	Stories	Lights	Windows	Area	Value
Crisor, Jacob		house & lot	40 x 20	wood & stone					450.00
		barn 1	50 x 25	log				148/148 A	4400.00
		barn 2	50 x 20	log					
	A50 B50 D55 E52 E53	note: two tracts of land; name also Crisher.							
Crocket, Andrew, heirs		house & lot	39 x 16	wood	1	3	33	2 A	200.00
	A45 B45 D49 E47	barn	45 x 16	old				173 A	1900.00
Crocket, James		house & lot	36 x 16	wood	1	1	9	2 A	130.00
		barn	25 x 12	old				146 A	900.00
	A44 B44 D48 E46	saw mill							
Crockett, George		house & lot	20 x 16	wood	2	6	63	2 A	150.00
								148 A	888.00
	A42 B42 D46 E44	note: name also Crocket							
Cunningham, James		house & lot	28 x 24	wood	1	4	51	2 A	300.00
	A31 B31 D35 E33	barn	60 x 22	log				98 A	1470.00
Deddo, John		house & lot	20 x 16	wood	1	3	18	2 A	200.00
		out house	20 x 18					94 A	1306.00
		smith shop	14 x 12						
		stable		old					
		forge and fore of hamer [?]							400.00
	A53 B53 D58 E56	note: name also Dedo							
Delap, John		house & lot	26 x 26	wood	2	7	75	2 A	410.00
		barn	50 x 18	old				278 A	4170.00
	A54 B54 D59 E57	still house	18 x 14						
Diller, Casper		house & lot	28 x 26	wood	2	11	114	2 A	410.00
		barn	80? x 22	log				177 A	2655.00
	A55 B55 D60 E58	still house	20 x 18						
Diller, Martin		house & lot	24 X 20	wood	1	3	28	2 A	250.00
Work, Peter		barn	66 x 18	log				111 A	1332.00
	A56 B56 D61 E59								
Dodds, Joseph		house & lot	24 x 18	wood	1	1	8	2 A	200.00
		out house	18 x 15	log					
		barn	50 x 20	log				158 A	1966.00
	A51 B51 D56 E54	note: Beam, Fish occupant of out house							
Douglass, James		house & lot	40 x 25	wood	2	21	278	2 A	500.00
		barn	25 x 25	log				48 A	1200.00
	A52 B52 D57 E55	saw mill							200.00
Eagy, Michael		tract						177 A	2194.00
	B61 E64								

Allen Township

Owner Occupant	Location Ref. Adjoining Owner	Structure	Dimensions	Descr.	Stories	Lights Windows	Area	Value
Eagy, Michael	mountain land B61 E65	tract					1278 A	262.00
Echelbarger, Christopher		house 1 & lot	24 x 24	wood	1	5 54	2 A	450.00
		wash house	20 x 15	stone				
		stable		log				
		barn	54 x 27	log			203 A	4060.00
		house 2 & lot	24 x 19	wood	2	7 70		250.00
	A60 B60 D65 D66 E63	notes first name Christopher in A & D, Stophel in B & E						
Eliot, Joseph		house & lot	20 x 16	wood	1	2 6	120 P	150.00
		out house	19 x 16					
	A58 B58 D63 E61	saw mill		unfinished				
Erwin, Samuel, Esq.		house & lot	25 x 25	wood	2	2 24	2 A	300.00
Greer, Samuel							98 A	1470.00
	A59 B59 D64 E62							
Everly, Henry		house & lot	30 x 18	wood	1	5 28	2 A	350.00
		out house	20 x 16					
	A57 B57 D62 E60	barn	50 x 24	log			198 A	2970.00
Feeman, Adam		house & lot	40 x 30	stone	1	7 48	2 A	1000.00
		barn	60 x 25	log			148 A	4440.00
	A60A B61A D67 E66	note: house value $100.00 in D; entries not numbered in A or B						
Free, Henry		house & lot	18 x 16	wood	1	2 10	1 A	100.10
	A61a B61b D69 (no entry in E)							
Frenkelbarger, George	in Lisburn	house & lot	26 x 22	wood	2	1	36 P	150.00
Hemphill, John		note: no property listed in B						
	A61 B61a D68 (no entry in E)							
Fridley, George		house & lot	20 x 18	wood	2	2 24	36 P	150.00
		wagon maker	20 x 16					
	A61B D70	shop						
Gatshall, Philip		house & lot	28 x 24	wood	2	5 60	2 A	300.00
		barn	54 x 20	log			98 A	1200.00
	A72 B70 D83 E77	note: name also Gutshall						

Allen Township

Owner / Occupant	Location Ref. / Adjoining Owner	Structure	Dimensions	Descr.	Stories	Windows Lights	Area	Value
Gees, John		house & lot 1	30 x 18	wood, old	1		2 A	150.00
		barn 1	84 x 25	log, bank			266/96 A	4288.00
		milk house	18 x 18	wood	1			
		[?]	33 x 30		2			
		house & lot 2	20 x 18	wood	1	2 18	2 A	150.00
		barn 2	15 x 18	log	2			
	A64 B64 D74 D75 E70 E71	note: two tracts; Snyder, Conrad, occupant of house 2						
Gees, Samuel Philips, Widow	4 D85	house & lot	25 x 20	wood	2	8 72	36 P	200.00
George, Martin	A67 B67 D78 E74	house & lot	24 x 22		1	2 18	2 A	150.00
		barn	30 x 13	log			4 A	50.00
Goodour, Peter		house & lot	28 x 26	wood	2	11 112	2 A	450.00
		barn	54 x 22	log			143/100 A	1290.00
		smith shop	18 x 15	stone				
	A73 B71 D84 E78	notes: only one value given for the two tracts; name also Goodyear, Goodoar, Goodyour						
Goosewelder, John		house & lot	28 x 24	wood	2	4 45	2 A	350.00
		barn	54 x 20	log, old			100 A	1200.00
	A66 B66 D77 E73	note: name also Goosewalder						
Graham, James	A70 B68 D81 E75	house & lot	25 x 22	wood	1	2 18	2 A	150.00
		barn	80 x 23	log			212 A	2632.00
Graham, John, heirs Mutchman, Man-- [?]	A71 B69 D82 E76	house & lot	28 x 24	stone	2	19 114	2 A	550.00
		barn	58 x 20	log			212 A	2632.00
Gregor, John		house & lot 1	25 x 20	wood	2	9 100	2 A	450.00
		kitchen	16 x 12	stone	1	2 12		
		barn 1	80 x 20	log, old			248 A	3610.00
		smith shop	16 x 12	old				
		house & lot 2	22 x 22	wood	2	3 44	2 A	250.00
		barn 2	45 x 22	log			113 A	
	A63 B63 D72 D73 E68 E69	notes: two tracts; Gregor, Adam, occupant of house 2 and barn 2: name also Greger; separate value not given for second tract						
Gregory, James	A62 B62 D71 E67	house & lot	35 x 16	wood	1	7 67	2 A	400.00
		barn	62 x 16	log			210 A	7380.00
		still house	24 x 20	old				
Grouse, John	A65 B65 D76 E72	house & lot	40 x 23	wood	1	6 69	2 A	250.00
		barn	60 x 24	log			178 A	2492.00

Allen Township

Owner / Occupant	Location Ref. / Adjoining Owner	Structure	Dimensions	Descr.	Stories	Windows	Lights	Area	Value
Grumbley, Adam	A68 B73[b] D79 E80	house & lot barn	22 x 12 45 x 15	wood old	1	2	18	2 A 298 A	150.00 3400.00
Grumley, Stophel	A69 B73[a] D80 E79	house & lot barn	20 x 18 45 x 15	wood old	1	2	12	2 A 48 A	150.00 250.00
Hair, Daniel	in Lisburn A86 B86 D97 E89	house & lot stable 1 sawmill stable 2 grist mill	45 x 21 20 x 16 25 x 18	wood wood	2	7	96	2 A 19 A	250.00 228.00 200.00 1500.00
Hare, Abraham	A76 B76 D87 E82	house & lot kitchen stone barn tan yard note: name also Hear	47 x 21 18 x 16 75 x 33	stone stone stone bank	2 1	11 2	240 24 wash house 340 A	2 A 340 A	1200.00 22 x 18 5260.00
Harkness, William	A83 B83 D94 E88	house & lot barn still house	40 x 30 95 x 30 24 x 22	stone stone bank	2	18	384	2 A 468 A	1200.00 6032.00
Heck, Jacob	A88 B88 D99 E90	house & lot barn smith shop note: half ownership in barn	22 x 18 70 x 30	wood stone bank	2	8	96	1 A 98 A	300.00 2180.00
Heck, John	A89 B89 D106 E91	house & lot out house barn note: half ownership of barn	22 x 18 18 x 15 70 x 30	wood stone bank	2	9	108	1 A 98 A	300.00 2180.00
Henry, Master [?] Markel, Mathias	in Lisburn A84 B84 D95 (no entry in E)	house & lot note: [last name of occupant is doubtful]	22 x 18	wood	1	2	24	36 P	100.10
Hewit, Michael Lemon, Daniel	A87 B74 D68 (no entry in E)	house & lot barn note: name appears as Hust in B and D	30 X 26 75 x 21	wood log	2	9	109	2 A 135 A	450.00 2200.00
Hickrenel, Abraham	in Lisburn A87 B87 D98 (no entry in E)	house & lot note: name Hickorynell in B, Hickremel in D	22 x 18	wood	2	2	24	36 P	100.10
Hickrenel, David	in Lisburn A85 B85 D96 (no entry in E)	house & lot note: Hickorynell in B	22 x 20	wood	1	2	12	36 P	100.10

Allen Township

Owner / Occupant	Location Ref. / Adjoining Owner	Structure	Dimensions	Descr.	Stories	Windows / Lights	Area	Value
Hickrennel, Frederick	A82 B82 D93 E87	house & lot	29 x 19	wood	2	9 108	36 P	200.00
		note: spelling of last name varies and is doubtful						
Hide, Abraham	A78 B78 D89 E84	house & lot barn	30 x 25 50 x 18	wood log	2	2 24	2 A 196 A	300.00 2744.00
Hollinger, Jacob	A80 B80 D91 E86	house & lot barn	20 x 18 50 x 18	wood log	1	3 24	2 A 80 A	150.00 960.00
		note: name also Holinger						
Hoover, Michael	A79 B79 D90 E85	house & lot barn	16 x 16 30 x 14	wood log	1	3 16	2 A 100 A	150.00 1200.00
		notes: name also Hover						
Houser, Martin		house & lot kitchen barn	20 x 20 20 x 15 90 x 24	stone wood log	1 1	4 40 3 39	2 A 128 A	600.00 1892.00
	A90 B90 D101 E92	note: name also Hauser; land is given as 228 A, value $1545.00 in E, [which seemingly places the value per acre too low]						
Hover, David	A77 B77 D88 E83	house & lot barn	25 x 18 50 x 18	wood log	2	2 15	2 A 109 A	250.00 1308.00
		notes: name also Hoover						
Hunter, William Ross, John	B91a E93	tract					53 A	424.00
Hutton, Solomon	A81 B81 D92 (no entry in E)	house & lot stable	22 x 20 15 x 10	wood log	2	7 75	36 P	200.00
Jones, William	A91 B91b D102 E94	house & lot out house	15 x 11 20 x 20	wood wood, unfinished	1 1	1 6	2 A	100.10
Kinour, Jacob Knisely, Jacob	A93 B93 D104 E96	house & lot barn	24 x 20 54 x 25	wood log	2	15 124	2 A 118 A	300.00 1416.00
		note: name also Kinewer						
Kisshecker, Nicholas		house & lot barn store room mill saw mill hemp mill oil mill	25 x 17 36 x 18 14 x 13 33 x 30	wood log wood stone	1 1	3 42 2 18	2 A 100 A	250.00 2000.00 2000.00 200.00 100.00 100.00
	A95 B95 D106 E98	note: spelling of last name varies; store room 15 x 13 in E						

Allen Township

Owner / Occupant	Location Ref. / Adjoining Owner	Structure	Dimensions	Descr.	Stories	Windows Lights		Area	Value
Kitch, John		house & lot	24 x 22	wood	2	8	75	2 A	400.00
		barn	60 x 20	log				128 A	1600.00
	A94 B94 C105 D97								
Knisley, Samuel		house & lot	30 x 25	wood	1	6	72	2 A	430.00
		out house	16 x 20						
		barn	60 x 27	log				113 A	1900.00
	A92 B92 D103 E95	mill	40 x 35	stone					1800.00
Laird, Hugh		house 1 & lot	24 x 21	wood	1	3	33	1 A	200.00
		barn	57 x 20	log				288 A	3500.00
		house 2 & lot	25 x 20	wood	1	3	18	1 A	200.00
	A98 B100 D110 E102	note: Laird, Samuel, occupant of house 2							
Lamb, John		house 1 & lot	28 x 22	wood	2	12	131	2 A	450.00
		kitchen	16 x 14	wood					
		store room	18 x 16	stone	1	2	8		
		milk house	22 x 16	stone	1				
		barn 1	64 x 30	log bank				298 A	4770.00
		house 2 & lot	18 x 16	wood	1	3	17		200.00
		barn 2		old					
	A97 B96 D108 D109 E99	note: name also Lam							
Lee, Timothy		house & lot	20 x 10	wood	1	3	20	2 A	150.00
	A100 B98 D112 E101	barn	40 x 15	old				49 A	700.00
Lidack, Adam		house & lot	22 x 20	wood	1	3	27	2 A	250.00
								148 A	1776.00
	A96 B97 D107 E100	oil mill		unfinished					
Long, Benjamin		house & lot	40 x 20	wood	2	8	45	2 A	550.00
	A102 B101 D115 E103							48 A	576.00
Long, Frederick		house 1 & lot	47 x 20	stone	1	11	116	2 A	1100.00
		house 2 & lot	22 x 18	wood	1	3	36	2 A	150.00
		barn	80 x 34	stone bank				226/173 A	5810.00
		note: Yeints, Henry, occupant of house 2 and 173 A; two tracts							
	A101 B102 D113 D114 E104 E105								
Long, John		house & lot	21 x 19	wood	1	2	24	36 P	150.00
	A99 B99 D111 (no entry in E)								
Mark, Henry		house & lot	24 x 20	wood	2	8	84	2 A	250.00
	A107 B107 D122 E112	barn	46 x 28	log				148 A	1800.00?
Markley, John		house & lot	25 x 22	wood	2	6	72	2 A	300.00
	A126a B127 D144 E132	barn	46 x 16	log				58 A	736.00

Allen Township

Owner / Occupant	Location Ref. Adjoining Owner	Structure	Dimensions	Descr.	Stories	Lights Windows	Area	Area	Value
Martin, Samuel		house 1 & lot	26 x 22	wood	2	7	87	2 A	350.00
		barn	80 x 22	log				370 A	5238.00
		house 2 & lot	20 x 18	wood	1	1	12		100.10
		tract						76 A	912.00
		note: Weaver, John, occupant of house 2 and tract of 76 A							
	A104 B104 D117 D118 E107 E108								
Marvet, Hartman		house & lot	22 x 20	wood	1	4	41	2 A	250.00
		barn	54 x 18	log				148 A	2220.00
	A113 B113 D130 E119	note: name variously as Morit, Mowat, Monet							
McCue, John		house & lot	24 x 24	wood	2	9	108	2 A	350.00
	A117 B117 D134 E123	stable	25 x 25	log				120 A	1960.00
McCue, Widow		house & lot	35 x 18	wood	1	3	22	2 A	200.00
		barn	54 x 20	log				130 A	1820.00
	A112 B112 D129 E118	note: Loyd, Jacob, occupant in B and D							
McDanel, John & McDanel, James		house & lot	30 x 26	wood, unfinished	2	10	120	2 A	350.00
		barn	60 x 22	log				430 A	6610.00
		still house	20 x 18						
		out house	18 x 16						
	A125 B126 D142 E131	note: Holmes, Thomas, occupant of out house; name also McDonnel							
McGrew, Archibald		house & lot	30 x 20	wood	1	4	36	2 A	250.00
		barn	60 x 25	log				116 A	1790.00
	A123 B123 D140 E129	note: name also Megrew							
McKinsey, John		house & lot	22 x 16	wood	1	3	21	2 A	100.10
	A118 B118 D135 E124	stable	22 x 20	wood				38 A	228.00
McMean, John		house & lot	25 x 22	wood	1	3	27	2 A	250.00
		out house	18 x 16						
		barn	45 x 25	log				117 A	1638.00
		hemp mill							75.00
	A122 B122 D139 E128	oil mill							75.00
McMean, William	in Lisburn	house & lot	25 x 20	wood	2	9	120	36 P	300.00
		kitchen	20 x 18	wood	1	3	27		
	A114 B114 D131 E120	stable	18 x 16					1 A	20.00
McNeal, Daniel		house & lot	21 x 17	wood	1	4	27	2 A	250.00
		out house	16 x 14						
	A105 B105 D119 E109	barn	38 x 24	log				118 A	1470.00

Allen Township

Owner Occupant	Location Ref. Adjoining Owner	Structure	Dimensions	Descr.	Stories	Windows Lights	Area	Value
McTeer, James		house & lot	30 x 22	wood	1	6 60	2 A	350.00
		kitchen	16 x 15	wood				
		barn	57 x 18	log			193 A	3138.00
		milk house	19 x 16	stone				
	A111 B112 D128 E116 E117							
McTeer, James Jr.	in Lisburn	house & lot	24 x 18	wood	2	5 56	108 P	300.00
		kitchen	18 x 18	wood				
		stable	18 x 16	log				
	A124 B124 D141 (no entry in E)							
McTeer, Samuel		house & lot	26 x 22	stone	1	4 48	2 A	600.00
		kitchen	16 x 12	wood	1	2 12		
		barn	40 x 20	log			138 A	2203.00
	A121 B121 D138 E127	tract					30 A	240.00
McTeer, William		house 1 & lot	25 x 25	wood	1	4 74	2 A	300.00
		kitchen	18 x 16	wood				
		barn 1	55 x 20	log			137 A	2194.00
		house 2 & lot	23 x 18	wood	1	2 18	2 A	200.00
		barn 2	60 x 18	log			91 A	910.00
		note: McTeer, James, occupant of house 2, tract of 91 A, and barn 2						
	A110 B110 D126 D127 E115							
Miller, Abraham		house & lot	26 x 20	wood	2	6 36	2 A	300.00
		barn	70 x 18	log			198 A	2516.00
		fulling mill						
	A119 B119 D136 E125	grist mill	22 x 18	unfinished				
Miller, Henry		house & lot	30 x 28	stone	2	10 130	2 A	1300.00
		kitchen	16 x 14	stone	1	1 12		
		barn	65 x 30	log bank			238 A	4784.00
	A103 B103 D116 E106	still house	20 x 22					
Miller, Rinehart		house & lot	30 x 26	wood	1	4 48	2 A	350.00
	A126 B125 D143 E130	barn	40 x 14	log			4 A	100.00
Miller, Thomas		house & lot	27 x 24	wood	1	3 28	2 A	250.00
	A116 B116 D133 E122	barn	64 x 27	log			148 A	1550.00
Mish, John		house & lot	30 x 28	stone	2	11 141	2 A	1000.00
Mish, Henry		barn	50 x 28	log bank			268 A	3852.00
	A115 B115 D132 E121	tanyard						
Morrison, Joseph		house & lot	24 x 21	wood	2	6 66	72 P	250.00
	A109 D125	stable	16 x 16	log				

Allen Township

Owner Occupant	Location Ref. Adjoining Owner	Structure	Dimensions	Descr.	Stories	Lights Windows	Area	Value
Myers, George Orres, Jacob & Smith, Peter		house 1 & lot barn 1 house 2 & lot barn 2 still house	22 x 18 40 x 18 25 x 25 16 x 18	wood stone log	1 2	2 8 8 88	2 A 289 A 2 A 218 A	200.00 4360.00 700.00 4624.00
		notes: Orres occupant of house 1, barn 1, and 289 A; Smith occupant						
		of house 2, barn 2, still house, and 218 A						
	A106 B106 D120 D121 E110	E111						
Myers, Jacob		house & lot barn	22 x 18 40 x 16	wood log, old	1	2 18	2 A 48 A	120.00 384.00
	A120 B120 D137 E126							
Myers, Joshua		house 1 & lot barn 1 house 2 & lot barn 2	22 x 10 60 x 24 26 x 22 60 x 22	wood log stone log	1 2	6 40 8 28	2 A 163 A 2 A 166 A	250.00 2930.00 700.00 2988.00
		note: Hover, Charles, occupant of house 2, 166 A, and barn 2.						
	A108 B108 D123 D124 E113	E114						
Negley, Eliab		house & lot barn	30 x 28 70 x 30	stone log bank	2	18 198	2 A 189 A	1000.00 3200.00
	A127 B128 D145 E133	note: name also appears as Neagley and Neagly						
Nesland, Daniel		house & lot	24 x 20	wood, unfinished	1	4	1 A	110.00
		note: name also appears as Naseland						
	A128 B129 C146 (no entry in E)							
Poorman, Christopher		house & lot barn	25 x 20 35 x 14	wood log	1	6 48	2 A 25 A	250.00 125.00
	A129 B131b D147 E135	note: number B131 is used twice						
Poorman, Stophel		house & lot	22 x 22	wood	1	2 16	2 A 94 A	250.00 750.00
	A130 B130 D148 E134							

13

Allen Township

Owner / Occupant	Location Ref. Adjoining Owner	Structure	Dimensions	Descr.	Stories	Lights Windows	Area	Value
Quigley, Christopher, Esq.		house 1 & lot	40 x 24	wood	1	5 61	2 A	450.00
		out house	18 x 16					
		barn 1	24 x 20	log			150 A	2100.00
		barn 2	30 x 20	log (1/2 interest)				
		saw mill		(1/2 interest)				20.00
		fulling mill		(1/2 interest)				100.00
Sipe, John		house 2 & lot	20 x 18	wood, unfinished	1		2 A	100.10
Erwin, William		house 3 & lot	18 x 16	wood	1	1 9	1 A	100.10
		tract					65 A	520.00
		tract					75 A	750.00
	A131 B131 D149 D150 D151 E136 E137							
Quigley, Henry		house 1 & lot	27 x 24	wood	2	7 72	2 A	400.00
		kitchen	16 x 14	wood	1	1 9	125 A	1750.00
		grist mill		(1/2 interest)				500.00
		saw mill		old, (1/2 interest)				20.00
		fulling mill		(1/2 interest)				100.00
Graham, Andrew		house 2 & lot	23 x 20	wood	1	2 12	1 A	150.00
Brawley, Daniel		out house 1	18 x 17					
Baughman, John		out house 2	18 x 14					
		tract 2					75 A	750.00
		tract 3					65 A	552.00
		tract 4					62 A	496.00
	A133 B133 D153 D154 E139 E140 E141 E142							
Quigley, James		house & lot	24 x 20	wood	1	4 48	2 A	250.00
Karlin, George		stable	17 x 14	wood			56 A	672.00
	A132 B132 D152 E138	grist mill		(1/2 interest)				500.00
Renninger, Conrad		house & lot	30 x 26	stone	2	13 174	2 A	1000.00
		kitchen	12 x 12	stone	1	1 9		
	A135 B135 D156 E144	barn	60 x 22	log			193 A	3474.00
Roseborough, Elenor		house & lot	30 x 20	wood	1	4 48	2 A	350.00
		barn	40 x 15	old			191 A	2865.00
		grist mill	40 x 20					700.00
	A134 B134 D155 E143	note: name also Rosebury and Roseberry						
Sands, George		house & lot	24 x 22	wood	1	2 24	1 A	150.00
		barn	29 x 22				50 A	750.00
	A146 B146 D173 E155	note: ownership of barn is probably 50%; see Sands, John						
Sands, John		house & lot	19 x 17	wood	1	1 12	1 A	150.00
	A145 B145 D172 E154	barn	29 x 22	log (1/2 interest)			50 A	750.00

Allen Township

Owner / Occupant	Location Ref. / Adjoining Owner	Structure	Dimensions	Descr.	Stories	Lights	Windows	Area	Value
Scoot, William		house 1 & lot	24 x 20	wood	1	4	24	2 A	250.00
		house 2 & lot	20 x 18	wood	1	3	36		120.00
		house 3 & lot	24 x 20	wood	2	5	60		120.00
		house 4 & lot	22 x 22	wood	1	2	24	2 A	150.00
		barn	64 x 30	log bank				310 A	2238.00
		tract						146 A	2190.00
		notes: occupants: none named for house 2; house 3, Scoot, Widow; house 4, Brindle, Peter; name also Scot							
	A142 B142 D166 D167 D168 D169 E151 E152								
Shelley, Jacob		house & lot	28 x 28	wood	1	5	60	2 A	450.00
		kitchen	12 x 14	wood	1	3	24		
		spring house	12 x 10	wood	1				
	A141 B141 C165 D150	barn	64 x 25	log bank				298 A	4370.00
Shelley, Jacob, Jr.		house & lot	30 x 27	wood	1	11	132	2 A	450.00
	A143 B143 C170 D153	barn	60 x 22	log				148 A	3000.00
Smith, George		house & lot	36 x 18	wood	1	4	36	2 A	250.00
	A137 B138a D161 E146	barn	40 x 18	log				92 A	1104.00
Smith, John		house & lot	28 x 26	wood, unfinished	2	2	24	72 P	150.00
	A147 D174								
Sollenberger, John		house & lot	16 x 15	wood	1	2	24	2 A	150.00
		barn	50 x 24	log				98 A	1176.00
		smith shop	20 x 15	log					
	A140 B140 D164 E149	note: name also Salinbarger, Sulenberger, Solenberger							
Sponsler, Charles		house & lot	20 x 18	wood	1	1	2	2 A	100.10
	A138 B138b D162 E147	barn	35 x 18	log, old				47 A	594.00
Springer, Jacob		house & lot	20 x 18	wood	1	2	12	2 A	100.10
	A144 B144 D171								
Starr, John / Snyder, Henry	in Lisburn	house 1 & lot	24 x 18	wood	1	9	91	36 P	150.00
		house 2 & lot	36 x 20	wood	2	4	42	36 P	200.00
		house 3 & lot	22 x 18	wood	1	3	23	36 P	150.00
		stable 1	18 x 15	wood					
		stable 2	16 x 14	wood					
		note: house 2 unoccupied; Hull, Henry, occupant of house 3							
	A135 B 136 D157 D159 (no entry in E)								
Stinespring, Henry		house & lot	18 x 15		1	4	36	2 A	100.10
	A136 B137 D160 D145	lot						40 P	50.00

Allen Township

Owner / Occupant	Location Ref. / Adjoining Owner	Structure	Dimensions	Descr.	Stories	Lights / Windows		Area	Value
Strock, Joseph		house & lot	28 x 20	wood	1	6	42	2 A	270.00
		barn	50 x 18	log				168 A	2016.00
	A139 B139 D163 E148	note: name also Strop							
Swetser, Frederick		house & lot	33 x 16	wood	1	5	60	2 A	250.00
		spring house	15 x 10	stone					
		barn	60 x 20	log bank				268 A	3952.00
	A148 B148 D175 E156	mill	35 x 35	stone					1600.00
Thomas, Martin		house & lot	30 x 27	stone	2	13	175	2 A	1000.00
		kitchen	18 x 15	stone					
	A149 B149 D176 E157	barn	56 x 22	log				278 A	5004.00
Umbarger, David		house & lot	26 x 22	wood	2	9	48	36 P	200.00
	A150 B150 D177 E158	smith shop	18 x 15	log					
Waggoner, Michael		house & lot	30 x 30	wood	2	11	150	2 A	550.00
	A165 B166 D194 E175	barn		old, falling down				158 A	1696.00
Wallace, Joseph &		house & lot	25 x 22	wood	1	3	24	2 A	250.00
Wallace, Samuel		barn	40 x 20	log				183 A	3000.00
		still house	18 x 16						
	A151 B151 D178 E159	granary	14 x 14						
Wallace, Moses		house & lot	22 x 20	wood	1	4	40	2 A	350.00
		barn	66 x 22	log				204 A	3722.00
	A157 B157 D168 E167	granary	13 x 13	stone					
Weaver, Conrad		house & lot	35 x 20	wood	1	5	45	2 A	300.00
	A161 B162 D190 E171	barn	40 x 18	log				92 A	1104.00
Weaver, Henry		house & lot	40 x 20	wood	1	4	56	2 A	350.00
	A160 B161 D189 E170	barn	70 X 22	log, old				148 A	1776.00
Weber, George		house & lot	24 x 18	wood	1	2	18	2 A	150.00
		barn	42 x 14	log				54 A	698.00
		still house	20 x 18						
	A156 B156 D185 E166	note: name also Webber							
Williams, John		house 1 & lot	28 x 26	wood	2	4	48	2 A	350.00
		kitchen	16 x 14	stone	1	2	18		
		stable		wood	1	1	6		
		barn	70 x 30	stone bank				246 A	4336.00
		house 2 & lot	30 x 28	wood	2	3	36	2 A	450.00
		house 3 & lot	16 x 18	wood	1	1	6	2 A	150.00
		still house	25 x 23	stone					
		tract 2						236 A	3540.00
		tract 3						171 A	2565.00
	A152 B152 D179 D180 D181 E160 E161 E162								

Allen Township

Owner / Occupant	Location Ref. / Adjoining Owner	Structure	Dimensions	Descr.	Stories	Lights	Windows	Area	Value
Williamson, John		house & lot	24 x 21	wood	1	4	40	2 A	350.00
		kitchen	16 x 22	wood	1	2	8		
		out house 1	24 x 21						
		out house 2	24 x 21						
		out house 3	18 x 16						
		barn	75 x 20	log				252 A	3340.00
	A159 B159 B160 D188 E169	note: Sheaver, Samuel is an ocupant of some part of the property							
Wilson, James		house & lot	20 x 15	wood	1	2	10	2 A	110.00
	A155 B155 D184 E165							8 A	150.00
Wilson, Widow		house & lot	28 x 24	wood	2	6	87	2 A	400.00
		kitchen	14 x 14	wood					
	A158 B158 D187 E168	barn	55 x 18	log				198 A	3200.00
Wise, Adam		house & lot	22 x 20	wood	1	3	36	2 A	300.00
	A164 B165 D193 E174	barn	30 x 14	log				21 A	252.00
Wise, Jacob		house & lot	33 x 25	wood	2	10	120	2 A	500.00
		kitchen	15 x 15	wood	1				
		barn	64 x 28	log				178 A	3304.00
	A154 B154 D183 E164	saw mill							300.00
Wolf, Jacob		house & lot	32 x 30	stone	2	14	196	2 A	1100.00
	A153 B153 D182 E163	barn	78 x 30	log bank				198 A	3168.00
Work, John		house & lot	38 x 18	wood	1	7	78	2 A	300.00
	A162 B163 D191 E172	barn	60 x 20	log				228 A	3420.00
Work, William		house & lot	35 x 20	wood	1	3	32	2 A	350.00
		barn	18 x 18	old				198 A	1584.00
	A163 B164 D192 E173	tract						200 A	3000.00

Carlisle Borough

CHAPTER II   CARLISLE BOROUGH

Owner / Occupant	Ref.	Location Adjoining Owner	Structure	Dimensions	Descr.	Stories	Lights Windows	Area	Area	Value
Adair, James Scranton, Hannah	A6 D6		house & lot	20 x 20	wood	1	3	27	26 P 121 F	110.00
Alexander, William, Esq.	A1 B1 D1	Hamilton, James, Esq.	house & lot kitchen store house barn & stable	33 x 16 20 x 18 22 x 13 50 x 20	stone stone wood wood	1 2	3 5	72 60	52 P 243 F 7 A	800.00 70.00
Anderson, John	A7 D7		house & lot kitchen stable	24 x 21 16 x 16 18 x 18	wood stone wood	2 1 1/2	6 2	68 21	52 P 243 F	540.00
Anderson, Joseph	A4 D4		house & lot kitchen	23 x 21 15 x 15	wood wood	2 1	6 1	72 9	52 P 243 F	300.00
Armor, Feby	B3		house lot	20 x 18					26 P 121 F	50.00 60.00
Armor, John	A3 B2 D3	other lot on High Street	house & lot kitchen stable lot	32 x 23 16 x 14 18 x 16	wood wood wood	2 1	10 1	156 12	52 P 243 F 52 P 243 F	600.00 200.00
Armor, William	A2 D2		house & lot kitchen shop stable	25 x 32 18 x 18 20 x 20 17 x 20	stone stone wood wood	2 1 1	11 2 4	204 18 51	52 P 243 F	1100.00
Armstrong, James, Dr.	A5 B4 D5	Lyon, William, & Miller, Robert, Esq.	house & lot kitchen stable 1 stable 2 stable 3 note: two 14 A tracts	30 x 31 21 x 21 19 x 19 15 x 15 30 x 20	stone wood wood wood wood	2 1	14 2	270 24	105 P 214 F 14 A 14 A	1600.00 140.00 140.00
Barber, John Nixon, John	A30 D30		house & lot stable	23 x 23 12 x 20	wood wood	1	4	48	52 P 243 F	150.00

Carlisle Borough

Owner / Occupant	Ref.	Location / Adjoining Owner	Structure	Dimensions	Descr.	Stories	Lights / Windows	Area		Value
Barkley, Robert			house 1 & lot	22 x 44	wood	2	19	228	52 P 243 F	500.00
			house 2	21 x 14	wood, small	1	3	10		
			carpenter shop	20 x 18	wood	1	5	60		
	A22 D22		stable	25 x 16	wood					
Bartholomy, Peter			house & lot	25 x 22	wood	2	8	81	52 P 243 F	400.00
	A21 D21		stable	16 x 13	wood					
Barton, William			house & lot	31 x 33	stone	2	10	234	40 P	800.00
Gray, Catharine			kitchen	13 x 10	stone	1	1	12		
			stable	20 x 15	wood					
	A24 D24		note: Barton is a resident of Lancaster County							
Barton, William			house & lot	20 x 30	wood	1	3	57	5 P 248 F	200.00
Murry, Andrew			kitchen	13 x 10	stone	1	1	12		
	A25 D25									
Beigle, William Henry			house & lot	19 x 20	wood	2	6	75	105 P 214 F	1100.00
Beigle, John			addition	17 x 25	stone	2	8	108		
			kitchen	23 x 19	wood	1	1	16		
			stable	24 x 22	stone					
	A10 D10		smith shop	12 x 28	wood					
Bigler, John			house & lot	22 x 22	wood	2	5	48	52 P 243 F	270.00
Schell, Henry			addition	12 x 22	wood	1	2	18		
	A16 D16		stable		wood					
Black, William			house & lot	37 x 17	wood	1	5	49	52 P 243 F	130.00
	A23 D23		stable	18 x 19	wood					
Blain, Alexander			house & lot	21 x 24	stone	2	12	129	105 P 214 F	800.00
Smith, John			kitchen	14 x 21	stone	1	1	15		
			stable	33 x 24	stone					
	A14 D14		smoke house	15 x 10	brick					
Blaine, Ephraim	B10	High Street Irvine, William, General	lot						105 P 243 F	300.00
Blaine, Ephraim			house & lot	18 x 20	wood	1	3	36	52 P 243 F	150.00
Ferguson, Colonel	A17 D17									
Blaine, Ephraim		Pomfret Street	house & lot	26 x 22	stone, unfinished	1			52 P 243 F	150.00
unoccupied	B9									

Carlisle Borough

Owner / Occupant	Ref.	Location / Adjoining Owner	Structure	Dimensions	Descr.	Stories	Windows Lights	Area	Area	Value
Blaine, James		on alley	house & lot	21 x 44	brick	2	16	348	14 P 74 F	1867.00
		Blaine, Robert	kitchen	40 x 16	stone	2	10	144		
			wash house	14 x 16	stone	1 1/4	2	21		
			stable & carriage house	24 x 37	stone				26 P 121 F	200.00
		other lot on alley	lot						24 P 86 F	30.00
	A27 B11 B12 D27									
Blaine, Robert		Louther Street	house	16 x 16						
Walker, John		Blain, James	lot						26 P 121 F	80.00
	B14									
Blaine, Robert			house & lot	33 x 44	brick	2	12	270	28 P	2400.00
Watt, David, Esq.		Blaine, James	kitchen	40 x 16	stone	2	10	144		
			wash house	14 x 16	stone	1 1/4	2	21		
			stable	24 x 29	stone					
	A28 B13 D28		lot						26 P 121 F	180.00
Blair, Isaiah, Dr.			house & lot	27 x 33	stone	2	8	186	23 P 218 F	1100.00
Hart, Anthony, Rev.			kitchen	21 x 11	wood	1	1	12		
			stable	18 x 18	wood					
	A26 D26		note: exemption claimed--rented by the German congregation							
Blair, William			house & lot	16 x 24	brick	2	8	98	52 P 243 F	800.00
			shop	16 x 24	brick	1	3	60		
	A13 D13		stable	22 x 18	wood					
Bonner, John			house & lot	18 x 18	wood	1	2	18	26 P 121 F	110.00
	A19 D19		stable	18 x 12	wood					
Boyd, Simon		Louther Street	house & lot	24 x 18	wood	1	5	60	52 P 243 F	700.00
		Eyler, Jacob	addition	24 x 9	stone	1	1	12		
			kitchen	26 x 8	wood	1	4	35		
			smith shop	28 x 27	stone					
			stable	20 x 16	wood					
			coal house	20 x 16	wood					
		Eyler, Jacob	lot						52 P 243 F	50.00
	A9 B5 D9									
Brown, Henry		South Street	house	30 x 15	wood	1	2	14		10.00
	B18		lot						52 P 243 F	40.00
Brown, John			house & lot	23 x 20	wood	2	5	51	26 P 121 F	200.00
McAlreavy, John			kitchen	18 x 14	wood	1	3	30		
	A18 D18		note: "sold Philip Grove"							

Carlisle Borough

Owner / Occupant	Ref.	Location / Adjoining Owner	Structure	Dimensions	Descr.	Stories	Lights Windows	Area	Value
Brown, William (tanner)		Bedford & Pomfret Streets McTeer, James	house	28 x 12	frame	2	11 133	52 P 243 F	1000.00
			kitchen	11 x 18	frame	1	1 12		
			shop	20 x 16	log				
			stable	30 x 18	log				
			tan yard		12 vats				
	A29 B15 D29		mill house	50 x 20	frame	1		52 P 243 F	500.00
Brown, William (tanner)		Rowney, James &	tract		unfinished			29 A	290.00
	B16	Beaker, John	note: unfinished house [?]						
Brown, William, Jr.		Hannover & South Streets	house & lot	20 x 24	frame	2	9 114	52 P 243 F	400.00
			work shop	30 x 21	wood	2	8 96		
			still house	17 x 15	wood				
			bark house	21 x 21	wood				
			mill house	24 x 20	wood				
			shade house	19 x 20					
			tanyard						
	A15 B7 D15		lot					52 P 243 F	
Buchanan, William		South Street Hamilton, James, Esq.	house & lot	22 x 17	wood	2	8 75	26 P 121 F	200.00
			lot					52 P 243 F	30.00
	A11 B6 D11								
Buchanan, William Gibson, Ann			house & lot	26 x 27	brick	2	10 192	26 P 121 F	800.00
			kitchen	13 x 17	wood	1 1/2	3 24		
			out house 1	17 x 24	wood	2	6 44		
	A12 D12		out house 2	22 x 12	brick	1	2 24		
Bullock, Moses Wendle, Michael			house & lot	18 x 20	frame	2	7 84	26 P 121 F	300.00
			kitchen	16 x 13	wood	1 1/2	4 36		
	A20 D20		stable	18 x 12	wood				
Burns, Mary			house	20 x 18	wood	1	2 14		10.00
	B17		lot					52 P 243 F	50.00
Butler, Richard, General, heirs Smith, Margaret			house & lot	27 x 22	wood	2	12 148	52 P 243 F	600.00
			back building & kitchen	34 x 16	wood	1	3 32		
			stable	14 x 12	wood				
	A8 D8		note: stable 18 x 18 in D						
Calhoun, Robert, heirs How, Catharine		East Street	house & lot	21 x 22	wood	1	4 32	52 P 243 F	200.00
			kitchen	17 x 22	wood	1	2 16		
	A51 B26 D51		lot		adj. other lot			158 P 84 F	90.00

Carlisle Borough

Owner / Occupant	Ref.	Location / Adjoining Owner	Structure	Dimensions	Descr.	Stories	Lights Windows	Area			Value
Calpatrick, James	A39 D39		house & lot	18 x 18	wood	1	2 17	52 P	243	F	110.00
Campbell, Elizabeth	B21	Louther Street	house lot	17 x 15				52 P	243	F	15.00 50.00
Cart, Jacob			house & lot	26 x 21	wood	2	7 66	52 P	243	F	600.00
			kitchen	26 x 21	wood	1	3 30				
			barn	63 x 23	wood						
			shade	12 x 20	wood						
	A45 B109 D45		building	75 x 16	wood, old						
Cart, Jacob, heirs			house & lot	22 x 22	wood	2	7 72	26 P	121	F	300.00
Cart, Christianna			kitchen	18 x 17	wood	1	2 24				
	A43 D43		stable	16 x 13	wood						
Cart, Jacob, heirs			house & lot	22 x 22	wood	1	3 36	26 P	121	F	200.00
Rhinehart, Frederick			kitchen	18 x 17	wood	1	3 34				
	A42 D42		stable	17 x 13	wood						
Carter, Andrew, heirs			house	21 x 20	wood	1 1/2	3 33				60.00
Carter, Margaret	B27		kitchen	12 x 12	wood	1	2 9	13 P	61	F	80.00
Chambers, Robert			house & lot	21 x 14	wood	2	5 63	52 P	243	F	500.00
Mitchell, James			kitchen	25 x 21	wood	1 1/2	5 39				
	A46 D46		stable	24 x 24	wood						
Chapman, John		Louther Street	house & lot	20 x 30	wood	1	3 36	52 P	243	F	130.00
		Anderson, Joseph	stable	15 x 18	wood						
			slaughter house	12 x 18	wood						
	A40 B22 D40							52 P	243	F	30.00
Collier, Hannah			house & lot	25 x 21	wood	2	10 132	52 P	243	F	300.00
	A48 D48		stable	17 x 15	wood						
Cooper, Charles			house & lot	16 x 24	wood	1	3 42	26 P	121	F	500.00
			kitchen	20 x 15	brick	1 1/2	6 72				
	A38 D38		stable	20 x 18	wood						
Cooper, Charles			house & lot	30 x 36	brick & stone	2	8 198	26 P	121	F	1500.00
		Lambuton, James	kitchen	24 x 16	stone	1 1/2	8 96				
	A37 B20 D37		stable	20 x 18	wood				5	A	50.00
Cope, Adam			house & lot	22 x 18	wood	2	8 88	52 P	243	F	400.00
			kitchen	16 x 18	wood	1	2 20				
			saddler shop	14 x 19	wood	1	4 36				
			stable	16 x 16	wood						
	A41 D41		shade	10 x 10	wood						

Carlisle Borough

Owner / Occupant	Location Ref. / Adjoining Owner	Structure	Dimensions	Descr.	Stories	Windows Lights	Area		Value
Craig, David		house & lot	18 x 20	stone	2	6 64	26 P 121 F		550.00
Spotwood, James		stable	7 x 18	wood					
		smoke house	18 x 13	stone	1	2 24			
	A31 D31	shade	30 x 12	wood	1	3 34			
Craighead, James		house & lot	38 x 18	wood	2	10 126	66 P 31 F		1000.00
		addition	23 x 8	brick	1	2 24			
		kitchen	22 x 14	wood	1	3 33			
		store house	19 x 22	brick	1	4 72			
	A49 D50	barn	35 x 27	wood					
Creigh, John		house & lot	30 x 38	brick	2	14 263	49 P 153 F		2000.00
		kitchen	23 x 16	stone	2	6 68			
		barn	25 x 37	wood					
	A32 D32	store house & stable	25 x 44	stone					
Creigh, John		house & lot	19 x 28	wood	2	8 84	52 P 243 F		600.00
Bayer, Frederick		kitchen	16 x 14	wood	1	1 9			
		shop	18 x 18	wood	1	2 40			
	A33 D33	stable	19 x 18	wood					
Creigh, John		house & lot	22 x 22	wood	2	8 84	52 P 243 F		200.00
Bolinger, Peter		stable	17 x 16	wood					
	A34 D34								
Creigh, John &	East Street	house & lot	27 x 24	wood	2	7 83	105 P 214 F		400.00
Kline, George		kitchen	15 x 24	stone	1	3 32	158 P 84 F		200.00
Haslet, Robert		stable	18 x 21	wood					
		tan house	60 x 21	wood, old					
	A52 B23 D52	note: house one story in D							
Crever, Jacob, Esq.	on alley	house	34 x 38	stone	2	13 276	56 P 60 F		2300.00
	Egolf, Michael	kitchen	17 x 38	brick	2	13 162			
		barn	60 x 20	wood			1 P 87 F		100.00
		warehouse	17 x 38	brick	1	2 52			
	Crever, John	tract					55 A		550.00
	A35 B19 D35								
Crever, Jacob, Esq.		house & lot	33 x 23	wood, part stone	1	4 96	52 P 243 F		300.00
Herwick, Jacob		kitchen	20 x 18	wood	1	2 24			
	A36 D36	back building	21 x 15	wood	1	3 28			

Carlisle Borough

Owner Occupant	Ref.	Location Adjoining Owner	Structure	Dimensions	Descr.	Stories	Lights Windows	Area		Value
Crever, John		East Street	house & lot	25 x 18	stone	2	6	66	26 P 121 F	600.00
		Craighead, James	stable	18 x 18	stone					
			barn	22 x 20	old logs					
			brew house	40 x 33	stone	2				
			malt house	40 x 35	stone	1				
		Crever, Jacob	tract						42 A	45.00
		Crever, Jacob	tract						25 1/2 A	225.00
	A50 B24 B25 D49									
Criswell, Samuel			house 1 & lot	23 x 18	wood	2	9	123	105 P 214 F	500.00
			kitchen	19 x 16	wood	1 1/2	2	18		
			stable	20 x 20	wood					
			house 2	17 x 17	wood, small	1	1	9		
			smith shop	20 x 34	stone & brick	2	7	104		
	A47 D47									
Croph, Casper			house	37 x 17	wood	2	11	126	52 P 243 F	300.00
			kitchen	15 x 15	wood	1	2	13		
	A44 D44		stable	17 x 14	wood					
Crous, Nicholas			house	17 x 18	wood	1	3	22		30.00
Barret, Richard			stable	15 x 15	wood				105 P 214 F	90.00
	B28									
Daugherty, Sarah		Pomfret Street	house	24 x 21						20.00
unoccupied		Burns, Mary							52 P 243 F	50.00
	B35									
Davidson, Robert, Rev.		High Street	house	30 x 39	brick	2	17	222	52 P 243 F	1300.00
		Duncan, John, heirs	kitchen	16 x 29	stone	2	9	84	52 P 243 F	150.00
	A56 B29 D56		stable	30 x 20						
Davidson, Robert, Rev.		Hamilton, James	tract						6 1/2 A	65.00
	B30									
Delaney, John		Bedford Street	house & lot	39 x 25	wood	1	5	68	52 P 243 F	800.00
		Dickinson College	shop	27 x 21	wood	1	6	109	52 P 243 F	50.00
			shade	15 x 10	wood	1	2	16		
			stable	18 x 20	wood					
		Pomfret Street	shop	11 x 12	wood					
		Collier, Hannah								
	A58 B33 B34 D58									
Delaney, John			house & lot	20 x 20	wood	1	4	39	52 P 243 F	150.00
Mathews, Adam			weaver shop	14 x 17	wood	1	1	6		
	A59 D59		stable	16 x 16	wood					

Carlisle Borough

Owner / Occupant	Location Ref. Adjoining Owner	Structure	Dimensions	Descr.	Stories	Lights Windows	Area		Value
Delaney, John Montgomery, Mary	A60 D60	house & lot stable 1 stable 2	25 x 21 18 x 18 14 x 7	wood wood wood	2	9	108	52 P 243 F	150.00
Denny, Ebenezer Denny, Agness	A53 D53	house & lot kitchen stable	20 x 18 12 x 8 15 x 10	wood wood wood	1 1	4 1	36 6	52 P 243 F	200.00
Dickson, Thomas Caldwell, Samuel	A62 D62	house & lot kitchen stable	18 x 21 17 x 21 18 x 15	wood wood wood	2 2	7 3	69 36	26 P 121 F	200.00
Dickson, Thomas Cockins, Vincent	A63 D63	house & lot stable	24 x 21 15 x 12	wood wood	2	6	72	26 P 121 F	200.00
Dill, John, Jr. Johnston, Hugh	A61 D61	house & lot	24 x 21	wood	1	4	32	52 P 243 F	300.00
Duncan, James, Esq.	B39	tract						50 A	500.00
Duncan, James, Esq. Kelly, Patrick	A67 D67	house & lot		log	1		28	52 P 243 F	110.00
Duncan, John, heirs	Louther Street Fossett, Robert B38	lot						52 P 243 F	30.00
Duncan, John, heirs McKinzie, Mrs.	A55 D55	house & lot kitchen	20 x 37 15 x 18	stone stone	2 1 1/2		216 25	16 P 44 F	1000.00
Duncan, John, heirs Thompson, William	A54 D54	house & lot kitchen hatter shop stable	24 x 30 27 x 18 30 x 10 18 x 11	brick wood wood wood	2 1 1	8 2 2	117 24 8	52 P 243 F	800.00
Duncan, Stephen Hearst, George	B37	house lot		log				52 P 243 F	15.00 60.00
Duncan, Stephen, Esq.	A64 D64	house kitchen store house stable note: stable is wood in D	40 x 37 20 x 28 34 x 26 29 x 26	stone stone stone stone	2 1 1/2		400 84	29 P 145 F	2400.00

Carlisle Borough

Owner / Occupant	Ref.	Location / Adjoining Owner	Structure	Dimensions	Descr.	Stories	Lights Windows	Area		Value
Duncan, Stephen, Esq. Duncan, James, Esq.	B36	South Street	house & lot					1 A	51 P 155 F	200.00
Duncan, Stephen, Esq. Greenfield, Richard	A66 D66		house & lot smith shop		frame wood			24	52 P 243 F	400.00
Duncan, Stephen, Esq. Reid, Francis	A65 D65		house & lot kitchen stable barn	31 x 36 18 x 24 22 x 28 61 x 26	stone stone stone log & stone	2 1 1/2		252 72	52 P 243 F	1200.00
Duncan, Thomas, Esq.		Pomfret Street Duncan, James, Esq.	house & lot kitchen & office stable carriage house	32 x 40 40 x 30 30 x 26 20 x 20	brick brick stone wood	2 2	12 19	252 324	52 P 243 F 52 P 243 F	3500.00 30.00
		Hughes, John Hughes, John	tract tract					40 A 9 A		400.00 90.00
	A57 B31 B32 D57									
Eby, Henry		Pomfret Street Scoby, James	house & lot stable carpenter shop	30 x 26 20 x 18 19 x 18	wood wood wood	2 1	10 3	96 22	105 P 214 F 52 P 243 F	400.00 40.00
	A69 B40 D69									
Eby, Moses			house & lot joiner shop stable	32 x 20 16 x 12 16 x 12	brick & wood wood wood	2 1	12 3	146 14	26 P 121 F	400.00
	A70 D70									
Egolf, Michael	A73 D73		house & lot kitchen stable	22 x 26 13 x 13 18 x 15	wood stone wood	2 1	7 2	90 16	19 P 227 F	350.00
Elliott, James	A71 D71		house & lot kitchen stable	24 x 23 17 x 15 21 x 16	wood brick wood	2 1	8 1	90 12	26 P 121 F	200.00
Elliott, John	A68 D68		house & lot kitchen stable slaughter house	36 x 15 15 x 13 11 x 12 16 X 16	wood wood wood brick	1 1	8 1	87 9	52 P 243 F	500.00

Carlisle Borough

Owner / Occupant	Ref.	Location / Adjoining Owner	Structure	Dimensions	Descr.	Stories	Windows	Lights	Area	Value
Eylor, Jacob (tailor)			house & lot	20 x 18	wood	1	1	12	52 P 243 F	150.00
			addition	9 x 18	stone	1	2	24		
	A72 D72		stable	14 x 12	wood					
Felter, Jacob			house & lot	35 x 18	wood	1	5	60	52 P 243 F	250.00
			stable	18 x 12	wood					
	A77 D77		workshop	18 x 21	wood	1	5	45		
Fossett, Robert Herron, David & Carten. John	A80 D80		house & lot	25 x 14	wood	1	1	8	52 P 243 F	110.00
Foster, Thomas		Hanover Street	house & lot	44 x 34	stone	2	17	360	38 P 214 F	3500.00
			kitchen	29 x 64	brick	2	24	576		
	A74 D74		smoke house	22 x 22	brick	1	1	18		
Foster, Thomas		Pomfret Street Gustine, Samuel	lot						52 P 243 F	50.00
	B41									
Foster, Thomas		Hannover Street adjacent other lot	stable	54 x 29	stone				52 P 243 F	1500.00
	B42		carriage house	43 x 23	wood					
Foulk, Stephen Forsyth, John			house & lot	22 x 22	wood	1	3	36	2 P 243 F	110.00
	A79 D79		kitchen	12 x 9	wood	1	1	4		
Foulk, Stephen Heigle, William			house & lot	31 x 34	stone	2	18	381	50 P	2000.00
			kitchen	17 x 20	stone	1	4	45		
			stable 1	34 x 23	stone					
	A78 D78		stable 2	19 x 18	stone					
Frank, Adam	A76 D76		house & lot	22 x 20	wood	2	5	66	52 P 243 F	250.00
Frank, Jacob			house & lot	25 x 22	wood	2	8	79	52 P 243 F	300.00
			kitchen	18 x 15	wood	1	2	21		
	A75 D75		stable	16 x 13	wood					
Freelin, Mary		Louther Street	house	15 x 15						20.00
	B43		lot						26 P 121 F	50.00
Galbraith, Alexander			house & lot	39 x 18	wood	1	4	33	52 P 243 F	150.00
			smith shop	23 x 18	wood					
	A83 D83		note: name also Galbreath							

Carlisle Borough

Owner Occupant	Location Ref. Adjoining Owner	Structure	Dimensions	Descr.	Stories	Lights Windows	Area	Value
Gamble, Widow Clark, Thomas A93 D93		house & lot	21 x 24	wood	1	2	18	52 P 243 F	110.00
Gaw, John Skinner, Robert B45		house lot	20 x 18	wood	1	3	22 52 P 243 F	20.00 80.00
Given, James A86 D86		house & lot kitchen stable	24 x 34 27 x 18 20 x 18	stone stone wood	2 2	8 8	162 96	26 P 214 F	1200.00
Given, James Hemming, Richard A87 D87		house & lot kitchen stable note: occupant's name may be Flemming	22 x 21 11 x 10 15 x 13	wood wood wood	1	3	30	35 P 243 F	120.00
Given, James Pope, John A88 D88		house & lot kitchen stable	26 x 31 15 x 17 18 x 18	stone stone wood	1 1	9 2	145 24	26 P 121 F	600.00
Given, James Stuart, George A89 D89		house & lot kitchen	23 x 19 19 x 11	wood wood	1 1	4 2	36 10	26 P 121 F	200.00
Gray, James Richardson, William B44	North Street	house lot	18 x 19				52 P 243 F	50.00 88.00
Gray, Widow Crouse, George A91 D91		house & lot out house	24 x 24 15 x 13	wood	2	9	80	52 P 243 F	400.00
Greenwood, John A90 D90		house & lot kitchen stable cooper shop	18 x 18 15 x 10 9 x 9 15 x 15	wood wood wood wood	1 1 1	7 2 3	54 10 14	52 P 243 F	300.00
Greenwood, John B107	Henderson, Matthew	house lot	18 x 16				5 A	20.00 50.00
Greer, Samuel Crouse, Jacob A84 D84		house & lot	16 x 16	wood	1	2	21	26 P 121 F	110.00

Carlisle Borough

Owner Occupant	Location Ref. Adjoining Owner	Structure	Dimensions	Descr.	Stories	Lights Windows	Area	Value
Greer, Samuel McMacken, James	A85 D85	house & lot stable	20 x 20 16 x 10	wood wood	1	4	42	26 P 121 F	110.00
Gregg, James, heirs Elliot, James	A92 D92	house & lot stable	22 x 22 18 x 12	wood wood	2	2	16	52 P 243 F	200.00
Gustine, Lemuel Swoap, Mary	A82 D82	house & lot kitchen stable	36 x 30 18 x 15 20 x 20	stone stone wood	2 1	12 3	274 21	52 P 243 F	1400.00
Gustine, Lemuel, Dr.	A81 D81	house & lot kitchen shade stable 1 stable 2	29 x 39 29 x 18 14 x 18 22 x 22 20 x 13	stone stone stone stone wood	2 1 1	9 3 2	216 45 30	26 P 121 F	2400.00
Hamilton, James	Davidson, Robert, Rev. B47	tract					6 1/2 A	65.00
Hamilton, James, Esq. Buchanan, William	South Street A95 B46 D95	house & lot kitchen office stable carriage house 1 carriage house 2 lot	30 x 36 28 x 36	brick brick brick stone stone stone	3 2 2	20 7 8	190 80 192	52 P 243 F 52 P 243 F	3500.00 38.00
Handle, Jacob Carothers, John, Esq.	A100 D100	house & lot	16 x 31	stone	2	6	126	14 P 14 F	700.00
Hare, Abraham	B52	house 1 kitchen stable house 2 lot note: house 2, walls only built	18 x 18 25 x 14 28 x 22 21 x 31	wood, old stone wood brick	1 2			26 P 121 F	400.00
Hare, Abraham Wise, George	A105 D105	house & lot kitchen stable	30 x 31 38 x 17 16 x 20	stone stone wood	2 2	10 7	225 127	26 P 121 F	1600.00
Harps, John, Rev.	A101 D101	house & lot stable	30 x 25 15 x 19	wood wood	2	5	80	105 P 214 F	200.00

Carlisle Borough

Owner / Occupant	Ref.	Location / Adjoining Owner	Structure	Dimensions	Descr.	Stories	Lights Windows	Area	Value
Haslet, Samuel		North Street	house	23 x 20					40.00
	B50	Rowan, David	lot					52 P 247 F	70.00
Hays, Joseph			house & lot	20 x 20	wood	2	8	99 52 P 243 F	1200.00
			addition	28 x 18	stone	2	6	72	
	A99 D99		stable	12 x 20	wood				
Heap, John, Esq.		South & East Sts.	lot					105 P 214 F	160.00
McManus, Charles		McClure, Charles	stable	15 x 15	wood				
	B51		still house	27 x 22	wood				
Holmes, Andrew			house & lot	24 x 24	wood	2	9	125 52 P 243 F	750.00
Wallace, Jonathan			addition	12 x 24	brick	2	5	74	
			kitchen	12 x 24	stone	1 1/2	4	42	
			stable 1	11 x 24	wood				
	A103 D103		stable 2	15 x 15	wood				
Holmes, John			house & lot	60 x 33	stone	2	22	504 52 P 243 F	3500.00
			kitchen	18 x 15	stone	1	1	16	
			store house	60 x 21	stone			2 A	30.00
	A98 B110 D98		& stable						
Holt, Elizabeth, heirs			house & lot	27 x 25	stone	2	11	252 52 P 243 F	1200.00
Oliver, John			kitchen	18 x 12	stone	1	1	12	
			store house	21 x 20	wood	1	4	48	
	A94 D94		stable	16 x 15	wood				
Hoosenight [?], Barbara		North Street	house	20 x 16					15.00
Lay [?], Mary			lot					52 P 243 F	50.00
	B8								
Hughs, John			house & lot	30 x 38	stone	2	6	130 22 P 10 F	1300.00
		Duncan, Thomas, Esq.	kitchen	28 x 18	stone	1 1/2	4	36	
	A96 B48 D96		stable	18 x 16	wood			26 A	260.00
Hughs, John, Esq.			house & lot	28 x 18	wood	1 1/2	10	90 4 P 111 F	400.00
Elliot, Ann			kitchen	16 x 16	stone	1 1/2	4	36	
	A97 D97								
Hunter, John		South Street	house & lot	38 x 22	brick	2	11	124 52 P 243 F	1730.00
		Rose, William	kitchen	24 x 18	stone	1	6	66	
			store house	22 x 14	brick	2	4	40	
	A104 B49 D104		barn	23 x 69	wood			52 P 243 F	30.00
Hutton, James			house & lot	20 x 16	wood	1	3	32 52 P 243 F	110.00
	A102 D102		shade	6 x 4	wood				

Carlisle Borough

Owner Occupant	Ref.	Location Adjoining Owner	Structure	Dimensions	Descr.	Stories	Lights Windows	Area	Value
Irvine, William, General		West & North Sts. Wallace, William	house & lot addition kitchen stable	30 x 22 32 x 22 18 x 16 20 x 20	stone brick stone wood	2 2 1	12 8 2	256 162 24	52 P 243 F 158 P 84 F	2000.00 90.00
	A106 B53 D106								
Iselt [?], John Sturm, George			house & lot kitchen stable	34 x 33 14 x 33 17 x 17	stone stone wood	2 2	8 6	198 64	26 P 121 F	1500.00
	A107 D107								
Jackson, Samuel		Pomfret Street other lot	house & lot stable lot	22 x 20 14 x 12	wood wood	1	2	24	52 P 243 F 52 P 243 F	150.00 30.00
	A109 B54 D109								
Johnston, Adam			house & lot kitchen stable out house 1 out house 2	23 x 20 21 x 15 18 x 17 17 x 17 17 x 17	wood wood wood wood wood	1 1	4 1	28 8	105 P 214 F	350.00
		Black, Robert Lyon, William	tract tract						22 A 5 A	220.00 50.00
	A110 B55 D110								
Jones, Thomas			house & lot stable	27 x 24 16 x 16	brick & wood wood	2	12	123	22 P 10 F	400.00
	A108 D108								
Keith, William			house & lot	15 x 24	stone	1	3	36	26 P 121 F	110.00
	A115 D115								
Keller, Leonard			house & lot kitchen hatter shop stable	23 x 28 22 x 20 21 x 17 18 x 18	wood wood wood wood	2 1 1	7 3 4	88 36 24	52 P 243 F	400.00
	A117 D117								
Kennedy, Hugh			house & lot kitchen stable	17 x 26 14 x 21 15 x 15	wood wood wood	1 1	5 4	60 33	52 P 243 F	320.00
	A114 D114								
Kerr, Andrew			house & lot kitchen smith shop stable	21 x 21 21 x 18 29 x 14 24 x 18	wood wood wood wood	1 1 1	5 2 3	57 24 17	35 P 71 F	300.00
	A116 D116								

Carlisle Borough

Owner / Occupant	Ref.	Location / Adjoining Owner	Structure	Dimensions	Descr.	Stories	Lights Windows	Area	Value
Kincaide, John Smiley, Thomas	A113 D113		house & lot kitchen hatter shop stable 1 stable 2	24 x 32 15 x 16 27 x 12 25 x 25	stone frame & brick wood wood wood	2 1 1	11 204 1 12 4 24	52 P 243 F	1000.00
Kline, George	A111 D111		house & lot kitchen & printing office smoke house stable	27 x 32 16 x 27 12 x 10 30 x 18	stone stone & brick brick & stone wood	2 2	7 152 9 132	26 P 121 F	900.00
Kline, George Irvine, Mrs.	A112 D112		house & lot	20 x 25	wood	2	9 104	52 P 243 F	180.00
Kreishner, John	A263 D263		house & lot	17 x 17	wood	1	3 30	52 P 243 F	110.00
Laird, Samuel, Esq.	A138 B64 B65 D138	on alley Weaver, Jacob South Street	house & lot kitchen workshop stable shade barn lot tract	30 x 30 23 x 19 24 x 20 16 x 23 45 x 18	stone stone brick stone frame, double adj. Robert Chambers adj. James Duncan, Esq.	2 2 1	12 172 5 51 6 72	30 P 26 P 121 F 52 P 243 F 25 A	1200.00 140.00 30.00 250.00
Laird, Samuel, Esq. Isett, John	A139 D139		house & lot kitchen stable note: house one story in D, two stories in A	29 x 22 21 x 11 16 x 23	stone brick stone	2 2	8 122 3 30	22 P 243 F	800.00
Lambuton, James	B60	Cooper, Charles	tract					15 A	150.00
Lambuton, James	A125 B59 D125	South Street Blaire, James	house & lot kitchen store house & stable	33 x 30 18 x 12 30 x 19	stone wood wood	2 1	11 276 1 12	28 P 269 F 52 P 243 F	1600.00 40.00
Lambuton, John Douglass, John	A127 D127		house & lot kitchen stable	23 x 34 17 x 15 22 x 18	stone stone wood	2 1	8 192 1 18	50 P	1600.00
Lambuton, John Martin, James	A26 D126		house & lot	13 x 21	wood	1	3 36	2 P 243 F	110.00

Carlisle Borough

Owner Occupant	Ref.	Location Adjoining Owner	Structure	Dimensions	Descr.	Stories	Lights Windows	Area	Value
Lechler, Henry			house & lot	17 x 26	stone	1 1/2	6	72	52 P 243 F	700.00
			kitchen	20 x 24	stone	1	2	24		
	A145 D145		shop	9 x 17	wood					
Lee, Richard, heirs			house & lot	27 x 19	wood	1	4	34	52 P 243 F	110.00
unoccupied			kitchen	13 x 13	wood	1	2	6		
	A136 D136		stable	10 x 9	wood					
Lee, Richard, heirs		North Street other lot	lot						52 P 243 F	30.00
	B111									
Lefever, George			house & lot	21 x 20	wood	1	6	51	26 P 121 F	300.00
	A135 D135		kitchen	20 x 14	brick	1	4	40		
Lefferry, David			house & lot	15 x 22	wood	1	3	28	52 P 243 F	200.00
			stable	16 x 20	wood					
	A132 D132		note: Leffery in C							
Legget, Patrick			house & lot	26 x 22	wood	2	8	68	52 P 243 F	250.00
	A137 D137		stable	14 x 14	wood					
Levy, William			house & lot	23 x 20	wood	2	9	98	52 P 243 F	400.00
Hays, Samuel & Foster [?], Jonathan			kitchen	18 x 15	stone	1	3	22		
	A133 D133									
Levy, William, Esq.			house & lot	20 x 24	wood	1	3	42	52 P 243 F	650.00
			kitchen	18 x 14	stone	2	4	42		
	A119 D119		shop	14 x 10	wood	1	3	31		
Leyburn, Robert			house & lot	30 x 21	wood	2	9	105	52 P 243 F	850.00
			kitchen	16 x 24	wood	1	4	36		
	A121 D121		barn	36 x 16	wood					
Lindsey, David		Pomfret Street Steel, John, Esq.	house & lot	25 x 20	wood	2	10	112	52 P 243 F	700.00
			kitchen	25 x 16	wood	1	4	38	52 P 243 F	
			stable	28 x 18	wood					
			shop 1	20 x 15	wood	1	2	18		
	A118 D118		shop 2	15 x 10	wood					
Lindsey, David		South Street Boyd, Simon	shop	15 x 16	wood					
			lot						52 P 243 F	50.00
	B56									
Lindsey, David		Pomfret Street Steel, John, Esq.	lot						52 P 243 F	30.00
	B57									

Carlisle Borough

Owner Occupant	Ref.	Location Adjoining Owner	Structure	Dimensions	Descr.	Stories	Lights Windows	Area	Value
Lindsey, Sidney			house	19 x 19					
			lot					52 P 243 F	50.00
	B63		note: claimed to be exempt from valuation, the owner not being taxed by the State for 15 years last past on account of his age and poverty.						
Loffman, Philip			house & lot	33 x 33	stone	2	9	210 52 P 243 F	1300.00
			kitchen	26 x 26	stone	2	8	84	
	A122 D122		stable	22 x 33	stone				
Logue, Adam			house & lot	22 x 20	wood	1	3	22 26 P 121 F	250.00
			wheelwright shop	22 x 22	frame & brick	2	9	81	
	A134 D134								
Logue, George, Esq.			house & lot	24 x 21	wood	2	8	92 44 P 21 F	650.00
			kitchen	16 x 24	wood	1	2	24	
			office	12 x 13	frame	1	2	24	
		Lambuton, James & Duncan, James	tract					10 A	100.00
	A140 B66 D140								
Logue, George, Esq.			house & lot	20 x 20	wood	1	6	66 17 P 172 F	170.00
Barnes, John			shade	11 x 20	wood				
	A142 D142								
Logue, George, Esq.			house & lot	18 x 20	stone	2	5	50 44 P 21 F	400.00
Sample, John			shade	11 x 7	stone	1	1	9	
			wheelwright shop		wood	1	8	54	
	A141 D141		stable	16 x 18	wood				
Logue, George, Esq.			house & lot	16 x 16	wood	1	3	22 52 P 243 F	170.00
Swalbridge, William			shade	10 x 16	wood				
	A143 D143								
Logue, George, Esq.			house & lot	20 x 24	frame	2	7	71 52 P 243 F	400.00
Webber, Mrs.			kitchen	12 x 12	frame	1	1	9	
	A144 D144		note: sold to Brown, Robert, cordwinder						
Louchridge, Abraham		South Street	house & lot	46 x 18	wood	1	7	42 40 P 255 F	1500.00
		McCune, William	barn	54 x 30	wood				
			shade	12 x 13	stone				
			stable	24 x 14	wood			52 P 243 F	250.00
	A128 B62 D128		still house	45 x 26	stone				
Louchridge, Abraham		Buchanan, William	tract					105 P 214 F	60.00
		Eby, Henry	tract					52 P 243 F	40.00
		Duncan, James, Esq.	tract					20 A	200.00
		Baker, John	tract					15 A	150.00
	B61								

Carlisle Borough

Owner / Occupant Ref.	Location Adjoining Owner	Structure	Dimensions	Descr.	Stories	Lights	Windows	Area	Value
Louchridge, Abraham Dawson, George & Smith, Eliphet A131 D131		house & lot kitchen	29 x 25 28 x 19	stone stone	2 2	12 7	169 87	6 P 91 F	700.00
Louchridge, Abraham Fishbaugh, Catharine A129 D129		house & lot kitchen	12 x 25 12 x 27	wood wood	2 1	5 2	93 8	2 P 205 F	400.00
Louchridge, Abraham McGinnis, John A130 D130		house & lot 30 D130	15 x 25	stone	2	7	128	2 P 235 F	400.00
Loudon, Archibald A120 D120		house & lot kitchen stable	25 x 25 13 x 13 18 x 18	wood wood wood	2 1	10 1	139 12	26 P 121 F	500.00
Lyon, William, Esq. A123 D123		house & lot barn kitchen office wood house	28 x 35 18 x [?] 14 x 20 20 x 18 16 x 18	stone wood stone stone wood	2 2 1	11 5 3	204 66 54	105 P 214 F	1600.00
Lyon, William, Esq. B58	Henderson, Matthew Armstrong, James Hamilton, James	tract 1 tract 2 tract 3						135 A 3 A 25 A	135.00 30.00 250.00
Lyon, William, Esq. Fleming, John A124 D124		house & lot kitchen	24 x 18 10 x 15	wood wood	1 1	3 1	36 8	52 P 243 F	200.00
Magaw, Robert, heirs Nisbet, Charles, Rev. A163 D163		house & lot kitchen stable	27 x 37 27 x 15 20 x 16	stone stone wood	2 1	8 3	162 42	26 P 121 F	1400.00
Mather, Jacob Patton, Mary A154 D154		house & lot kitchen stable	27 x 24 24 x 23 19 x 14	stone stone wood	2 1	13 4	144 23	52 P 243 F	800.00
McCartney, Patrick McCauley, John A178 D178		house & lot stable	25 x 21 28 x 8	wood wood	2	8	81	52 P 243 F	300.00
McCauley, John B77		house lot note: This property claimed to be exempted from valuation, the owner being a soldier of the United States.	17 x 14	wood				26 P 121 F	20.00 50.00

Carlisle Borough

Owner Occupant	Ref.	Location Adjoining Owner	Structure	Dimensions	Descr.	Stories	Lights Windows	Area	Value
McClure, Charles		Pomfret & Pitt Sts.	lot					1 A 51 P 155 F	120.00
		East Street Heep, John	lot					105 P 214 F	60.00
	B74								
McClure, Charles Davis, James	A168 B73 D168	High Street other lot	house & lot wood house stable	36 x 30 21 x 17 31 x 26	stone wood wood	2	18	214 52 P 243 F 52 P 243 F	800.00 40.00
McClure, Charles McCullough, Francis	A169 D169		house & lot work shop	15 x 18 26 x 12	wood wood	1 1	1 2	12 152 P 243 F 18	110.00
McCormick, James, Esq.	A167 D167		house & lot kitchen stable	24 x 36 24 x 14 40 x 20	stone stone wood	2 1	9 1	168 52 P 243 F 12	1000.00
McCoskey, Samuel A.			house & lot kitchen	25 x 23 12 x 19	brick stone & brick	2 2	13 7	294 40 P 93	2000.00
			smoke house stable	14 x 8 41 x 22	brick brick				
		Davidson, Robert, Rev.	tract					5 A	50.00
		Duncan, James, Esq.	tract					10 A	100.00
	A181 B76 D181								
McCoskey, Samuel A.	A182 D182		house & lot kitchen	18 x 33 12 x 14	brick stone	2 1	10 1	164 12 P 243 F 12	1000.00
McCoy, John	A170 D170		house & lot kitchen stable	33 x 20 15 x 19 23 x 19	wood wood wood	1 1	4 2	46 52 P 243 F 20	500.00
McCullough, Hugh McBride, Robert	A177 D177		house & lot weaver shop stable	23 x 20 16 x 23 20 x 22	wood stone & brick wood	2 1	7 4	84 105 P 214 F 32	400.00
McCune, Esq., heirs Weakley, Nathaniel	A180 D180		house & lot kitchen stable	38 x 33 26 x 21 26 x 57	stone wood stone	2 1	17 2	310 52 P 243 F 36	1700.00
McCune, William	B79	South Street Louthridge, Abraham	house lot	21 x 16				52 P 243 F	10.00 40.00
McCurdy, John	A183 D183		house & lot smith shop	22 x 26 22 x 16	wood wood	2	9	106 52 P 243 F	650.00

Carlisle Borough

Owner Occupant	Location Ref. Adjoining Owner	Structure	Dimensions	Descr.	Stories	Lights Windows	Area	Value
McDonald, John Shoutz, Nicholas	A184 D184	house & lot piazza kitchen stable	22 x 21 15 x 6 15 x 17 15 x 20	wood wood stone wood	2 1 1	7 2 1	76 27 9	52 P 243 F	800.00
McDonald, Margaret	Johnston, Adam A179 B75 D179	house & lot addition stable	36 x 25 28 x 16 20 x 20	wood stone wood	2 2	11 8	132 103	52 P 243 F 9 A	500.00 90.00
McGinnis, John Rouse, Martin	A172 D172	house & lot	19 x 17	wood	1	3	18	105 P 214 F	150.00
McKinley, Daniel Leyburn, James	A174 D174	house & lot stable	24 x 21 15 x 15	wood wood	2	10	93	39 P 182 F	250.00
McKinley, Henry	A171 D171	house & lot kitchen	22 x 26 13 x 14	stone stone	2 1	8 1	112 4	52 P 243 F	540.00
McManis, Charles	A173 D173	house & lot kitchen stable	30 x 24 18 x 21 20 x 12	wood wood wood	1 1	4 3	48 36	26 P 121 F	150.00
McMurry, Thomas	A166 D165	house & lot	22 x 19	wood	1	4	20	105 P 214 F	140.00
McMurry, William Boden, Hugh	A175 D175	house & lot kitchen stable	27 x 22 30 x 26 18 x 15	wood stone wood	2 1	8 3	74 36	52 P 243 F	540.00
McPherson, William	A185 D185	house & lot kitchen stable	20 x 20 16 x 15 24 x 14	brick wood wood	2 1	7 2	90 24	26 P 121 F	350.00
McTeer, James Thomas, George	A176 D176	house & lot kitchen stable	32 x 30 14 x 14 19 x 19	brick wood wood	2 1	11 1	228 8	52 P 243 F	600.00
Miller, Jeremiah	A152 D152	house & lot kitchen stable	22 x 24 14 x 22 20 x 20	wood stone wood	2 1	8 3	92 28	26 P 121 F	450.00
Miller, Jeremiah	A153 D153	house & lot	25 x 32	wood	2	10	114	26 P 121 F	450.00
Miller, John, heirs Miller, John	A146 D146	house & lot kitchen store house	27 x 38 22 x 18 25 x 32	stone stone stone	2 1	15 3	382 36	52 P 243 F	2200.00

Carlisle Borough

Owner / Occupant	Ref.	Location / Adjoining Owner	Structure	Dimensions	Descr.	Stories	Lights Windows	Area		Value
Miller, Michael	A149 D149		house & lot kitchen	20 x 23 14 x 12	wood wood	2 1	8 1	100 9	26 P 121 F	200.00
Miller, Michael Guthrie, Robert D.	A150 D150		house & lot shop	16 x 20 13 x 23	wood wood	1 1	2 4	24 49	26 P 121 F	200.00
Miller, Philip Miller, Jeremiah, Sr.	A155 D155		house & lot work shop stable	16 x 26 26 x 24 18 x 18	stone wood wood	2 1	6 4	72 48	52 P 243 F	600.00
Miller, Robert, Esq.	B71	East Street Miller, William	lot						105 P 214 F	100.00
Miller, Robert, Esq.	B72	McClure, Charles Pattison, Charles & Duncan, Thomas, Esq.	tract tract						20 A 25 A	200.00 250.00
Miller, Robert, Esq.	A164 B70 D166	High & East Streets	house & lot 1 kitchen stable barn house 2	34 x 33 21 x 18 24 x 30 60 x 21 20 x 22	stone stone frame stone wood, old	2 2	17 6	324 55	79 P 92 F 1 A 51 P 155 F	1300.00 800.00
Miller, Robert, Esq. Brown, Robert	A165 D165		house & lot note: D shows Magaw, Robert as an owner	20 x 20	wood	2	7	72	26 P 121 F	300.00
Miller, William	A161 B68 D161	East Street Miller, Robert, Esq.	house 1 & lot kitchen stable tan yard currying shop bark shade mill house house 2	28 x 28 19 x 18 24 x 24 52 x 22 54 x 20 27 x 24 21 x 20	stone brick stone wood wood wood	2 1	11 1	147 12	52 P 243 F 105 P 213 F	950.00 1100.00 40.00
Mitchell, James, heirs Miller, Jeremiah	B67	Hanover Street Miller, Jeremiah	house	19 x 19					52 P 243 F	9.00
Montgomery, John, Esq.	A162 B69 D162	High & Pitt Streets Levis, William, Esq.	house & lot kitchen barn	43 x 39 36 x 20 60 x 21	stone stone wood, old	2 2	21 12	533 153	46 P 76 F 105 P 214 F	3200.00 600.00

Carlisle Borough

Owner / Occupant	Ref.	Location / Adjoining Owner	Structure	Dimensions	Descr.	Stories	Lights Windows	Area		Value
Moore, William (blacksmith)			house & lot	21 x 17	stone	2	7	60	52 P 243 F	700.00
			kitchen	12 x 16	wood	1	1	9		
			smith shop	24 x 20	wood	1	1	12		
	A151 D151		stable	16 x 16	wood					
Moore, William Glenn, John			house & lot	25 x 27	stone	2	11	165	52 P 243 F	1200.00
			kitchen	12 x 15	wood	1	1	6		
	A160 D160		barn	60 x 18	wood					
Moore, William Goebell, Henry			house & lot	34 x 35	stone	2	11	258	26 P 121 F	1400.00
			kitchen	24 x 20	stone	2	4	48		
	A159 D159									
Moore, William Greason [?], Robert			house & lot	27 x 36	stone	2	7	144	26 P 121 F	1400.00
			kitchen	18 x 27	stone	2	4	54		
	A158 D158		stable	12 x 26	wood					
Moore, William Keigley, Jacob			house & lot	29 x 25	wood	1 1/2	8	87	52 P 243 F	500.00
			kitchen	29 x 14	wood	1	2	24		
	A156 D156									
Moore, William unoccupied			house & lot	20 x 24	brick	2	8	96	26 P 121 F	400.00
	A157 D157		stable	9 x 18	wood					
Moorhead, James Allspaugh, George	A148 D148		house & lot	24 x 20	wood	2	9	93	39 P 182 F	200.00
Musselman, Jacob Stinicke, Charles			house & lot	29 x 41	brick	2	11	264	26 P 121 F	1500.00
	A147 D147		stable	12 x 16	wood					
Nailor, Thomas, heirs	A187 D187		house & lot	24 x 20	wood	1	3	18	105 P 214 F	110.00
			stable	14 x 12	wood					
Nelson, Nancy O'Bryan, Margery	B82	South Street	house	23 x 20						40.00
			lot						52 P 243 F	70.00
Nisbit, Charles, Rev., D. D.	B83	South Street Hamilton, James, Esq.	lot						105 P 214 F	60.00
Noble, John		Pomfret Street Steel, John	house & lot	26 x 18	brick	2	8	102	52 P 243 F	800.00
			stable	33 x 18	wood					
			slaughter house	22 x 18	stone					
	A186 B80 D186		lot						52 P 243 F	50.00

Carlisle Borough

Owner Occupant	Ref.	Location Adjoining Owner	Structure	Dimensions	Descr.	Stories	Lights Windows	Area	Value
Noble, John		Lyon, William, Esq.	tract					8 A	80.00
		Alexander, William, Esq.	tract					8 A	80.00
	B81								
Officer, John			house & lot	25 x 21	stone	2	7 67	52 P 243 F	700.00
			piaza	8 x 21	stone	1	1 9		
			out house	18 x 18	wood	2	9 84		
			carpenter shop	30 x 18	wood	1	10 96		
	A189 D189		stable	19 x 18	wood				
Orwan, John			house & lot	20 x 20	wood	1	3 30	52 P 243 F	150.00
	A188 D188		stable	12 x 10	wood				
Paddow, Peter			house & lot	18 x 21	wood	2	5 72	26 P 121 F	450.00
			addition	15 x 18	wood	1	3 26		
			kitchen	9 x 9	wood	1	1 9		
			kiln house	21 x 21	wood				
			out house	16 x 16	wood	1	2 18		
	A191 D191		potash works	16 x 16	wood	1	4 36		
Pattison, Charles			house & lot	24 x 24	wood	2	11 135	52 P 243 F	700.00
		Miller, Robert, Esq.	kitchen	15 x 15	wood	1	2 18		
			stable	34 x 18	wood			7 1/4 A	72.50
	A194 B86 D194		shop	20 x 18	wood	1	4 45		
Pattison, George			house & lot	24 x 20	wood	2	7 73	52 P 243 F	700.00
		Crever, John	kitchen	24 x 13	wood	1	4 27		
			barn	28 x 22	wood			12 A	120.00
	A193 B85 D193		shop	18 x 20	wood	1	5 93		
Pendergrass, Margaret			house & lot	23 x 20	wood	1	2 13	26 P 121 F	110.00
	A196 D196								
Philips, Robert, heirs			house & lot	21 x 18	wood	2	4 48	52 P 243 F	300.00
		Bullock, Moses	shade	21 x 12	wood	1	2 10		
			work shop	14 x 12	wood	1	3 18		
	A195 D195		stable	14 x 14	wood				
Pollock, James			house 1 & lot	24 x 26	wood	2	11 140	105 P 214 F	1600.00
			addition	45 x 20	brick	2	14 324		
			house 2	21 x 24	wood, small	1	3 45		
			barn 1	45 x 18	wood				
			barn 2	42 x 18	stone				
	A192 B84 D192		tract					16 A	160.00

Carlisle Borough

Owner / Occupant	Location Ref. Adjoining Owner	Structure	Dimensions	Descr.	Stories	Lights / Windows		Area	Value
Pollock, John		house 1 & lot	20 x 15	stone	2	7	72	52 P 243 F	450.00
		stable	18 x 16	wood					
	A190 D190	house 2	20 x 18	wood, unfinished					
Postlethwait, Samuel, Esq.		house & lot	30 x 38	brick	2	6	150	26 P 121 F	1400.00
		kitchen	28 x 18	stone	1 1/2	4	36		
	A197 D197	stable	28 x 18	wood					
Quigley, Michael	A198 D198	house & lot	30 x 20	wood	1	4	42	26 P 121 F	120.00
Rainey, William		house & lot	29 x 20	wood	1	11	68	52 P 243 F	550.00
		barn	20 x 50	wood					
		cooper shop	17 x 16	wood	1	3	15		
	Cart, Jacob	tract 1						20 A	200.00
	Montgomery, John, Esq.	tract 2						17 A	170.00
	A202 B87 D202								
Rainey, William		house & lot	26 x 26	wood	2	10	102	26 P 121 F	1400.00
Bigler, John		addition	11 x 26	wood	1	3	36		
		kitchen	34 x 19	stone & wood	2	8	93		
		wood house	19 x 10	stone					
		stable 1	40 x 25	stone					
	A204 D204	stable 2	21 x 10	wood					
Rainey, William		house & lot	13 x 26	stone	2	7	79	26 P 121 F	550.00
Dunlap, Daniel		kitchen	14 x 40	wood	1	7	72		
		shade & storehouse	15 x 10	wood					
	A203 D203	note: D indicates that shade and storehouse are two separate structures.							
Ramsey, Archibald		house & lot	25 x 19	wood	2	7	96	26 P 121 F	600.00
	A199 D199	kitchen	9 x 15	wood	1	1	12		
Ramsey, James, heirs	Pomfret Street	house	15 x 15						10.00
Jones, Joshua		lot						52 P 243 F	30.00
	B90								
Ramsey, James, heirs		house & lot	16 x 16	wood	1	2	15	26 P 121 F	105.00
Maxwell, William	A201 D201								
Ramsey, James, heirs		house & lot	22 x 22	wood	2	7	72	26 P 121 F	240.00
Williams, Samuel & Levinger, Mrs.		kitchen	12 x 10	wood	1	1	9		
	A200 D200								

Carlisle Borough

Owner Occupant	Ref.	Location Adjoining Owner	Structure	Dimensions	Descr.	Stories	Lights Windows	Area	Value
Randle, Agness	B93	South Street	house lot	25 x 20	wood			52 P 243 F	50.00 80.00
Rannels, Ruth McCoskey, Samuel	B78	High Street McCoskey, Samuel	house lot		old			52 P 243 F	150.00
			note: [this entry is alphabetized under M; owner and occupant may be reversed]						
Reid, James	A205 D205		house & lot kitchen smith shop coal house stable	27 x 24 22 x 11 20 x 31 22 x 12 17 x 17	stone stone stone wood wood	2 1	10 1	142 12	52 P 243 F	800.00
Reighter, John Reighter, Henry & Moore, Ralph	A212 D212		house & lot kitchen stable	29 x 33 18 x 15 18 x 15	stone wood wood	2 1	15 1	306 12	52 P 243 F	600.00
Reisinger, Adam	A210 D210		house & lot kitchen out house	22 x 22 9 x 9 22 x 22	brick wood wood	2 1	6	72	52 P 243 F	300.00
Rhine, Henry Fossett, Robert	A213 B92 D213	East Street	house & lot kitchen stable	33 x 22 46 x 21 15 x 15	stone stone wood	1 1/2 1	11 6	132 72	52 P 243 F 158 P 84 F	600.00 120.00
Rhine, John	A208 D208		house & lot kitchen stable potter house	27 x 23 15 x 18 16 x 20 18 x 21	wood wood wood wood	2 1	8 3	88 36	52 P 243 F	500.00
Ritner, Michael	A211 D211		house 1 & lot house 2 house 3 stable	28 x 24 24 x 19 20 x 20 15 x 21	wood wood, old wood, unfinished wood	2	8	103	52 P 243 F	350.00
Robison, Elizabeth	A207 D207		house & lot kitchen	24 x 20 18 x 18	wood wood	2 1	4 1	40 9	52 P 243 F	400.00
Rose, William	B91	South Street	house stable	15 x 14 15 x 14				26 P 121 F	20.00 40.00
Rowan, David	A206 D206		house 1 & lot kitchen barn house 2	22 x 22 22 x 18 24 x 18 18 x 18	wood wood wood wood, small	2 1 1	5 2 2	60 21 21	52 P 243 F	550.00

Carlisle Borough

Owner Occupant	Ref.	Location Adjoining Owner	Structure	Dimensions	Descr.	Stories	Lights Windows		Area	Value
Rowan, David		North & Pitt	house	25 x 21	wood					30.00
			stable	14 x 16	wood				105 P 214 F	90.00
		Laird, Samuel,	tract						7 A	70.00
	B88	Esq.	note: [tract may not be adjacent to other property]							
Rowney, James			house & lot	26 x 17	stone	1	2	24	52 P 243 F	200.00
		Brown, William	tract						10 A	100.00
	A209 B89 D209									
Scandinger heirs		Louther Street	house	26 x 14	wood					30.00
Dimsey, George			lot						52 P 243 F	70.00
	B95									
Scoby, James			house & lot	22 x 21	wood	1	6	68	26 P 121 F	400.00
			piazza	12 x 12	wood	1	1	8		
			kitchen	19 x 12	stone	1	2	24		
	A222 D222		stable	12 x 12	wood					
Seewright, Gilbert		Louther Street	house	20 x 15	wood					50.00
Bone, Betsey			addition	13 x 13	stone					
	B96		lot						26 P 121 F	70.00
Seewright, Gilbert			house	17 x 17	wood					30.00
McGunnegle [?], Patrick			stable 1	15 x 15	wood					
			stable 2	12 x 17	wood					
	B97		lot						26 P 121 F	50.00
Shram, Joseph			house & lot	18 x 27	brick	2	9	111	19 P 226 F	500.00
	A229 D229		stable	18 x 18	wood					
Shram, Joseph			house & lot	28 x 36	brick	2	14	312	26 P 121 F	1400.00
Bouvard, Charles			kitchen	16 x 18	wood	1	2	18		
			stable	18 x 18	wood					
			tan house	50 x 28	brick					
			tan yard							
		other lot	mill house &	60 x 23	wood				13 P 61 F	700.00
	A230 B100 D230		bark shade							
Shram, Philip, heirs			house & lot	18 x 25	wood	1	3	28	19 P 226 F	110.00
Wright, Joshua										
	A231 D231									
Smith, James		North Street	house	14 x 12						50.00
(cooper)			stable	14 x 11					52 P 243 F	80.00
	B101		cooper shop	16 x 16						
Smith, John (blacksmith)			house & lot	30 x 30	stone	2	10	202	26 P 121 F	800.00
Henry, John & others			kitchen	20 x 18	stone	1	2	24		
	A223 D223									

Carlisle Borough

Owner / Occupant / Ref.	Location / Adjoining Owner	Structure	Dimensions	Descr.	Stories	Lights Windows	Area	Value
Smith, John (blacksmith) / A224 D224		house & lot / smith shop / stable	22 x 13 / 15 x 15 / 15 x 15	brick / wood / wood	1 1/2	4	36	26 P 121 F 300.00
Smith, John (tailor) / A225 D225		house & lot / stable	22 x 15 / 14 x 16	brick / wood	2	6	77	26 P 121 F 300.00
Snider, George / A214 D214		house & lot / kitchen / stable	26 x 21 / 18 x 11 / 20 x 18	wood / wood / wood	2 / 1	10 / 2	123 / 18	52 P 243 F 400.00
Steel, Ephraim / A232 D232		house & lot / kitchen / smoke house	28 x 41 / 29 x 24 / 13 x 30	stone / stone / stone	2 / 2	16 / 11	310 / 136	17 P 172 F 2600.00
Steel, Ephraim / Gibson, Widow / A233 D233		house & lot	24 x 24	stone	1 1/2	4	28	17 P 172 F 500.00
Steel, Ephraim / Smith, John (shoemaker) / A234 D234		house & lot / kitchen	24 x 24 / 16 x 30	stone / stone	1 1/2 / 1	4 / 6	28 / 72	17 P 172 F 500.00
Steel, John, Esq. / Hoffer, Isaac / A221 D221		house & lot	19 x 19	wood	1	4	40	26 P 121 F 150.00
Steel, John, Esq. / McCartney, Patrick / A220 D220		house & lot	12 x 30	wood	1	2	14	105 P 214 F 150.00
Steel, Joseph / A219 D219		house & lot / kitchen / stable	25 x 21 / 24 x 18 / 16 x 16	wood / stone / wood	2 / 1	8 / 2	100 / 24	19 P 227 F 300.00
Stevenson, George, Dr. / Williams, Isaac / A218 B98 D218	Pitt Street / Rowan, David	house & lot / kitchen / note: Stephenson in D	23 x 20 / 18 x 16	stone / wood	1 / 1	7 / 2	78 / 10	52 P 243 F 400.00 / 52 P 243 F 50.00
Stuart, James / Blaine, Lue [?] / B99	Louther Street / other lot	house / lot / stable	18 x 18 / / 15 x 7	wood				52 P 243 F 70.00
Stuart, James, heirs / Eckles, Francis / A228 D228		house & lot / kitchen / stable	25 x 25 / 15 x 15 / 16 x 15	stone / stone / wood	2 / 1	8 / 1	138 / 12	52 P 243 F 400.00

Carlisle Borough

Owner / Occupant / Ref.	Location / Adjoining Owner	Structure	Dimensions	Descr.	Stories	Lights Windows	Area	Value
Stuart, James, heirs Osburn, Robert A227 D227		house & lot stable	36 x 15 15 x 7	wood wood	1	5	42 52 P 243 F	200.00
Stuart, Samuel Cowper, Frederick A215 D215		house & lot kitchen stable	34 x 23 15 x 12 30 x 24	stone stone stone	1 1	5 1	69 52 P 243 F 12	700.00
Stuart, Samuel Ruff [?], Catherine A217 D217		house & lot note: [name of occupant may be Russ]	20 x 18	wood	1	5	34 26 P 121 F	150.00
Stuart, Samuel unoccupied A216 D216		house 1 & lot house 2 kitchen stable	24 x 24 18 x 18 18 x 18 15 x 18	stone wood, old stone wood	2 1	9 2	120 26 P 121 F 24	200.00
Sturm, George Williams, Charles A226 B94 D226	Iselt, John	house 1 & lot addition stable house 2 kitchen	20 x 16 16 x 14 16 x 13 26 x 33 18 x 22	wood stone wood stone unfinished only walls built	2 1 2	5 1	56 17 P 172 F 15 22 P 250 F	350.00 800.00
Templeton, John Beigle, William A237 D237		house & lot kitchen	25 x 23 15 x 15	wood wood	2 1	7 1	72 26 P 121 F 9	140.00
Templeton, John Beigle, William J. A236 D236		house & lot kitchen stable	30 x 33 27 x 21 30 x 24	stone stone wood	2 1	7 6	157 26 P 121 F 58	1200.00
Thomas, John Haynes, Godfrey A238 D238		house & lot stable note: Thomas a resident of Philadelphia	28 x 16 15 x 15	wood wood	1	4	48 105 P 214 F	250.00
Thomas, John Underwoood, James A253 D253		house & lot stable	27 x 25 17 x 17	stone wood	1	6	88 52 P 243 F	250.00
Thompson, Alexander A235 B102 D235	Louther Street	house & lot stable note: lots adjacent	21 x 20 15 x 15	wood wood	1	3	36 52 P 243 F 52 P 243 F	200.00 40.00
Uhler, Frederick A240 D240		house & lot stable	37 x 20 18 x 18	wood wood	1	5	58 52 P 243 F	250.00

Carlisle Borough

Owner Occupant	Location Ref. Adjoining Owner	Structure	Dimensions	Descr.	Stories	Lights Windows	Area	Value
Uhler, Frederick Girling, William A241 D241		house & lot kitchen stable	28 x 33 25 x 20 18 x 18	brick stone wood	2 1 1/2	8 5	180 51	26 P 121 F 1300.00
Underwood, John A239 D239		house & lot kitchen addition stable	24 x 21 12 x 12 18 x 20 12 x 15	wood wood wood wood	1 1 1	5 1 3	52 6 36	52 P 243 F 250.00
Vanlier, Christopher, heirs Fass, Peter A242 D242		house & lot addition stable	23 x 21 18 x 18 15 x 13	wood wood wood	1 1	4 2	38 24	105 P 214 F 300.00
Vanlier, Christopher, heirs Vanlier, Elizabeth A243 D243		house & lot kitchen stable	40 x 24 33 x 21 55 x 20	stone wood wood	2 1	12 3	261 39	52 P 243 F 1200.00
Wallace, William A250 B104 D250	North Street Irving, William, General	house & lot kitchen 1 kitchen 2 shop stable	60 x 40 20 x 30 16 x 13 16 x 18 50 x 30	stone stone stone wood wood	2 2 1 2	21 5 1 7	480 90 20 84	52 P 243 F 3000.00 52 P 243 F 30.00
Watson, Allen Baird, James & Beacom, John A244 D244		house & lot kitchen stable	18 x 15 15 x 21 18 x 16	wood stone wood	2 2	5 6	68 72	26 P 121 F 550.00
Waugh, William Anderson, Joseph A247 D247		house & lot stable	25 x 16 17 x 8	stone wood	2	9	100	17 P 172 F 200.00
Waugh, William Duncan, James, Esq. B106		tract					20 A	200.00
Waugh, William Jordan, Agness A248 D248		house & lot note: house is stone in D	33 x 24	wood	1	6	68	17 P 172 F 160.00
Waugh, William Magauran, Edward A246 D246		house & lot kitchen stable	24 x 30 15 x 12 15 x 15	stone stone wood	2 1	9 1	198 15	17 P 172 F 1000.00

Carlisle Borough

Owner / Occupant	Ref.	Location / Adjoining Owner	Structure	Dimensions	Descr.	Stories	Windows / Lights	Area	Value
Weaver, Jacob		North Street / Hutton, James	house 1 & lot	18 x 24	stone	2	8 / 78	52 P 243 F	800.00
			house 2	18 x 24	wood, unfinished	1	3 / 36		
			stable	15 x 15	wood				
			wash & wood house	24 x 9	wood				
			workshop	18 x 18	wood	1	2 / 12		
			thrashing floor	18 x 11	wood			52 P 243 F	30.00
	A249 B103 D249								
Wilson, Hugh			house & lot	23 x 40	brick	2	11 / 231	52 P 243 F	1800.00
			kitchen	21 x 16	stone	1	2 / 30		
			piaza	10 x 8	stone	1			
	A245 D245		stable	20 x 15	wood				
Wiser, Jacob			house & lot	21 x 27	wood	2	6 / 60	52 P 243 F	400.00
			kitchen	15 x 12	wood				
	A254 D254		stable	18 x 24	wood				
Wiser, Jacob / Brandt, Jacob			house & lot	27 x 31	brick	2	11 / 216	13 P 61 F	800.00
			kitchen	31 x 17	brick	1 1/2	8 / 96		
	A255 D255		stable	30 x 18	wood				
Wiser, Jacob / Young, Robert & Musselman, David			house & lot	30 x 16	wood	1 1/2	10 / 88	13 P 61 F	200.00
			kitchen	15 x 16	wood	1	2 / 24		
	A156 D256								
Wishong, Conrad			house & lot	19 x 19	wood	1	3 / 30	26 P 121 F	150.00
	A251 D251		stable	23 x 18	wood				
Wood, Alexander, heirs / Hunter, Elizabeth			house & lot	29 x 25	brick	2	12 / 145	22 P 10 F	250.00
	A152 D252								
Wood, Margaret			house & lot	25 x 19	wood	1	7 / 60	26 P 121 F	250.00
	A257 D257		smoke house	12 x 9	stone	1			
Wray, John		Blaine, Robert	house & lot	27 x 33	frame	2	9 / 252	52 P 243 F	1400.00
			kitchen	25 x 16	stone & brick	1	3 / 38		
			stable	14 x 18	wood				
	A259 D259		hatter shop	20 x 20	wood				
Wray, John		Blaine, Robert	tract					15 A	150.00
	B105								

Carlisle Borough

Owner / Occupant	Ref.	Location / Adjoining Owner	Structure	Dimensions	Descr.	Stories	Windows / Lights	Lights	Area	Value
Wright, Robert			house & lot	33 x 26	brick	2	5	60	52 P 243 F	300.00
	A258 D258		note: nine windows without any glass							
Yaley, John			house & lot	16 x 33	wood	1	3	30	52 P 243 F	110.00
Gould, Stophel			stable	15 x 12	wood					
	A261 D261		note: Yaley resident of York Co.							
Young, Joseph			house & lot	19 x 19	wood	1	2	18	52 P 243 F	300.00
			kitchen	19 x 12	stone	1	2	18		
			shop	20 x 12	wood	1	1	15		
	A260 D260		stable	16 x 12	wood					
Zeigler, Mark			house & lot	24 x 24	wood	2	14	186	52 P 243 F	700.00
	A262 D262									

Dickinson Township

CHAPTER III DICKINSON TOWNSHIP

Owner Occupant	Ref.	Location Adjoining Owner	Structure	Dimensions	Descr.	Stories	Lights Windows	Area	Area	Value
Alexander, John			house 1 & lot	28 x 21	wood	1 1/2	5	48	2 A	300.00
			kitchen	21 x 14	wood	1	1	12		
			room	21 x 9	stone	1	2	24		
			granary	14 x 16	wood	1				
			milk [?] house	16 x 12	stone					
			still house							
			barn	55 x 28					370 A	4880.00
	A4 D4 E4		house 2							
Alexander, William			house							
Alexander, John		Lee, John &	tract						370 A	4940.00
	E5	Thomas	still house							
Armstrong, James			house & lot	30 x 36	stone	2	12	217	2 A	1000.00
Sample, Robert		Miller, John	kitchen	28 x 29	stone	1	2	18		
	A5 D5 E6		barn	60 x 28					292 A	5578.00
Arthur, John			house 1 & lot	32 x 24	wood	2	11	109	2 A	380.00
		Lusk, William	kitchen	24 x 18	wood	1 1/2	4	31		
			barn	72 x 22					310 A	4870.00
			house 2	20 x 22						
			spring house	14 x 12	stone					
			grist mill	45 x 40	stone					
	A1 D1 E1		saw mill							
Arthur, John		mountain land	house & lot	30 x 18	wood	1 1/2	5	48	10 P	101.00
Barr, John									1915 A	638.00
	A3 D3 E3		note: six surveys							
Arthur, John		Cumberland Furnace	house & lot	24 x 18	wood	1 1/2	5	42	10 P	110.00
Herman, Daniel									5 A 42 P	42.00
	A2 D2 E2									
Brown, Joseph			house & lot	18 x 18	wood	1 1/2	3	10	2 A	102.00
		Gourd, Joseph	barn	40 x 18					198 A	599.00
	A6 D6 E7									
Buchanan, Thomas, & Co.	D8	South Mountain	tracts	20 surveys					8000 A	1000.00
Calvert, James			house & lot	18 x 18	wood	1 1/2	2	18	1 A 24 P	200.00
	A10 D10		w. shop	18 x 12	wood	1	2	14		
Camp, Christopher			house & lot	20 x 24	wood	2	2	16	2 A	120.00
	A9 D9									

49

Dickinson Township

Owner / Occupant	Ref.	Location / Adjoining Owner	Structure	Dimensions	Descr.	Stories	Windows	Lights	Area	Value
Camp, Stophel	E11	Clopper, John	barn	45 x 24					198 A	436.00
			note: [may be the same person as in AD9]							
Carruthers, Sarah	A11 D11 E14	Marlin, Joshua	house & lot barn	29 x 27 40 x 16	stone	2	5	60	1 A 50 P 278 A	300.00 3108.00
Caupher, George	A12 D12 E15	Weakley, Robert	house 1 & lot house 2 lot	20 x 18	wood	1	1	4	1 A 3 A 44 P	101.00 40.00
Cerfass, Daniel	A13 D13 E16	McCallister, Andrew	house & lot kitchen barn	36 x 27 20 x 18 65 x 30	stone stone	2 1	11 3	232 36	2 A 45 A	1200.00 725.00
Clark, John	E13	Mathers, Joseph	house stable		old				100 A	914.00
Clopper, John	E12	Purcell, John	barn smith shop	40 x 16					100 A	176.00
Cochran, Robert	A7 D7 E9	Arthur, John	house & lot	30 x 18	wood	1 1/2	2	11	2 A 161 A 59 P	105.00 595.00
Criswell, Robert	A8 D8 E10	Hutton, John	house & lot	21 x 21	wood	1 1/2	3	19	2 A 26 A 120 P	130.00 107.00
Dixon, John	A14 D14 E17	Maxwell, Robert	house & lot barn	36 x 17 50 x 25	wood	1 1/2	4	24	2 A 282 A	120.00 594.00
Donaldson, Andrew	A15 D15 E18	Sprout, John	house & lot barn	23 x 20 58 x 20	wood	1 1/2	3	12	2 A 145 A	110.00 1180.00
Dull, Conrad Hartman, Adam	A16 D16 E19	Ege, Thornburgh, & Aitkin	house & lot barn & sawmill workshop & stable	26 x 20	wood	2	2	24	2 A 307 A	120.00 466.00 155.00
			note: total value of outbuildings $155.00							
Eckles, Nathaniel	E28	Sprout, John	house 1 house 2						100 A	816.00

Dickinson Township

Owner / Occupant	Ref.	Location / Adjoining Owner	Structure	Dimensions	Descr.	Stories	Windows	Lights	Area	Value
Ege, Michael			house & lot	38 x 18	wood	1	7	46	2 A	300.00
		McBride,	kitchen	18 x 15	wood	1	2	8		
		Alexander	office	16 x 12	wood	1	3	30		
			s. house	24 x 19	stone	2	3	36	205 A	3105.00
			furnace							2000.00
			saw mill							100.00
			smith shop							50.00
			spring house							20.00
	A17 D17 E20		houses		7 houses					262.00
Ege, Michael		South Mountain	tracts		4 surveys				2206 A	4412.00
		Arthur, John								
	E21									
Ege, Michael		on South Mountain	tracts		15 surveys				5118 A	1479.00
	E22									
Ege, Thornburgh, & Aitkin		South Mountain							4843 A	1815.00
	E25									
Ege, Thornburgh, & Aikin			house & lot	28 x 22	wood	2	9	140	2 A	500.00
			kitchen	19 x 16	wood	1	2	21		
Blackford,		South Mountain	houses		20 houses					630.00
Benjamin & others		Creek	barn & stable							80.00
			counting house	25 x 22	stone	2	6	93		
			smoke house	24 x 18	wood					
			smith shop & coal house							100.00
			store house							40.00
			furnace							2500.00
			grist mill							200.00
			saw mill							50.00
									135 A	3610.00
	A18 D18 E23		note: store house appears to be prefixed by "pot"							
Ege, Thornburgh, & Aitkin		South Mountain	house							
			barn	48 x 22					100 A	280.00
Cough, George										
	E24									
Ege, Thornburgh, & Aitkin			house & lot	23 x 19	wood	1	3	26	1 A	110.00
									205 A	3105.00
Peterson, Israel										
	A19 D19									

Dickinson Township

Owner Occupant	Ref.	Location Adjoining Owner	Structure	Dimensions	Descr.	Stories	Windows Lights		Area	Value
Ewing, John		Hays, John	house 1 & lot	37 x 20	wood	1 1/2	5	37	2 A	150.00
			barn	55 x 20					238 A	2450.00
			house 2							
			still house							
	A21 D21 E27		weaver shop							
Ewing, William			house & lot	24 x 27	stone	2	9	53	2 A	500.00
		Galbreath,	kitchen	16 x 16	stone	1 1/2	3	28		
		Samuel	barn						152 A 80 P	612.00
			stable							
			wash house	23 x 14	wood	1				
	A20 D20 E26		milk house	16 x 18	wood					
Fenner, Godfrey		McTaggart, Hugh	tract						150 A	150.00
	E31									
Filson, Samuel		Yellow Breeches	house							
Elliott, James		Creek	tract						31 A	320.00
	E30									
Filson, Samuel			house & lot	35 x 22	wood	2	3	33	2 A	120.00
Filson, James		Norton, Thomas	barn	50 x 20					172 A	1584.00
	A22 D22 E29		hatter shop							
Fulton, Francis		Ewing, John	tract						125 A	1000.00
	E32									
Funk, Daniel		Purcel, John	house						200 A	205.00
	E33 (no entry in D)		tract							
Galbreath, Joseph		King, David	house						97 A	688.00
	E38		stable	16 x 14						
Galbreath, Samuel			house & lot	25 x 22	wood	2	5	50	2 A	130.00
Duncan, Joseph			barn	40 x 20					95 A	950.00
	A25 D25 E37									
Galbreath, Samuel			house & lot	25 x 20	wood	1	3	12	2 A	120.00
Fulton, Francis		King, David	houses		3 houses					
	A24 D24 E35		barn	45 x 22					230 A 73 P	1915.00
Galbreath, Samuel			stable	25 x 18					120 A	1090.00
Fulton, Francis										
	E36									

Dickinson Township

Owner Occupant	Location Ref. Adjoining Owner	Structure	Dimensions	Descr.	Stories	Windows	Lights	Area	Value
Gibson, John	Myers, George E44	house barn	59 x 25					219 A	2330.00
Glenn, Alexander	Patterson, Robert A29 D29 E43	house & lot kitchen barn still house	22 x 21 22 x 22	wood wood	1 1 1/2	2 1	16 6	2 A 198 A	115.00 2025.00
Glenn, Elizabeth	Glenn, Thomas E42	house barn	35 x 18					15 A	240.00
Glenn, Thomas	Harper, John A27 D27 E40	house 1 & lot stable house 2	21 x 18 23 x 17 18 x 16	wood	1 1/2	3	27	2 A 98 A	120.00 1030.00
Goorly, John	Patterson, Thomas E45	house 1 house 2 stable saw mill						160 A	1560.00
Gourd, Joseph	Brown, Joseph A23 D23 E34	house & lot stable	20 x 19	wood	1 1/2	1	9	2 A 78 A	101.00 244.00
Greer, Thomas Greer, James	Myers, George A26 D26 E39	house 1 & lot stable house 2 barn weaver shop	22 x 21 75 x 30	wood	1 1/2	2	8	2 A 598 A	101.00 6302.00
Griger, John Dooey, Peter	Moore, John A28 D28 E41	house & lot stable	29 x 24 29 x 20	wood	1 1/?	4	27	2 A 398 A	130.00 3590.00
Grupe, Philip	McTaggart, Hugh E47	house stable saw mill						400 A	600.00
Grupe, Philip	Parcell, John E46	barn	40 x 20					200 A	430.00
Haft, John	Sprout, John A40 D40 E61	house & lot barn	22 x 20 45 x 20	wood	1 1/2	2	10	2 A 128 A	110.00 1064.00

Dickinson Township

Owner / Occupant	Ref.	Location Adjoining Owner	Structure	Dimensions	Descr.	Stories	Windows Lights		Area	Value
Harper, John		Patterson, Robert	house 1 & lot	25 x 19	wood	1 1/2	3	21	2 A	105.00
			barn	49 x 21					118 A	1024.00
	A32 D32 E51		still house							
Harper, John, Jr. / Neal, Thomas	E52	Wizor, Jacob	house tract						100 A	800.00
Harper, John, Sr.		Glenn, A.	house & lot	20 x 15	wood	1	4	21	2 A	105.00
			kitchen	15 x 15	wood	1				
	A34 D34 E54		barn	40 x 17					98 A	922.00
Harper, John, Sr.	E55	Ege, Michael	tract						100 A	75.00
Hartman, Henry		Waltimyer, L.	house & lot	24 x 24	wood	1 1/2	3	12	2 A	101.00
	A31 D31 E50		barn	40 x 18					48 A	58.00
Hays, John		Ewing, John	house & lot	32 x 27	stone	2	9	117	2 A	600.00
			stable							
			barn						92 A 86 P	1024.00
	A33 D33 E53		milk house	18 x 16	wood	1				
Hesson, Jack	E49	Camp, Christopher	house tract						150 A	200.00
Houk, Adam	E60	South Mountain	tract						60 A	45.00
Houk, Adam, Sr.	A38 d38		house & lot	20 x 30	stone	2	8	105	2 A	200.00
Houke, Adam		Woods, Samuel	house 1 & lot	16 x 14	wood	1	3	20	2 A	105.00
			kitchen	14 x 11	wood	1				
			barn 1	72 x 18					309 A	2632.00
			house 2							
			barn 2	60 x 24						
			still house							
	A39 D39 E59		note: Houke, Adam, Jr. occupant of house 2 & barn 2							
Huston, John		Woodburn, J.	house & lot	35 x 20	wood	2	12	144	2 A	200.00
	A35 D35 E56		barn	43 x 16					264 A	2157.00

Dickinson Township

Owner / Occupant	Ref.	Location / Adjoining Owner	Structure	Dimensions	Descr.	Stories	Windows	Lights	Area	Value
Huston, William		Beatty, William	house & lot	33 x 21	wood	1 1/2	3	36	2 A	250.00
			kitchen	16 x 16	wood					
	A36 D36 E57		barn	60 x 20					198 A	2238.00
Huston, William			house 1 & lot	20 x 18	wood	1 1/2	1	3	2 A	102.00
Piper, James		Ewing, W.	house 2							
	A37 D37 E58		smith shop						23 A	361.00
Hutton, John			house & lot	22 x 22	wood	2	2	18	2 A	130.00
		Patterson,	kitchen	16 x 22	wood	1 1/2				
		Thomas	barn	21 x 52					178 A	762.00
	A30 D30 E48		workshop	27 x 14	wood	1				
King, David			house 1 & lot	22 x 22	wood	1 1/2	2	21	2 A	110.00
		Ramsey, Nathan	house 2							
			barn						234 A	1056.00
	A41 D41 E62		saw mill							
King, David			house							
Reed, David		Moore, John	tract						200 A	1640.00
	E63									
Kitters [?], John		South Mountain	tract						2700 A	675.00
	E64									
Lamerson, Joshua [?]			house & lot	23 x 20	wood	1	4	40	2 A	110.00
Bockley [?], David		Houke, Adam	stable						163 A	499.00
	A48 D48 E74									
Lee, John			house & lot	27 x 25	wood	2	6	23	2 A	120.00
		Greer, Thomas	kitchen	18 x 15	wood	1				
	A47 D47 E73		barn	63 x 22					298 A	2722.00
Lee, Thomas			house & lot	24 x 21	wood	1 1/2	3	21	2 A	115.00
		Line, Abraham	kitchen	24 x 14	wood	1 1/2				
	A43 D43 E68		barn	40 x 24					298 A	3005.00
Line, Abraham			house & lot	28 x 30	stone	1 1/2	5	75	2 A	300.00
		Alexander, John	barn	56 x 30					176 A 80 P	2438.00
	A44 D44 E69									
Line, John			house & lot	33 x 22	stone	2	14	234	2 A	500.00
		Line, Abraham	kitchen	21 x 21	stone	2	4	48		
	A45 D45 E70		barn	60 x 32					176 A 80 P	2428.00

Dickinson Township

Owner / Occupant	Ref.	Location Adjoining Owner	Structure	Dimensions	Descr.	Stories	Windows	Lights	Area	Value
Line, William		McCallister, A.	house & lot	20 x 24	wood	1	4	44	2 A	220.00
			kitchen	20 x 16	wood	1	2	14		
			room	30 x 10	stone	1	3	27		
			barn	60 x 26					248 A	3294.00
			work shop	20 x 13	wood	1	1	4		
	A46 D46 E71		saw mill							
Line, William Bigler	E72	Stewart, Samuel	house tract						150 A	1450.00
Lusk, William		Arthur, John	house 1 & lot	42 x 20	brick	2	15	284	2 A	700.00
			kitchen	30 x 24	wood	2	9	108		
			smoke house	10 x 12	brick					
			barn	48 x 17					347 A	3480.00
	A42 D42 E65		house 2							
Lusk, William	E67	South Mountain	tract						200 A	100.00
Lusk, William, Esq. Bradley, Thomas	E66	King, David	house tract						400 A	610.00
Marlin, Joshua		McCulloch, John	house & lot	28 x 26	wood	2	6	40	2 A	150.00
			barn	44 x 18					240 A	2190.00
	A56 D56 E86									
Masoner, Jacob	E82	McTaggart, Hugh	house tract						50 A	55.00
Mathers, James		Clark, John	house & lot	18 x 16	wood	1 1/2	1	9	2 A	102.00
			stable	20 x 15					128 A	1014.00
	A55 D55 E85									
Maxwell, Robert		Dixon, John	house & lot	24 x 12	wood	2	3	14	2 A	101.00
			barn	40 x 18					298 A	616.00
			work shop	16 x 16	wood					
	A52 D52 E80									
McBride, Alexander Jr.		Ege, Michael	house & lot	24 x 22	wood	1 1/2	4	42	80 P	160.00
			kitchen	16 x 12	wood				80 P	20.00
	A58 D58 E88		stable	16 x 16						
McBride, Alexander Sr.		Lusk, William	house & lot	28 x 24	wood	2	4	48	2 A	120.00
	A57 D57 E87								197 A	1773.00

Dickinson Township

Owner Occupant	Location Ref. Adjoining Owner	Structure	Dimensions	Descr.	Stories	Windows	Lights	Area	Value
McCullogh, John	Weakley, Samuel A62 D62 E93	house & lot kitchen barn	20 x 25 26 x 21 66 x 18	stone wood	2 2	10 2	120 12	2 A 252 A	350.00 2298.00
McCullogh, John	Aitken, John E94	tract						48 A	384.00
McDonald, William	Glenn, Thomas A53 D53 E83	house & lot house 2 smith shop	18 x 17	wood	1 1/2	1	9	2 A 4 A 100 P	101.00 80.00
McFarlane, William	South Mountain E92	tract						100 A	50.00
McKinstry, James	Harper, John A54 D54 E84	house 1 & lot barn house 2	24 x 21 48 x 19	wood	2	8	26	2 A 248 A	200.00 2297.00
McTaggart, Hugh	Masoner, Jacob E81	house tract						250 A	270.00
Miller, William McIntire, Andrew	Miller, John A51 D51 E79	house 1 & lot kitchen barn milk house house 2	24 x 22 22 x 20 80 x 28 18 x 16	wood wood stone wood	1 1/2 1	3	16	2 A 371 A	400.00 7249.00
Moore, James	E90	barn stable 1 stable 2 smith shop		unfinished				296 A	2553.00
Moore, James Aitken, William	A59 D59	house & lot kitchen	51 x 37 26 x 20	stone stone	2 1 1/2	27 3	482 42	2 A	1600.00
Moore, James Weebley, George	A60 D60	house & lot	25 x 20	wood	1 1/2	3	18	2 A	110.00
Moore, John	Griger, John A49 D49 E75	house 1 & lot houses barn still house grist mill saw mill & cooper shop note: $1450.00 is the value of both mills	49 x 31 80 x 30 50 x 40	stone 4 houses stone stone stone	2	20	123	2 A 181 A	600.00 50.00 2200.00 1450.00

Dickinson Township

Owner / Occupant	Ref.	Location Adjoining Owner	Structure	Dimensions	Descr.	Stories	Windows	Lights	Area	Value
Moore, John Crosby, William	A50 D50	Griger, John	house & lot	26 x 22	wood	1	2	15	2 A	110.00
Moore, John Kincaid, James	E77	Woodburn, Samuel	house tract						281 A	2579.00
Moore, John Moore, William	E78	Galbreath, Samuel	tract grist mill saw mill still house						46 A	408.00 40.00
Moore, John Turner, William	E76	Ramsey, Nathan	house tract						374 A	3423.00
Moore, William, Sr.	D89	Woodburn, Samuel	tract						120 A	960.00
Myers, George	A61 D61 E91	Gibson, J.	house 1 & lot kitchen barn milk house stable work shop house 2	30 x 20 15 x 15 50 x 22	stone log	2 1	5 1	60 9	2 A 298 A	500.00 3671.00
Narns, John	A63 D63 E95	Ege, Thornburgh, & Aitkin	house & lot barn	20 x 18 50 x 28	wood	1 1/2	3	24	2 A 78 A	101.00 98.00
Neel, Sarah	A65 D65 E97	Woodburn, Samuel	house & lot room wash house barn smith shop	20 x 22 22 x 12 14 x 11	wood wood wood	1 1/2 1 1	2 1	10 9	2 A 213 A	130.00 2398.00
Norton, Thomas	A64 D64 E96	Filson, Samuel	house 1 & lot barn house 2	45 x 18 58 x 24	wood	1 1/2	4	40	2 A 208 A	120.00 1592.00
Parcel, John	A67 D67 E99	Funk, D.	house 1 & lot barn house 2	26 x 18 34 x 18	wood	1	3	22	2 A 198 A	101.00 1446.00

Dickinson Township

Owner Occupant	Location Ref. Adjoining Owner	Structure	Dimensions	Descr.	Stories	Lights Windows		Area	Value
Patterson, Josiah	Glenn, A. A69 D69 E101	house & lot kitchen barn	18 x 18 18 x 18 56 x 20	wood wood	1 1/2 1	4	29	2 A 113 A	110.00 1057.00
Patterson, Obediah	Goorley, John A70 D70 E102	house & lot stable	23 x 21 16 x 15	wood	1 1/2	1	4	2 A 188 A	101.00 1326.00
Patterson, Robert	Hays, John E105	house grist mill						33 A 60 P	1283.00
Patterson, Robert	Gourd, Joseph E106	tract						15 A	45.00
Patterson, Robert, Jr.	A68 D68	house & lot kitchen	28 x 26 20 x 18	stone wood	2	9	92	2 A	400.00
Patterson, Robert. Sr.	Glenn, A. E100	tract						83 A 120 P	1004.00
Patterson, Thomas	Norton, Thomas A66 D66 E98	house & lot barn milk house	42 x 18 60 x 30 10 x 12	wood stone	1 1/2 1	4	24	2 A 298 A	120.00 2444.00
Pepper, Philip	Woods, Samuel A71 D71 E103	house & lot barn still house	28 x 25	wood stone stone	2	4	40	2 A 255 A	120.00 2675.00
Pope, John, heirs	Ege, Thornburgh, & Aitkin E104	tract						150 A	300.00
Rainy, William	Line, William E111	tract						40 A	480.00
Ralston, Andrew	Waltimyer, Ludwick A72 D72 E107	house & lot	25 x 21	wood	1 1/2	2	9	2 A 200 A	105.00 400.00
Ramsey, Nathan	Varnes, Jacob A74 D74 E109	house 1 & lot stable barn house 2	50 x 20	wood	1	4	26	2 A 298 A	120.00 2146.00

Dickinson Township

Owner / Occupant	Ref.	Location / Adjoining Owner	Structure	Dimensions	Descr.	Stories	Windows Lights	Area	Value
Ramsey, Nathan / White, John	E110	mountain	house tract					86 A	232.00
Rowan, William	A73 D73 E108	Ewing, John	house & lot barn note: Roan in E	20 x 17 44 x 18	wood	1	4 18	2 A 166 A	105.00 1348.00
Smith, John	A75 D75 E112	Marlin, Joshua	house 1 & lot house 2	28 x 20	stone	2	8	2 A 145 A	150.00 1170.00
Sowers, John	A77 D77 E114	Houke, Adam	house 1 & lot house 2 barn	25 x 20 60 x 18	wood	1 1/2	2 20	2 A 204 A	120.00 876.00
Sprout, John	A76 D76 E113	Haft, John	house 1 & lot house 2 barn	30 x 28 60 x 20	stone	2	9 60	2 A 318 A	200.00 2902.00
Steep, Jacob / Carson, Samuel	A80 D80		house & lot kitchen	20 x 16 16 x 14	wood wood	1 1/2 1	3 12	2 A	110.00
Steep, Jacob / Palsley, John	A79 D79 E116	Barnes, Jacob	house & lot barn note: owner is Steep, John in E	31 x 15	wood	1	4 12	2 A 296 A	103.00 928.00
Stewart, Samuel	A78 D78 E115	Galbreath, Joseph	house & lot stable 1 stable 2 cooper shop note: name also Stuart	24 x 20	wood	2	2 27	2 A 183 A	120.00 1777.00
Turner, Joseph	A81 D81 E117	Eckles, Nathan	house 1 & lot kitchen stable house 2 smith shop	22 x 18 15 x 15	wood wood	1 1/2 1	2 9 1 4	2 A 148 A 40 P	110.00 1209.00
Varnes, Jacob	A82 D82 E118	Houke, Adam	house & lot barn hemp mill	32 x 23	wood	1 1/2	4 40	2 A 198 A	150.00 1766.00
Varnes, Jacob	E119	South Mountain	house tract					200 A	305.00
Waltimyer, Ludwick	A83 D83 E120	Ralston, Andrew	house & lot	25 x 21	wood	1 1/2	1 6	2 A 198 A	110.00 396.00

Dickinson Township

Owner / Occupant	Ref.	Location Adjoining Owner	Structure	Dimensions	Descr.	Stories	Lights Windows	Area	Area	Value
Weakly, Edward		Weakly, Joseph	house & lot	24 x 24	wood	2	4	42	2 A	300.00
			kitchen	15 x 15	wood	1	1	4		
	A87 D87 E126		room	24 x 12	wood	1	2	18	150 A	1200.00
Weakly, Edward	E127	South Mountain	stable						200 A	220.00
Weakly, Edward Righter, John		Weakly, Joseph	house & lot	22 x 22	wood	1	3	36	2 A	101.00
			stable							
			barn	56 x 22					396 A	3154.00
			grist mill							
	A88 D88 E125		saw mill							
Weakly, James		Moore, William	house 1 & lot	30 x 30	stone	2	14	212	2 A	600.00
			kitchen	30 x 15	stone	1	4	44		
			stable						419 A 80 P	5848.00
			house 2							
	A85 D85 E122		milk house	25 x 15	stone	1				
Weakly, Robert		Pepper, Philip	house & lot	50 x 22	wood	1	7	60	2 A	150.00
			barn						155 A	1275.00
	A89 D89 E128		fulling mill							
Weakly, Samuel		Lusk, William	house & lot	40 x 35	brick	2	16	318	2 A	1500.00
			kitchen	30 x 18	brick	1	6	90		
			barn						480 A 80 P	4840.00
			milk house	16 x 14	stone	1				
	A95 D95 E134		smoke house	18 x 14	stone	1				
Weakly, Samuel Erwin, Agnes			house 1							
			house 2							
	E135		still house						118 A	1246.00
Whitmore, Baltzer		Ewing, John	house & lot	24 x 20	wood	1	1	12	2 A	101.00
	A84 D84 E121		barn	44 x 19					177 A 80 P	1259.00
Wizer, Jacob Mill, William		Halder, John	house							
	E136		tract						114 A	878.00
Woodburn, John		Neal, John	house 1 & lot	24 x 24	wood	2	7	84	2 A	200.00
			house 2							
			barn						198 A	2408.00
	A86 D86 E123		shop							
Woodburn, Samuel		Moore, John	house							
	E124		tract						180 A	2010.00

Dickinson Township

Owner Occupant	Ref.	Location Adjoining Owner	Structure	Dimensions	Descr.	Stories	Lights Windows		Area	Value
Woods, Jane	E132	Woods, Samuel, Sr.	stable						219 A	2195.00
Woods, Samuel, Jr.	A90 D90 E129	Houke, Adam	house & lot kitchen stable 1 stable 2 barn milk house	27 x 24 24 x 19 12 x 12	stone wood stone	2 1 1/2 1	8	88	2 A 219 A	450.00 2469.00
Woods, Samuel, Jr. Smith, Benjamin	A91 D91 E130	Lusk, William	house 1 & lot house 2 barn	18 x 16	wood	1 1/2	3	18	2 A 249 A	101.00 2012.00
Woods, Samuel, Sr. Woods, Nathan	A94 D94		house & lot	32 x 22	stone	1 1/2	5	87	2 A	200.00
Woods, Samuel, Sr. Woods, Samuel Jr.	A93 D93 E133	Pepper, Philip	house 1 & lot house 2 milk house oil mill	30 x 25 20 x 18	wood wood	2 1	4	66	2 A 716 A	150.00 6464.00
Woods, Thomas, heirs Woods, Jane	A92 D92 E131	Woods, Samuel	house 1 & lot house 2 barn note: first name of owner is William in E	40 x 18	wood	1 1/2	4	24	2 A 221 A	110.00 3270.00

East Pennsboro Township

CHAPTER IV EAST PENNSBORO TOWNSHIP

Owner Occupant	Location Adjoining Owner	Structure	Dimensions	Descr.	Stories	Windows Lights	Area	Value
Adams, Abraham	Hawke, John A7 D7 E7	house & lot out house tan yard	42 x 29	stone & log	1	10 118	2 A 117 A	1000.00 1270.00
Adams, Abraham Wolf, David	McGuire, James A8 D8 E8	house & lot	28 x 20	sq. log	1	3 36	2 A 200 A	400.00 2000.00
Anderson, James List, George	Rennox, John A1 D1 E1	house & lot	33 x 30	stone	2	14 173	2 A 148 A	1000.00 1776.00
Ansberger, Henry	Adams, Abraham A5 D5 E5	house & lot note: house 26 x 26 in C	26 x 24	sq. log	1	4 37	2 A 41 A	400.00 987.00
Armstrong, Andrew	Stony Ridge A3 D3 E3	house & lot note: description appears to be "scutched" log	40 x 20	? log	1	4 21	2 A 298 A	300.00 3576.00
Armstrong, John	Stony Ridge A2 D2 E2	house & lot	36 x 17	sq. log	1	4 45	2 A 120 A	400.00 1440.00
Atchley, Thomas	Conodoguinet A6 D6 E6	house & lot out house note: Auchley in D	30 x 18	sq. log	1	5 36	2 A 129 A	400.00 1161.00
Aukerman, Paul	Susquehanna A4 D4 E4	house & lot note: name also Aucument	26 x 22	sq. log	1	4 40	2 A 20 A	400.00 240.00
Barnhart, John	Sheely, Andrew A12 D12 E12	house & lot note: name also appears as Barrenhart	29 x 27	sq. log	1	4 30	2 A 98 A	400.00 980.00
Bashore, Daniel	Roop, Jonas A15 D15 E15	house & lot	28 x 24	sq. log	1	5 60	2 A 128 A	400.00 1280.00
Bashore, Daniel Bashore, Michael	Roop, Jonas A16 D16 E16	house & lot note: in D house is 1 story, 2 windows, 12 lights	28 x 24	sq. log	1	4 48	2 A 125 A	400.00 1125.00
Bell, James	Brodpecker, David A21 D21 E21	house & lot out house note: Brodpecker is not listed as a property owner	28 x 22	sq. log	2	7 66	2 A 153 A	450.00 1377.00

East Pennsboro Township

Owner / Occupant	Ref.	Location / Adjoining Owner	Structure	Dimensions	Descr.	Stories	Windows	Lights	Area	Value
Bell, James		Stony Ridge	house & lot	43 x 34	stone	2	22	283	2 A	2200.00
			out house 1						348 A	4176.00
			out house 2							
	A27 D27 E25		out house 3							
Bell, Robert			house & lot	40 x 22	sq. log	1	4	36	2 A	400.00
		Brodpecker, David							148 A	1332.00
	A20 D20 E20		note: Brodpecker is not listed as a property owner							
Benage, George		Mannor	house & lot	20 x 18	log	1	2	8	2 A	300.00
	A26 D26 E26								28 A	336.00
Bloser, Christley			house & lot	28 x 24	sq. log	1	2	12	2 A	400.00
		Byers, Stephen							138 A	1242.00
	A17 D17 E17		note: name also appears as Blazor							
Boar, William			house & lot	28 x 26	sq. log	2	12	108	2 A	600.00
		Saylor, Matthias	out house						348 A	4176.00
	A25 D25 E24		note: name also appears as Bear							
Bosler, John			house & lot	30 x 20	sq. log	1	6	48	2 A	400.00
		Trimble, John							218 A	1962.00
	A19 D19 E19									
Bower, Elizabeth			house & lot	28 x 26	log	1	3	36	2 A	250.00
		Longstaff, Martin	stable						132 A	1320.00
	A10 D10 E10									
Bower, George			house & lot	26 x 22	sq. log	2	9	105	2 A	500.00
		Longstaff, Martin							103 A	1030.00
	A9 D9 E9									
Bowman, John		publick land	house & lot	41 x 30	stone & log	2	24	284	2 A	2350.00
			out house 1						190 A	5700.00
	A14 D14 E14		out house 2							
Bowman, Samuel		State Road	house & lot	35 x 30	sq. log	2	15	111	2 A	800.00
			out house 1	15 x 12	stone	1	2	12		100.00
			out house 2	20 x 20	sq. log	1				100.00
									8 A	240.00
	A13 D13 E13		note: outhouse 2 stone in D							
Brinizer, John			house & lot	24 x 20	sq. log	2	6	57	2 A	340.00
		Philips, John	stable						148 A	1184.00
	A11 D11 E11		note: name also Briniser							

East Pennsboro Township

Owner / Occupant	Ref.	Location / Adjoining Owner	Structure	Dimensions	Descr.	Stories	Lights	Windows	Area	Value
Buddorff, Leonard	A24 D24 E23	Carothers, Andrew	house & lot note: Budorf in D; Buttorf in E	25 x 20	sq. log	1	5	20	2 A 220 A	450.00 1540.00
Burkholder, Wilbrick	A28 D28 E27	Colberts Run	house & lot out house 1 out house 2 mill	28 x 28	stone & log stone	1	6	48	2 A 200 A	700.00 2400.00
Butner, Jacob	A22 D22 E22	Clendennon, John	house & lot out house	42 x 24	sq. log	1	8	66	2 A 257 A	600.00 1799.00
Butner, Jacob, Jr.	A23 D23		house & lot	23 x 18	sq. log	1	3	28	2 A	200.00
Byers, Stephen	A18 D18 E18		house & lot out house	40 x 18	sq. log	1	4	36	2 A 148 A	400.00 1480.00
Carnes, Richard	A46 D46 E44	Anderson, James	house & lot	28 x 26	sq. log	1	6	57	2 A 70 A	500.00 490.00
Carothers, Andrew	A44 D44 E42		house & lot note: neighbor in E is Carothers, Andrew	18 x 16	sq. log	1	4	31	2 A 200 A	450.00 1600.00
Carothers, James & Carothers, William	A45 D45 E43	Orr, John	house & lot note: only William listed as owner in E	50 x 20	sq. log	1	6	56	2 A 155 A	500.00 1860.00
Carothers, Thomas McElwain, Gail [?]	A32 D32		house & lot out house	24 x 20	log	1	3	24	1 A	110.00
Carothers, Thomas Mulholm, Rudy	A30 D30 E29	Douglas, John	house & lot out house 1 out house 2 note: house lot 2 A in D; occupant Zonizer, Robert in E; name also appears as Crothers	22 x 16	frame	2	5	60	1 A 278 A	500.00 3336.00
Carothers, Thomas Thompson, Robert	A31 D31		house & lot	24 x 16	log	1	2	18	1 A	200.00
Chain, Martha	A35 D35 E32	Douglass, John	house & lot	24 x 24	sq. log	1	4	36	2 A 125 A	500.00 2500.00

East Pennsboro Township

Owner Occupant	Ref.	Location Adjoining Owner	Structure	Dimensions	Descr.	Stories	Lights	Windows	Area	Value
Clendennon, Samuel		Haugh, Widow	house & lot out house 1 out house 2	40 x 22	sq. log	1	2	18	2 A 160 A	400.00 1130.00
	A39 D39 E37		note: Clandinen in A; Clendenon in E							
Clendenon, John, Esq.		Butorf, Leonard	house & lot	25 x 25	sq. log	1	3	30	2 A 200 A	450.00 2000.00
	A42 D42 E40		note: name also Clandinen							
Clendenon, John, Esq. Frederick, Peter		Haugh, Widow	house & lot	22 x 25	sq. log	1	2	18	2 A 160 A	400.00 1120.00
	A40 D40 E38		note: name also Clandinen							
Clendenon, John, Esq. Shoop, Abraham		Haugh, Widow	house & lot out house 1 out house 2	25 x 22	sq. log	1	1	4	2 A 150 A	400.00 1050.00
	A41 D41 E39		note: Clandinen in A							
Coffman, Christley		Stayman, Joseph	house & lot	41 x 36	stone	2	18	392	2 A 163 A	1500.00 3260.00
	A36 D36 E33		note: Christly in E							
Coffman, Christley		Stayman, Joseph	house & lot out house	28 x 20	stone & log	1	4	48	2 A 183 A	700.00 3660.00
	A37 D37 E34									
Contz, George		Byers, Stephen	house & lot	30 x 26	sq. log	2	5	49	2 A 100 A	400.00 1200.00
	A38 D38 E36		note: Countz in E							
Cress, Henry Switzer, Frederick		Carothers, Andrew	house & lot	16 x 16	log	1	2	10	2 A 80 A	300.00 320.00
	A43 D43 E41									
Crum, Dolly		Kistle, Jacob	tract						20 A	40.00
	E35									
Culbertson, Agness		Urrie, Thomas	house & lot out house	30 x 26	stone	2	10	129	2 A 215 A	1400.00 3010.00
	A34 D34 E31		note: adjoining land of Urrie is in Middleton twp.							
Culbertson, Samuel		Urrie, Thomas	house & lot out house 1 out house 2	52 x 20	stone	2	14	166	2 A 300 A	1400.00 4500.00
	A33 D33 E30		note: adjoining land of Urrie is in Middleton twp.							
Culp, Jacob		Kritzer, Nicholas	house & lot out house 1 out house 2	26 x 21	sq. log	2	10	120	72 P 5 A	600.00 60.00
	A29 D29 E28									

East Pennsboro Township

Owner / Occupant	Ref.	Location / Adjoining Owner	Structure	Dimensions	Descr.	Stories	Windows	Lights	Area	Value
Denny, Jane	A47 D47 E45	Culbertson, Samuel	house & lot	22 x 18	log	1	4	16	2 A 58 A	100.10 406.00
Dicky, James	A52 D52 E51	Stony Ridge	house & lot	42 x 17	sq. log	1	4	32	2 A 120 A	400.00 720.00
Dill, Michael	A50 D50 E49	Wharton, Thomas	house & lot	22 x 26	sq. log	1	4	28	2 A 170 A	450.00 1190.00
Dodds, Mary	A51 D51 E50	Greason, William	house & lot out house	16 x 14	log	1	1	4	2 A 69 A	200.00 621.00
Donaldson, Thomas	A48 D48 E46	Conodoguinet Creek	house & lot	32 x 22	sq. log	1	4	48	2 A 170 A	500.00 2040.00
Donaldson, Thomas	E47	North Mountain	tract						75 A	75.00
Douglass, John	A49 D49 E48	Carothers, Thomas	house & lot out house	24 x 24	stone	2	7	30	2 A 127 A	800.00 2540.00
Echelberger, Stophel	A54 D54 E54	Mannor of Lowther	house & lot out house	43 x 31	sq. log	1	6	64	2 A 100 A	500.00 2000.00
Ely, Jacob	A62 D62 E58	Waugh, Samuel	house & lot note: Ealy in E	33 x 22	sq. log	1	2	24	2 A 75 A	350.00 525.00
Emminger, Andrew	A58 D58 E56	Fisher, Leonard	house & lot	43 x 24	sq. log	1	11	112	2 A 175 A	500.00 2040.00
Emminger, Conrad	A55 D55 E55	Fisher, Leonard	house & lot	35 x 22	sq. log	1	7	36	1 A 180 A	400.00 2160.00
Emminger, Conrad / Speice, John	A57 D57		house & lot note: name also appears as Speece	24 x 15	log	1	2	10	80 P	110.00
Emminger, Susannah	A56 D56		house & lot	24 x 20	sq. log	1	6	28	80 P	300.00

East Pennsboro Township

Owner / Occupant	Ref.	Location / Adjoining Owner	Structure	Dimensions	Descr.	Stories	Lights / Windows		Area	Value
Ertford, Dewalt	A60 D60 E57	Conodoguinet Creek	house & lot out house saw mill	26 x 24	sq. log	2	6	90	1 A 50 A	600.00 900.00
Ertford, Dewalt	A61 D61		house & lot	20 x 18	sq. log	1	2	12	1 A	100.10
Everly, John	A59 D59 E57	Galbraith, Andrew	house & lot out house	40 x 32	stone	2	14	230	2 A 279 A	1500.00 4722.00
Evers, Philip	A53 D53 E53	Snider, Philip	house & lot	28 x 24	sq. log	1	3	36	2 A 40 A	400.00 240.00
Ferguson, Andrew	A68 D68 E64	Reed, James	house & lot note: Fargison in A and D	36 x 18	sq. log	1	2	21	2 A 160 A	400.00 1220.00
Fisher, Leonard	A63 D63 E60	Sheely, Michael	house & lot out house	28 x 26	sq. log	2	2	18	2 A 80 A	200.00 960.00
Fisher, Leonard / Willis, Abraham	A64 D64 E61	Sheely, Michael	house & lot	24 x 20	sq. log	1	2	18	160 A	250.00 1920.00
Fisher, Samuel	A69 D69 E65	Mannor of Lowther	house & lot out house	38 x 16	sq. log	2	9	87	2 A 50 A	450.00 1500.00
Fisher, Thomas & James	A66 D66 E59	Longnecker, Abraham	house & lot out house	26 x 24	log	1	5	48	2 A 80 A	300.00 960.00
Forney, Jacob	A65 D65 E62	Hoge, David	house & lot out house	30 x 26	sq. log	1	6	48	2 A 161 A	450.00 1932.00
Frederick, Peter	A67 D67 E63	North Mountain	house & lot	26 x 20	log	1	1	4	2 A 202 A	100.10 404.00
Galbraith, Andrew, Esq.	A71 D71 E67	Galbraith, John	house & lot out house 1 out house 2	26 x 24	sq. log	1	6	72	2 A 354 A 80 P	600.00 7080.00
Galbraith, John	A70 D70 E66	Pollock, Oliver	house & lot out house	55 x 33	stone	2	18	372	2 A 393 A	1500.00 7074.00

East Pennsboro Township

Owner Occupant	Location Ref. Adjoining Owner	Structure	Dimensions	Descr.	Stories	Lights	Windows	Area	Value
Geddis, Samuel, heirs Campbell, Ennis	Adams, Abraham A81 D81 E75	house & lot	38 x 20	sq. log	1	5	54	2 A 127 A	400.00 1524.00
Gilson, Richard	Conodoguinet Creek A77 D77 E73	house & lot out house	30 x 26	stone	2	9	135	2 A 222 A	1000.00 2664.00
Ginger, Ludwick	Dell, Michael A80 D80 E74	house & lot out house	24 x 20	sq. log	1	2	9	2 A 8 A	200.00 40.00
Greson, William	A79 D79	house & lot note: Greason in D	18 x 16	log	1	2	8	2 A	200.00
Greson, William	A78 D78 E76	house & lot fulling & grist mill note: Greason in D	40 x 16	log	1	6	34	2 A 181 A	300.00 1467.00
Grice, John	Fisher, Leonard A73 D73 E69	house & lot out house note: Grist in E	22 x 18	sq. log	1	5	36	2 A 12 A	200.00 144.00
Grouse, John Miller, Jacob	Mann, George A76 D76 E72	house & lot	34 x 16	log	1	1	6	2 A 250 A	200.00 3450.00
Grouse, Simon	Fisher, Leonard A74 D74 E70	house & lot out house	40 x 24	stone	2	5	52	2 A 244 A	1000.00 2928.00
Grumley, Frederick	Roop, Jonas A75 D75 E71	house & lot out house	24 x 20	sq. log	2	10	105	2 A 54 A	500.00 540.00
Gunkle, Michael	Anderson, James A72 D72 E68	house & lot out house	22 x 18	sq. log	1	2	12	2 A 104 A	300.00 1040.00
Harman, Christly Wolf, John	Dewalt, John A90 D90 E91	house & lot out house note: first name also appears as Christy	20 x 18	log	1	1	6	2 A 130 A	100.10 1300.00
Harman, Martin, Jr.	Dicky, James A95 D95 E86	house & lot out house	20 x 18	sq. log	1	2	15	2 A 130 A	200.00 1040.00
Harman, Martin, Sr.	Junkin, Joseph A98 D98 E80	house & lot out house 1 out house 2	30 x 28	stone	2	8	84	2 A 300 A	1200.00 3600.00

East Pennsboro Township

Owner / Occupant	Location / Adjoining Owner	Structure	Dimensions	Descr.	Stories	Lights Windows	Area	Value
Harshbarger, Ann	Mannor of Lowther	house & lot	27 x 25	sq. log	2	10 124	2 A	550.00
							97 A	1940.00
	A97 D97 E88	note: Harshbarger, Widow in E						
Hawk, George		house & lot	24 x 16	sq. log	1	3 18	2 A	300.00
	Humes, James						69 A	414.00
	A92 D92 E83							
Hawk, John		house & lot	30 x 28	log [?]	1	4 42	2 A	500.00
	Adams, Abraham	out house		rotten [?]			276 A	2760.00
	A83 D83 E92							
Hawk, Michael		house & lot	28 x 26	sq. log	2	5 54	2 A	400.00
	Longsdorf, Martin						192 A	1920.00
	A99 D99 E90	note: Halk in D						
Hawk, Michael Longsdorf, Ann		house & lot	20 x 18	sq. log	1	4 24		200.00
	A100 D100	note: Halk in D						
Hawker, John		house & lot	34 x 24	log	1	3 36	2 A	300.00
	Whitehall, Robert	out house					237 A 120 P	3792.00
	A84 D84 E78	note: Halker in D						
Hoge, David, Esq.		house & lot	30 x 22	sq. log	2	11 119	2 A	650.00
	Hoge, Jonathan,	out house 1						
	Esq.	out house 2					300 A	5100.00
	A87 D87 E97							
Hoge, John, Rev.		house 1	24 x 18	log	1	2 12		
	Pollock, Oliver	house 2						
		house 3						120.00
		out house 1						
		out house 2					188 A	3384.00
		note: house 1 description appears to be "rotten logs", value "not						
	A82 D82 E77	worth $100; houses 2 and 3 valued at $120 for both						
Hoge, Jonathan, Esq.		house & lot	26 x 24	sq. log	2	8 82	1 A	500.00
	A86 D86 E94	out house					274 A	4932.00
Hoge, Jonathan, Esq. Monosmith, Peter	Hoge, Jonathan, Esq.	house & lot	20 x 18	sq. log	1	3 18	1 A	100.10
	A85 D85							
Hoge, Jonathan, Jr.	State Road	house & lot	40 x 32	stone	2	14 230	2 A	1600.00
	A88 D88 E89						200 A	3200.00
Houser, Martin		house & lot	24 x 18	sq. log	1	2 12	2 A	300.00
	Barnhart, John						150 A	1500.00
	A101 D101 E93							

East Pennsboro Township

Owner Occupant	Ref.	Location Adjoining Owner	Structure	Dimensions	Descr.	Stories	Lights Windows	Area	Value
Humes, James	A91 D1 E82	Swarts, John	house & lot	42 x 20	log	1	5 42	2 A 278 A	400.00 2224.00
Hursh, Jacob	A89 D89 E81	North Mountain	house & lot out house	22 x 20	log	1	3 24	2 A 55 A	300.00 275.00
Huston, John	A93 D93 E84	Stayman, Joseph	house & lot	30 x 24	sq. log	2	7 84	2 A 123 A 80 P	600.00 1230.00
Huston, John Fisher, Thomas	A96 D96 E87	North Mountain	house & lot	26 x 22	sq. log	1	2 18	2 A 150 A	400.00 1200.00
Huston, Jonathan	A94 D94 E85	Stayman, Joseph	house & lot out house 1 out house 2	18 x 16	log	1	2 13	2 A 123 A	200.00 1230.00
Irvin, Armstrong	A104 D104 E99	Armstrong, Andrew	house 1 & lot out house house 2 still house note: Irwin in D; house 1 20 x 36 in D	30 x 26 24 x 15	stone stone	2 1	8 96 2 18	2 A 96 A	1000.00 1152.00 200.00
Irvin, James	A105 D105 E100	Conodoguinet Creek	house & lot still house	35 x 20	sq. log	1	6 56	2 A 180 A	500.00 1900.00
Irvin, John	A103 D103 E98	Armstrong, Andrew	house & lot out house still house note: Irwin in D	20 x 20	sq. log	1	5 46	2 A 96 A	400.00 1152.00
Irvin, William	A102 D102 E97	Armstrong, Andrew	house & lot note: Irwin in D	20 x 18	sq. log	1	2 24	2 A 96 A	400.00 1152.00
Junken, Benjamin	A108 D108		house & lot out house 1 out house 2 note: house lot 1 A in D	43 x 32	stone	2	20 223	2 A	1500.00
Junken, Benjamin Evers, John	A107 D107 E96	State Road	house & lot out house note: house lot 1 A in D	30 x 28	stone	2	14 110	2 A 200 A	800.00 2400.00
Junken, Joseph	A106 D106 E95	State Road	house & lot out house	38 x 26	stone	2	13 150	2 A 200 A	1200.00 2400.00

East Pennsboro Township

Owner Occupant	Ref.	Location Adjoining Owner	Structure	Dimensions	Descr.	Stories	Windows Lights		Area	Value
Keller, Henry		Culbertson, Widow	house & lot	32 x 30	stone	1	8	96	2 A	800.00
	A115 D115 E101								200 A	1600.00
Kelso, William		Susquehanna	house & lot	54 x 21	sq. log	2	14	114	2 A	1000.00
			out house 1	35 x 18	stone	1	5	54		
			out house 2							700.00
									168 A	3360.00
	A111 D111 E104		note: value of both out houses is $700.00							
Keys, James, Jr.			house & lot	22 x 22	log	1	1	4	2 A	200.00
	A112 D112		out house							
Kimble, Samuel			house & lot	32 x 26	sq. log	2	10	136	2 A	700.00
	A114 D114		out house							
Kinsey, Jacob			house & lot	13 x 18	sq. log	1	2	21	2 A	200.00
	A113 D113		out house							
Kissel, Jacob, Jr.	E106	North Mountain	tract						10 A	20.00
Kissel, Jacob, Sr.		North Mountain	house & lot	18 x 16	log	1	2	8	2 A	100.10
			out house						30 A	60.00
	A110 D110 E105		note: name also Kistle							
Kritzer, Nicholas		Morton, Edward	house & lot	60 x 50	sq. log	2	20	212	2 A	1200.00
									349 A	6980.00
	A116 D116 E102		note: entry says two houses but only one listed							
Krutzer, Adam		Mannor of Lowther	house & lot	38 x 33	stone	2	24	378	1 A	1300.00
			house 2 & lot	25 x 25	sq. log	2	10	105	1 A	400.00
			house 3 & lot	24 x 24	sq. log	1	3	27		100.10
									250 A	4500.00
	A109 D109 E103		notes: Kritzer in E; Yengst, John, occupant of house 2; Yengst, Jacob, occupant of house 3							
Lantz, Philip			house & lot	30 x 28	sq. log	1	4	30	2 A	400.00
	A123 D123									
Leirston, Jacob			house & lot	30 x 26	stone	2	12	220	1 A	800.00
	A121 D121									
Leirston, Jacob			house & lot	30 x 28	sq. log	1	2	24	1 A	300.00
	A122 D122									
Longnecker, Abraham			house & lot	33 x 33	stone	1	9	108	2 A	900.00
	A119 D119		out house							

East Pennsboro Township

Owner Occupant	Location Ref. Adjoining Owner	Structure	Dimensions	Descr.	Stories	Windows Lights	Area	Value
Longnecker, Joseph	A120 D120	house & lot out house	22 x 18	sq. log	1	1 4	2 A	250.00
Longsdorff, Adam	A124 D124	house & lot out house 1 out house 2 note: name also appears as Longstorf	25 x 22	sq. log	2	7 69	2 A	600.00
Longstorff, Martin	A117 D117	house & lot out house	28 x 26	sq. log	1	5 51	2 A	500.00
Lootz, George	A126 D126	house & lot out house	20 x 18	sq. log	1	4 24	2 A	300.00
Loudon, Archibald	A125 D125	house & lot note: value $150.00 in A	37 x 20	sq. log	1	8 67	2 A	450.00
Loudon, Matthew	A118 D118	house 1 & lot out house house 2	28 x 24 18 x 16	stone stone	2 1	11 136	2 A	1300.00 100.10
Mann, George	A141 D141	house & lot out house	28 x 28	log	1	5 85	2 A	500.00
Martin, Edward	A134 D134	house & lot out house	30 x 24	stone	2	11 238	1 A	1300.00
Martin, Edward Armstrong, James	A135 D135	house & lot	20 x 18	sq. log	1	2 24	1 A 80 P	150.00
Martin, Edward Armstrong, John	A136 D136	house & lot	28 x 20	sq. log	1	6 48	80 P	300.00
McCalister, Archibald Goodshal, Goodley	A146 D146	house & lot	20 x 18	log	1	2 18	2 A	300.00
McClure, Thomas	A129 D129	house & lot	24 x 21	log	1	3 30	2 A	200.00
McConnel, Mathew	A147 D147	house & lot out house	21 x 18	log	1	2 16	80 P	200.00
McCormick, Robert	A127 D127	house & lot out house	46 x 20	sq. log	1	6 66	2 A	500.00
McCormick, William	A128 D128	house & lot	25 x 25	sq. log	1	8 80	2 A	500.00

East Pennsboro Township

Owner Occupant	Location Ref. Adjoining Owner	Structure	Dimensions	Descr.	Stories	Lights Windows		Area	Value
McGuire, James	A142 D142	house & lot out house 1 out house 2	36 x 20	sq. log	1	6	48	2 A	400.00
Megaugh, Anthony	A130 D130	house & lot	20 x 18	log	1	1	4	2 A	100.10
Miller, Jacob	A132 D132	house & lot out house	36 x 30	sq. log	1	15	180	2 A	700.00
Miller, John	A139 D139	house & lot	28 x 26	brick	2	9	148	2 A	1200.00
Miller, John	A140 D140	house & lot	16 x 16	brick	1	2	12		100.10
Miller, Peter	A133 D133	house & lot	25 x 20	log	1	2	16	2 A	100.10
Miller, William	A145 D145	house & lot out house 1 out house 2	28 x 26	sq. log	1	4	40	2 A	400.00
Moor, Andrew	A137 D137	house & lot out house	41 x 31	stone	2	14	156	1 A	1400.00
Moor, Andrew Holts, John	A138 D138	house & lot	25 x 26	log	1	2	12	1 A	100.10
Moor, Howard	A143 D143	house & lot	23 x 20	sq. log	1	4	34	1 A	400.00
Moor, Howard Black, William	A144 D144	house & lot	20 x 18	log	1	3	24	1 A	200.00
Myre, George	A131 D131	house & lot	30 x 27	sq. log	2	6	66	2 A	600.00
Nidigh, Abraham	A148 D148	house & lot	28 x 18	sq. log	1	3	60	2 A	500.00
Nidigh, Abraham Monosmith, Isaac	A149 D149	house & lot	28 x 26	sq. log	1	6	66	2 A	500.00
Noble, James	A150 D150	house & lot	20 x 20	log	1	1	8	2 A	200.00

East Pennsboro Township

Owner Occupant	Location Ref. Adjoining Owner	Structure	Dimensions	Descr.	Stories	Windows Lights	Area	Value
Ober, John	A157 D157	house & lot	28 x 20	sq. log	1	2 24	2 A	300.00
Oliver, John Buchanan, James	A151 D151	house & lot	36 x 18	sq. log	1	6 52	2 A	400.00
Orr, John	A155 D155	house & lot out house	32 x 18	sq. log	1	4 16	2 A	400.00
Orr, Widow	A152 D152	house & lot	26 x 26	sq. log	1	6 56	2 A	400.00
Orr, Widow	A153 D153	stone kiln	35 x 25		1			200.00
Orr, Widow	A154 D154	out house note: [listed as an out house but assessed as a dwelling]	18 x 16	sq. log	1			100.10
Orr, Widow & John	A156 D156	house & lot	18 x 14	log	1	1 4	2 A	300.00
Parker, Andrew	A163 D163	house & lot	30 x 30	stone	1	11 135	2 A	800.00
Paxton, Samuel	A168 D168	house & lot	23 x 21	sq. log	1	3 21	2 A	500.00
Philip, John	A165 D165	house & lot	32 x 28	sq. log	1	2 12	2 A	200.00
Phisick, Edmund Johnston, John	A166 D166	house & lot	30 x 26	sq. log	1	2 18	2 A	300.00
Pile, Laurence	A167 D167	house & lot out house	20 x 18	log	1	2 8	2 A	200.00
Pollock, Oliver	A158 D158	house & lot note: [listed as an out house but assessed as a dwelling]	40 x 34	stone	3	21 358	2 A	1400.00
Pollock, Oliver	A159 D159	house & lot out house note: [listed as an out house but assessed as a dwelling]	19 x 20	stone	2			200.00
Pollock, Oliver	A160 D160	house & lot note: [listed as an out house but assessed as a dwelling]	46 x 20	stone	2	6 64		600.00

East Pennsboro Township

Owner Occupant	Location Ref. Adjoining Owner	Structure	Dimensions	Descr.	Stories	Lights Windows		Area	Value
Pollock, Oliver Briggs, David	A161 D161	house & lot out house 1 out house 2 horse shed	40 x 33 28 x 18 20 x 20 60 x 12	stone stone stone stone	2 1 2 1	20 3 5 1	350 32 60 9	2 A	2000.00 200.00 200.00
Pope, Nicholas	A162 D162	house & lot	34 x 22	log	1	4	40	2 A	450.00
Prats, Simeon	A164 D164	house & lot out house	30 x 28	sq. log	1	4	48	2 A	500.00
Quigley, James	A171 D171	house & lot	40 x 18	sq. log	2	4	24	1 A	300.00
Quigley, John, deceased Slone, William	A172 D172	house & lot	24 x 18	sq. log	1	3	18	2 A	300.00
Quigley, Mary	A169 D169	house & lot	34 x 16	sq. log	1	5	42	2 A	400.00
Quigley, William	A170 D170	house & lot out house	21 x 18	sq. log	2	7	78	1 A	500.00
Redsecker, Nicholas	A184 D184	house & lot out house	24 x 19	sq. log	1	2	16	1 A	400.00
Redsecker, Nicholas Shoop, Jacob	A187 D187	house & lot out house [?]	27 x 17	sq. log	1	2	18	1 A	200.00
Reed, John	A185 D185	house & lot note: entry lists two houses, but information is given only for one	47 x 16	sq. log	2	7	60	2 A	500.00
Reese, Jeremiah	A183 D183	house & lot note: name also appears as Reece	30 x 28	sq. log	2	10	147	2 A	650.00
Reese, Solomon	A181 D181	house & lot out house note: name also appears as Reece	25 x 20	sq. log	1	4	28	2 A	400.00
Renix, John	A173 D173	house & lot note: dimension of 24 feet is doubtful	24 x 18	sq. log	2	6	48	2 A	400.00
Roop, Jonas, Jr.	A175 D175	house & lot out house	40 x 22	sq. log	1	7	72	2 A	500.00
Roop, Jonas, Sr.	A174 D174	house & lot out house	36 x 32	stone	2	13	174	2 A	1000.00

East Pennsboro Township

Owner Occupant	Location Ref. Adjoining Owner	Structure	Dimensions	Descr.	Stories	Lights Windows		Area	Value
Roop, Martin	A176 D176	house & lot note: [valuation seems excessive]	16 x 13	sq. log	1	2	24	2 A	1000.00
Roopley, Conrad	A186 D186	house & lot out house note: name also appears as Rooply	35 x 30	sq. log	2	14	168	2 A	500.00
Roopley, John	A179 D179	house & lot	24 x 18	sq. log	2	7	78	2 A	500.00
Roopley, John Strong, Francis	80 D180	house & lot	28 x 30	sq. log	1	8	96	2 A	300.00
Rooply, Frederick	A178 D178	house & lot out house	30 x 25	sq. log	1	4	48	2 A	500.00
Rooply, Jacob	A177 D177	house & lot out house	35 x 30	sq. log	2	10	110	2 A	600.00
Rooply, Michael	A182 D182	house & lot	29 x 26	sq. log	1	4	48	2 A	350.00
Sailor, Mathias	A214 D214	house & lot out house	26 x 22	sq. log	2	11	109	2 A	500.00
Sample, John & Charles	A212 D212	house & lot	40 x 24	sq. log	1	6	72	2 A	550.00
Seerer, George	A194 D194	house & lot	30 x 28	sq. log	2	12	144	2 A	600.00
Sheely, Andrew	A198 D198	house & lot	30 x 25	sq. log	1	10	120	2 A	600.00
Sheffer, John	A207 D207	house & lot	30 x 25	sq. log	2	8	94	1 A	600.00
Sheffer, John Loudon, Anthony	A208 D208	house & lot	24 x 17	sq. log	1	2	16	1 A	100.10
Shelly, Michael	A188 D188	house & lot	30 x 25	sq. log	1	5	40	2 A	450.00
Shippen, Joseph Henry, James 	A196 D196	house & lot out house 1 out house 2	20 x 18	sq. log	1	2	24	2 A	400.00

East Pennsboro Township

Owner Occupant	Location Ref. Adjoining Owner	Structure	Dimensions	Descr.	Stories	Lights Windows	Area	Value
Shoop, Jacob	A211 D211	house & lot	27 x 21	sq. log	1	4 48	2 A	400.00
Shoop, John	A191 D191	house 1 & lot house 2 out house	33 x 28 18 x 15	stone stone	2 1	11 186 2 24	2 A 2 A	1000.00 300.00
Snider, Philip	A215 D215	house & lot	36 x 34	stone	2	18 230	2 A	1000.00
Snively, Henry	A189 D189	house & lot	30 x 28	sq. log	2	11 132	2 A	600.00
Snively, Jacob	A213 D213	house & lot out house	40 x 30	sq. log	2	17 204	2 A	600.00
Snively, John	A190 D190	house & lot	30 x 24	sq. log	1	4 48	2 A	500.00
Stakemiller, Valentine	A210 D210	house & lot	24 x 22	sq. log	1	1 8	2 A	200.00
Stayman, John	A201 D201	house & lot out house	36 x 30	sq. log	2	17 204	2 A	550.00
Stayman, John Cough, Joseph	A203 D203	house & lot	20 x 18	log	1	2 12	1 A	200.00
Stayman, Joseph	A192 D192	house & lot	36 x 30	stone	2	20 267	2 A	1200.00
Stayman, Joseph Smith, Henry	A193 D193	house & lot	20 x 15	sq. log	1	2 12	2 A	300.00
Steel, Ephraim Prats, Samuel	A197 D197	house & lot	30 x 28	sq. log	1	5 60	2 A	500.00
Stier, John, deceased Coover, -----	A199 D199	house & lot note: name also appears as Star	45 x 35	stone	2	15 253	1 A	1300.00
Stier, John, deceased Cress, Henry	A202 D202	house & lot out house note: [confused with A203, Stayman, John]	26 x 24 28 x 12	sq. log stone	1 2	2 6 1 12	1 A	400.00 150.00

East Pennsboro Township

Owner Occupant	Location Ref. Adjoining Owner	Structure	Dimensions	Descr.	Stories	Lights Windows	Area	Value
Stier, John, deceased Miller, Melchor	A200 D200	house & lot	22 x 24	log	1	3 / 18	1 A	300.00
Strome, Samuel	A206 D206	house & lot out house	19 x 26	sq. log	1	2 / 12	2 A	400.00
Swarts, John	A204 D204	house & lot out house	38 x 28	sq. log	2	11 / 117	2 A	800.00
Swarts, Leonard	A195 D195	house & lot	30 x 26	sq. log	1	4 / 42	2 A	500.00
Swats, George	A209 D209	house & lot	30 x 25	sq. log	1	4 / 36	2 A	500.00
Swiler, Christley	A205 D205	house & lot out house	20 x 20	sq. log	1	3 / 24	2 A	300.00
Titler, Balsor	A216 D216	house & lot out house	29 x 25	sq. log	1	4 / 12	2 A	500.00
Trimble, George	A217 D217	house & lot	28 x 18	sq. log	1	3 / 30	1 A	300.00
Trimble, John	A218 D218	house & lot	40 x 20	sq. log	1	3 / 36	1 A	300.00
Vanderau, Adam May, Frederick	A219 D219	house & lot	29 x 19	sq. log	1	5 / 44	2 A	500.00
Walker, David	A246 D246	house & lot out house	40 x 26	stone	2	16 / 179	2 A	1500.00
Walker, David Walker, William	A247 D247	house & lot out house	26 x 16	stone	1	6 / 72	2 A	600.00
Walker, John	A230 D230	house & lot out house	18 x 28	frame	2	10 / 135	2 A	300.00
Walker, John Brewkirk, David	A231 D231	house & lot note: occupant name also appears as Braikark [?]	18 x 20	sq. log	1	3 / 30	2 A	300.00

East Pennsboro Township

Owner Occupant	Location Adjoining Owner	Structure	Dimensions	Descr.	Stories	Lights Windows	Area	Value
Walker, John, Esq. Carothers, Thomas | A229 D229	house & lot out house 1 out house 2 out house 3	43 x 22	stone	2	16	321	2 A	1800.00
Walters, Joseph A235 D235		house & lot	17 x 24	log	1	2	16	2 A	300.00
Warton, Thomas A239 D239		house & lot note: house is stone in D	24 x 22	sq. log	1	1	12	2 A	400.00
Waugh, James A244 D244		house & lot	24 x 24	sq. log	1	1	9	1 A	300.00
Waugh, John A243 D243		house & lot out house 1 out house 2	30 x 20	sq. log	1	3	14	1 A	500.00
Waugh, Samuel A242 D242		house & lot	20 x 18	sq. log	1	2	8	2 A	400.00
Waugh, Samuel, Rev. A240 D240		house & lot out house	30 x 28	sq. log	2	12	241	1 A	800.00
Waugh, Samuel, Rev. Junkin, Benjamin A241 D241		house & lot	28 x 24	log	1	2	16	1 A	100.10
Whitehill, Robert A221 D221		house & lot out house 1 out house 2	30 x 30	stone	2	14	208	2 A	1400.00
Widle, Martin A236 D236		house & lot out house 1 out house 2	22 x 15	sq. log	1	7	52	2 A	300.00
Wiley, Robert A237 D237		house & lot out house	22 x 18	sq. log	1	1	4	2 A	300.00
Wiley, Robert A238 D238		house & lot	30 x 25	stone	1	4	48		500.00
Williamson, Thomas A220 D220		house & lot out house	30 x 20	sq. log	2	8	96	2 A	700.00
Wilson, Isabella A245 D245		house & lot out house 1 out house 2	22 x 18	log	1	4	36	2 A	400.00

East Pennsboro Township

Owner Occupant	Location Ref. Adjoining Owner	Structure	Dimensions	Descr.	Stories	Lights Windows	Area	Value
Wilson, Joseph, deceased Fostler, Peter	A234 D234	house & lot out house	16 x 14	log	1	3	16	2 A	300.00
Witt, Nicholas	A232 D232	house & lot out house note: name may be Wilt	33 x 24	stone & log	1	5	62	80 P	600.00
Wolf, Abraham	A248 D248	house & lot	36 x 30	sq. log	1	5	60	1 A	500.00
Wolf, Abraham Lootz, George	A249 D249	house & lot	30 x 14	log	1	2	12	1 A	150.00
Womeldorff, Eve	A233 D233	house & lot out house	30 x 16	log	1	5	28	2 A	300.00
Wormley, Hartley	A223 D223	house & lot out house	26 x 28	sq. log	2	20	270	2 A	800.00
Wormley, Jacob	A222 D222	house & lot out house	30 x 27	sq. log	2	10	120	2 A	600.00
Wormley, John	A224 D224	house & lot	30 x 16	sq. log	1	4	48	80 P	450.00
Wormley, John Coffman, Andrew	A226 D226	house & lot	15 x 16	log	1	1	4	1 A	100.10
Wormley, John Martin, Thomas	A225 D225	house & lot out house	24 x 20	sq. log	2	6	72	80 P	500.00
Wormley, John Rinegar, Martin	A227 D227	house & lot	30 x 26	sq. log	1	8	96	2 A	500.00
Wormly, George	A228 D228	house & lot out house 1 out house 2	27 x 34	sq. log	1	6	72	2 A	700.00
Young, Alexander	A250 D250	house & lot unspecified	30 x 20	sq. log	1	5	39	2 A	500.00

Frankford Township

CHAPTER V FRANKFORD TOWNSHIP

Owner Occupant	Location Adjoining Owner	Structure	Dimensions	Descr.	Stories	Lights Windows	Area	Value
Albert, Henry		house & lot	26 x 22	log	1 1/2	5 60	2 A	224.00
	Bowman, John	barn	35 x 20	log			13 A 120 P	164.00
		wagon maker shop	20 x 18	log				
	A4 B4 D4 E4							
Alter, Jacob	on Conodoguinet Cr.	house & lot	30 x 28	log	2	9 100	2 A	320.00
	Wilson, Matthew	stable	26 x 26	log				
	A1 B1 D1 E1	barn	60 x 30	brick under part			270 A	2700.00
Alter, John	on Conodoguinet Cr.	house & lot	24 x 24	log	1 1/2	3 32	2 A	174.00
	Galbreath,	kitchen	14 x 12					
	William	barn	48 x 24	brick under part			66 A	924.00
	A2 B2 D2 E2							
Armstrong, James, heirs	adj. the Mountain Snyder, Philip	house & lot spring house	20 x 20	log, old wood	1 1/2	3 12	2 A	110.00
Miller, Robert		barn	45 x 18	log, very old			198 A	990.00
(% Brown, John)		shop		wood				
A3 B3 D3 E3		note: land is very stony						
Bell, John		house 1 & lot	26 x 22	log	1 1/2	4 20	2 A	168.00
	Officer,	out house	15 x 13	wood				
	Alexander	barn	50 x 18	log, old, cabin			226 A	2147.00
		still house						
		shop		cabin				
		house 2	18 x 14	log				50.00
	A7 B10 D7 E10	note: house 2 occupied by Brown, Kathrine						
Benedum, George		house & lot	26 x 22	log	2	7 75	2 A	320.00
	Jumper, Jacob	barn	38 x 20				38 A	532.00
		tan house 1	20 x 20					
		tan house 2	18 x 18					
	A6 B9 D6 E9	tan yard		small				
Bigler, William Henry	on Conodoguinet Cr. McDanel, John	tract					14 A	240.00
unoccupied		note: a piece of meadowland purchased from John McDanel						
B12 E12								
Bowman, Jacob	on Conodoguinet Cr.	house & lot	26 x 26	log	2	8 78	2 A	324.00
	Hervey, Andrew & McDanel, John	barn	74 x 36	log			209 A	2508.00
	A9 B11 D9 E11							
Brown, John		house	22 x 20	log, very old				60.00
	Gillespie,	stable 1		cabin				
	George	stable 2		cabin				
	B8 E8	barn	60 x 24	log			207 A	2207.00

Frankford Township

Owner / Occupant	Ref.	Location / Adjoining Owner	Structure	Dimensions	Descr.	Stories	Lights	Windows	Area	Value
Burkholder, Abram		on Conodoguinet Cr.	house & lot	28 x 23	log	2	8	40	2 A	220.00
		McFarlane, Widow	barn	40 x 20	log, very old				198 A	1828.50
	A8 B13 D8 E13									
Butler, Thomas, Col.		adj. the Mountain	house & lot	24 x 24	log	2	8	100	2 A	224.00
Bloser, Peter		Painter, Martin	barn	60 x 22					328 A	3608.00
		& Butler land	spring house							
	A5 B5 D5 E5		note: half the glass broke							
Butler, Thomas, Col.		adj. the Mountain	house	18 x 18	old					
Bloser, Peter		Painter, Martin	stable						168 A	840.00
		& other Butler	note: land stony							
	B6 E6	land								
Butler, Thomas, Col.		adj. the Mountain	cabin	20 x 18						20.00
Kline, George		Painter, Martin							200 A	120.00
		& other Butler	note: land stony; in care of Sample, Robert, Esq.; land value $100 in							
	B7 E7	land	E [the three surveys belonging to Col. Thomas Butler join]							
Campbell, John			house 1 & lot	24 x 22	log	1 1/2	3	22	2 A	180.00
		Shambaugh,	stable	13 x 16	cabin					
		Philip	barn 1	28 x 16	log				371 A 120 P	2974.00
			barn 2	24 x 14	cabin					
			house 2	26 x 20	cabin					40.00
	A12 B16 D12 E16		note: Campbell, Robert occupant of cabin; name also Campble							
Carothers, John		on Conodoguinet Cr.	cabin	small						10.00
Cook, John		Love, John							42 A	504.00
	B18 E18									
Clark, George		on Conodoguinet Cr.	house & lot	22 x 20	log	1 1/2	3	22	2 A	140.00
		Carothers, John	barn	50 x 20	log, part uncovered				128 A	1336.00
	A13 B17 D13 E17		note: 125 A in B & E							
Connelly, Joseph		on Conodoguinet Cr.	house & lot	40 x 22	log	1 1/2	6	60	2 A	220.00
		Johnston, James	stable	15 x 13	log, old					
			barn	50 x 18	log, old				141 A	1410.00
	A10 B14 D10 E14		still house	21 x 21	log					
Cosh, Philip			house & lot	22 x 18	log, old	1 1/2	3	32	2 A	120.00
		Jumper, Conrod	barn	64 x 26	under part stone				248 A	2356.00
	A11 B15 D11 E15									
Dixon, Barnabas			cabin	18 x 16						10.66
		Geddis, James	stable	very small					10 A 100 P	40.00
	B22 E22		note: land very stony							

Frankford Township

Owner Occupant	Ref.	Location Adjoining Owner	Structure	Dimensions	Descr.	Stories	Lights Windows	Area	Value
Douglass, William		Logan, John	house & lot spring house	40 x 18	log wood	1 1/2	4 36	2 A	218.00
	A15 B20 D15 E20		barn stable	50 x 20 small	log, old			158 A	1422.00
Douglass, William Gormley, Thomas	B20 B21 E21	on the Mountain	house tract	18 x 16				60 A	50.00 30.00
Dunbar, John unoccupied	B23 E23	adj. the Mountain McDowell, John	tract note: land stony; unimproved					200 A	100.00
Dunn, Nicholas	A14 B19 D14 E19	Lemon, Jacob	house & lot barn	30 x 20 35 x 22	log, old log, old	1 1/2	3 26	2 A 92 A	136.00 736.00
Ebright, Philip	B29 E29	on Conodoguinet Cr. Officer, Alexander	cabin spring house barn note: land stony	30 x 20 small 24 x 18				120 A	80.00 120.00
Eiley, Philip	A19 B30 D19 E30	Hoopstater, Jacob	house & lot cabin barn saw mill note: Clemens, James, occupant of cabin; saw mill dry 3 mos. of year	24 x 22 18 x 16 45 x 20	log log	1 1/2	3 36	2 A 68 A	168.00 20.00 612.00
Ernest, John	B24 E24	on Conodoguinet Cr. Wilson, Matthew	house barn	20 x 20 45 x 18	log, very old log, old			100 A	50.00 1100.00
Espy, Thomas	A17 B26 D17 E26	adj. the Mountain Espy, William	house & lot spring house stables barn	24 x 22 50 x 24	log wood 4, old, cabin log	1 1/2	3 24	2 A 148 A	172.00 888.00
Espy, Thomas	B27 E27	adj. the Mountain Espy, William	tract note: the greater part of the land is stony and poor					200 A	100.00
Espy, Widow	A16 B25 D16 E25	Graham, Arthur	house 1 & lot kitchen barn house 2 note: Conaway, George, occupant of house 2	24 x 22 18 x 16 60 x 18 20 x 20	log wood, old log, old log, old	1 1/2	4 33	2 A 114 A	192.00 60.00 940.50 60.00

Frankford Township

Owner / Occupant	Ref.	Location / Adjoining Owner	Structure	Dimensions	Descr.	Stories	Lights Windows		Area	Value
Espy, William		Laird, James	house & lot	22 x 20	log	1 1/2	3	24	2 A	132.00
			spring house							
			barn	52 x 20	log				98 A	588.00
			still house							
	A18 B28 D18 E28		cabin	20 x 18						
Galbreath, William			house 1 & lot	24 x 24	log	1	3	27	2 A	174.00
Pilgrim, Henry		Alter, John	barn 1	50 x 25	log				230 A	2760.00
			barn 2	20 x 18	log					
			house 2	20 x 18	wood					80.00
			cabin 1		old					2.00
			cabin 2		old					2.00
			note: Galbreath listed as occupant in B; Wickline ocupant of cabin							
	A27 B40 D27 E40		1, Lepard, of cabin 2							
Geddis, James		on Conodoguinet Cr.	house & lot	24 x 20	log	1 1/2	4	22	2 A	189.00
		Johnston, James	out house	14 x 12	wood					
	A21 B33 D21 E33		barn	56 x 22	log				268 A	1876.00
Geddis, James			house & lot	20 x 20	log	1 1/2	3	16	2 A	124.00
McCauley, William		Bell, John &	barn	40 x 20	log				221 A	1547.00
		Varner, George								
	A22 B34 D22 E34									
Gees, Peter			house	18 x 18	log					60.00
		Butler, Thomas,	barn	22 x 18					21 A	105.00
	B43 E43	Esq.								
George, Martin			house 1 & lot	24 x 20	log	1 1/2	3	33	2 A	204.00
Martin, George &		Painter,	stable	small						40.00
George Jr.		Martin	barn	50 x 20	log				118 A	1298.00
	A23 B35 D23 E35		house 2	20 x 16	log					40.00
George, Martin		at the Mountain	tract						50 A	50.00
		Varner, George								
	B36 E36									
Gerish, Hanicle			house & lot	20 x 16	log	1 1/2	3	18		112.00
		Musselman,	kitchen		old					
		Jacob	barn	16 x 14	log, old				45 A	270.00
	A20 B32 D20 E32									
Gillespie or Syke		adj. the Mountain	house	18 x 18	log					75.00
Lodorus, Joseph		Gees, Peter							209 A	209.00
	B44 E44		note: land stony							
Gillespie, George			house & lot	30 x 20	log	2	5	48	2 A	214.00
		Gillespie,	cabin	25 x 18						40.00
		Widow	barn	70 x 18					198 A	1881.00
	A25 B38 D25 E38		note: Plunket, Isaac occupant of cabin.							

Frankford Township

Owner Occupant	Ref.	Location Adjoining Owner	Structure	Dimensions	Descr.	Stories	Lights Windows	Area	Area	Value
Gillespie, Widow		Lime, Michael	house & lot	20 x 20	log	1 1/2	4	39	2 A	164.00
			out house	14 x 12	wood					
			barn	40 x 20	log				172 A	1204.00
			cabin		old					
	A24 B37 D24 E37		note: Fortney, Melchor occupant of cabin.							
Graham, Arthur		McDowell, Samuel	house & lot	20 x 20	log	1 1/2	4	39	2 A	144.00
			barn	58 x 26	log				154 A	1541.00
	A28 B41 D28 E41		smith shop	18 x 18	log					
Graham, Isaiah Steel, John		adj. the Mountain Gillespie, Widow	house & lot	20 x 18	log	1 1/2	1	9	2 A	106.00
									128 A	384.00
	A29 B42 D29 E42		note: part of land stony							
Gregory, Widow vacant		Lindsay, Robert	cabin		old					
			tract						30 A	60.00
	B31 E31		note: waste, the land poor							
Gustine, Lemuel, Dr. Templeton, William		Parker, William	house 1 & lot	24 x 24	stone	2	8	96	2 A	428.00
			out house	20 x 13	wood					
			barn	58 x 20	log, old				129 A	1706.00
			house 2	20 x 12	old					
	A26 B39 D26 E39		note: house 2 and out house may be the same structure							
Hannah, William		Rachford, Hugh	house & lot	24 x 22	log	2	7	48	2 A	216.00
			cabin		old					
			barn	50 x 18	log				148 A	1184.00
	A31 B46 D31 E46		weaver shop							
Harvey, Andrew Harvey, Andrew & Harvey, William		Bowman, Jacob	house & lot	40 x 18	log	1	4	32	2 A	204.00
			out house	16 x 16	wood					
			stables		3, log, old					
	A30 B45 D30 E45		barn	50 x 18					194 A 80 P	2334.00
Hoopstater, Jacob		Lepard, Henry	house & lot	25 x 22	log	1	5	48	2 A	174.00
			cabin		old					6.00
			barn	45 x 18	log				48 A	576.00
	A32 B47 D32 E47		note: Lutz [?], John occupant of cabin; house consumed by fire May 16, 1799							
Hyser, Rudolph		Panter, John	house & lot	28 x 22	log	1 1/2	2		2 A	108.00
			barn	54 x 20	log				81 A	648.00
	A33 B48 D33 E48									
Johnston, James		on Conodoguinet Cr. Geddis, James	house 1 & lot	24 x 22	log	2	5	45	2 A	216.00
			out house	22 x 10	wood					
			spring house							
			barn	50 x 20	log, old				184 A	1518.00
			house 2	20 x 18	log, old					50.00
	A37 B52 D37 E52		note: Lemon, John, occupant of house 2							

Frankford Township

Owner Occupant	Ref.	Location Adjoining Owner	Structure	Dimensions	Descr.	Stories	Lights Windows	Area	Value
Johnston, James			cabin		very old				
Clemons, Benjamin		Laird, James	barn	50 x 20	log			175 A	1750.00
	B53 E53								
Jumper, Conrad			house & lot	30 x 20	log	1 1/2	7 61	2 A	220.00
		McDanel, John	out house	10 x 13	wood				
			out house	10 x 20	wood				
			stable	25 x 20	log				
			barn	50 x 18	log			308 A	4928.00
			grist mill	45 x 20	stone				
			saw mill	small					
			cabin	small					
			notes: Cox, William occupant of cabin. The mills are "as loss chd [charged?] at half the sum."						
	A34 B49 D34 E49								
Jumper, Conrad		adj. the Mountain	house & lot	20 x 18	log	1	3 30	1 A	101.00
Miller, -----		Espy, William	stable	small					
			barn	54 x 20	log			120 A	1831.50
			cabin 1	14 x 14					20.00
			cabin 2		very old				.50
	A35 B50 D35 E50		note: the land poor and stony; occupant in A35 is "The Miller"						
Jumper, Jacob			house & lot	20 x 20	log	1	4 29	2 A	193.00
		Jumper, Conrad	barn	50 x 18				198 A	1832.00
			cabin 1		shell				50.00
			cabin 2		very old				
			still house						
	A36 B51 D36 E51		note: Jumper, Abram, occupant of cabin 2						
Kearn, Henry			house & lot	22 x 22	log	1 1/2	3 32	2 A	195.00
		Logan, Henry	stable	very small	log			8 A 120 P	87.50
	A43 B61 D43 E61								
Kennedy, Thomas, Esq.			house & lot	36 x 20	log, old	1 1/2	8 80	2 A	189.00
		Hanna, William	out house						
			barn 1	double	log, old			248 A	1612.00
			barn 2	double	log, old				
	A41 B58 D41 E58		note: Crow is listed as occupant in D						
Kennedy, Thomas, Esq.		at the Mountain Graham, Isaiah	tract					136 A	136.00
			note: unimproved land						
	B60 E59								

Frankford Township

Owner Occupant	Ref.	Location Adjoining Owner	Structure	Dimensions	Descr.	Stories	Windows Lights	Area	Value
Kennedy, Thomas, Esq. Bower, Henry	A42 B59 D42 E60	Gillespie, George	house & lot out house barn	26 x 24 40 x 20	log log, old	2	6 72	2 A 154 A	222.00 1694.00
King, John	A38 B54 D38 E54	Rufner, Conrod	house & lot stable note: the land poor	20 x 18 small	log log	1 1/2	3 24	2 A 15 A 80 P	130.00 77.50
Kinsemore, John	B63 E63	Gees, Peter	house	18 x 18	log			21 A	60.00 105.00
Klay, John	A40 B57 D40 E57	Hyser, Rudolph	house & lot barn	30 x 24 54 x 20	log log	2	5 56	2 A 148 A	216.00 1221.00
Klay, Mathias	B55 E55	adj. the Mountain Snider, George	cabin barn	20 x 15 48 x 28	log			130 A	30.00 1300.00
Kraft, Ralph	A39 B56 D39 E56	Nickey, George	house & lot stable note: this property is exempt from State and County taxes, the owner being poor and lame [The valuation is listed in the exempt column.]	30 x 24 small	log log	1 1/2	3 45	2 A 28 A	189.00 224.00
Kulp, Simon vacant	B62 E62	McDowell, Samuel	tract note: unimproved					6 A	60.00
Lackey, Alexander	A44 B64 D44 E64	McClure, Robert	house 1 & lot stable barn still house house 2 cabin note: Woods, Robert, occupant of house 2; Jamison, Robert, of cabin.	32 x 20 60 x 25 20 x 20 20 x 18	log cabin log, old cabin small	1 1/2	4 20	2 A 307 A	191.00 2532.75 50.00 30.00
Lackey, Alexander	B65 E65	at the Mountain Laird, James	tract					200 A	100.00
Laird, James	A52 B76 D52 E76	Johnston, James	house & lot barn	24 x 24 52 x 24	log log	1 1/2	4 36	2 A 221 A	154.00 1547.00

Frankford Township

Owner / Occupant	Location / Adjoining Owner	Structure	Size	Descr.	Stories	Lights / Windows	Area	Value
Laird, James	adj. the Mountain other Laird property B77 E77	tract					153 A	306.00
Layman, Abram	Harvey, Andrew A46 B67 D46 E67	house & lot barn	20 x 18 25 x 28	log log	1 1/2	3 18	2 A 58 A	162.00 464.00
Lemon, Adam	on Conodoguinet Cr. Geddis, James A53 B79 D53 E79	house & lot barn shop	24 x 22 50 x 20	log log cabin	2	5 48	2 A 43 A	214.00 301.00
Lemon, Jacob	Dunn, Han--- [?] A47 B68 D47 E68	house & lot cabin barn note: Harper, Ebenezer, occupant of cabin	32 x 18 20 x 14 52 x 20	log poor, very old log	1 1/2	3 36	2 A 73 A	162.00 10.00 584.00
Lepard, Henry	Connelly, Joseph B70 E70	house 1 house 2 barn note: barn with [?] in one end	20 x 18 22 x 20 20 x 18	log, new log			30 A	20.00 240.00
Lepard, John vacant	Lepard, Henry B71 E71	tract note: unimproved					22 A	110.00
Limes, Michael	adj. the Mountain Snider, Philip A45 B66 D45 E66	house & lot barn	22 x 20 52 x 21	log log	1 1/2	3 33	2 A 120 A	187.00 840.00
Lindsay, Robert	Lindsey, William A49 B72 D49 E72	house & lot cabin barn	28 x 25 58 x 21	log old log	2	9 108	2 A 147 A	266.50 1215.00
Lindsay, Widow	Lindsey, Robert B73 E73	house	20 x 18	old			73 A	20.00 602.50
Lindsay, William	Geddis, James A50 B74 D50 E74	house & lot barn	34 x 20 56 x 20	log log	1	5 40	2 A 115 A	191.00 949.00

Frankford Township

Owner / Occupant	Ref.	Location / Adjoining Owner	Structure	Dimensions	Descr.	Stories	Lights / Windows		Area	Value
Logan, Alexander		Logan, John	house & lot	27 x 25	log	1	4	36	2 A	216.50
			stable	20 x 20	log					
			spring house							
			barn	45 x 28	log				378 A	3118.50
			cabin		old					50.00
	A51 B75 D51 E75		note: Bradley, Robert, occupant of cabin							
Logan, Henry			house	20 x 20	log, old					50.00
Anderson, John		Wilson, Matthew	barn	50 x 20	log, old				206 A	1236.00
	B78 E78									
Logan, John			house & lot	28 x 24	log	1 1/2	7	49	2 A	316.50
		Lindsey,	kitchen	20 x 16						
		William	spring house							
			barn	52 x 22	log				290 A	2392.50
			cabin		old					1.00
	A48 B66 D48 E66		note: Cowan, Robert, occupant of cabin							
McClure, Robert, heirs			house & lot	26 x 24	log	2	4	42	2 A	222.00
Ward, Philip &		Lackey,	out house	16 x 12	wood					
Wilson, Henry		Alexander	barn	50 x 20	log, old				245 A	2695.00
	A56 B83 D56 E83		note: in care of McClure, William & Laird, James							
McDanel, John			house & lot	24 x 18	log	2	9	112	2 A	232.00
		Jumper, Conrod	out house	18 x 12						
			out house	22 x 12						
			spring house							
	A54 B80 D54 E80		barn	60 x 55	frame, old				184 A	2944.00
McDowell, John			house & lot	28 x 22	log	1	5	39	2 A	197.00
			stable	20 x 12						
	A55 B81 D55 E81		barn	60 x 22	log				262 A	2882.00
McDowell, John		adj. the Mountain	tract						85 A	42.50
		Logan, Alexander								
	B82 E82									
McDowell, Samuel			house & lot	22 x 20	log	1 1/2	1	9	2 A	132.00
		Espy, Widow	barn	54 x 20	log				198 A	1188.00
	A58 B85 D58 E85									
McFarlane, Widow			house & lot	30 x 20	log	1 1/2	4	30	2 A	180.00
		Burkholder,	barn		very old, almost rotten				198 A	1188.00
		Abram								
	A57 B84 D57 E84									
Musselman, Jacob		on Conodoguinet Cr.	tract						200 A	2000.00
vacant		Clark, George	wash house		old					
	B87 E87									

Frankford Township

Owner Occupant	Ref.	Location Adjoining Owner	Structure	Dimensions	Descr.	Stories	Lights Windows	Area	Value
Myers, Bostain		Shambaugh, Philip	cabin stable note: name also Myres	20 x 12 small				15 A	20.00 150.00
	B86 E86								
Nickey, George		Sansbaugh, Christy	house & lot stable barn	24 x 22 small 55 x 25	log log	2	3 36	2 A 148 A	189.00 1110.00
	A59 B88 D59 E88								
Officer, Alexander		adj. the Mountain Bell, John	house & lot out house stable barn note: part very stony	26 x 22 10 x 22 20 x 18 20 x 18	log wood log log	1 1/2	3 36	1 A 243 A	206.00 1579.50
	A60 B89 D60 E89								
Officer, Alexander Patton, William			house & lot	30 x 16	log	1	3 27	1 A	106.00
	A61 D61								
Painter, John		Jumper, Jacob	cabin barn	20 x 18 28 x 20	log			80 A	75.00 640.00
	B94 E94								
Painter, Martin		Butler, Thomas, Esq.	house 1 & lot stable barn shop house 2	46 x 24 60 x 30 18 x 16 20 x 18	log log, old under part stone log log	1 1/2	7 58	2 A 128 A	220.00 1344.00 75.00
	A64 B93 D64 E93								
Parker, William		Jumper, Jacob	house & lot barn fulling mill cabin note: Cohan, Charles, occupant of cabin; dry more than half the year	16 x 14 30 x 18 22 x 20	log, old log	1	2 20	2 A 98 A	100.50 784.00 6.00
	A63 B92 D63 E92								
Patton, Robert Crane, Richard		Nickey, George	house 1 stable 1 house 2 cabin stable 2 note: Womer, Henry, occupant of house 2; Smith, Samuel, of the cabin	30 x 16 16 x 16	log, old old log old old			273 A	50.00 40.00 10.00 2252.25
	B95 D95								
Popenmyre, Gabriel		Hanna, William	house & lot stable barn	36 x 20 20 x 16 54 x 20	log log log	1 1/2	5 42	2 A 178 A	218.00 1646.50
	A62 B90 D62 E90								
Porter heirs Horner, Henry		Wilson, Matthew	house barn	30 x 20 48 x 22	log log			155 A	75.00 1715.00
	B91 E91								

Frankford Township

Owner / Occupant	Ref.	Location / Adjoining Owner	Structure	Dimensions	Descr.	Stories	Lights Windows	Area	Value
Ratchford, Hugh	B96 E96	Worst, Jacob	house barn cabin 1 cabin 2	27 x 23 58 x 22	log, old log			130 A	60.00 780.00
Rhine, Henry vacant	B98 E98	Parker, William	tract note: unplatted					16 A 80 P	132.00
Rufner, Conrod	A65 B97 D65 E97	Wallace, John	house & lot barn note: barn built since October	24 x 22	log	1 1/2	4 42	2 A 101 A	185.00 606.00
Sansebaugh, Christy	A70 B104 D70 E104	Patton, Robert	house & lot out house barn cabin	20 x 18 12 x 10 48 x 20 16 x 14	log log, old	1 1/2	3 24	2 A 90 A	135.00 675.00
Shambaugh, George	A66 B99 D66 E99	Clay, John	house & lot barn	28 x 16 30 x 14	log log	1 1/2	4 29	2 A 98 A	166.00 784.00
Shambaugh, Philip	A72 B106 D72 E106	Jumper, Jacob	house & lot barn	28 x 24 40 x 18	log log	1 1/2	4 32	2 A 88 A	190.00 704.00
Sharp, John	A73 B107 D73 E107	Wallace, John	house & lot barn	22 x 20 56 x 20	log log	1 1/2	3 18	2 A 170 A 80 P	172.00 1875.50
Snider, Christy	A67 B100 D67 E100	adj. the Mountain Snider, George	house & lot barn	24 x 22 50 x 20	log log, old	2	3 36	2 A 98 A	187.00 588.00
Snider, Christy	B101 E101	adj. the Mountain	tract					50 A	175.00
Snider, George	A68 B102 D68 E102	Wax, Peter	house & lot barn 1 barn 2 note: [location of barns ambiguous; both are on this tract in D102, but one may be on B103]	35 x 20 50 x 20 45 x 18	log log log	2	12 118	2 A 296 A	268.00 2368.00
Snider, George Snider, George, Jr.	A69 B103 D69 E103	adj. the Mountain	house & lot cabin note: Stone, Hugh, occupant of cabin	20 x 16		1 1/2	2 20	2 A 175 A	100.50 10.00 175.00

Frankford Township

Owner / Occupant	Ref.	Location / Adjoining Owner	Structure	Dimensions	Descr.	Stories	Windows Lights	Area	Value
Snider, Philip	A74 B108 D74 E108	Armstrong, James, heirs	house & lot barn still house	26 x 27 56 x 20 20 x 16	 log, old log	2	8 96	2 A 120 A	213.00 780.00
Souther, Jacob	A71 B105 D71 E105	Logan, Alexander	house & lot barn	26 x 24 45 x 20	log log	1 1/2	4 42	2 A 117 A	190.00 819.00
Speck	A75 B109 D75 E109	Popenmyer, Gabriel	house & lot stable note: no first name given	22 x 22 small	log log	1 1/2	3 32	2 A 3 A 120 P	186.00 37.50
Varner, George	B110 E110	adj. the Mountain Painter, Martin	cabin 1 cabin 2 tract		old old			 50 A	 100.00
Waggoner, Jacob	B122 E122	Patton, Robert	wash cabin tract	small				100 A	1000.00
Wallace, John	A81 B120 D81 E120	Sharp, John	house & lot barn	20 x 20 60 x 20	log log	1 1/2	3 18	2 A 158 A	188.00 1027.00
Wallace, Patrick	A78 B114 D78 E114	McClure, Robert, heirs	house & lot out house barn	28 x 20 18 x 16 50 x 20	log log	1 1/2	4 22	2 A 204 A	192.00 2040.00
Wallace, Patrick	B115 E115	adj. the Mountain Laird, James	cabin		new			119 A	119.00
Wax, Peter	A77 B112 D77 E112	Douglass, William	house & lot out house barn	24 x 20 10 x 26 50 x 18	log, old log	1 1/2	3 22	2 A 136 A	118.00 1224.00
Wax, Peter	B113 E113	adj. the Mountain	tract					100 A	100.00
Wilson heirs Sharp, John	B117 E117	Sharp, John	house barn	 58 x 20	old, almost rotten log			 235 A	20.00 1527.50

Frankford Township

Owner Occupant	Ref.	Location Adjoining Owner	Structure	Dimensions	Descr.	Stories	Lights Windows	Area	Value
Wilson, Joseph			house & lot	27 x 15	log	2	4	48	2 A	195.00
		Alter, Jacob	stable	14 x 14	log				3 A	30.00
	A82 B121 D82 E121		smith shop	16 x 14	log					
Wilson, Matthew			house & lot	24 x 22	log	1	5	30	2 A	191.00
		Logan, Henry	stable 1	small	log					
			barn	60 x 20	log				183 A	1555.50
			cabin		old					
			stable 2	small	log					
	A80 B118 D80 E118		note: Thomas, John, occupant of cabin							
Wilson, Matthew			house		log					40.00
McCrae, William		Butler, Thomas	barn	66 x 30	log, new, not yet covered				155 A	1615.00
	B119 E119									
Wilson, Samuel			house & lot	43 x 21	log	1 1/2	5	24	2 A	174.00
		Espy, Thomas	spring house							
	A76 B111 D76 E111		barn	56 x 22	log				169 A	1183.00
Worst, Jacob			house & lot	30 x 20	log	1 1/2	3	30	2 A	163.00
		Brown, John	stable	20 x 16	log					
	A79 B116 D79 E116		barn	59 x 20	log				198 A	1287.00

Hopewell Township

CHAPTER VI   HOPEWELL TOWNSHIP

Owner / Occupant	Location / Adjoining Owner	Structure	Dimensions	Descr.	Stories	Lights / Windows	Area	Area	Value
Boyd, Abraham B3 E3	adj. No. Mountain	cabin	14 x 16					100 A	10.00 55.00
Boyd, Adam Louther, Joseph B2 E2	adj. No. Mountain Wilson, Nathaniel	house stable note: stable dimensions may be 18 x 20	18 x 20 16 x 20	cabin cabin				200 A	20.00 825.00
Boyd, James A1 B1 D1 E1	adj. No. Mountain Hannah, Samuel	house & lot barn	22 x 22 22 x 60	log	1 1/2	1	12	1 A 149 A	200.00 1140.00
Brady, Joseph B4 E4	Mustard, Archibald	cabin barn	16 x 16 18 x 20					100 A	10.00 630.00
Brotherton, Samuel B5 E5	Miller, Loudwick & Morrett, Nicholas	house barn house 2 note: Maxwell, John, occupant of house 2	20 x 20 22 x 60 14 x 15	log, old log cabin				380 A	10.00 3075.00 5.00
Clark, George B9 E9		cabin 1 cabin 2 barn note: $130 is written immediately after house description but not in amount column	16 x 10 25 x 30 18 x 54	log, unfinished log				100 A	10.00 1190.00
Cooper, Robert, Dr., D. D. A3 B6 D3 E6	Trimble, William & McCormick, Widow	house & lot kitchen barn	28 x 31 18 x 18 20 x 66	stone stone log	2 1	10	127	1 A 206 A	650.00 1748.00
Cunningham, Adam A2 B7 D2 E7	Robertson, John & McCune, John	house & lot barn	20 x 20 24 x 55	log log	1 1/2	2	15	1 A 139 A	120.00 1450.00
Cunningham, John B8 E8	Conodoguinet Creek Cooper, Robert, Dr.	house barn	18 x 18 20 x 20	cabin				50 A	10.00 540.00
Duncan, John A6 B12 D6 E12	McEntire, Robert & Gibb, John	house & lot kitchen barn house 2 note: area 149 A, value $1170.00 in E	12 x 18 18 x 18 20 x 80 16 x 16	log log log log	1 1/2 1 1/2	3	32	1 A 169 A	400.00 1343.00 50.00

Hopewell Township

Owner / Occupant	Ref.	Location / Adjoining Owner	Structure	Dimensions	Descr.	Stories	Windows	Lights	Area	Value
Duncan, John		on Conodoguinet Cr.	house & lot	20 x 22	log	1 1/2	3	27	1 A	200.00
Waddle, James		Gibb, John	barn	20 x 40	log				149 A	940.00
	A7 B13 D7 E13		house 2	12 x 12	log					5.00
Dysert, Benjamin			house & lot	27 x 27	log	2	10	105	1 A	450.00
		Brotherton, Saml.	kitchen	20 x 20		1				
		& Dysert, James	barn	20 x 60	log				228 A	2115.00
	A4 B10 D4 E10		grain house							
Dysert, James			house & lot	26 x 26	log	1 1/2	3	65	1 A	300.00
		Dysert, Benjamin	barn	14 x 24					230 A	1856.00
		& Montgomery,	cabin		log					
		William								
	A5 B11 D5 E11									
Erwin, Samuel			house	18 x 20	log					90.00
		Woods, John &							179 A	1170.00
		Mustard, Archibald								
	B14 E14									
Fogelsonger, Jacob			house	16 x 20	log					50.00
		Woods, John &	barn	18 x 22	log				95 A	650.00
		Duncan, John								
	B15 E15									
Gibb, John		on Conodoguinet Cr.	house & lot	18 x 18	log	1 1/2	2	16	1 A	150.00
		Duncan, John	kitchen	18 x 20	log	1 1/2				
	A9 B17 D9 E17		barn	20 x 50					149 A	1242.00
Gilbert, George			house & lot	22 x 20	log	1 1/2	3	20	1 A	120.00
		Wills, John &	kitchen	22 x 14	log	1 1/2				
		Montgomery, Wm.	barn	20 x 60	log				179 A	1492.00
	A8 B16 D8 E16		cabin	18 x 20	log					10.00
Gilbreath, Hannah			cabin	18 x 20						15.00
		Wilson,	barn	21 x 28	log				80 A	520.00
		Nathaniel &								
	B18 E18	Miller, Ludwick								
Hannah, Ezekiel			house & lot	26 x 26	log	1 1/2	4	48	1 A	250.00
Hannah, Samuel		Peebles, Robert	barn	21 x 56	log				225 A	1870.00
		& Dysert,	cabin	16 x 16	log					10.00
		Benjamin								
	A13 B23 D13 E23									
Hannah, Samuel			house & lot	29 x 29	stone	2		107	1 A	400.00
		Miller, Ludwick	kitchen	20 x 20	log	1				
		& Montgomery,	barn	30 x 80	log				233 A	2269.00
		William	tan house	18 x 14	log					
	A11 B21 D11 E21		tan yard							

Hopewell Township

Owner / Occupant	Ref.	Location / Adjoining Owner	Structure	Dimensions	Descr.	Stories	Lights / Windows	Area	Value
Hannah, Samuel		mountain land	house & lot	18 x 20	wood	1 1/2	4 / 42	1 A	120.00
Long, John								50 A	50.00
	A12 B22 D12 E22		note: value $40.00 in B						
Hefflefinger, Martin &			house 1	20 x 20	old				10.00
Hefflefinger, Frederick		McClelland, Thomas & Dysert, Benjamin	house 2	27 x 27	unfinished				30.00
			cabin		log				15.00
			barn	22 x 60	log			190 A	1810.00
	B26 E26		note: Hefflefinger, Frederick occupant of house 2 and cabin						
Hefflefinger, Philip		adj. No. Mountain Mitchell, John	cabin	18 x 20	old				10.00
	B19 E19							200 A	410.00
Hemphill, James		on Conodoguinet Cr. Cooper, Doctor	house & lot	24 x 21	log	1 1/2	4 / 36	1 A	200.00
			kitchen	24 x 21	log	1 1/2			
			barn 1	20 x 54	log			272 A	2780.00
	A17 B29 D17 E29		barn 2	20 x 40	log				
Hemphill, James			house & lot	18 x 20	log	1 1/2	2 / 18	1 A	150.00
Orbison, Adam			kitchen	12 x 12	log	1			
	A18 D18								
Henderson, James		on Conodoguinet Cr. Hemphill, James	house & lot	18 x 24	log	1 1/2	3 / 27	1 A	200.00
			barn	20 x 58	log			99 A	1078.00
			cabin	12 x 15	log				10.00
	A15 B27 D15 E27		note: Walker, Frank, occupant of cabin						
Henderson, James		on Conodoguinet Cr. McKee, James	house & lot	24 x 20	log	1 1/2	2 / 30	1 A	200.00
Henderson, Samuel			kitchen	20 x 20	log	1 1/2			
			barn	20 x 58	log			99 A	1040.00
			cabin	15 x 15					10.00
	A16 B28 D16 E28		note: Beaty, James, occupant of cabin						
Hess, John		McClelland, Thomas & Morrett, Nicholas	house & lot	24 x 24	log	1 1/2	3 / 19	1 A	150.00
			kitchen	10 x 22	log	1			
			barn	23 x 58	log			199 A	1025.00
	A10 B20 D10 E20								
Hill, Henry		adj. No. Mountain Whisler, John	cabin	16 x 16					10.00
	B31 E31		stable		old, cabin			50 A	60.00
Hiry, Christopher		Simmeral, John & Clark, George	house	18 x 20	log				90.00
Bowers, John			stable	small				23 A	230.00
	B30 E30								

97

Hopewell Township

Owner / Occupant	Location Ref. / Adjoining Owner	Structure	Dimensions	Descr.	Stories	Lights Windows		Area	Value
Holler, Henry		house	20 x 20	log, old					30.00
	Piper, William	barn	20 x 55	log				161 A	1051.00
	& Thompson, William	cabin	20 x 13	log					15.00
	B25 E25	note: East, Stophel, occupant of cabin							
How, Henry	on Conodoguinet Cr.	house & lot	18 x 24	brick	1 1/2	2	30	1 A	250.00
	Wills, John	stable	24 x 24						
	A14 B24 D14 E24	barn	20 x 60	log				169 A	1810.00
Hunter, Joseph		house & lot	24 x 21	log	1 1/2	4	36	1 A	200.00
Mason, Isaac	McKee, John &	stable		old				35 A	90.00
	Whisner, John	house 2	20 x 20	cabin					10.00
	B32 E32								
Laughlin, John		house & lot	22 x 24	log	2	7	75	1 A	400.00
McClure, James	Cooper, Robert	kitchen	22 x 24	log	1 1/2				
	& Wills, David	barn	20 x 56	log				349 A	3301.00
	A19 B33 D19 E33								
Lesher, Gasper		house	20 x 24	old, cabin					30.00
	Simmerel, Martin	kitchen		old, cabin					
	& Woods, John	barn	20 x 24	log				100 A	660.00
	B34 E34								
Mason, Isaac		cabin	16 x 16						10.00
	Whisner, John &	still house		old, cabin				50 A	90.00
	Mitchell, John								
	B51 E51								
McClelland, Thomas		house & lot	28 x 32	log	2	6	57	1 A	450.00
	McKinney, Joseph	kitchen	18 x 18	log	1				
	& Wherry, Samuel	barn	24 x 60	log				249 A	2331.00
	A21 B36 D21 E36								
McCormick, Elizabeth	Rocksburgh Road	house & lot	24 x 24	log	1 1/2	6	60	1 A	300.00
	Cooper, Robert	kitchen	18 x 18	log					
	A25 B41 D25 E41	barn	20 x 60	log				199 A	1672.00
McDonald, Rebecca		house	20 x 22	log					50.00
	Peebles, Robert	barn	16 x 25	log				18 A	191.00
	& Rogers, Richard								
	B39 E39								
McEntire, Robert		house & lot	20 x 22	log	1 1/2	4	27	1 A	200.00
	Cunningham, Adam	barn	20 x 37					62 A	474.00
	& Duncan, John								
	A27 B45 D27 E45								

Hopewell Township

Owner / Occupant	Ref.	Location / Adjoining Owner	Structure	Dimensions	Descr.	Stories	Lights Windows	Area	Value
McEntire, William			house & lot	22 x 24	log	1 1/2	5 48	1 A	200.00
		Cooper, Robert	stable	16 x 16	log			9 A	92.00
		& Rogers, Richard							
	A24 B40 D24 E40								
McKee, John			house & lot	24 x 24	log	1 1/2	5 30	1 A	400.00
		McKinney, David	kitchen	23 x 18	log	1 1/2			
		& Wherry, Samuel	barn	20 x 56	log			194 A	1816.00
	A20 B35 D20 E35								
McKinney, David			house & lot	18 x 20	log	1 1/2	2 18	1 A	220.00
		McKee, John &	kitchen	20 x 20	log	1 1/2			
		McKinney,	barn	24 x 24	log			359 A	3321.00
		Joseph	house 2	18 x 20	log				50.00
			cabin	16 x 16					10.00
			note: McCalmont, Alexander, occupant of house 2; Thompson, Robert, of						
	A29 B48 D29 E48		cabin						
McKinney, Joseph			house & lot	24 x 24	log	1 1/2	6 70	1 A	400.00
		McKinney, David	kitchen	23 x 24	log	1 1/2			
		& McClelland,	barn	22 x 60	log			359 A	3325.00
		Thomas	house 2		[?]				10.00
			cabin	16 x 16					10.00
	A30 B49 D30 E49		note: Jackson, William, occupant of cabin; house 2 razed to the ground						
McKinney, Joseph		mountain land	house	16 x 16	cabin				10.00
Cloyd, Solomon			stable	18 x 20				150 A	100.00
	B50 E50		note: late survey						
Miller, Ludwick			house & lot	24 x 24	stone	1 1/2	5 60	1 A	430.00
		Hannah, Samuel	kitchen	18 x 15	log	1			
		& Brotherton,	stable	20 x 30	log				
		Samuel	barn	24 x 60				185 A	1775.00
	A26 B43 D26 E43								
Miller, Ludwick		mountain land	tract					70 A	60.00
	B44 E44								
Mitchell, John			house & lot	22 x 20	log	1 1/2	2 10	1 A	180.00
		Morrette,	kitchen	22 x 13	log	1 1/2			
		Nicholas &	barn	22 x 56	log			239 A	1691.00
		Brotherton, James							
	A23 B38 D23 E38								
Mountgomery, William			house & lot	24 x 24	log	1 1/2	4 30	1 A	120.00
Holmes, George		Dysert, James	barn	22 x 22	old, cabin			249 A	2010.00
		& Gilbert,	cabin	18 x 18					8.00
		George	note: Gormin, Archibald, occupant of cabin						
	A31 B42 D31 E42								

Hopewell Township

Owner Occupant	Location Ref. Adjoining Owner	Structure	Dimensions	Descr.	Stories	Windows	Lights	Area	Value
Morrette, Nicholas		house & lot	28 x 30	log	2	6	72	1 A	350.00
	McClelland, Thomas & Mitchell, John	barn	22 x 60	log				249 A	1783.00
	A22 B37 D22 E37								
Mustard, Archibald		house	18 x 18						80.00
	Sharp, James & Thompson, William	stable	18 x 18						
		barn	20 x 40	log				100 A	736.00
	B47 E47								
Myers, John	on Conodoguinet Cr.	house & lot	18 x 26	log	1 1/2	3	36	1 A	220.00
	McEntire, William	kitchen	17 x 20	log	1				
		barn	20 x 20	log				55 A	580.00
	A28 B46 D28 E46								
Nesbet, Francis	on Conodoguinet Cr.	house & lot	20 x 26	brick	1 1/2	2	27	1 A	200.00
owner & Duffy, John	Piper, William	kitchen	12 x 20	log	1				
		barn	22 x 58	log				99 A	758.00
		cabin	16 x 16						8.00
	A32 B52 D32 E52	note: name also Nisbit, Nesbit							
Over, John	on Conodoguinet Cr.	house	28 x 30	unfinished					80.00
	Cooper, Robert	spring house							
	B54 E54	barn	28 x 30	log				103 A	1150.00
Overline, Adam		house & lot	24 x 16	log	1 1/2	3	28	1 A	250.00
	Trimble, William	kitchen	12 x 20	log	1 1/2				
	& Wallace, James	barn	17 x 49	log				159 A	1332.00
	A33 B53 D33 E53								
Peebles, Robert		house & lot	24 x 24	log	1 1/2	6	52	1 A	350.00
	Smith, Hugh &	kitchen	16 x 17	log	1				
	Hannah, Ezekiel	barn	21 x 56	log				159 A	1312.00
	A34 B55 D34 E55								
Piper, James		house	15 x 15	cabin					10.00
	Piper, William & Erwin, Samuel	weaver shop	10 x 12	cabin				13 A	101.00
	B56 E57								
Piper, William		house & lot	24 x 24	log	1 1/2	3	36	1 A	120.00
	Nesbet, Francis & Holler, Henry	barn	20 x 53	log, old				211 A	1493.00
	B35 B57 D35 E56								

Hopewell Township

Owner Occupant	Ref.	Location Adjoining Owner	Structure	Dimensions	Descr.	Stories	Lights	Windows	Area	Value
Quigley, Robert		on Conodoguinet Cr. Sharp, James	house & lot	18 x 24	log	1 1/2	7	57	1 A	300.00
			kitchen	15 x 18	log	1				
			barn	20 x 50	log				251 A	3327.00
			house 2	18 x 20	unfinished					20.00
			cabin	15 x 15						10.00
			grist mill		unfinished					
			still house		old, cabin					
	A36 B58 D36 E58		note: Galbreath, Samuel, occupant of cabin							
Robison, John			house & lot	22 x 24	log	1 1/2	5	39	1 A	120.00
		Duncan, John	barn	24 x 50	log				128 A	816.00
		McEntire, Robert	still house	15 x 12						
	A38 B60 D38 E60									
Rogers, Richard		on Conodoguinet Cr. Peebles, Robert	house & lot	25 x 25	log	2	10	120	1 A	500.00
			kitchen	15 x 18	log	1				
			stable	12 x 20						
			barn	20 x 60	cabin				599 A	6200.00
Smith, Henry			house 2	18 x 20						20.00
Early, Robert			cabin 1	16 x 16						10.00
Wilson, John			cabin 2	16 x 16						10.00
			saw mill							
	A37 B59 D37 E59		smith shop		cabin					
Sharp, James			house & lot	18 x 20	log	1 1/2	3	27	1 A	300.00
			kitchen	18 x 20	log	1 1/2				
			barn	22 x 80	log				399 A	2901.00
	A47 B71 D47 E71		cabin	16 x 16						8.00
Shumaker, John		on Conodoguinet Cr. Cooper, Doctor	house & lot	28 x 30	log	1 1/2	6	62	1 A	400.00
			kitchen	14 x 15	log	1				
			barn	30 x 77	log				199 A	2125.00
			house 2	19 x 22	log					20.00
			house 3	16 x 18						15.00
	A43 B67 D43 E67		note: Byers, John, occupant of house 2; name also Shoemaker							
Simmeral, John			house & lot	24 x 24	log	1 1/2	4	26	1 A	250.00
		Sharp, James & Simmeral, Martha	barn	16 x 40	log				169 A	1730.00
	A46 B70 D46 E70									
Simmeral, Martha			house & lot	27 x 27	log	2	9	46	1 A	300.00
		Simmeral, John	kitchen	15 x 15	log	1				
		& Lesher, Gasper	barn	18 x 20	log				149 A	1520.00
			smith shop	19 x 15						
	A45 B69 D45 E69		cabin	16 x 16						15.00

Hopewell Township

Owner / Occupant	Ref.	Location / Adjoining Owner	Structure	Dimensions	Descr.	Stories	Windows Lights	Area	Value
Slusher, Philip		Hannah, Samuel & Miller, Ludwick	house & lot	26 x 28	log	1 1/2	4 48	1 A	250.00
			barn	30 x 60	under part stone			111 A	998.00
			house 2	16 x 18					12.00
	A39 B61 D39 E61								
Slusher, Philip		mountain land	tract					40 A	40.00
	B62 E62								
Smith, Hugh		Rogers, Richard & Peebles, Robert	house & lot	24 x 24	log	1 1/2	4 42	1 A	350.00
			kitchen	24 x 14	log	1			
			barn	24 x 65	log			149 A	1292.00
			still house	16 x 18	old				
	A40 B63 D40 E63								
Smith, Samuel		adj. No. Mountain McKinney, David	house & lot	27 x 29	log	2	9 98	1 A	450.00
			kitchen	16 x 23	log	1			
			barn	22 x 47	log			309 A	2851.00
	A41 B64 D41 E64		grain house	14 x 18					
Smith, Samuel		mountain land	tract					200 A	150.00
	B65 E65								
Snody, John		Thompson heirs & McKinney, David	house & lot	24 x 28	log	2	6 66	1 A	350.00
			kitchen	11 x 20	log	1			
			barn	18 x 18	log			149 A	1212.00
	A48 B72 D48 E72								
Sowers, Barnhart		Laughlin, John & Hemphill, James	house & lot	22 x 24	log	1 1/2	2 18	1 A	120.00
			kitchen	10 x 12	log	1			
			barn	20 x 54	log			119 A	1012.00
			house 2	16 x 18					20.00
	A42 B66 D42 E66		note: Wiley, Robert, occupant of house 2						
Sterrett, Robert		on Conodoguinet Cr. Sharp, James	house & lot	26 x 30	stone	2	9 130	1 A	500.00
			house 2	20 x 24	log				30.00
	A44 B68 D44 E68		grist mill	30 x 45	under part stone, upper frame			149 A	2077.00
Thompson heirs / Kennedy, Gilbert		Wills, David & McKinney, David	house & lot	24 x 24	log	2	4 36	1 A	300.00
			barn	22 x 62	log			259 A	2122.00
	A49 B73 D49 E73		note: [Andrew Thompson, died 1793]						
Thompson, William		Sharp, James & Holler, Henry	house	16 x 16	cabin				20.00
			barn	20 x 60	log			119 A	903.00
	B76 E76								

Hopewell Township

Owner / Occupant	Ref.	Location / Adjoining Owner	Structure	Dimensions	Descr.	Stories	Lights	Windows	Area	Value
Trimble, William		Cooper, Robert & Overline, Adam	house & lot	23 x 26	log	2	4	26	1 A	300.00
			kitchen	12 x 20	wood	1				
			spring house							
			barn	22 x 58	log				176 A	1468.00
	A50 B74 D50 E74		still house							
Trimble, William	B75 E75	mountain land	tract note: late survey						150 A	90.00
Wallace, James		Overline, Adam & McKee, John	house & lot	26 x 26	log	1 1/2	5	52	1 A	300.00
			kitchen	12 x 26	log	1				
			stable	20 x 18	log					
	A54 B82 D54 E82		barn	22 x 16	log				166 A	1554.00
Wherry, Samuel		McKee, John & McClelland, Thomas	house & lot	22 x 24	log	1 1/2	3	18	1 A	120.00
			barn	24 x 54	log				255 A	2405.00
	A55 B83 D55 E83		still house		old, cabin					
Whisner, John		adj. No. Mountain Morrett, Nicholas	cabin	16 x 16	old					4.00
	B80 E80								89 A	300.00
White, David		adj. No. Mountain	house & lot	20 x 22	log	1 1/2	3	13	1 A	120.00
			kitchen	12 x 15	log	1				
			barn	24 x 24	log				174 A	730.00
	A56 B84 D56 E84		still house		old					
Wills, David		Rogers, Richard & Thompson heirs	house & lot	20 x 20	log	1 1/2	3	36	1 A	250.00
			kitchen	25 x 20	log	1 1/2				
			barn	26 x 60	log				299 A	2821.00
			cabin	16 x 16	old					8.00
	A51 B77 D51 E77		note: Morrison, James, occupant of cabin							
Wills, John		on Conodoguinet Cr. Rogers, Richard	house & lot	20 x 20	log	1 1/2	2	12	1 A	250.00
			barn	20 x 56					233 A	2360.00
			shade	10 x 20	log	1				
			cabin	16 x 16						10.00
	A53 B81 D53 E81		note: Grogin, Charles, occupant of cabin							
Wilson, Nathaniel / Cloyd, John		Mitchell, John & Brotherton, Samuel	house & lot	28 x 30	log	2	3	36	1 A	250.00
			barn	22 x 56	log				79 A	593.00
	A52 B78 D52 E78									
Wilson, Nathaniel / Brown, Hugh		North Mountain Boyd, James	house	20 x 20						20.00
	B79 E79								269 A	558.00

103

Hopewell Township

Owner		Location	Structure	Dimensions	Descr.	Stories	Lights Windows		Area	Value
Occupant	Ref.	Adjoining Owner								
Woods, John, Esq.		on Conodoguinet Cr.	house	25 x 25	wood	2	5	27	1 A	400.00
		Sharp, James	barn 1	24 x 48	log				299 A	2592.00
			barn 2	14 x 44	log					
			still house	20 x 18	cabin					
			cabin	16 x 18						
	A57 B85 D57 E85		note: Wesley, John, occupant of cabin							

Middleton Township

CHAPTER VII   MIDDLETON TOWNSHIP

Owner Occupant	Ref.	Location Adjoining Owner	Structure	Dimensions	Descr.	Stories	Windows	Lights	Area	Value
Alexander, William	E2	Postlethwaite, Samuel	tract						28 A 138 P	346.35
Apple, John	A1 D1 E4	South Mountain	house & lot stable	20 x 20 12 x 12	wood	1	1	4	2 A 48 A	150.00 96.00
Armpister, Jacob	A3 D3 E5		house & lot stable grist mill	22 x 18 10 x 12 50 x 35	wood stone [?]	1	3	28	2 A 8 A	150.00 64.00
Armstrong, James, Dr. Kernan, John	A2 D2 E1	Duncan, James	house & lot barn	24 x 20 50 x 16	wood	2	8	98	2 A 240 A	450.00 2880.00
Armstrong, John	D3	Sample, Joseph	tract						122 A	1220.00
Baker, Catharine, Widow	A22 D22 E20	Blaine, Alexander	house & lot barn	30 x 20 80 x 36	stone stone	1	5	90	2 A 314 A	1000.00 5210.00
Baker, Catharine, Widow Wolf, Philip	A23 D23		house & lot	30 x 18	wood	1	6	54	2 A	350.00
Baker, John	A29 D29 E15	Mitchell, Ross	house & lot barn	25 x 20 80 x 22	wood	2	7	69	2 A 198 A	500.00 3120.00
Blaine, Alexander	A24 D24 E18	Swanger, Paul	house & lot barn	50 x 18 60 x 20	wood	1	7	84	2 A 278 A	700.00 4230.00
Blaine, Alexander Bellow, Cornelius	A25 D27 E19	Swanger, Paul	house & lot	24 x 20	wood	1	2	8	2 A 198 A	300.00 2376.00
Blaine, Ephraim, Colonel	A8 D8 E6	Letort Springs	house & lot kitchen barn nursery saw mill fulling mill grist mill	45 x 25 18 x 16 100 x 40 15 x 15 50 x 36	wood wood stone wood stone	2 1 1	18 2 3	228 18 40	2 A 589 A	1000.00 15602.00

Middleton Township

Owner / Occupant	Location Ref. / Adjoining Owner	Structure	Dimensions	Descr.	Stories	Lights / Windows		Area	Value
Blaine, Ephraim, Col.	A12 D12	house & lot	22 x 18	wood	1	4	42	2 A	220.00
Blaine, Ephraim, Col. Carlisle, Daniel	A9 D9	house & lot	24 x 20	wood	2	5	45	2 A	400.00
Blaine, Ephraim, Col. Hoffer, Melchor	A10 D10	house & lot	22 x 19	stone	1	4	48	2 A	400.00
Blaine, Ephraim, Col. Stephens, John	A11 D11	house & lot	20 x 16	wood	1	4	48	2 A	200.00
Blaine, James Hunter, James	A21 D21 E15	house & lot	20 x 18	wood	1	1	4	2 A 178 A	100.10 2146.00
Blaine, James Fury, John	Lyon, Samuel A19 D19 E14	house & lot barn	20 x 26 64 x 30	wood stone	2	4	42	2 A 296 A	500.00 7940.00
Blaine, James McKinley, John	A20 D20	house & lot	20 x 18	wood	1			2 A	100.10
Blaine, Robert	Mitchell, Ross A13 D13 E7	house & lot barn grist mill saw mill	57 x 28 80 x 17 40 x 36	wood stone	2	17	174	2 A 490 A	700.00 7000.00
Blaine, Robert Briggs, Robert	A15 D15	house & lot	24 x 19	wood	1	2	24	2 A	200.00
Blaine, Robert Craig, John	A18 D18	house & lot	18 x 16	wood	1	1	6	2 A	100.10
Blaine, Robert Cryser, Sebastian	A16 D16	house & lot	18 x 16	wood	1	1	4	2 A	100.10
Blaine, Robert Sponsler, Nicholas	mountain land A14 D14 E8	house & lot	27 x 20	stone	2	5	60	2 A 298 A	300.00 298.00

Middleton Township

Owner / Occupant	Location Ref. / Adjoining Owner	Structure	Dimensions	Descr.	Stories	Lights / Windows		Area	Value
Blaine, Robert Surhots [?], Lar- [?]	A17 D17	house & lot	24 x 18	wood	1	2	12	2 A	100.10
Bower, Martin	Logue, George A6 D6 E10	house & lot barn	40 x 16 84 x 24	wood	1	5	40	2 A 153 A	300.00 1224.00
Bricker, John	Dickey, George A4 D4 E9	house & lot barn	35 x 17 65 x 30	wood	1	5	44	2 A 221 A	400.00 2210.00
Bricker, John Hendricks, John	A5 D5	house & lot	16 x 15	wood	1	1	4	2 A	100.10
Brown, Henry Warsham, Philip	Sample, Joseph A28 D28 E17	house & lot barn	50 x 20 60 x 22	wood	1	2	8	2 A 198 A	300.00 1804.00
Burkholder, Christopher	Ritchey, Thomas A27 D26 E13	house & lot barn saw mill still house	27 x 22 62 x 26	wood	2	12	104	2 A 198 A	400.00 1488.00
Burkholder, John	Craighead, Thomas & John A26 D25 E12	house & lot barn	40 x 24 68 x 21	wood	1	5	44	2 A 218 A	600.00 2280.00
Byers, Jacob	Clark, William A7 D7 E11	house & lot barn	27 x 24 46 x 27	wood	2	7	79	2 A 98 A	450.00 784.00
Campbell, Robert	Cornman, Valentine A38 D38 E36	house & lot	30 x 20	wood	1	1	4	2 A 198 A	200.00 1584.00
Caul, John	Keehl, Francis A49 D49 E42	house & lot barn grist mill saw mill	23 x 20	wood	2	7	45	2 A 58 A	500.00 1114.00
Chambers, Robert	Williamson, David A32 D32 E21	house & lot barn	20 x 20 58 x 22	wood	1	5	60	2 A 228 A	400.00 2130.00
Chambers, Robert Richwine, Christopher	Irwin, Samuel A33 D33 E22	house & lot barn	31 x 20 83 x 22	wood	1	2	13	2 A 216 A	400.00 2642.00

Middleton Township

Owner / Occupant	Ref.	Location / Adjoining Owner	Structure	Dimensions	Descr.	Stories	Lights / Windows		Area	Value
Chambers, William		Blaine, Ephraim	house & lot	40 x 36	stone	2	13	128	2 A	2000.00
			kitchen	24 x 20	stone	1	4	48		
	A30 D30 E23		barn	77 x 30	stone				229 A	4522.00
Chambers, William			house & lot	16 x 16	wood	1	1	4	2 A	200.00
Comfort, Andrew		Lyon, Samuel							113 A	1356.00
	A31 D31 E24									
Clark, William			house & lot	40 x 20	wood	1	5	45	2 A	450.00
		Templeton, John	kitchen	20 x 17	stone	1	2	18		
			barn	60 x 22					198 A	1746.00
			tract	274 A	mountain land					
	A46 D38 D39 E46		note: two D entries, but only one land value given							
Clouser, John		Eliot, David	house & lot	22 x 20	wood	1	2	24	2 A	300.00
			barn	20 x 20					92 A	786.00
	A51 D51 E29									
Clouser, Margaret		Clouser, John	house & lot	21 x 26	wood	1	4	20	2 A	300.00
			barn	34 x 20					298 A	2086.00
	A50 D50 E28									
Cooper, Adam		Kenny, Robert	house & lot	24 x 28	wood	2	3	36	2 A	300.00
			barn						218 A	1994.00
	A35 D35 E42		saw mill							
Cooper, Adam			house & lot	22 x 20	wood	1	3	16	2 A	200.00
Drayer, Peter										
	A36 D36									
Cornman, John		Stuart, John	house & lot	28 x 24	wood	2	9	108	2 A	420.00
			barn	64 x 30					198 A	1634.00
	A52 D52 E25									
Cornman, Valentine		Campbell, R.	house & lot	30 x 18	wood	2	4	22	2 A	400.00
			barn	55 x 22					138 A	1184.00
	A39 D39 E37									
Cort, Jacob		Steel, John	tract						45 A	540.00
	E26		note: owner deceased							
Cory, Henry		Leonard, Widow	house & lot	18 x 16	wood	1	2	8	2 A	200.00
									73 A	584.00
	A37 D37 E32									
Craighead, Gilson		Wolf, John	house & lot	28 x 32	brick	2	14	300	2 A	1200.00
			barn	52 x 18					334 A	5140.00
			fulling mill							
	A43 D43 E34		saw mill							

Middleton Township

Owner / Occupant	Location Ref. / Adjoining Owner	Structure	Dimensions	Descr.	Stories	Windows	Lights	Area	Value
Craighead, Gilson Dunn, Andrew	A44 D44	house & lot	24 x 20	wood	1	2	18	2 A	110.00
Craighead, John		house & lot	30 x 28	stone	2	10	32	2 A	1200.00
	Peters, Richard, Esq.	kitchen	18 x 15	wood	1	1	12		
		barn	60 x 30	stone				180 A	2490.00
	A34 D34 E30	still house	30 x 20						
Craighead, Richard Craighead, Thomas	Peters, Richard E33	barn	60 x 30					178 A	2236.00
Craighead, Thomas Dixon, Andrew	A41 D41	house & lot	20 x 20	wood	1	2	12	2 A	150.00
Craighead, Thomas Yengst, William	A42 D42	house & lot kitchen	30 x 28	stone	2	12	130	2 A	1200.00
Craighead, Thomas, Jr.		house & lot	28 x 32	brick	2	20	328	2 A	1700.00
	Craighead, Gilson	kitchen stable	18 x 18	brick	2	8	72		
		grist mill	40 x 36	stone					
	A45 D45 E35	sawmill						22 A	2864.00
Craighead, Thomas, Sr.		house & lot	30 x 33	brick	2	22	300	2 A	1400.00
	Burkholder, John	kitchen barn	20 x 16 27 x 30	brick stone	2			382 A	3280.00
	A40 D40 E31	smith shop							
Craine, Richard	Fought & Crane A47 D47 E40	house & lot	28 x 24	wood	?	3	27	2 A 396 A	350.00 2428.00
Craine, Richard Craine, George	A48 D48	house & lot	20 x 18	wood	1	1	4	2 A	100.10
Crane & Fought	Gay, Thomas E41	tract						198 A	1386.00
Creigh, John	Postlethwaite, Samuel E27	tract						56 A	672.00

Middleton Township

Owner / Occupant	Ref.	Location / Adjoining Owner	Structure	Dimensions	Descr.	Stories	Windows / Lights		Area	Value
Dale, George		South Mountain	house & lot	24 x 18	wood	1	1	4	2 A	110.00
	A59 D59 E53		note: name also Deal						298 A	447.00
Davidson, Patrick			house & lot	20 x 20	wood	1	1	6	2 A	300.00
Zigler, Jacob			kitchen							
	A63 D63 E47		barn	56 x 20					258 A	2104.00
Davidson, Robert, Rev.			house & lot	20 x 15	stone	1	2	24	2 A	300.00
Carson [?], James		Blaine, Alexander							118 A	1770.00
	A62 D62 E43		note: this land is attached to the Presbyterian Church; glebe land							
Davis, Elijah		South Mountain	house & lot	20 x 19	wood	1	1	2	2 A	100.10
	A58 D58 E52								48 A	96.00
Denny, Daniel			house & lot	28 x 34	wood & stone	2	5	50	2 A	600.00
Denny, John		Peters, Richard								
			barn	72 x 30	stone				238 A	3256.00
	A67 D67 E44		note: Denny, John, not named as occupant in E							
Denny, William			house & lot	20 x 16	wood	1	1	12	2 A	400.00
		Ramsey, Samuel	kitchen						198 A	2376.00
	A68 D68 E45		stable							
Dickey, George			house & lot	23 x 20	wood	1	2	18	2 A	360.00
		Ege, Michael	barn	50 x 20					192 A	2416.00
	A55 D55 E50									
Dicky, George			house & lot	20 x 18	wood	1	2	8	2 A	100.10
Humes, Thomas										
	A56 D56									
Dicky, Margaret			house & lot	20 x 18	wood	1	2	18	2 A	110.00
		Dicky, George							78 A	624.00
	A57 D57 E51									
Diller, Benjamin			house & lot	18 x 18	wood	1	2	12	2 A	100.10
		Diller, Martin							114 A	1710.00
	A65 D65 E49									
Diller, David & Martin			house & lot	30 x 24	stone	2	18	359	2 A	1300.00
		Miller, John	barn	70 x 30	stone				227 A	3845.00
			wash house	15 x 14	stone	1	1	9		
			store house		stone					
	A64 D64 E48		note: Diller, David, not listed in E							

Middleton Township

Owner / Occupant	Ref.	Location / Adjoining Owner	Structure	Dimensions	Descr.	Stories	Lights / Windows		Area	Value
Douglass, John		Waggoner, Jacob	house & lot	15 x 14	wood	1	2	5	2 A	200.00
	A60 D60 E56		barn	50 x 20					148 A	1184.00
			wash house							
Duncan, James, Esq.			house & lot	30 x 25	brick	2	12	124	2 A	550.00
Lipe, Peter		Miller, Matthew	barn	60 x 20					198 A	2576.00
	A69 D69 E54									
Duncan, James, Esq.			house & lot	24 x 20	wood	2	8	102	2 A	300.00
Nimans, George		Lyon, William	barn	50 x 20					198 A	2384.00
	A70 D70 E55									
Duncan, Thomas			house & lot	58 x 20	wood	2	15	180	2 A	600.00
Long, Benedict		Irwine, General	barn	48 x 23					186 A	2820.00
	A53 D53 E58									
Duncan, Thomas			house & lot	21 x 24	wood	1	3	24	2 A	350.00
Lukes, Daniel		Young, Peter	barn	58 x 22					306 A	3722.00
	A54 D54 E59									
Dunn, Jacob			house & lot	24 x 20	wood	1	3	36	2 A	400.00
		Caul, John	barn	56 x 22					123 A	1054.00
	A61 D61 E57		still house	20 x 20						
Eckart, Jonas		Harper's Gap	house & lot	28 x 22	stone	1	5	48	2 A	700.00
			barn	60 x 20					163 A	1364.00
	A79 D79 E66		still house	26 x 22						
Ediburn, Jacob			house & lot	26 x 20	wood	1	5	44	2 A	350.00
		Davidson, Patrick	barn	46 x 16					98 A	814.00
	A80 D80 E64									
Ege, Michael			house & lot	40 x 50	brick	2	30	700	2 A	4500.00
	A71 D71		kitchen	26 x 40	brick	2	15	200		
Ege, Michael			house & lot	22 x 20	wood	1	3	24	2 A	100.10
Day, John										
	A73 D73									
Ege, Michael			house & lot	24 x 20	wood	1	1	4	2 A	110.00
Foster, Thomas		Dickie, George	barn	80 x 30					5819 A	10026.50
			slitting mill							
			grist mill	40 x 36	stone					
			saw mill							
	A74 D74 E68		forge & steel furnace							

Middleton Township

Owner / Occupant	Ref.	Location Adjoining Owner	Structure	Dimensions	Descr.	Stories	Lights Windows	Area	Value
Ege, Michael McGowan, Robert	A72 D72		house & lot	22 x 20	wood	1	3	24	2 A	100.10
Ekhart, Conrad	A78 D78 E65	Davidson, Patrick	house & lot	30 x 24	wood	2	5	60	2 A 193 A	400.00 1544.00
Elliot, David	A77 D77 E61	Sanderson, William	house & lot barn still house	39 x 20 70 x 20 24 x 16		1	8	81	2 A 212 A	420.00 1746.00
Elliot, James	A76 D76 E60	Wolf, John	house & lot kitchen barn	24 x 20 15 x 15 60 x 18	wood wood	2 1	7 2	84 12	2 A 290 A	400.00 2350.00
Elter, Samuel	A75 D75 E67	McCormack, Hugh	house & lot stable	20 x 18	wood	1	2	8	2 A 48 A	150.00 384.00
Eversole, Jacob	A81 D81 E63	Urie, Thomas	house & lot barn w. house still house smith shop	25 x 20 66 x 30 22 x 18 20 x 18	wood stone stone	1	2	18	2 A 178 A	400.00 3120.00
Eversole, John Whitmire, Jacob	A82 D82 E62	Chambers, William	house & lot barn note: Ebersole in E; occupant not named in E	26 x 21 56 x 20	wood	1	4	40	2 A 111 A	300.00 2028.00
Fireovid, John	A86 D86 E70	Weaver, William	house & lot barn still house	22 x 24	wood	1	3	30	2 A 126 A	250.00 1260.00
Fleming, James	A85 D85 E72	Miller, Matthew	house & lot	22 x 16	wood	1	2	18	2 A 165 A	300.00 1980.00
Fleming, John	A88 D88 E69	Sanderson, John	house & lot kitchen barn	30 x 24 16 x 16 68 x 22	wood wood	2	10	114	2 A 196 A	550.00 2352.00

Middleton Township

Owner / Occupant	Ref.	Location Adjoining Owner	Structure	Dimensions	Descr.	Stories	Windows	Lights	Area	Value
Fleming, John Kenned, Archibald	A89 D89		house & lot	16 x 18	wood	1	1	4	2 A	100.10
Fosler, George	A83 D83 E71	Lyon, Samuel	house & lot barn w. house	26 x 24 19 x 15	wood decayed stone	1	6	38	2 A 171 A	450.00 2776.00
Fosler, George Frank, Daniel	A84 D84		house & lot	22 x 20	wood	1	2	18	2 A	150.00
Fought, Frederick Crane, Benjamin	A87 D87		house & lot kitchen note: occupant Craine in A	40 x 18 12 x 12	wood wood	1	8	96	2 A	400.00
Fought, Jacob	A90 D90 E74	Leonard, Widow	house & lot barn smith shop note: house 22 x 20 in A	20 x 20 50 x 20 20 x 16	wood	1	2	8	2 A 73 A	300.00 654.00
Foulk, Stephen	A91 D91 E73	McClure, Charles	house & lot spring house barn	30 x 24 15 x 20 60 x 26	stone stone stone	2	12	153	2 A 146 A	1500.00 2052.00
Foulk, Stephen	A92 D92		house & lot	25 x 18	stone	1	4	42	2 A	500.00
Garvin, Henry	A96 D96 E80	Elliot, James	house & lot	20 x 16	wood	1	2	5	2 A 21 A	150.00 84.00
George, David	A97 D97 E81	Smith, James	house & lot	24 x 22	wood	1	2	16	2 A 114 A	300.00 1140.00
Giffen, James	A93 D93 E78	Weaver, William	house & lot spring house barn	30 x 22 18 x 18 72 x 28	wood wood	1	3	36	2 A 182 A	200.00 1970.00
Giffen, James Giffen, Widow	A94 D94		house & lot	16 x 18	wood	1	2	18	2 A	200.00
Giffen, Samuel	A95 D95 E79	Weaver, William	house & lot	20 x 18	wood	1	2	24	2 A 4 A	200.00 40.00

Middleton Township

Owner / Occupant	Ref.	Location / Adjoining Owner	Structure	Dimensions	Descr.	Stories	Windows	Lights	Area	Value
Glenn, John	E77	Lyon, William	tract						148 A	1776.00
Gregg, Andrew Lose, George	A99 D99 E76	Chambers, Robert	house & lot kitchen barn	31 x 23 15 x 12 45 x 18	wood wood	2	2	24	2 A 198 A	450.00 2376.00
			note: Lose not listed in E; kitchen in A, spring house in D							
Gregg, John	A100 D100 E75	Gregg, Andrew	house & lot kitchen barn	27 x 19 15 x 12 40 x 20	wood wood	1	4	54	2 A 120 A	350.00 990.00
			note: kitchen in A, spring house in D							
Guy, Thomas	A98 D98 E82	Patton, Robert	house & lot barn	28 x 24	wood	2	4	42	2 A 321 A	400.00 2568.00
Hafson, Jonathan	A117 D117 E90	Hoge, James	house & lot	25 x 24	wood	2	8	64	2 A 196 A	350.00 2352.00
Hafson, Jonathan Bell, James	A118 D118		house & lot	22 x 20	wood	1	3	27	2 A	250.00
Hamilton, James, Esq. Bidleman, Adam	A108 D108 E89	Scott, Andrew	house & lot barn b. proof [?]	36 x 24 28 x 16	stone old stone	2 1	22 4	276 96	2 A 262 A	1400.00 2630.00
Hamilton, James, Esq. Wolf, Valentine	A109 D109 E88	McClure, Charles	house & lot barn	50 x 20	stone	1	11	171	2 A 134 A	1200.00 1540.00
Hedrick, George	A106 D106 E83	Irwin, James	house & lot barn	26 x 20 72 x 32	wood stone	1	2	16	2 A 233 A	400.00 5060.00
Hedrick, John	A107 D107		house & lot	40 x 20	wood	1	3	22	2 A	300.00
Heger, John	A113 D113 E86	Wolf, Jacob	house & lot barn	24 x 20 56 x 20	wood	1	2	17	2 A 112 A	350.00 946.00
Henderson, Benjamin	A111 D111 E96	Holmes, John	house & lot barn	24 x 20	wood stone & wood	2	6	54	2 A 98 A	400.00 1276.00

Middleton Township

Owner / Occupant	Ref.	Location / Adjoining Owner	Structure	Dimensions	Descr.	Stories	Windows Lights	Area	Value
Henderson, Matthew		near Carlisle	house & lot	20 x 20	brick	1	4 48	2 A	1000.00
			kitchen	20 x 15	wood				
			wash house	22 x 16	stone				
			barn	70 x 30	stone			256 A	6998.00
			grist mill						
	A115 D115 E85		still house	20 x 15					
Henderson, Matthew			house & lot	22 x 20	stone	1	2 8	2 A	100.10
Sweny, Hugh									
	A116 D116								
Hinkle, Philip			house & lot	30 x 22	wood	2	4 36	2 A	400.00
		Taylor, John	barn	60 x 22				135 A	1160.00
	A103 D103 E94								
Hock, Henry			house & lot	19 x 24	wood	1	4 12	2 A	350.00
		Smith, Hugh	kitchen	15 x 15	wood	1	2 12		
	A112 D112 E92		barn		decayed			98 A	814.00
Hogg, James			house & lot	30 x 20	wood	1	2 8	2 A	260.00
		Wolf, John						178 A	1958.00
	A119 D119 E91		note: name also Hoge						
Hogg, James			house & lot	20 x 18	wood	1	2 12	2 A	100.10
Swanger, Michael									
	A120 D120								
Holmes, Andrew		Bonny Brook	house & lot	80 x 25	stone	1	5 60	2 A	1600.00
			kitchen	20 x 25	stone	1	2 44		
			room	15 x 25	stone	1	2 36		
			wash house	24 x 10	stone	1	1 3		
			barn	80 x 30	stone			296 A	4052.00
			milk house	15 x 15	stone	1	1 8		
			still house	27 x 24					
	A101 D101 E93		note: milk house has 2 windows in D						
Holmes, Andrew			house & lot	25 x 18	wood	1	2 8	2 A	200.00
Nagle, John									
	A102 D102								
Holmes, John		Carlisle	house & lot	24 x 20	wood	1	3 27	2 A	300.00
	A110 D110 E95							198 A	2376.00
Holmes, Jonathan		near Carlisle	house & lot	36 x 20	stone	2	16 193	2 A	1600.00
			kitchen	18 x 18	stone	1	1 12		
	A114 D114 E84		barn	60 x 20				246 A	3796.00
Holmes, William			house & lot	34 x 21	stone	2	10 32	2 A	1200.00
		McClure, Charles	barn	60 x 30	stone			148 A	2076.00
	A105 D105 E87								

Middleton Township

Owner / Occupant	Ref.	Location / Adjoining Owner	Structure	Dimensions	Descr.	Stories	Lights Windows		Area	Value
Hunter, John Deirdorf, Isaac	A104 D104 E97	Blaine, James	house & lot barn	18 x 18 60 x 20	wood	1	2	8	2 A 312 A	250.00 3794.00
Irwin, James	A123 D123 E98	Sample, Joseph	house & lot kitchen wash house barn note: wash house is stone in D	33 x 30 15 x 15 14 x 14 70 x 28	stone stone wood	2	12	155	2 A 240 A	1500.00 3690.00
Irwin, Samuel, Esq.	A125 D125 E99	Miller, Matthew	house & lot kitchen barn	26 x 24 22 x 18 73 x 25	wood stone	2 2	7 4	63 41	2 A 219 A	500.00 2390.00
Irwin, William, General Ensminger, Chris.	A122 D122		house & lot	25 x 20	wood	1	5	39	2 A	300.00
Irwin, William, General Taylor, William	A121 D121 E100	Blaine, James	house & lot kitchen spring house barn 1 barn 2 note: kitchen is 31 x 21 in D	45 x 44 34 x 21 14 x 12 54 x 20 54 x 20	stone stone stone	2 1	31 4	675 28	2 A 346 A	3500.00 5290.00
Johnston, William	A124 D124 E101	South Mountain	house & lot	20 x 19	wood	1	1	4	2 A 68 A	200.00 68.00
Kelly, Francis	A127 D127 E109	Taylor, John	house & lot barn	20 x 20 50 x 18	wood	2	7	72	2 A 98 A	300.00 644.00
Kennedy, Joseph	A139 D139 E111	Guy, Thomas	house & lot	24 x 24	wood	2	3	27	2 A 138 A	350.00 966.00
Kenny, Robert	A136 D136 E108	Smyth, Hugh	house & lot barn 1 barn 2	25 x 16	wood wood wood	1	2	4	2 A 294 A	100.10 3060.00
Kenny, Robert Shimp, Widow	A137 D137		house & lot	20 x 20	wood	1	2	24	2 A	250.00
Kenny, Robert Stukey, John	A138 D138		house & lot	24 x 20	wood	1	1	3	2 A	200.00

Middleton Township

Owner Occupant	Ref.	Location Adjoining Owner	Structure	Dimensions	Descr.	Stories	Windows	Lights	Area	Value
Kibler, George		Bower, Martin	house & lot	20 x 18	wood	1	1	8	2 A	300.00
			barn	50 x 20					98 A	814.00
	A132 D132 E107									
Kiehl, Francis		Caul, John	house & lot	28 x 26	wood	1	5	38	2 A	400.00
			barn						168 A	1380.00
	A129 D129 E103		smith shop							
Kincaid, John		Blaine, Robert	house & lot	20 x 20	wood	2	2	8	2 A	300.00
	A126 D126 E110								148 A	1184.00
Kitch, Martin		Fleming, John	house & lot	38 x 22	wood	2	9	95	2 A	400.00
			barn	90 x 20					158 A	1314.00
	A131 D131 E106									
Kittera, John W.		South Mountain	house & lot	30 x 35	stone	1	6	84	2 A	1200.00
			stable							
			forge & furnace						3450 A	5000.00
			grist mill							
			saw mill							
	A134 D134 E105		houses		14, for workmen					
Kittera, John W. Grosscoat, Jacob			house & lot	24 x 24	wood	1	3	36	2 A	200.00
	A135 D135		note: house is 24 x 26 in C							
Kline, John		Kinkle, Philip	house & lot	24 x 20	wood	2	9	100	2 A	400.00
			barn	50 x 20					148 A	1214.00
	A128 D128 E102									
Kosh, Michael		Wolf, Jacob	house & lot	30 x 20	wood	1	6	28	2 A	400.00
			barn	56 x 20					118 A	934.00
	A130 D130 E104									
Krips, Joseph		White, Davis	house & lot	30 x 23	wood	1	4	28	2 A	450.00
			barn	65 x 25					133 A	1410.00
	A133 D133 E112		still house	25 x 20						
Laird, Matthew		Ramsey, Samuel	house & lot	36 x 18	wood	1	7	38	2 A	450.00
			kitchen	10 x 18	wood					
			barn	70 x 30	stone				278 A	4736.00
			milk house	15 x 15	stone					
			grist mill	40 x 30	stone					
	A144 D144 E120		still house	30 x 20	stone					
Laird, Samuel Dice, Martin		Lyon, William	house & lot	25 x 20	wood	1	2	16	2 A	300.00
			barn	50 x 20					98 A	1196.00
	A149 D149 E129									

Middleton Township

Owner Occupant	Ref.	Location Adjoining Owner	Structure	Dimensions	Descr.	Stories	Lights	Windows	Area	Value
Lamberton, James		road to Croghan's Gap	house & lot kitchen barn	25 x 24 16 x 12 48 x 30	wood wood	2	5	60	2 A 115 A	500.00 950.00
	A155 D155 E124									
Lamberton, Simon		Lamberton, James	house & lot barn	25 x 20 60 x 26	wood	1	6	54	2 A 128 A	400.00 1054.00
	A156 D156 E125									
Lane, Widow Geerhart, Peter			house & lot	24 x 19	wood	1	2	12	2 A	200.00
	A158 D158									
Lane, Widow Kitch, David		Eckhart, Jonas	house & lot barn note: house 25 x 25 in D	22 x 25 50 x 20	wood	2	8	96	2 A 258 A	450.00 2094.00
	A157 D157 E122									
Leonard, Jane, Widow		Wolf, Jacob	house & lot barn	25 x 20 50 x 20	wood	2	10	120	2 A 98 A	500.00 824.00
	A140 D140 E113									
Leonard, Philip		Kline, John	house & lot kitchen	22 x 19 14 x 12	wood wood	2	10	120	2 A 64 A	300.00 512.00
	A152 D152 E114									
Loghridge, Abraham Mathews, James		Steel, John	house & lot barn	20 x 20 50 x 20	wood	1	4	32	2 A 67 A	200.00 830.00
	A146 D146 E117									
Logue, George, Esq. Day, John			house & lot	20 x 18	wood	1	2	12	2 A	100.10
	A154 D154									
Logue, George, Esq. Love, Elijah		Bower, Martin	house & lot	24 x 22	wood	1	3	22	2 A 218 A	300.00 1744.00
	A153 D153 E121									
Lose, Jacob		Wolf, Jacob	house & lot barn	30 x 24 50 x 20	wood	2	7	84	2 A 106 A	500.00 898.00
	A142 D142 E116									
Lose, Jacob Mark, Christian			house & lot	15 x 18	wood	1	1	4	2 A	100.10
	A143 D143									
Love, James Yells, John		Kittera, John W.	house & lot barn saw mill	18 x 18 40 x 20	wood	1	1	4	2 A 298 A	100.10 443.00
	A147 D147 E126									
Love, John		South Mountain	house & lot barn	30 x 20 50 x 20	wood	1	3	14	2 A 348 A	200.00 716.00
	A148 D148 D127									

Middleton Township

Owner / Occupant	Ref.	Location / Adjoining Owner	Structure	Dimensions	Descr.	Stories	Windows / Lights	Area	Value
Lutz, Balser Lutz, Jacob	A141 D141 E115	Waggoner, Jacob	house & lot note: Luts in C	20 x 28	wood	1	3 / 36	2 A 48 A	300.00 384.00
Lyon, Samuel	A145 D145 E118	Chambers, William	house & lot kitchen barn note: [it is unclear how E118 and E119 relate to AD145 and AD150; see also Lyon, William, note]	40 x 25 26 x 18 80 x 34	wood wood stone	1 1	17 / 129 8 / 27	2 A 301 A	700.00 5868.00
Lyon, Samuel	E119	Elliot, James	tract					165 A	330.00
Lyon, William Gray, Alexander	A150 D150 E128	Glenn, John	house & lot barn note: Lyon, Samuel, in D	24 x 20 56 x 20	wood	2	6 / 48	2 A 228 A	400.00 2766.00
Lyon, William Hunter, John	A151 D151 E123	Searight, Gillis	house & lot barn	20 x 20 50 x 20	wood	2	6 / 48	2 A 342 A	400.00 4134.00
Mahaffey, Andrew	A190 D190 E155	White, David	house & lot	26 x 24	wood	2	4 / 40	2 A 98 A	300.00 980.00
Mahaffey, John	A191 D191 E156	White, David	house & lot	22 x 18	wood	1	4 / 40	2 A 98 A	300.00 980.00
Mahaffey, Margaret	A189 D189 E147	White, David	house & lot	24 x 20		1	3 / 9	2 A 186 A	120.00 1302.00
Mahaffey, Margaret Mercer, Henry	A188 D188		house & lot	20 x 16	wood	1		2 A	100.10
Malter, Jacob	A159 D159 E135	Henderson, Matthew	house & lot barn	24 x 20 40 x 20	wood	1	2 / 8	2 A 215 A	100.10 4300.00
Malter, Jacob	A160 D160 E136	Miller, Robert	house & lot barn	30 x 25 50 x 25	wood	2	16 / 129	2 A 228 A	500.00 2330.00
McBeath, Alexander Brats, John	A171 D171 E138	Kenny, Robert	house & lot barn note: McBeath, Andrew, in E	29 x 32 50 x 20	brick	2	8 / 164	2 A 246 A	1200.00 3690.00

Middleton Township

Owner Occupant	Location Ref. Adjoining Owner	Structure	Dimensions	Descr.	Stories	Lights Windows	Area	Value
McBeath, Alexander Wibley, Jacob A172 D172	Kenny, Robert	house & lot	28 x 20	wood	1	3 54	2 A	200.00
McClintock, John Cooper, Adam A182 D182 E144		house & lot barn	22 x 30 60 x 25	wood	1	1 9	2 A 248 A	350.00 2272.00
McClure, Charles Holmes, William A196 D196 E153		house & lot kitchen spring house barn still & dwelling note: stone building occupied as a still and dwelling house	48 x 20 28 x 16 24 x 19 60 x 30	stone stone stone stone stone	2 1 1	15 210 2 24 5 60	2 A 532 A	1600.00 6984.00
McClure, Charles Egolf, Henry E151	Carlisle	tract					16 A 120 P	153.00
McClure, Charles Herwick, Mrs. A187 D187		house & lot	20 x 20	wood	1	3 27	2 A	150.00
McClure, Charles Hopple, Christopher A186 D186 E152	Kittera, John W.	house & lot saw mill	20 x 16	wood	1	1 4	2 A 532 A	100.10 532.00
McClure, Charles Stephens, Evan E154	Carlisle	grist mill	64 x 37	stone			37 A	4166.00
McClure, Charles Swanger, Christopher A185 D185 E149	Ege, Michael	house & lot note: house 20 x 16 in D	20 x 18		1	2 12	2 A 223 A	200.00 2676.00
McClure, Charles Swanger, Jacob A197 D197 E150	Foulke, Stephen	house & lot barn	27 x 24	stone	2	8 74	2 A 168 A	1000.00 2046.00
McCormack, Hugh Blaine, Robert A195 D195 E143		house & lot kitchen barn	24 x 18 15 x 12 25 x 22	wood wood	2 1	6 72 2 12	2 A 150 A	500.00 1530.00
McCormack, Sarah, Widow Blaine, Robert A183 D183 E142		house 1 & lot house 2 & lot barn note: total value of two houses is $300.00	18 x 18 18 x 18	wood wood wood & stone	1 1	2 12 2 12	2 A 150 A	300.00 1540.00

Middleton Township

Owner / Occupant	Location Ref. / Adjoining Owner	Structure	Dimensions	Descr.	Stories	Windows	Lights	Area	Value
McFeely, John	Ramsey, Samuel A184 D184 E145	house & lot barn	24 x 22 60 x 28	wood	1	2	18	2 A 188 A	350.00 2296.00
McKee, Jane, Widow	placed between AD178 and AD179, but not numbered	house & lot	22 x 22	wood	2	2	18	2 A	300.00
McKee, Jane, Widow McKee, William	A178 D178	house & lot	20 x 18	wood	1	1	4	2 A	100.10
Miller, John	Diller, Martin A165 D165 E148	house & lot kitchen barn note: house has 13 windows in D	28 x 32 20 x 19 64 x 30	stone stone stone	2 2	18 9	144 78	2 A 342 A 80 P	1500.00 5430.00
Miller, John Boggs, Francis	A166 D166	house & lot	24 x 20	wood	1	2	17	2 A	120.00
Miller, Matthew	Irwin, General A167 D167 E139	house & lot kitchen barn	30 x 32 20 x 26 96 x 34	brick brick brick	2 2	25	428	2 A 742 A	1700.00 11630.00
Miller, Matthew Blaine, James	A168 D168	house & lot	20 x 20	wood	1	2	12	2 A	100.10
Miller, Matthew Boring, Nathaniel	A169 D169	house & lot	20 x 18	wood	1	3	27	2 A	110.00
Miller, Matthew Philips, Daniel	A170 D170	house & lot	18 x 16	wood	1	2	8	2 A	100.10
Miller, Robert Mower, George	Wise, Jacob A192 D192 E141	house & lot barn	30 x 20 40 x 20	stone	2	7	66	2 A 212 A	450.00 2574.00
Miller, Robert Sallender, Christopher	McCormack, Hugh A193 D193 E140	house & lot barn	33 x 33 60 x 20	wood	2	4	48	2 A 154 A	350.00 1560.00
Mitchell, Ross	Blaine, Robert A164 D164 E146	house & lot barn still house	20 x 20 82 x 36 40 x 24	wood & stone stone stone	1	4	33	2 A 222 A	200.00 3780.00

Middleton Township

Owner Occupant	Location Ref.	Adjoining Owner	Structure	Dimensions	Descr.	Stories	Lights Windows		Area	Value
Montgomery, John Smith, Henry		Waggoner, Jacob A161 D161 E132	house & lot	16 x 15	wood	1	1	4	2 A 171 A	110.00 256.50
Montgomery, John, Esq. Croney, Thomas		Gregg, John A163 D163 E134	house & lot barn	24 x 20 60 x 18	wood	1	3	19	2 A 248 A	300.00 2024.00
Montgomery, John, Esq. Latshaw, Peter	State Road Happy Retreat [?] A162 D162 E133		house & lot kitchen barn storehouse	22 x 25 12 x 25 16 x 16	brick wood wood	2 1	11 2	147 12	2 A 78 A	1250.00 966.00
Moore, William		Peters, Richard, Esq. A173 D173 E131	house & lot wash house barn grist mill saw mill	48 x 30 24 x 20 80 x 30	stone wood stone stone	2	19	298	2 A 814 A	1800.00 7602.00
Moore, William Graham, William	A176 D176		house & lot	20 x 18	wood	1	1	4	2 A	200.00
Moore, William Mathew, Agness	A177 D177		house & lot	18 x 16	wood	1	1	4	2 A	100.10
Moore, William Moore, Robert	A175 D175		house & lot	24 x 20	wood	1	3	27	2 A	250.00
Moore, William Ramsey, David	A174 D174		house & lot	16 x 18	wood	1	1	4	2 A	110.00
Moreland, James		Chambers, Robert A194 D194 E130	house & lot barn	18 x 16 50 x 20	wood	1	1	4	2 A 148 A	100.10 1184.00
Morrison, Robert		Smith, Hugh A179 D180 E137	house & lot kitchen barn wash house	25 x 19 20 x 17 56 x 25 20 x 17	wood wood wood	1	2	21	2 A 221 A	400.00 1381.00
Morrison, Robert Hart, David	A180 D179		house & lot	24 x 20	wood	1	2	6	2 A	110.00

Middleton Township

Owner / Occupant	Ref.	Location / Adjoining Owner	Structure	Dimensions	Descr.	Stories	Windows	Lights	Area	Value
Morrison, Robert Huston, Samuel	A181 D181		house & lot	24 x 20	wood	1	2	10	2 A	110.00
Noar, Frederick	A198 D198 E157	Clouser, Widow	house & lot kitchen barn	26 x 24 16 x 16 60 x 22	wood wood	1	4	35	2 A 398 A	400.00 3622.00
		note: name also Noaire and Noire								
Parkison, Richard	A201 D201 E159		house & lot barn	22 x 24 60 x 22	wood	2	2	18	2 A 183 A	500.00 2775.00
Patterson, William	A199 D199 E160	Ramsey, Samuel	house & lot barn	30 x 25 65 x 20	wood	2	8	84	2 A 178 A	500.00 2166.00
Patton, Robert	A203 D203 E161	Waggoner, Jacob	house & lot barn tract	24 x 20 40 x 20	wood mountain land	1	2	24	2 A 294 A 120 P 120 A	300.00 2672.00
		note: separate value not stated for mountain land								
Patton, Robert Stuart, William	A204 D204		house & lot	18 x 15	wood	1	2	6	2 A	100.10
Peters, Richard, Esq. Close, Samuel	A202 D202 E162	Moore, William	house & lot barn	27 x 27 60 x 20	wood	2	6	48	2 A 398 A	500.00 4816.00
		note: Close occupant in A & D; Boggs, Francis occupant in E								
Pollinger, Abraham Shaffer, Peter	A205 D205 E163	Diller, Martin	house & lot	20 x 20	wood	1	2	18	2 A 114 A	100.10 1710.00
Postlethwaite, Samuel Hamute [?], John	A200 D200 E158	Blaine, Ephraim	house & lot barn	16 x 16 40 x 20	wood	1	3	27	2 A 60 A	200.00 750.00
Rainy, William	E174	Creigh, John	tract						38 A	370.00
Ralston, Andrew	A207 D207 E165	South Mountain	house & lot	25 x 20	wood	1	1	4	2 A 98 A	200.00 490.00
Ramsey, Samuel	A209 D209 E171	Land, Matthew	house & lot wash house barn	40 x 20 18 x 18 60 x 30	wood stone	1 2	3	25	2 A 198 A	550.00 2416.00

Middleton Township

Owner / Occupant	Ref.	Location / Adjoining Owner	Structure	Dimensions	Descr.	Stories	Windows Lights	Area	Value
Randolph, Ichabod		Fleming, John	house 1 & lot	18 x 18	wood	1	5 / 20	2 A	300.00
			house 2	18 x 18	wood	1	5 / 20		
			barn	25 x 20				148 A	1480.00
	A212 D212 E170		note: Randolph, Archibald, owner in E (barn & 148 A); total value of two houses is $300.00						
Randolph, Jacob		Kincaide, John	house & lot	22 x 18	wood	1	1 / 12	2 A	300.00
			kitchen	15 x 18	wood				
	A213 D213 E169		barn	50 x 20				148 A	1480.00
Randolph, Paul		Fleming, John	house & lot	24 x 20	wood	1	1 / 12	2 A	300.00
	A211 D211 E168		barn	25 x 20				148 A	1480.00
Reighter, George		Moore, William	house & lot	26 x 22	wood	2	10 / 90	2 A	500.00
			barn					216 A	1812.00
	A214 D214 E167		saw mill						
Ritchey, Thomas		White, David	house & lot	26 x 18	wood	1	1 / 9	2 A	300.00
	A208 D208 E166		barn		wood & stone			198 A	1240.00
Roush, Henry		Bower, Martin	house & lot	20 x 20	wood	1	2 / 18	2 A	300.00
	A210 D210 E173							48 A	384.00
Rowan, David / Dice, Conrad		Wise, Jacob	house & lot	22 x 20	wood	1	6 / 72	2 A	250.00
	A206 D206 E164		barn	50 x 20				148 A	1816.00
Rupard, John / Lechter, Casper		Smith, Hugh	house & lot	25 x 28	wood	1	6 / 64	2 A	300.00
			barn	56 x 24				138 A	1154.00
	A215 D215 E172		note: owner deceased; no occupant listed in E						
Sample, Joseph		Irwin, James	house & lot	28 x 33	stone	2	9 / 171	2 A	1500.00
			kitchen	26 x 26	stone	1	3 / 36		
			barn	57 x 26				206 A	3140.00
	A233 D233 E176		wash house	14 x 16	stone	1			
Sanderson, John, Jr. [?]		Sanderson, William	house & lot	20 x 38	wood	1	4 / 28	2 A	300.00
			grist mill					276 A	2728.00
	A216 D216 E183		still house						
Sanderson, John, Jr. [?]			house & lot	16 x 20	wood	1	1 / 4	2 A	100.10
	A217 D217								
Sanderson, John, Sr. [?]		Fleming, John	house & lot	28 x 20	wood	2	6 / 72	2 A	450.00
	A218 D218 E184		barn	54 x 18				158 A	1580.00

Middleton Township

Owner / Occupant	Ref.	Location / Adjoining Owner	Structure	Dimensions	Descr.	Stories	Lights / Windows	Area	Value
Sanderson, Robert		Davidson, Robert, Rev.	house & lot	20 x 24	wood	1	5	45	2 A	300.00
			kitchen	20 x 18	wood					
			barn	30 x 20					133 A	2015.00
	A239 D239 E179									
Sanderson, William		Elliot, James	house & lot	26 x 20	wood	1	3	33	2 A	400.00
			kitchen	17 x 18	wood					
			barn						138 A	1154.00
	A222 D222 E186									
Scott, Andrew		Hamilton, James	house & lot	24 x 20	wood	1	2	12	2 A	300.00
			barn						116 A	1412.00
	A221 D221 E175									
Searight, Gilbert		Denny, Daniel	house & lot	24 x 22	wood	2	6	45	2 A	400.00
			kitchen	14 x 12	wood	1	1	6		
			barn	56 x 26					596 A	7152.00
	A230 D230 E181									
Searight, Gilbert / Gibson, John			house & lot	20 x 18	wood	1	2	16	2 A	200.00
	A231 D230									
Shaffer, Rudolph			house & lot	40 x 18	wood	2	5	54	2 A	400.00
	A230a, no entry in D									
Shaffer, Rudolph / Shaffer, John		Miller, John	house & lot	18 x 16	wood	1	2	12	2 A	150.00
			barn 1						220 A	2740.00
			barn 2							
	A232 D232 E190		still house							
Singer, Henry		Elliot, David	house & lot	40 x 20	wood	1	3	14	2 A	250.00
			barn	45 x 20					53 A	454.00
	A238 D238 E182									
Slonaker, William		Byers, Jacob	house & lot	24 x 20	wood	1	3	37	2 A	300.00
			barn	40 x 18					38 A	304.00
	A223 D223 E185									
Smith, David		Whitmer, Jacob	house & lot	28 x 24	wood	2	8	96	2 A	500.00
			kitchen	15 x 24	wood					
			barn	50 x 20					195 A	2945.00
	A219 D219 E189		note: kitchen 15 x 12 in D							
Smith, David / Weaver, Philip			house & lot	30 x 15	wood	1	3	20	2 A	200.00
	A220 D220									
Smith, Esther		Diller, Martin	house & lot	40 x 18	stone	1	6	72	2 A	1050.00
			barn	80 x 30	stone				246 A	4190.00
	A235 D235 E191									

Middleton Township

Owner / Occupant	Ref.	Location / Adjoining Owner	Structure	Dimensions	Descr.	Stories	Lights / Windows		Area	Value
Smith, Esther Koonts, David	A236 D236		house & lot	24 x 20	wood	1	1	4	2 A	120.00
Smith, Hugh		Kenny, Robert	house & lot kitchen wash house barn still house	30 x 30 18 x 18 12 x 18 55 x 22 25 x 27	stone wood stone stone	2 1 1	10 1 1	145 12 4	2 A 222 A	1400.00 1708.00
	A237 D237 E188									
Smith, James	A224 D224 E178	Bonny Brook	house & lot barn	34 x 28 27 x 24	stone	1	6	81	2 A 218 A	1050.00 2616.00
Speck, Frederick		Cooper, Adam	house & lot barn still house	24 x 28 60 x 22 18 x 30	wood	2	10	104	2 A 198 A	600.00 2060.00
	A234 D234 E177		note: Spack in A							
Steel, John, Esq.		Blaine, Ephraim	house & lot barn	58 x 18	wood wood & stone	1			2 A 225 A	400.00 2760.00
	A227 D227 E187									
Steel, John, Esq. Spiker, Ebenezer	A228 D228		house & lot	14 x 14	wood	1	1	6	2 A	100.10
Stuart, Elizabeth		Templeton, John	house & lot barn	30 x 20 42 x 20	wood	1	2	16	2 A 184 A	200.00 1472.00
	A229 D229 E180									
Swanger, Paul		Hamilton, James	house & lot barn	28 x 26 50 x 20	wood	1	3	36	2 A 160 A	400.00 1950.00
	A225 D225 E192									
Swanger, Paul Foster, Joseph	A226 D226		house & lot	24 x 18	wood	1	3	27	2 A	150.00
Taylor, John		Kelly, Francis	house & lot barn	27 x 22 24 x 16	wood	2	7	84	2 A 88 A	400.00 704.00
	A241 D241 E194									
Templeton, John		Clark, William	house & lot barn tract	30 x 18 56 x 20	wood mountain land	1	4	24	2 A 198 A 50 A	400.00 1699.00
	A240 D240 E195		note: value not given for mountain land							
Thompson, Abraham		Love, John	house & lot	24 x 20	wood	1	2	12	2 A 48 A	150.00 444.00
	A242 D242 E193									

Middleton Township

Owner Occupant	Ref.	Location Adjoining Owner	Structure	Dimensions	Descr.	Stories	Lights Windows		Area	Value
Urie, Thomas		Smith, Esther	house & lot	28 x 32	stone	2	10	126	2 A	1400.00
			kitchen	18 x 20	stone	1	2	24		
			spring house	12 x 14	stone					
			barn	60 x 30	stone				198 A	3720.00
	A276 D276 E196		note: Yury in D							
Waggoner, Jacob		Patton, Robert	house & lot	28 x 19	wood	2	3	24	2 A	600.00
			wash house	16 x 17	wood					
			spring house	12 x 12	wood					
			barn 1						298 A	4000.33
			barn 2							
			tract 2		mountain land				200 A	
	A271 D271 E207		note: value of tract 2 not given							
Waltimire, Ludwick		Ralston, Andrew	house & lot	25 x 20	wood	1	3	14	2 A	150.00
									98 A	490.00
	A257 D257 E217									
Weaver, William		Giffen, James	house & lot	40 x 20	wood	1	4	48	2 A	250.00
			barn	60 x 24					120 A	1000.00
	A274 D274 E198									
Wetmire, Jacob Angeny, Isaac			house & lot	26 x 21	wood	1	4	40		
	A263a, no entry in D		note: value scratched out; entry may have been intended to be erased							
White, David		Craighead, Gilson	house & lot	32 x 27	stone	1	6	71	2 A	1050.00
			barn	75 x 40					248 A	4320.00
			grist mill							
	A259 D259 E219		saw mill							
White, David Carothers, Alexander	E220	Smith, James	tract						100 A	1200.00
Williamson, David		Mitchell, Ross	house & lot	24 x 22	wood	2	5	47	2 A	400.00
			barn						231 A	2802.00
	A268 D268 E200		still house							
Williamson, David Morrison, James	A269 D269		house & lot	15 x 18	wood	1	1	4	2 A	100.10
Wilson, Archibald Fisher, James	A264 D264		house & lot	26 x 20		1	2	7	2 A	300.00
			note: owner deceased							
Wilson, Joseph		Wilson, Richard	house & lot	30 x 16	wood	1	1	4	2 A	110.00
	A267 D267 E202									

Middleton Township

Owner / Occupant	Ref.	Location / Adjoining Owner	Structure	Dimensions	Descr.	Stories	Windows	Lights	Area	Value
Wilson, Richard	E201	Wilson, Joseph	tract note: owner deceased						246 A	1968.00
Wilson, Widow	A265 D265		house & lot	22 x 20	wood	1	1	4	1 A	120.00
Wise, Jacob	A251 D251 E213	Hamilton, James	house & lot barn	32 x 25 62 x 26	wood	1	5	58	2 A 295 A	600.00 3610.00
Wise, Jacob Wise, Jacob, Jr.	A252 D252 E214	Rowan, David	house & lot note: Jr. is owner in E	24 x 18	wood	1	3	24	2 A 98 A	100.10 1176.00
Witmer, Jacob	A247 D247		house & lot	32 x 27	wood	1	1	12	2 A	350.00
Witmer, Jacob Witmer, John	A248 D248 E212	Chambers, William	house & lot barn	25 x 25 65 x 27	wood	1	4	48	2 A 129 A	200.00 2352.00
Witsel, Jacob	A272 D272 E208	Bower, Martin	house & lot barn	26 x 20 56 x 20	wood	2	5	44	2 A 98 A	350.00 834.00
Wolf, Andrew	A256 D256 E216	Love, John	house & lot kitchen barn	20 x 18 30 x 12 20 x 20	wood wood	1	1	4	2 A 148 A	100.10 250.00
Wolf, Henry	A260 D260 E221	Miller, Robert	house & lot	24 x 22	wood	2	6	72	2 A	250.00
Wolf, Henry	A258 D258 E218	Ritchey, Thomas	house & lot	18 x 18	wood	1	2	12	2 A 48 A	100.10 96.00
Wolf, Jacob	A249 D249		house & lot	25 x 24	wood	1	5	54	2 A	350.00
Wolf, Jacob, Jr.	A261 D261 E199	Keihl, Francis	house & lot barn	30 x 18 60 x 20	wood	1	3	28	2 A 128 A	400.00 1054.00
Wolf, Jacob, Sr.	E203	Kiehl, Francis	barn	55 x 21					110 A	920.00

Middleton Township

Owner / Occupant	Ref.	Location / Adjoining Owner	Structure	Dimensions	Descr.	Stories	Windows	Lights	Area	Value
Wolf, John	A245 D245 E197	Fleming, John	house & lot barn	28 x 22 50 x 20	wood	1	5	45	2 A 146 A	350.00 1510.00
Wolf, John	A253 D253 E215	Craighead, Gilson	house & lot barn	41 x 26 60 x 30	wood & stone stone	2	6	60	2 A 228 A	600.00 3000.00
Wolf, John Runion, Richard	A246 D246		house & lot	20 x 16	wood	1	1	6	2 A	100.10
Wolf, John Stewick, Joseph	A254 D254		house & lot	25 x 16	wood	1	3	22	2 A	100.10
Wolf, Philip George, Mary	A255 D255 E205	Hager, John	house & lot	24 x 20	wood	2	10	90	2 A 68 A	350.00 544.00
Wonderlich, Daniel	A244 D244 E210	Fosler, George	house & lot barn	24 x 20 50 x 20	wood	1	4	16	2 A 96 A	200.00 1390.00
Wonderlich, Daniel Wood, Joseph	A243 D243		house & lot	29 x 24	wood	2	15	180	2 A	600.00
Wonderlich, David	A266 D266 E206	Waggoner, Jacob	house & lot out house barn	24 x 20 15 x 10 56 x 20		1	4	36	2 A 118 A	400.00 994.00
Wonderlich, Frederick	A250 D250 E204	Giffen, James	house & lot barn	26 x 22 56 x 20	wood	1	3	36	2 A 188 A	450.00 1930.00
Wonderlich, John	A263 D263 E209	Walter, Jacob	house & lot barn	30 x 20	wood decayed	1	3	28	2 A 56 A	150.00 870.00
Wonderlich, John	A270 D270 E211	McCormark, Hugh	house & lot barn	26 x 20 60 x 20	wood	2	7	84	2 A 166 A	400.00 1710.00
Wonderlich, John Rhine, Samuel	A262 D262		house & lot	20 x 15	wood	1	1	8	2 A	150.00
Wyncoop, Jacob	A273 D273		house & lot	18 x 20	wood	1	4	48	2 A	200.00

Middleton Township

Owner Occupant	Ref.	Location Adjoining Owner	Structure	Dimensions	Descr.	Stories	Windows	Lights	Area	Value
Young, Peter			house & lot	30 x 20	wood	1	4	48	2 A	310.00
		Duncan, Thomas	barn	50 x 20					157 A	1924.00
	A275 D275 E222									
Zigler, Andrew			house & lot	24 x 20	wood	2	5	43	2 A	450.00
		Davidson,	kitchen	20 x 16	wood	1	2	8		
		Patrick	wash house	20 x 18	stone	2				
	A278 D278 E223		barn	48 x 20					298 A	2484.00
Zigler, Jacob		South Mountain	house & lot	20 x 20	wood	1	1	4	2 A	100.10
	A277 D277 E224								48 A	96.00

Mifflin Township

CHAPTER VIII   MIFFLIN TOWNSHIP

Owner / Occupant	Location / Adjoining Owner	Structure	Dimensions	Descr.	Stories	Lights / Windows	Area	Value
Allen, Hugh, heirs of / Allen, John / B1 E1	on Three Square Hollow Road / Brison, Samuel	house 1 / house 2 / stable / note: $80.00 is total value for both houses	24 x 20 / 20 x 20 / 22 x 22	wood / wood / logs			200 A	80.00 / / 1720.00
Barnett, John / / A4 B4 D4 E4	on Big Run / McCormack, Samuel	house & lot / stable	24 x 20 / small	wood	1 1/2	3 18	2 A / 100 A	100.50 / 600.00
Barnett, John / Hadden, Thomas / A5 D5		house & lot / stable	22 x 20	wood	1 1/2	3 18	2 A / 100 A	100.50 / 600.00
Barr, Robert / / A13 B11 D13 E11	/ Laughlin, Hugh	house & lot / kitchen / barn / still house	22 x 18 / / 60 x 22 / 16 x 16	wood / wood / wood / wood	1 1/2	3 30	2 A / / 100 A	200.00 / / 1120.00
Bell, Andrew / / A8 B8 D8 E8	on Three Square Hollow Road / Hannah, Samuel	house & lot / kitchen / cabin / barn / tan house / bark house	24 x 24 / 12 x 20 / 20 x 18 / 60 x 22 / 22 x 20 / 24 x 24	wood / wood / wood / wood / wood, 8 vats	2 / 1	1 12	2 A / / / 430 A	300.00 / / 25.00 / 4136.30
Bell, John / / A12 B9 D12 E9	[undecipherable] / Bell, Walter	house & lot / barn / tanhouse	24 x 18 / 68 x 24 / 64 x 20	wood / wood / 5 vats	1 1/2	3 29	2 A / 190 A	150.00 / 2293.30
Bell, Walter / A11 D11		house & lot	22 x 15	wood	1 1/2	2 18	2 A	100.50
Bell, Walter / Holmes / / A9 B10 D9 E10	on Upper Run / Montgomery, William	house & lot / barn / stable / still house / [?] / note: Holmes occupant in B & E; Bell, in B; none listed in E; undecipherable structure appears in B	27 x 21 / 116 x 28 / 18 x 16 / 17 x 17 / 10 x 10	wood / wood / / wood / wood	1 1/2	[?] [?]	2 A / 180 A	300.00 / 2244.60
Bell, Walter / Syphir [?] / A10 D10		house & lot / kitchen	24 x 24	wood / wood	2	4 29	2 A	250.00
Bowman, Jacob / Colpt, Simon / / A2 B3 D2 E3	/ [?], Andrew	house & lot / barn / note: on road from Schoulars mill to Carlisle	24 x 17 / 53 x 20	wood	1 1/2	3 18	2 A / 113 A	100.50 / 1398.94

Mifflin Township

Owner Occupant	Ref.	Location Adjoining Owner	Structure	Dimensions	Descr.	Stories	Lights Windows	Area	Value
Bowman, Joseph & Bear, Samuel			house & lot	20 x 20	wood	1 1/2	3 18	2 A	110.50
			barn	60 x 20	wood			113 A	1342.30
Summers, Andrew		Dagon, Jacob	cabin	20 x 20					25.00
	A1 B2 D1 E2		note: on road from Schoulars mill to Carlisle						
Brittain, Adam		on road leading	house & lot	37 x 23	wood	1 1/2	6 72	2 A	280.00
		to Newville	barn	60 x 22	wood			150 A	1565.00
		Kennedy, Thomas	cabin	18 x 16	wood				10.00
	A3 B6 D3 E6								
Bryson, Samuel		on Three Square	house & lot	24 x 24	wood	2	5 60	2 A	300.00
		Hollow Road	kitchen	22 x 14	wood	1			
		Williamson, David	barn	62 x 22	wood			120 A	1380.00
	A7 B7 D7 E7								
Buck, George		joining the North	house 1 & lot	42 x 22	wood	1 1/2	8 54	2 A	280.00
		Mountain	barn 1	56 x 22	wood			300 A	2528.00
		McFarlane, John	house 2	22 x 18	wood				70.00
	A6 B5 D6 E5		barn 2	24 x 24					
Carnahan, Robert		on Conodoguinet Cr.	house & lot	24 x 22	wood	1	1 6	2 A	100.50
		Brison, Samuel	barn	60 x 20	wood			140 A	1637.00
			cabin 1	28 x 24					
	A15 B14 D15 E14		cabin 2	28 x 24	total value of both cabins				26.00
Casper, Nicholas			barn	24 x 22				100 A	850.00
		Felair, Jacob							
	B12 E12								
Chrislip, Charles			house 1 & lot	22 x 18	wood	1 1/2	1 8	2 A	100.75
		Morrow, John	house 2	26 x 24	stone				
			barn	60 x 22				100 A	1260.00
	A14 B15 D14 E15		smith shop	16 x 16					
Christian, Ludwig			cabin	28 x 24	wood				50.00
		Exolf, Michael	stable	20 x 18				80 A	390 00
	B13 E13								
Dagon, Jacob		on road from Adam	house	22 x 20	new				
		Brittain's to	barn	50 x 20				40 A	574.00
		Newville	cabin	20 x 14					10.00
		Jacob, Thomas							
	B16 E16								
Davidson, John		on Three Square	house	27 x 24	wood				
		Hollow Road	kitchen						
		Laughlin, Hugh	barn	58 x 20	wood			240 A	2489.00
	B19 E19		cabin	20 x 15					10.00

Mifflin Township

Owner / Occupant	Ref.	Location / Adjoining Owner	Structure	Dimensions	Descr.	Stories	Windows	Lights	Area	Value
Devalt, John	B18 E18	on Big Run / Dibbs, John	cabin / stable	22 x 20 / 20 x 12	wood				100 A	12.00 / 318.00
Dibbs, Abraham	B17 E17	near Big Run / Devalt, John	cabin	18 x 18	wood				5 A	8.00 / 31.00
Donnnel, Francis	A16 D16		house & lot	25 x 20	wood	1 1/2	1	8	2 A	100.75
Elliott, Alexander	A17 B20 D17 E20	on road leading from McCormick Gap to Newville / Mitchell, Samuel	house & lot / kitchen / barn / cabin	24 x 24 / / 60 x 24 / 14 x 12	wood / wood / wood	2	3	33	2 A / / 193 A	280.00 / / 1925.00 / 5.00
Ensminger, Jacob	A19 B22 D19 E22	Grouse, Jacob	house & lot / barn / wagonmaker shop	26 x 20 / 45 x 24 / 22 x 22	wood	1 1/2	4	36	2 A / 74 A	200.00 / 931.66
Esrig, Jacob	A18 B21 D18 E21	Walker, James	house & lot / kitchen / barn	18 x 18 / / 33 x 18	wood / wood / wood	1	3	38	2 A / / 19 A	100.75 / / 224.46
Fealair, Andrew	A23 B26 D23 E26	Morrow, John	house & lot / barn / cabin	20 x 20 / 64 x 25 / 12 x 10	wood	1 1/2	4	33	2 A / 148 A	150.00 / 1680.16 / 10.00
Fealair, Christopher	A20 B23 D20 E23	Gillespie, Nathaniel	house & lot / barn	32 x 30 / 80 x 32	wood / wood	2	4	40	2 A / 137 A	350.00 / 1724.83
Fealair, Jacob	A24 B27 D24 E27	Lusk, Robert, Morrow, John & Martin, Paul	house & lot	20 x 18	stone	2	2	24	2 A / 173 A	140.00 / 1859.75
Fenton, Samuel	A21 B24 D21 E24	Reed, John	house & lot / barn / note: on road from George Kneller to Newville	28 x 23 / 60 x 22	wood / wood	2	4	29	2 A / 165 A	300.00 / 1857.90
Findley, Samuel	B28 E28	on Sulpher Spring [?] / Moffett, William	house / cabin 1 / cabin 2 / barn	24 x 24 / 44 sq. ft. / 44 sq. ft. / 45 x 18	wood, new / / / wood				153 A	601.29

Mifflin Township

Owner / Occupant	Ref.	Location / Adjoining Owner	Structure	Dimensions	Descr.	Stories	Lights	Windows	Area	Value
Findley, Samuel	B29 E29	Murray, Thomas	tract						91 A	182.00
Fite, Jacob	A22 B25 D22 E25	Haun, Jacob	house & lot barn	25 x 24 50 x 26	wood	1 1/2	3	36	2 A 88 A	200.00 869.44
Gander, Peter	B30 E30	on Big Run Wallace, John	grist mill saw mill oyler [?] mill	30 x 26	wood				51 A	584.42
Gault, James & Alexander Mather, Robert	A29 B35 D29 E35	on Conodoguinet Cr. Barr, Robert	house & lot spring house barn weaver shop	23 x 18 small 44 x 16	wood wood wood	1 1/2	3	18	2 A 298 A	100.75 3635.60
Gees, Christopher heirs of Shannon, James	B38 E38	on Whiskey Run McElwain, Joseph	cabin barn	20 x 20 80 x 22	wood wood				198 A	20.00 2352.24
Gees, Conrad	A38 B33 D38 E33	on Conodoguinet Cr. Reed, John	house 1 & lot house 2 house 3 barn still house smith shop weaver shop note: $60.00 is total value of houses 2 and 3	42 x 20 20 x 15 14 x 16 60 x 25 16 x 16 16 x 16	wood wood wood wood wood	1 1/2	5	48	2 A 170 A	300.00 60.00 2051.26
Gees, Conrad	B34 E34	mountain land Patton, John & Greger, Abraham	tract						50 A	150.00
George, Jacob	B32 E32	Chrislip, Charles	cabin barn	20 x 18 36 x 18	wood wood				 51 A	50.00 304.96
Gillespie, Nathaniel	A26 B37 D26 E37	on Big Run Gillespie, Robert	house & lot kitchen barn tan house & bark mill	29 x 23 56 x 22 40 x 22	wood wood wood 6 vats	2	8	64	2 A 198 A	350.00 2576.98
Gillespie, Robert	A25 B36 D25 E36	on Big Run Elliot, Alexander	house & lot kitchen barn cabin	28 x 26 44 x 22 18 x 18	wood wood wood	2	9	102	2 A 298 A	400.00 3497.40 20.00

Mifflin Township

Owner Occupant	Ref.	Location Adjoining Owner	Structure	Dimensions	Descr.	Stories	Lights Windows		Area	Value
Greger, Abraham			house & lot	25 x 24	wood	1 1/2	6	72	2 A	320.00
		Patten, John	barn	54 x 26	wood				98 A	941.80
	A27 B31 D27 E31		smith shop	22 x 18	wood					
Grouse, Jacob			house & lot	26 x 20	wood	1 1/2	2	24	2 A	200.00
		Ensminger, Jacob	barn	66 x 24	wood				128 A	1399.14
		Wolf, Joseph								
	A28 B39 D28 E39									
Hamilton, James		at Mountain's foot	barn	70 x 26					468 A	4104.36
Hamilton, George		Weaver, Wendal								
	B48 E48									
Harper, James		on Big Run	house 1 & lot	22 x 22	wood	2	3	27	2 A	300.00
		Harper, William	kitchen		wood					
			spring house	small	stone					
			barn	56 x 25	wood				173 A	2169.42
	A33 B42 D33 E42		house 2	22 x 20	wood					30.00
Harper, William		on Big Run	house & lot	24 x 21	wood	1 1/2	4	42	2 A	300.00
		Harper, James	kitchen		wood					
	A34 B43 D34 E43		barn	66 x 24	wood				148 A	1978.76
Haun, Jacob		on Middle Run	house & lot	27 x 21	wood	1 1/2	3	24	2 A	160.00
		Fite, Jacob	barn	44 x 18	wood				44 A	335.72
	A32 B45 D32 E45									
Hauser, John		on Middle Run	barn	44 x 18	wood				18 A	275.94
		Knettle, George	smith shop	14 x 14						
	B44 E44									
Hendricks, John		at Mountain's foot	cabin	22 x 16						16.00
Kingler, Henry		Patten, John	stable	16 x 16	wood				103 A	411.45
	B49 E49									
Hoover, Frederick		on Big Run	cabin	22 x 18	wood					20.00
		Barnett, John	barn	44 x 15	wood				45 A	402.50
	B41 E41									
Houts, Henry,		on Three Square	house 1 & lot	30 x 22	wood	2	8	66	2 A	350.00
heirs of		Hollow Road	barn	70 x 28					198 A	2128.30
Weaver, Vandal		Bell, Walter	house 2	22 x 18	wood					30.00
	A35 B47 D35 E47		smith shop	15 x 15						
Hudley, Samuel			house & lot	28 x 24	wood	1 1/2	3	36	2 A	200.00
		Ensminger, Jacob	barn	45 x 20					148 A	873.30
	A31 B46 D31 E46									

135

Mifflin Township

Owner / Occupant	Ref.	Location / Adjoining Owner	Structure	Dimensions	Descr.	Stories	Windows Lights		Area	Value
Hunter, William		on road to Newville Kennedy, Thomas	house & lot kitchen barn	28 x 26 53 x 24	wood wood wood	2	8	96	2 A 147 A	350.00 1195.38
	A30 B40 D30 E40									
Jacob, Thomas		on Conodoguinet Cr. Wilson, Samuel	house & lot barn cabin 1 cabin 2	38 x 18 48 x 18 18 x 18 22 x 18	wood total value of both cabins	1 1/2	4	48	2 A 208 A	280.00 2773.93 32.00
	A36 B50 D36 E50									
Kennedy, Thomas Donnall, Thomas		on Big Run Scoullar, John	house & lot wing barn cabin	26 x 18 18 x 12 50 x 20	wood wood	1 1/2 2	2 11	16 12	2 A 163 A	300.00 1620.00 10.00
	A40 B51 D40 E51									
Kish, heirs of Shannon, James			house & lot	24 x 18	wood	1 1/2	2	16	2 A	100.50
	A39 D39									
Knettle, George		on Middle Run Hauser, John	house & lot barn smith shop	39 x 20 75 x 22 15 x 15	wood wood	1 1/2	5	40	2 A 158 A	280.00 1855.46
	A37 B52 D37 E52									
Laughlin, Alexander		on Upper Run Thompson, Matthew	house & lot kitchen barn saw mill note: house 30 x 30 in A	30 x 18 29 x 17 60 x 28	wood wood	2 1	2 2	27 20	2 A 295 A	200.00 3537.16
	A42 B54 D42 E54									
Laughlin, Hugh		on Upper Run Hauser, John	house & lot kitchen barn merchant mill	26 x 26 23 x 17 60 x 28 36 x 26	wood wood wood wood	2 1	7 2	64 10	2 A 298 A	300.00 4225.74
	A41 B53 D41 E53									
Leeper, William		adj. the mountain Patten, John	tract						162 A	324.00
	B56 E56									
Lusk, Robert		McElwain, Andrew	house spring house barn	28 x 19 12 x 12 70 x 19	wood stone wood	2	5	27	2 A 135 A	280.00 1551.15
	A43 B55 D43 E55									
Marshall, John		Marshall, William	house & lot kitchen barn still house malt ---- [?]	24 x 24 60 x 20 26 x 16	wood wood wood	1 1/2 1	4	13	2 A 190 A	250.00 1045.00
	A58 B76 D58 E76									
Marshall, William		Gees, Conrad	house & lot pump house barn	30 x 18 58 x 20	wood wood wood	1	2	12	2 A 67 A	100.10 586.92
	A59 B77 D59 E77									

Mifflin Township

Owner Occupant	Ref.	Location Adjoining Owner	Structure	Dimensions	Descr.	Stories	Lights Windows	Area	Value
Martin, Paul, Jr.	A65 D65		house & lot	20 x 18	wood	1	1 6	2 A	100.50
Martin, Paul, Sr.		Weaver, Wendel	house & lot spring house stable 1 barn cabin	36 x 20 20 x 20 20 x 20 18 x 16	wood wood	1 1/2	3 18	2 A 390 A	200.00 2623.50 20.00
	A64 B85 D64 E85		stable 2	20 x 20					
Mathers, Thomas		on Middle Run Thompson, Andrew	house 1 & lot barn house 2	27 x 24 58 x 20	wood wood new	1 1/2	4 36	2 A 98 A	280.00 1004.50
	A60 B78 D60 E78		weaver shop						
McClintock, Alexander [?], heirs of	B70 E70	McClintock, Sarah & McDannell, Daniel	tract					110 A	1171.60
McClintock Alexander [?], heirs of	B71 E71	near the Mountain McDannell, Daniel	tract					105 A	200.00
McClintock, Sarah	A54 B69 D54 E69	Harper, James	house & lot barn	26 x 24 60 x 22	wood	1 1/2	4 48	2 A 108 A	270.00 1177.20
McCormick, Joseph	A51 D51		house & lot	27 x 22	wood	1 1/2	3 30	2 A	250.00
McCormick, Samuel		on Big Run Harper, James	house & lot barn 1 barn 2 merchant mill	27 x 22 60 x 25 60 x 30 34 x 26	wood wood wood wood	2	4 26	2 A 198 A	250.00 3009.60
	A49 B67 D49 E67		saw mill						
McCormick, Thomas	A50 D50		house & lot	28 x 27	wood	1 1/2	5 43	2 A	270.00
McCoy, Archibald	B84 E84	Felair, Jacob	house tract		new			100 A	840.00
McDaniel, Daniel		Harper, James	house & lot barn cabin	40 x 26 70 x 28 18 x 16	wood	1 1/2	6 58	2 A 350 A	290.00 3630.00 10.00
	A52 B88 D52 E88								

Mifflin Township

Owner / Occupant	Ref.	Location / Adjoining Owner	Structure	Dimensions	Descr.	Stories	Lights	Windows	Area	Value
McDaniel, Daniel	B89 E89	mountain land / Buck George & Wolf, Michael	tract / note: this land was surveyed by a deputy under Mr. Henderson and ----- McDannel; both firmly believe that he will be agreaved by the inaccuracy of the survey						127 A	381.00
McDannell, Joseph	B63 E63	at Mountain's foot / Dewalt, James	house / stable / still house	18 x 18 / 20 x 18 / 30 x 20	wood / wood / wood				50 A	35.00 / 178.00
McElheny, Hugh	A44 B57 D44 E57	near Whiskey Run / Stevenson, James	house & lot / barn	24 x 24 / 56 x 20	wood	1 1/2	4	30	2 A / 98 A	140.00 / 980.00
McElheny, Samuel	A45 B59 D45 E59	on Whiskey Run / McLaughlin, Daniel	house & lot / stable / note: house 24 x 26 in D	29 x 20 / 20 x 18	wood / wood	1 1/2	3	25	2 A / 80 A	100.75 / 700.00
McElheny, Samuel, heirs of / McElheny, Mabel	B58 E58	on Whiskey Run / Shannon, John	house / barn	22 x 20 / 24 x 22	wood				88 A	50.00 / 713.84
McElwain, Andrew	A61 B81 D61 E81	/ Lusk, Robert	house & lot / barn / still house	27 x 16 / 75 x 20 / 16 x 16	wood / wood	1 1/2	2	16	2 A / 263 A	150.00 / 2606.85
McElwain, Andrew heirs of / Lightcap, William	A47 B62 D47 E62	on Conodoguinet Cr. / Gees, Conrad	house & lot / kitchen / barn	25 x 24 / / 60 x 20	wood / wood / wood	2	4	34	2 A / 269 A	270.00 / 3193.30
McElwain, James	A62 B82 D62 E82	/ Williamson, David	house & lot / barn	42 x 19 / 56 x 18	wood & stone / wood	1 1/2	1	12	2 A / 121 A	180.00 / 1179.75
McElwain, Joseph	A46 B61 D46 E61	on Conodoguinet Cr. / Morrow, Samuel	house & lot / pump house / barn / tan vats	27 x 17 / small / 60 x 20	wood / wood / / 6 vats	1 1/2	4	24	2 A / 100 A	250.00 / 1300.00
McFarlane, James	A48 B66 D48 E66	on Big Run / Wolf, Conrad	house & lot / barn	24 x 22 / 40 x 18	wood	1	1	6	2 A / 140 A	100.50 / 395.00
McFarlane, John	A53 B68 D53 E68	on Big Run / Buck, George	house & lot / barn / still house	30 x 28 / 68 x 20 / 16 x 16	wood / wood / wood	2	4	36	2 A / 198 A	350.00 / 2391.84

Mifflin Township

Owner / Occupant	Ref.	Location / Adjoining Owner	Structure	Dimensions	Descr.	Stories	Windows Lights	Area	Value
McLaughlin, Daniel		on Whiskey Run Williamson, David	house 1 house 2 stable	20 x 20 24 x 24 20 x 20	wood wood, new wood			110 A	80.00 1143.00
	B60 E60								
McNickle, Alexander		on Big Run Harper, William	house 1 & lot house 2 barn	32 x 22 16 x 12 60 x 22	wood	1 1/2	5 48	2 A 63 A	300.00 918.54
	A55 B72 D55 E72		note: barn 56 x 22 in E						
Miller, Philip		Christian, Ludwig	house stable	24 x 18 18 x 16	wood			40 A	40.00 290.00
	B79 E79		note: land value $190.00 in E						
Minor, Michel		on Big Run Wallace, John	cabin stable	26 x 26 24 x 28				128 A	10.00 389.36
	B64 E64								
Mitchell, John		Fenton, Samuel	house 1 & lot barn house 2	26 x 24 56 x 22 16 x 22	wood wood	1 1/2	4 33	2 A 88 A	250.00 923.68 10.00
	A57 B74 D57 E74								
Mitchell, John		high in the mountain Farland, James	tract					167 A	417.40
	B75 E75								
Mitchell, Samuel		on Big Run Elliot, Alexander	house & lot barn	26 x 24 60 x 24	wood wood	1 1/2	4 36	2 A 115 A	200.00 1265.00
	A56 B73 D56 E73								
Moffett, William		on Big Run Fenton, Samuel	cabin barn	38 x 20 40 x 16				130 A	40.00 560.60
	B87 E87								
Montgomery, William		on Upper Run Sterrett, David	house & lot kitchen barn	44 x 20 58 x 20	wood wood wood	1 1/2	10 60	2 A 158 A	330.00 1832.40
	A66 B86 D66 E86								
Morrow, John		Felair, Andrew	house & lot barn	20 x 20 22 x 22	wood wood	1	1 9	2 A 98 A	100.25 891.60
	A63 B83 D63 E83								
Morrow, Samuel			house & lot kitchen	26 x 24	wood wood	2	3 36	2 A	300.00
	A67 D67								
Morrow, Samuel McCune, Samuel			house & lot	17 x 15	wood	1	2	2 A	100.50
	A68 D68								

Mifflin Township

Owner / Occupant	Ref.	Location / Adjoining Owner	Structure	Dimensions	Descr.	Stories	Windows	Lights	Area	Value
Murray, Thomas		on Big Run	cabin	22 x 18						12.00
		Sanders, Frederick	barn	36 x 26					100 A	266.00
	B65 E65									
Myres, John		on Whiskey Run	house	24 x 18	wood					30.00
		Unanks, Henry	barn	18 x 18	wood				100 A	460.00
	B80 E80		note: name also Mires							
Newton, Conrad		on Whiskey Run	house & lot	22 x 20	wood	1 1/2	3	24	2 A	100.50
		McLaughlin, Daniel	barn	50 x 22					73 A	818.16
	A72 B92 D72 E92									
Nicholson, James		on Whiskey Run	house & lot	26 x 26	stone	2	4	12	2 A	500.00
		Stevenson, James	kitchen				[?]	4		
			[?] cellar				1	9		
			barn 1	55 x 20	wood				287 A	3387.60
	A69 B90 D69 E90		barn 2	62 x 22	wood	2	10	72		
Nicholson, James / Ohenbaugh, Henry			house & lot	44 x 20	wood	1 1/2	5	45	2 A	250.00
			kitchen		wood			14		
	A70 D70									
North, Jacob		on Whiskey Run	house & lot	24 x 22	wood	1 1/2	3	22	2 A	100.50
		Penney, Jacob	barn	55 x 20	wood				240 A	1890.00
			cabin	16 x 16						10.00
	A71 B91 D71 E91		smith shop							
Patterson, Andrew			house & lot	41 x 24	wood	1 1/2	6	55	2 A	300.00
		Stevenson, William	kitchen		wood					
			barn	62 x 22	wood				188 A	2058.00
	A77 B96 D77 E96		cabin	20 x 18						10.00
Patton, John			house & lot	40 x 20	stone & wood	1 1/2	3	40	2 A	250.00
		Penney, Jacob								
	A75 B94 D75 E94		barn	60 x 22					241 A	1928.00
Penney, Jacob		on Whiskey Run	house & lot	26 x 24	wood	1 1/2	1	12	2 A	100.50
		Patton, John	stable	22 x 20	wood				114 A	866.40
	A76 B95 D76 E95									
Purdy, James			house & lot	24 x 24	wood	1 1/2	2	24	2 A	200.00
	A74 D74									
Purdy, John			house & lot	28 x 24	wood	1 1/2	4	36	2 A	250.00
		Harper, James	barn	62 x 22	wood				242 A	1476.20
	A73 B93 D73 E93		weaver shop							

Mifflin Township

Owner Occupant	Ref.	Location Adjoining Owner	Structure	Dimensions	Descr.	Stories	Windows Lights		Area	Value
Realing, Joseph		on Middle Run Shannon, John	house & lot kitchen	30 x 22 small	wood wood	2	6	72	2 A	330.00
	A80 B99 D80 E99		barn	66 x 20	wood				184 A	2024.00
Reed, John		on Middle Run Fenton, Samuel	house & lot	26 x 20	stone & wood	1 1/2	4	30	2 A	330.00
			kitchen		wood					
	A78 B97 D78 E97		barn	62 x 22	wood				178 A	2146.68
Renard, John		on Middle Run Weaver, Philip	house & lot barn	30 x 18 42 x 18	wood wood	1	4	27	2 A 17 A	100.50 173.91
	A79 B98 D79 E98									
Roberts, John		on Big Run Donnall, Francis	house stable	23 x 18 16 x 12	wood				8 A	50.00 145.40
	B100 E100									
Salsburg, heirs of Fentonbinder, Martin		Wolf, Joseph	house stable	20 x 20 18 x 15	wood wood				94 A	60.00 539.56
	B110 E110									
Sanders, Frederick		on Big Run Moffett, William	cabin stable	22 x 18 16 x 16	wood				50 A	12.00 170.00
	B105 E105									
Schoular, John		on Big Run Reed, John	house & lot	28 x 28	stone & wood	2	8	84	2 A	350.00
			cabin	20 x 18						20.00
			barn	66 x 22	stone & frame				194 A	2987.00
			merchant mill	40 x 32						
	A81 B103 D81 E103		saw mill							
Sensebaugh, John		on Big Run Gillespie, Nathaniel	house & lot kitchen barn still house	26 x 23 16 x 16 81 x 20 18 x 18	wood wood	2 1	5 1	57 8	2 A 125 A	250.00 1320.00
	A89 B101 D89 E101		smith shop	15 x 15						
Shannon, John		on Whiskey Run Stevenson, James	house & lot barn	30 x 24 64 x 24	wood wood	2	3	24	2 A 182 A	250.00 2009.28
	A88 B112 D88 E112									
Shenenberger, Jacob		Yecovah, Philip	house stable	28 x 24 22 x 20	wood, new wood				136 A	734.40
	B106 E106									

Mifflin Township

Owner / Occupant	Location / Ref. / Adjoining Owner	Structure	Dimensions	Descr.	Stories	Lights / Windows	Area	Value
Snider, David		cabin 1	18 x 18					
Ress, Hugh	Purdy, John	cabin 2	18 x 20					32.00
		stable	22 x 18	wood			100 A	516.00
	B104 E104	note: $32.00 is total value of both cabins						
Sterrett, David	on Upper Run	house & lot	40 x 30	wood	2	20 48	2 A	1050.00
	Montgomery,	kitchen	30 x 20	brick	1	2 9		
	William	stable	15 x 15					
		smoke house		stone	1 1/2	2 6		
		barn 1	84 x 30	stone			338 A	5435.04
		merchant mill	45 x 26	wood				
		barn 2		log, old				
	A83 B108 D83 E108	note: name also Starrett						
Sterritt, David		house & lot	27 x 20	wood	1 1/2	4 36	2 A	200.00
Walker, James								
	A84 D84							
Stevenson, James	on Whiskey Run	house & lot	32 x 22	wood	1 1/2	4 35	2 A	280.00
	Shannon, John	spring house	15 x 12	stone	[?]	4 8		
	A85 B111 D85 E111	barn	67 x 27	wood			233 A	2691.15
Stevenson, William		house & lot	24 x 22	wood	2	4 39	2 A	300.00
	Patterson,	kitchen		wood				
	Andrew	barn	54 x 18	wood			157 A	1482.08
	A90 B107 D90 E107							
Stewart, James,	Three Square	house & lot	22 x 20	wood	1	2 12	2 A	100.50
heirs of	Hollow Road	cellar		wood				
Carnahan, James	Barr, Robert	stable		old			118 A	944.00
	A82 B109 D90 E109							
Stoke, Reverend	on Whiskey Run	house & lot	26 x 16	wood	1	2 10	2 A	100.25
Allen, William	Shannon, John	barn	50 x 20				72 A	624.80
	A87 B102 D87 E102	cabin	24 x 20					16.00
Stoke, Reverend		house & lot	39 x 20	wood	1 1/2	3 36	2 A	160.00
Koogan, John								
	A86 D86							
Thompson, Andrew	on Middle Run	house & lot	24 x 22	wood	1 1/2	3 22	2 A	250.00
	Realing, Joseph	barn 1	78 x 24	wood			314 A	3689.50
	A92 B113 D92 E113	barn 2	50 x 20	wood, old				
Thompson, Matthew	on Conodoguinet Cr.	house & lot	28 x 30	stone	2	11 126	2 A	650.00
	Laughlin,	barn 1	100 x 35	brick, not finished			223 A	3865.88
	Alexander	barn 2	60 x 20	wood, old [?]				
		house 2	30 x 22	old				
		cabin	16 x 12					50.00
	A91 B114 D91 E114	note: total value of house 2 and cabin $50.00						

Mifflin Township

Owner / Occupant	Ref.	Location / Adjoining Owner	Structure	Dimensions	Descr.	Stories	Windows	Lights	Area	Value
Unanks, Henry		Myers, John	cabin	20 x 18						10.00
			stable	16 x 12	wood				101 A	343.50
	B115 E115									
Walker, James		on Middle Run	house & lot	20 x 18	wood	1	3	30	2 A	150.00
		Smith, George	kitchen	small	wood					
	A96 B121 D96 E121		barn	64 x 18					98 A	1107.40
Wallace, John		on Big Run	cabin	18 x 19						12.00
		Hoover,	barn	18 x 20					100 A	374.00
		Frederick	still house	16 x 16						
	B127 E127									
Weaver, Martin		Walker, James	barn	48 x 18	wood				23 A	325.91
	B122 E122									
Weaver, Philip		on Middle Run	house 1 & lot	28 x 24	wood	2	5	40	2 A	300.00
		Thompson, Andrew	barn	60 x 24	wood				82 A	975.80
			house 2	18 x 16	wood					
	A95 B120 D95 E120		still house	16 x 16						
Weaver, Vandal			house & lot	34 x 28	stone	2	3	45	2 A	450.00
			barn	70 x 26	wood				356 A	3880.40
	A97 B126 D97 E126		stable	20 x 18	wood					
Weaver, Vandal / Weaver, Peter			house & lot	22 x 18	wood	1	3	18	2 A	110.00
	A98 D98									
Williamson, David		on Three Square	cabin 1	18 x 18						
		Hollow Road	cabin 2	15 x 12						20.00
		Morrow, Samuel	barn 1	70 x 26	wood					
			barn 2	55 x 20					348 A	4354.36
	B125 E125		note: $20.00 is total value of both cabins							
Wilson, Samuel, Rev.		on Conodoguinet Cr.	house & lot	34 x 30	stone	2	14	75	2 A	800.00
		Jacob, Thomas	kitchen	20 x 20	stone	1 1/2	3	12		
	A93 B116 D93 E116		barn	55 x 24					148 A	1835.20
Wise, Philip		on Big Run	house 1 & lot	39 x 22	wood	1 1/2	6	52	2 A	280.00
		Harper, William	kitchen		wood					
			barn	60 x 21	wood				238 A	2925.96
	A94 B118 D94 E118		house 2	20 x 16						30.00
Wolf, Conrad		on Big Run	cabin	20 x 18						20.00
		Zigler, Henry	barn	38 x 18	wood				10 A	90.00
	B117 E117									

Mifflin Township

Owner Occupant	Ref.	Location Adjoining Owner	Structure	Dimensions	Descr.	Stories	Lights	Windows	Area	Value
Wolf, Henry		on Big Run	cabin	20 x 18						20.00
		Zigler, Henry	smith shop	16 x 16					14 A	51.20
	B119 E119									
Wolf, Joseph		on Middle Run	house	22 x 18	wood					60.00
		Grouse, Jacob	barn	52 x 18					10 A	120.00
	B123 E123									
Wolf, Michel		near the mountain	house	28 x 18	wood, new					60.00
		McDaniel, Daniel	stable	18 x 18					100 A	497.00
	B124 E124									
Yecovah, Peter			house	20 x 20						25.00
		Martin, Paul	stable	16 x 10					12 A	81.80
	B129 E129									
Yecovah, Philip			house & lot	22 x 22	wood	1 1/2	2	12	2 A	100.50
		Shenenberger, Jacob	wagon maker shop						134 A	683.40
	A99 B128 D99 E128									
Zigler, Henry		on Big Run	house & lot	24 x 21	wood	1 1/2	2	12	2 A	120.00
		Barnett, John	barn	50 x 21	wood				129 A	965.50
	A101 B131 D101 E131		cabin	14 x 12						2.00
Zigler, John		on Big Run	house & lot	30 x 20	wood	1	4	45	2 A	150.00
		Donnall, Francis	barn	70 x 24	wood				142 A	1680.16
	A100 B130 D100 E130		cabin	18 x 15						20.00

CHAPTER IX NEWTON TOWNSHIP

Owner Occupant	Ref.	Location Adjoining Owner	Structure	Size	Descr.	Stories	Lights Windows	Area	Value
Aikman, John			house & lot	20 x 30	log	1 1/2		2 A	102.00
		Weir, George,	spring house	16 x 16	log				
		heirs	stable	14 x 11	log				
			barn		log, old, little or no value			148 A	1036.00
	A2 B2 D2 E2		note: rate $7.00						
Anderson, James		Newville	house 1	26 x 24	new, stone				
		Brown, James	house 2	18 x 14	log				20.00
			lot					40 P	250.00
	B1 E1		note: house 1 covered and floors laid						
Andrew, Lodewick			house & lot	24 x 24	log	2	10 102	40 P	150.00
		Weir, George,	barn		log, old				
	A1 D1	heirs							
Beatty, James		on the Shater [?]	house	28 x 28	new,	2			
		Quigley, John			unfinished, covered				
			stable	20 x 18	log			107 P 120 F	1400.75
	B7 E7		cabin	18 x 15					3.00
Binder, Peter			house & lot	27 x 26	stone	2	8 102	40 P	500.00
McCally, Patrick			stable	15 x 15	stone	2	5 19		
	A3 D3		shop	20 x 15	wood	1	2 12		
Boyd, Elizabeth		Newville	house	21 x 17	log	1	3 6		45.00
		Kennedy, Thomas						25 P	50.00
	B5 E5								
Boyd, William		on Conodoguinet Cr.	house & lot	24 x 24	log	1	5 48	2 A	200.00
		Mickey, James	stable	30 x 20	log, new				
			barn	60 x 30	old, log			248 A	2876.80
			cabin	16 x 12	old				8.00
	A7 B6 D7 E6		note: rate $11.60						
Brown, James		on Big Spring	house & lot	28 x 26	stone	2	9 99	2 A	700.00
		Carson, John	wing	16 x 12	stone	1 1/2	1 6		
			spring house		stone				
			stable	14 x 12	log				
			barn	45 x 14	log			35 A 111 P	477.58
	A9 B10 D9 E10		note: rate $13.38						
Brown, James		Newville	house & lot	27 x 24	stone, unfinished,			120 P	500.00
		McLaughlin's mill	dam		principal part of stone				
	B12 E12				work done				
Brown, James		Newville	lot					40 P	50.00
		Ross, James							
	B11 E11								

Newton Township

Owner / Occupant	Ref.	Location / Adjoining Owner	Structure	Dimensions	Descr.	Stories	Windows Lights	Area	Value
Brown, James			house & lot	18 x 18	log	1 1/2	1 4	2 A	102.00
Doud, James		McCracken, William	wing	17 x 9	log	1	2 8		
			barn	55 x 16	log			184 A 10 P	1522.19
			note: land is of good quality, but half is so rocky as not to be arable; rate $8.27						
	A10 B13 D10 E13								
Brown, William		Newville	house & lot	21 x 19	log	2	5 60	40 P	280.00
		Dunbar, John	house		log, shell				
			stable	14 x 14	log			40 P	60.00
	A5 B4 D5 E4		smith shop	26 x 19	stone				
Bryson, Hugh			house & lot	24 x 23	log	2	8 81	40 P	380.00
Shannon & Bryson			kitchen	16 x 11	stone				
	A6 D6		stable	14 x 14	log				
Buchanan, Thomas			house	18 x 18	log				30.00
		Patterson, James						400 A	1628.00
	B9 E9								
Buchanan, Thomas		pine land	house	20 x 18	log				30.00
Cooper, Henry		Watt, David	barn	60 x 25	log, old			350 A	875.00
			saw mill						100.00
	B8 E8		note: rate $2.50						
Byerly, Andrew		road from Carlisle to Shippensburg via Walnut Bottom Patterson, James	house 1 & lot	25 x 24	frame	2	10 114	2 A	350.00
			house 2	27 x 24	new, log, unfinished				
			barn	30 x 13	log			111 A	610.50
	A8 B3 D8 E3		note: rate $5.50						
Calbreath, Duncan			house & lot	18 x 20	log	2	5 30	40 P	102.00
	A13 D13								
Carnahan, Adam, heirs		on Conodoguinet Cr. Wilson, William	house & lot	38 x 19	log	1 1/2	5 34	2 A	250.00
			barn	60 x 20	log, old			133 A	1649.20
Carson, Elisha			note: rate $12.40						
	A15 B21 D15 E21								
Carson, John		on Big Spring McFarlane, William	house & lot	22 x 20	log	2	4 28	2 A	300.00
			wing	18 x 10	log	1			
			kitchen	20 x 18	log	1	1		
			barn	60 x 20	log, new			175 A	1548.75
	A16 B22 D16 E22		note: rate $8.85						
Carson, John			house & lot	20 x 18	log	1	1 6	2 A	102.00
Lancaster, John		Thompson, Alexander	wing	15 x 10	log			172 A	1126.60
			stable	16 x 16	log, old				
	A17 B23 D17 E23		note: rate $6.55						

Newton Township

Owner Occupant	Ref.	Location Adjoining Owner	Structure	Dimensions	Descr.	Stories	Lights	Windows	Area	Value
Chapman, James Chapman, William	A11 D11		house & lot stable	26 x 15 10 x 10	log log	1	3	18	40 P	150.00
Clark, Thomas Brattan, John	A18 D18		house & lot	25 x 21	log	2	10	120	40 P	300.00
Clark, Thomas, Sr.	B14 E14	Newville, Main & West Streets	house note: erected since the 1st of October ult.		small stone				40 P	20.00
Cooper, John	A14 B20 D14 E20	on Conodoguinet Cr. Speck, Bernard	house & lot barn 1 barn 2 cabin note: Love, George, occupant of cabin; rate $12.75 [$3417.00]	30 x 26 small 20 x 18	log log, old	2	5	54	2 A 268 A	300.00 3685.00 20.00
Crone, John	B19 E19	Newville Hollar, Peter	lot						40 P	10.00
Crowel, Samuel	A12 B15 D12 E15	Newville Presbyterian Church	house & lot kitchen stable 1 stable 2	26 x 28 16 x 16 40 x 30 18 x 16	log stone stone wood	2 1	10 1	129 6	40 P 40 P	600.00 200.00
Crowel, Samuel	B16 E16	Newville other Crowel lot (B15)	lot						40 P	10.00
Crowel, Samuel	B17 E17	out lot near Newville other Crowel lot (B16)	lot note: rate $26.50						3 A 9 P	80.99
Crowell, Samuel	B18 E18	on Conodoguinet Cr. near Newville Esrig, Simon	tract note: rate: $16.00 [$164.50]		meadow ground				10 A 45 P	169.00
Davidson, John	A19 B24 D19 E24	Newville	house & lot kitchen spring house stable mill house shop tan yard	23 x 22 20 x 15 15 x 14 16 x 13 27 x 20 27 x 20	log stone stone log log log 18 vats	1 1/2 1	6 2	63 12	40 P 40 P	400.00 260.00

Newton Township

Owner / Occupant	Ref.	Location / Adjoining Owner	Structure	Dimensions	Descr.	Stories	Windows Lights	Area	Value
Davidson, John	B25 E25	out lot near Newville / Woodburn, James	lot note: rate $20.00					2 A 40 P	45.00
Davis, Adam Allen, Robert	B34 E34	in the pines / McElroy, John	house note: rate $2.00		old, gone to wreck			180 A	6.00 360.00
Dearmin, Henry	B28 E28	Newville / Wallace, Hugh	house weaver shop	19 x 17 12 x 9	log log			40 P	40.00 60.00
Dedwiler, Jacob	A22 B29 D22 E29	on Green Spring / Thompson, Alexander	house & lot kitchen smoke house barn note: rate $12.25	21 x 21 16 x 12 16 x 12 70 x 20	log log log log	2	5 60	2 A 180 A	300.00 2205.00
Donally, Barney	B33 E33	Millford (lot)	house note: on Thomas Buchanan's land	16 x 13	log			47 P	13.00 18.00
Duck, George Rhode, Frederick	A24 B31 D24 E31	Hollar, Peter	house 1 & lot kitchen stable house 2 note: rate $11.75	28 x 24 24 x 9 24 x 20 18 x 17	log log log log	1 1/2	3 36	2 A 128 A	155.00 1504.00 40.00
Duck, William Swigard, Joseph	A23 B30 D23 E30	Kilgore, Robert	house 1 & lot stable barn house 2 note: B and E give Duck as occupant	20 x 20 17 x 16 50 x 20 18 x 16	log log log, new log	1 1	1 8	2 A 100 A	102.00 1310.00 40.00
Dunbar, John	A20 B27 D20 E27	Newville / Peck, Philip	house & lot kitchen stable	26 x 25 18 x 13 21 x 21	frame log log	2 1	7 105 1 9	40 P 40 P	400.00 12.00
Dunbar, John	B26 E26	out lot near Newville / McKibben, Jeremiah	tract note: rate $21.30					5 A	106.50
Dunbar, John Dunning, Agnes	A21 D21		house & lot	28 x 22	log	1	2 15	40 P	150.00
Duncan, Thomas	A25 B32 D25 E32	on State Road / Peebles, Robert	house & lot kitchen barn note: rate $12.65	30 x 28 18 x 15 60 x 22	log log log	2	9 117	2 A 216 A 80 P	500.00 2378.72

Newton Township

Owner / Occupant	Ref.	Location / Adjoining Owner	Structure	Dimensions	Descr.	Stories	Lights / Windows		Area	Value
Early, Hugh		Millford	house	26 x 26	log					60.00
			kitchen	15 x 13	log				47 P	70.00
	B35 E35		note: on Thomas Buchanan's land							
Esrig, Simon		on Conodoguinet Cr.	house & lot	36 x 18	log	1 1/2	3	27	2 A	140.00
		Walker, John	barn	53 x 20	log				89 A	1172.00
			dairy	15 x 13	stone					
			smith shop	23 x 16	log					
	A26 B36 D26 E36		note: rate $14.00 [$1246.00]							
Ferguson, William			house & lot	21 x 20	log	2	6	54	40 P	300.00
	A28 D28		shop	19 x 18	log	1	2	4		
Fox, John		Newville	house & lot	22 x 18	log	2	5	48	40 P	300.00
		Sharp, Alexander	kitchen	16 x 12	log	1	1	8		
			joiner shop	30 x 8	frame					
			lot						4 P	100.00
	A27 B37 D27 E37		note: joiner shop is on small lot							
Gammel, Benjamin		Newville	lot						40 P	80.00
		Mitchell, Samuel								
	B39 E39									
Geddes, John, Esq.		out lot near	house & lot	30 x 27	stone	2	8	155	40 P	600.00
		Newville	kitchen	20 x 18	stone					
		Woodburn, James	stable	20 x 18	log				4 A 68 P	117.70
	A29 B38 D29 E38		note: rate $26.60							
Harper, James			house & lot	26 x 24	log	2	9	108	40 P	300.00
Cooper, David			shop	12 x 12	log					
	A30 D30									
Hawthorn, James			house 1	26 x 18	log					
		McCollom, John	house 2	34 x 17	log, nearly gone to wreck					37.00
			barn		log, old, nearly gone to wreck				331 A	4038.20
	B44 E44		note: rate $12.20; value of $37 is total for both houses							
Hazleton, Hamilton		Milford	house	24 x 18	log					45.00
	B45 E45								24 P	50.00
Hollar, Peter			house & lot	25 x 20	log	1 1/2	2	24	2 A	125.00
		Peck, George	stable	16 x 12	log				22 A	258.50
	A34 B43 D34 E43		note: rate $11.75							
Hollar, Peter		Newville	lot						40 P	10.00
	B42 E42	Waggoner, Philip								
Holmes, Hugh		out lot near	house & lot	24 x 22	log	2	8	90	40 P	260.00
		Newville	stable	12 x 12	log				1 A 40 P	37.50
	A33 B47 D33 E47		note: rate $20.00 [$25.00]							

Newton Township

Owner Occupant	Ref.	Location Adjoining Owner	Structure	Dimensions	Descr.	Stories	Windows Lights	Area	Value
Hoon, Stophel	B41 E41	Newville McMeeken, William	lot					40 P	18.00
Houser, John	A31 D31		house & lot shop	23 x 21 12 x 12	log wood	2	8 96	40 P	300.00 25.00
Howard, Nicholas	A32 B40 D32 E40	Newville Peck, Philip	house wing	19 x 16 19 x 20	log log	2 1	5 72 2 6	40 P 40 P	150.00 25.00
Hunter, Joseph	A35 B46 D35 E46	Conodoguinet Cr. Walker, William	house & lot addition kitchen barn note: rate $11.55	20 x 18 13 x 8 20 x 18 56 x 20	log log log log	1 1/2 1 1/2	1 8 1 6	2 A 109 A	160.00 1258.95
Jamison, John Pettigrew, James	A36 B48 D36 E48	McCormick, Robert	house 1 & lot kitchen stable barn house 2 note: rate $12.40	30 x 19 15 x 14 24 x 13 62 x 20 25 x 20	log stone log log, a pretty good building log	2	7 84	2 A 498 A	160.00 6175.20 50.00
Kennedy, Thomas	A37 B49 D37 E49	Newville Holmes, Hugh	house 1 & lot kitchen stable house 2 note: first story of house 2 finished	26 x 24 15 x 14 24 x 13 28 x 17	log stone wood log, unfinished, with cellar	2	7 81	40 P 40 P	300.00 80.00
Kennedy, Thomas	B50 E50	Newville Roberts, John	lot					40 P	14.00
Kilgore, Jesse	A40 B54 D40 E54	Micky, James	house & lot stable barn note: rate $11.50	26 x 24 20 x 12 62 x 20	log log, old log, old	2	3 24	2 A 207 A 120 P	300.00 2389.12
Kilgore, Robert	B53 E53	Duck, William & Kilgore, William	house & lot stable 1 stable 2 stable 3 note: rate $12.75	20 x 18 25 x 18 25 x 24 28 x 18	log log log log			140 A 24 P	50.00 1786.90
Kilgore, William	A39 B52 D39 E52	Scrogs, James	house & lot wing barn note: rate $14.75	20 x 18 18 x 10 60 x 20	log log	2 1	1 4	2 A 172 A	160.00 2537.00

Newton Township

Owner Occupant	Ref.	Location Adjoining Owner	Structure	Dimensions	Descr.	Stories	Windows	Lights	Area	Value
Kipford, Abram		on Conodoguinet Cr. Cooper, John	house & lot barn	20 x 20 50 x 24	log log	1 1/2	1	12	2 A 70 A	120.00 922.50
	A38 B51 D38 E51		note: rate $11.75 [$822.50]							
Lammond, James			house & lot	18 x 16	log	2	4	31	40 P	102.00
	A42 D42									
Lightcap, Solomon, Jr. Anderson, John			house & lot wing stable	22 x 17 22 x 10 14 x 12	log log log	2 1	5 3	43 18	40 P	200.00
	A43 D43									
Lightcap, Solomon, Jr. Lightcap, Samuel		road from Newville to Specks Mill Morrow, John	house & lot barn	21 x 21 48 x 19	log log	1 1/2	3	36	2 A 48 A	120.00 480.00
	A44 B55 D44 E55		note: rate $10.00							
Lightcap, Solomon, Sr. Lightcap, Solomon		Sharp, Robert & Morrow, John	house & lot wing barn dairy	20 x 20 20 x 12 50 x 20	log log log, old log	1 1/2 1	3 1	21 9	2 A 141 A	130.00 1269.00
	A45 B56 D45 E56									
Lusk, Robert Clark, Thomas			house & lot stable still house	38 x 28 21 x 20 18 x 18	stone stone & log stone	2	8	102	46 P	600.00
	A41 D41									
Martin, Thomas McCoy, Archibald			house & lot kitchen stable still house	28 x 24 14 x 14 16 x 12	stone stone stone stone	2 1	8 1	102 9	40 P	600.00
	A48 D48									
Maxwell, William		Newville Hoon, Stophel	lot lot		adjacent lots				40 P 40 P	17.00 21.00
	A61 B62 D61 E62									
McAvoy, John McAvoy, Margaret		Newville	house	16 x 15	log	1	1	12	40 P	65.00 80.00
	B87 E87									
McCann, Robert Patton, Andrew		Newville	house stable	24 x 18 17 x 12	log log				40 P	50.00 60.00
	B70 E70									
McCollum, John		on great road Carlisle to Shippensburg Thrush, Barney	house 1 house 2 barn	18 x 16 30 x 30 60 x 20	log stone, new, unfinished log				140 A 80 P	2412.38
	B80 E80		note: rate $17.17; house 2 lower story finished							

Newton Township

Owner / Occupant	Ref.	Location / Adjoining Owner	Structure	Dimensions	Descr.	Stories	Lights / Windows	Area	Area	Value
McCormick, Robert		Hawthorn, James	house	20 x 19	old & decayed					10.00
			barn	20 x 16	log, old				100 A 29 P	1112.00
	B79 E79		note: rate $9.20 [$921.66]							
McCoy, Archibald		Newville	house & lot	26 x 24	stone, new, unfinished, roof on				40 P	200.00
	B58 E58									
McCoy, James		Newville	house	18 x 17	log	1	2	12		50.00
	B57 E57								40 P	70.00
McCracken, William		on Big Spring / Brown, James	house & lot	43 x 18	stone & wood	1	6	87	2 A	500.00
			kitchen	20 x 16	stone	2	6	21		
			barn	50 x 18	small logs				152 A 40 P	3197.25
			grist mill							2000.00
			saw mill							100.00
	A67 B84 D67 E84		note: rate $21.00							
McCulloch, James		Jamison, John, Rev.	house 1 & lot	20 x 18	log	1 1/2	2	15	2 A	160.00
			kitchen	24 x 18	log	1 1/2	1	4		
			cabin	16 x 14						
			barn	50 x 23	log				309 A	3862.50
			house 2	21 x 18	log					50.00
	A64 B78 D64 E78		note: Mikesell, Andrew, occupant of house 2; rate $12.50							
McCune, Hugh		McCune, Samuel	house & lot	21 x 21	log	1 1/2	3	16	2 A	102.00
			barn	32 x 16	log				96 A	1036.00
	A68 B85 D68 E85		note: rate $11.00 [$1056.00]							
McCune, John		Sterrett, James	house & lot	20 x 18	log	1 1/2			2 A	135.00
			barn	20 x 20	log, new				106 A	1245.50
	A62 B75 D62 E76		note: rate $11.75							
McCune, Mary		Kilgore, Jesse	house & lot	29 x 24	log	2	4	38	2 A	180.00
			stable	18 x 18	log, old					
			barn	60 x 20	log				328 A	3936.00
	A61 B74 D61 E74		note: rate $10.65 [$3493.20]							
McCune, Mary / Peetry, George		Aikman, John	house	23 x 21	log, old					25.00
			barn	40 x 20	log, old				128 A	901.00
	B75 E75		note: rate $6.35 [$812.80]							
McCune, Samuel		McCune, John	house & lot	25 x 23	log	1 1/2	4	41	2 A	200.00
			barn	50 x 20	log				106 A	1256.10
	A63 B77 D63 E77		note: rate $11.85							
McElroy, John		Ross, Simon	house & lot	28 x 26	log	2	10	132	2 A	460.00
			barn	60 x 20	log				276 A 58 P	3233.43
	A65 B81 D65 E81		note: rate $11.70							

Newton Township

Owner / Occupant	Ref.	Location / Adjoining Owner	Structure	Size	Descr.	Stories	Windows Lights	Area	Value
McFarlane, William		McKibben, Jeremiah	house & lot	22 x 19	log	1 1/2	8 80	2 A	460.00
			wing	19 x 14	log	1	3 12		
			kitchen	14 x 12	log	1			
			smoke house	14 x 10	stone				
			barn	80 x 30	stone			345 A	6210.00
			dairy	18 x 12	stone				
			grist mill		log				
			fulling mill		log				
			sawmill						
	A51 B63 D51 E63		note: rate $18.00						
McFarlane, William		on Big Spring Carson, John & McGuffin, Joseph, heirs	tract					73 A	876.00
	B66 E66		note: rate $12.00						
McFarlane, William		Newville Weaver, John	lot					40 P	16.00
	B64 E64								
McFarlane, William		road from Mount Rock by Newville to McCallister Gap McKibben & Sharp, Alexander	cabin 1						
			cabin 2						20.00
			barn	42 x 20	log			196 A	2694.80
	B65 E65		note: Carter, Samuel, occupant of cabin 1; Dumon, Christy of cabin 2 rate $13.80						
McFarlane, William Crawford, James	A53 D53		house & lot	20 x 17	log	1	1 12	2 A	102.00
McFarlane, William Davis, Francis	A52 D52		house & lot	26 x 22	log	2	3 30	2 A	200.00
McGuffin, James		on Conodoguinet Cr. Speck, Barnhart	house & lot	21 x 18	log	1 1/2	4 32	2 A	280.00
			kitchen	24 x 21	log	1	1 12		
			barn	64 x 20	log, new, unfinished			157 A	1020.50
			still house	22 x 20	log				
	A55 B68 D55 E68		note: rate $6.50						
McGuffin, Joseph, heirs McMullen, Robert		on Big Spring McFarland, William	house	20 x 18	log				50.00
			cabin						10.00
								73 A	753.56
	B82 E82		note: rate $10.32						

Newton Township

Owner Occupant	Ref.	Location Adjoining Owner	Structure	Size	Descr.	Stories	Lights Windows		Area	Value
McKain, William	B60 E60	Newville Lusk, Robert	lot						32 P	16.00
McKeehan, George	B59 E59	Newville Over, David	lot						40 P	30.00
McKibben, Jeremiah		on Big Spring McFarlane, William & lots in Newville	house & lot	30 x 28	stone	2	14	190	40 P	1200.00
			addition	14 x 18	log	1	1	12		
			kitchen	17 x 12	log	1 1/2	2	6		
			smoke house	12 x 12	stone					
			store house	22 x 17	log	2	4	12		
			barn	60 x 23	log				134 A	2010.00
	A57 B69 D57 E69		note: rate $15.00							
McKibben, Jeremiah			house & lot	21 x 17	log	2	4	45	2 A	220.00
			wing	25 x 20	log	1	2	12		
	A58 D58		kitchen	14 x 10	log	1				
McMeekin, William			house & lot	19 x 19	log	2	7	76	40 P	180.00
	A46 D46		kitchen	16 x 14	log	1				
McMonagle, William			house & lot	24 x 22	log	2	7	63	40 P	150.00
	A47 D47		stable	10 x 10	log					
McMonagle, William	B86 E86	Newville	house	13 x 13	log	1	1	6	60 P	40.00 50.00
Micky, David		on Green Spring Micky, James & Scrogs, James	house & lot	30 x 21	log	2	4	42	2 A	400.00
			spring house	12 x 12	log					
			barn	60 x 26	log				141 A	1804.80
	A56 B71 D56 E71		note: rate $12.80							
Micky, James		on Green Spring Scrogs, James	house & lot	26 x 22	log	2	2	24	2 A	210.00
			kitchen	24 x 12	log	1				
			barn	64 x 26	log				141 A	1804.80
			cabin	18 x 18						10.00
	A59 B72 D59 E72		note: rate $12.80							
Micky, Robert		Vanderbelt, Cornelius	house 1 & lot	30 x 27	stone	2	11	147	2 A	500.00
			house 2	33 x 28	stone, new, unfinished					
			barn	52 x 20	log, old				298 A	5066.00
	A60 B73 D60 E73		note: rate $17.00							
Miller, George		Duck, William	house & lot	24 x 20	log				2 A	150.00
			barn	? x 16	log				43 A 80 P	538.90
	A66 B83 D66 E83		note: rate $12.37; text reads barn 3 x 16							

Newton Township

Owner Occupant	Ref.	Location Adjoining Owner	Structure	Size	Descr.	Stories	Lights Windows	Area	Value
Mitchell, Samuel Hays, John	A49 D49		house & lot stable 1 stable 2	23 x 21 12 x 12 12 x 12	log log log	2	9	90	40 P	300.00
Montgomery, James	A50 D50		house & lot	24 x 23	log	2	7	69	40 P	150.00
Morrow, John	A54 B67 D54 E67	Lightcap, Solomon	house & lot spring house stable note: rate $9.00	24 x 22 10 x 10 14 x 10	log log log	1 1/2	3	24	2 A 205 A	120.00 1845.00
Nettle, Henry	A69 D69		house & lot kitchen stable shop coal house	19 x 18 18 x 18 12 x 12 28 x 20	log log log stone frame	2 1	7 2	72 8	40 P	400.00
Norton, Thomas Neil, Lawrence	A70 D70		house & lot	28 x 22	stone	2	13	145	40 P	200.00
owner not known Butler, James	A4 D4		house & lot	16 x 19	log	2	5	57	40 P	115.00
Over, David	A71 D71		house & lot kitchen	26 x 24 12 x 12	log stone	2 1	7	84	40 P	250.00
Patterson, James	A75 B91 D75 E91	road Carlisle to Shippensburg via Walnut Bottom Byerly, Andrew	house & lot spring house barn note: rate $12.25	29 x 28 16 x 16 50 x 21	stone stone log	2 2	8 1	96 12	2 A 227 A	800.00 2780.75
Patterson, James Fulton, William	A76 D76		house & lot	18 x 18	stone & log	1 1/2	1	4	2 A	101.00
Peck, George	A73 B88 D73 E88	Sharp, Alexander	house & lot barn note: rate $12.25	23 x 20	log old, nearly gone to wreck	1 1/2	2	12	2 A 157 A 120 P	190.00 1932.43
Peck, Philip	A72 D72		house & lot kitchen stable	30 x 20 15 x 14 29 x 20	stone stone stone	2 1	5 1	27 12	40 P	630.00
Peck, Philip	B94 E94	out lot near Newville	lot note: rate $23.00						3 A 25 P	72.58

Newton Township

Owner Occupant	Ref.	Location Adjoining Owner	Structure	Size	Descr.	Stories	Lights Windows	Area	Value
Peck, Philip	B95 E95	Newville Montgomery, James	lot		unimproved			40 P	20.00
Peebles, John F. Irvin, James	A77 B93 D77 E93	State Road seven miles below Shippensburg Brown, James	house 1 & lot addition kitchen barn joiner shop house 2 note: rate $9.25	30 x 21 19 x 12 24 x 20 16 x 14	stone log log old, gone to wreck log, little value log, old	2 1 1	6 99 2 18	2 A 200 A	800.00 1850.00 40.00
Peebles, Robert	A74 B90 D74 E90	head of Big Spring McCracken, William	house & lot kitchen stable shop bark house tan yard	26 x 18 16 x 16 25 x 20 24 x 20 30 x 20	log log log log frame, without board 18 vats	2 2	9 120 1 12	2 A 2 A 40 P	450.00 260.00
Peebles, Robert	B89 E89	on State Road Duncan, Thomas, Esq.	tract note: rate $10.50		unimproved			125 A	1312.50
Piper, Samuel	A78 B92 D78 E92	on Big Spring McCracken, William	house 1 & lot house 2 grist mill still house note: rate $17.50; cellar under half of house	30 x 15 30 x 21 20 x 18	log stone, unfinished, roof on half interest log	1	2 21	2 A 277 A	180.00 500.00 4847.50
Quigley, John Ryan, Timothy	B96 E96	on State Road Beatty, James	cabin note: rate $12.10		old			100 A 40 P	8.00 1213.20
Rheem, Abram	A83 B98 D83 E98	Scroggs, James & Peck, George	house & lot kitchen barn note: rate $13.40	20 x 18 18 x 10 42 x 18	log log log	1 1	3 27	2 A 48 A	120.00 643.20
Rhine, Stephen	A80 B97 D80 E97	Newville Clark, Thomas	house & lot kitchen stable store house lot	20 x 18 16 x 12 23 x 18 20 x 15	log log log log	2 1 1	4 54 1 1 2 15	40 P 40 P	400.00 16.00
Rhodes, Jacob	A85 B99 D85 E99	McCulloch, James	house & lot stable barn note: barn first story stone, other wood; rate $12.75	27 x 21 60 x 23	log, old stone	2 1	3 30	2 A 202 A 24 P	110.00 2577.40

Newton Township

Owner Occupant	Ref.	Location Adjoining Owner	Structure	Size	Descr.	Stories	Windows	Lights	Area	Value
Rightmire, Lewis		on Big Spring McCracken, William	house & lot barn smith shop cabin	22 x 18 32 x 20 20 x 14 16 x 14	log log log	1 1/2	2	10	2 A 83 A 127 P	115.00 754.14 8.00
	A86 B100 D86 E100		note: rate $9.00							
Rippey, William		in North Mountain Kline, George	tract		unimproved				524 A	262.00
	B102 E102									
Roberts, John King, Nicholas			house & lot	22 x18	stone & log	2	4	35	80 P	160.00
	A84 D84									
Robinson, Andrew Shoop, Christian			house & lot stable	22 x 20 18 x 15	log log	2	6	63	40 P	250.00
	A81 D81									
Ross, James			house & lot stable	20 x 17 16 x 16	stone log	2	5	56	40 P	150.00
	A82 D82									
Ross, Simon		McElroy, John	house & lot kitchen barn	21 x 14 14 x 14 24 x 20	log log, old log	2	4	30	2 A 257 A	102.00 2865.55
	A79 B101 D79 E101		note: rate $11.15							
Scrogs, Alexander Young, John		Piper, Samuel	house & lot stable	22 x 18	stone & log old	2	2	17	2 A 6 A	240.00 69.96 10.00
	A94 B116 D94 E116		note: a small lot which he sold to Bower, Daniel, & which he again purchased; rate $11.66							
Scrogs, Alexander, heirs		on Green Spring Thompson, Alexander	house & lot barn	40 x 20 50 x 20	log log	1 1/2	4	24	2 A 168 A	250.00 2318.40
	A88 B103 D88 E103		note: rate $13.81							
Scrogs, Alexander, heirs			house & lot	24 x 22	log	2	4	48	40 P	250.00
	A89 D89									
Scrogs, James		on Green Spring Kilgore, William	house & lot wing spring house store house barn	28 x 17 12 x 17 12 x 8 18 x 14 60 x 21	log log log log log	1 1/2 1	3 2	21 13	2 A 180 A	200.00 3024.00
	A93 B104 D93 E104		note: rate $16.80							
Scrogs, James		Newville Lamond, James	lot		unimproved				40 P	14.00
	B105 E105									

Newton Township

Owner / Occupant	Ref.	Location / Adjoining Owner	Structure	Size	Descr.	Stories	Lights / Windows		Area	Value
Scrogs, James	B106 E106	Newville / Houser, John	lot		unimproved				40 P	25.00
Sharp, Alexander		Thompson, William	house & lot	26 x 20	stone	2	7	93	2 A	600.00
			addition	15 x 10	log					
			kitchen	20 x 17	log	1	2	6		
			barn	60 x 30	stone				196 A	3136.00
			still house	24 x 22	log, new					
	A90 B107 D90 E107		note: rate $16.00							
Sharp, Alexander	B110 E110	on Conodoguinet Cr. / Micky, David	tract		mostly good meadow land				18 A	306.00
			note: rate $17.00							
Sharp, Alexander / Fields, John		Thompson, William & other Sharp property	house & lot	24 x 22	log	2	3	32	2 A	200.00
									198 A	2755.00
	A91 B108 D91 E108		note: rate $14.50 [$2871.00]							
Sharp, Alexander / McCreary, James		Carson, John & other Sharp property	house & lot	24 x 22	log	2	6	63	40 P	300.00
			kitchen	10 x 10	log				150 A	1800.00
			stable	10 x 12	log					
	A92 B109 D92 E109		note: rate $12.00							
Sharp, Robert		on Conodoguinet Cr. / McGuffin, James	house & lot	18 x 18	log, old	1	2	5	2 A	140.00
			wing	16 x 10	log	1	1	12		
			spring house	17 x 17	stone & log					
			barn	55 x 28	log				200 A	2120.00
			still house	18 x 18	log					
	A95 B117 D95 E117		note: rate $10.60							
Sharp, Robert		on Conodoguinet Cr. / Hunter, Joseph & other Sharp, Robert, property	tract						165 A	2227.50
	B118 E118		note: rate $13.50							
Sharp, Robert / Orr, Widow	A96 D96		house & lot	24 x 24	log	2	3	36	2 A	200.00
Smith, John		Peebles, John	cabin	16 x 12						7.00
	B115 E115		note: rate $8.07						101 A 108 P	820.50

Newton Township

Owner Occupant	Ref.	Location Adjoining Owner	Structure	Size	Descr.	Stories	Windows	Lights	Area	Value
Speck, Bernard		on Conodoguinet Cr. Cooper, John	house & lot spring house barn grist mill saw mill	30 x 20 12 x 12 60 x 21	log stone log	1	6	48	2 A 85 A	200.00 2629.50 2200.00 100.00
	A97 B119 D97 E119		note: rate $42.70 [$3629.50]							
Sterrett, James		McCune, Samuel	house & lot kitchen barn	25 x 25 18 x 10 60 x 20	log log log	2 1 1/2	4 2	38 18	2 A 93 A	250.00 1506.60
	A98 B111 D98 E111		note: rate $16.20							
Sterrett, James		Sterrett, Thomas	tract						116 A	1160.00
	B112 E112		note: rate $10.00							
Sterrett, Thomas		Sterrett, James	house & lot wing barn	25 x 21 23 x 13 60 x 20	log log log, old	1 1/2 1	6 3	46 14	2 A 171 A	200.00 2565.00
	A87 B113 D88 E113		note: rate $15.00							
Sterrett, Thomas		Sterrett, James	tract						121 A	1270.50
	B114 E114		note: rate $10.50							
Thomson, Alexander		on Green Spring Scrogs, Alexander & Davidson, Jacob	house & lot wing barn smith shop still house	30 x 21 30 x 13 70 x 20 25 x 14 25 x 20	log stone log log stone	2 1	9 3	96 12	2 A 328 A	400.00 4592.00 50.00
	A101 B121 D101 E121		note: rate $14.00							
Thomson, Ann		Millford Buchanan, Thomas	house & lot	36 x 20	log				 47 P	25.00 30.00
	B125 E125		note: on Thomas Buchanan's land.							
Thomson, Matthew Martin, Thomas			house & lot kitchen stable stable or shop	34 x 22 12 x 10 12 x 14 12 x 30	log stone log frame	2 1	12 1	158 12	40 P	800.00
	A99 D99									
Thomson, Matthew		out lot near Newville	lot						1 A 148 P	49.40
	B126 E126		note: rate $26.00							
Thomson, Samuel		Newville, Main St. Dunbar, John Kibben farm	lot 1 lot 2						40 P 4 A 30 P	8.00 125.62
	B120 E120		note: lot 2 is an out lot near Newville; rate $30.00 (on out lot)							

Newton Township

Owner Occupant	Ref.	Location Adjoining Owner	Structure	Size	Descr.	Stories	Lights Windows		Area	Value
Thomson, Samuel	A100 D100		house & lot	24 x 18	log	2	8	78	40 P	150.00
Thomson, William		Sharp, Alexander	house & lot	32 x 28	stone	2	8	111	2 A	600.00
			kitchen	18 x 16	stone	1	1	12		
	A102 B122 D102 E122		barn note: rate $14.40	60 x 20	log				163 A	2347.20
Thrush, Barney		McCollum, John	house & lot	20 x 17	log	1 1/2	1	9	2 A	120.00
	A103 B123 D103 E123		smith shop note: rate $15.50						5 A 54 P	82.71
Thrush, Leonard		on State Road McCollum, John	house		old & decayed					10.00
	B124 E124		barn note: rate $12.10	60 x 22	log				97 A	1173.70
Vanderbelt, Cornelius		Micky, Robert	house & lot	24 x 23	log	2	2	12	2 A	200.00
			barn	50 x 20	log, old				270 A	3307.50
	A104 B127 D104 E127		cabin note: rate $12.25	12 x 16	log, old					8.00
Vanderbelt, Jacob		on Big Spring McCracken, William	house & lot	20 x 18	log	1	2	8	2 A	102.00
			stable	20 x 16	log					
	A105 B128 D105 E128		barn note: rate $8.60	42 x 20	log				97 A 25 P	835.53
Waggoner, Philip	B135 E135	Newville McAvoy, John	lot						40 P	10.00
Walker, John		on Conodoguinet Cr. Esrig, Simon	house & lot	26 x 24	log	1 1/2	2	13	2 A	160.00
			spring house	14 x 12	log					
			stable	18 x 14	log					
	A114 B146 D114 E146		barn note: rate $12.64	52 x 18	log				93 A	1175.52
Walker, Joseph, heirs Shannon, Leonard		on Conodoguinet Cr. Walker, William	house	28 x 18	log, wreck					33.00
			cabin	18 x 16						
	B143 E143		barn note: combined value of house & cabin is $33	56 x 24	log				147 A	1587.60

Newton Township

Owner / Occupant	Location Ref.	Adjoining Owner	Structure	Size	Descr.	Stories	Windows	Lights	Area	Value
Walker, William	on Conodoguinet Cr.	Hunter, Joseph	house & lot	19 x 19	log	1 1/2	2	13	2 A	266.00
			kitchen	23 x 19	log	1 1/2				
			barn	60 x 20	log				178 A	2136.00
			still house	18 x 16	log					
			cabin	20 x 18						20.00
	A111 B142 D111 E142		note: rate $12.00							
Wallace, Hugh	out lot near Newville	McKibben's farm	house & lot	20 x 18	log	1 1/2	3	22	40 P	115.00
			stable	18 x 12	log				3 A 33 P	75.70
	A115 B145 D115 E145		note: rate $22.00 [$70.54]							
Watts, David, Esq. / Buchanan, Thomas		Buchanan, Thomas, sawmill tract of	house & lot	32 x 22	log	2	4	48	2 A	150.00
			cabin	18 x 16	log					12.00
									256 A	2321.92
	A109 B140 D109 E140		note: rate $9.07							
Weaver, John	Newville	Dunbar, John	lot						40 P	16.00
	B134 E134									
Weir, George, heirs / Weir, Margaret		Kilgore, Jesse	house 1 & lot	22 x 21	log	1 1/2	3	22	2 A	300.00
			kitchen	22 x 21	log	1	1	9		
			barn	50 x 20					180 A	1710.00
			house 2		log, old, unoccupied, out of repair					50.00
	A108 B139 D108 E139		note: rate $8.50; [$1530.00]							
Wilson, Samuel, Rev. / Trotter, Richard			house & lot	21 x 20	log	1 1/2			40 P	120.00
			stable	20 x 20	log, old					
	A112 D112									
Wilson, Samuel, Rev.	out lot near Newville		house & lot	26 x 25	log	2	9	114	2 A	400.00
			kitchen	18 x 16	log	1	1	8	8 A	176.00
	A113 B144 D113 E144		note: rate $22.00							
Wilson, William	on Conodoguinet Cr.	Carnahan, Adam, heirs	house & lot	39 x 20	log	1	3	18	2 A	200.00
			barn	53 x 20	log				65 A 80 P	712.50
	A107 B138 D107 E138		note: rate $12.50 [$818.75]							
Wilson, William		Cooper, John	house	20 x 17	log, clapboard roof					55.00
									53 P	60.00
	B137 E137									
Wolf, Sophia	Newville	Rhine, Stephen	house	16 x 12	log				40 P	50.00
			stable	12 x 12	log					
	B129 E129									

Newton Township

Owner / Occupant	Ref.	Location / Adjoining Owner	Structure	Size	Descr.	Stories	Lights	Windows	Area	Value
Woodburn, James			house 1 & lot	33 x 20	log	2	9	96	80 P	400.00
		Clark, Robert	wing	16 x 14	log	1	2	12		
			kitchen	12 x 12	log	1				
			stable	18 x 12	log				124 A	1414.00
			house 2	18 x 18	log	1 1/2				50.00
	A106 B133 D106 E133		note: rate $12.00; [$1488.00]							
Woodburn, James		out lot near Newville	lot						7 A 78 P	201.97
		Geddes, John, Dr.	note: rate $27.00							
	B132 E132									
Woodburn, James		Newville	stable	22 x 24	log				40 P	160.00
		Clark, Thomas								
	B130 E130									
Woodburn, James		out lot near Newville	lot						3 A 71 P	92.96
		Davidson, John								
	B131 E131		note: rate $27.00							
Woodburn, Matthew			house & lot	22 x 20	log, old	2	3	16	2 A	102.00
		Patterson, James	barn	52 x 20	log				239 A	2031.50
			cabin	18 x 16						6.00
	A110 B141 D110 E141		note: rate $8.50							
Work, James heirs			house	22 x 22	log					50.00
Steel, John		McGuffin, James	stable	18 x 18	log, old				138 A	877.68
	B136 E136		note: rate $6.36							

Southampton Township

CHAPTER X   SOUTHAMPTON TOWNSHIP

Owner / Occupant	Location / Adjoining Owner	Structure	Dimensions	Descr.	Stories	Windows / Lights	Area	Value
Achison, Thomas D11		house & lot	16 x 16	wood	1	2 13	61 P	110.00
Addams, Matthew D7		house & lot kitchen stable	22 x 24 12 x 18 18 x 18	wood	1	3 36	30.5 P	250.00
Addams, Matthew Faughner, John D8		house & lot	18 x 18	wood	1	2 8	61 P	120.00
Admiston, Elizabeth D10		house & lot	22 x 18	stone	1	2 18	61 P	120.00
Aikey, Alexander D9		house & lot stable	26 x 16 12 x 12	wood wood	1	2 24	61 P	150.00
Aitken, Robert unoccupied B4 E4	South Mountain Nicholson, Jane & Nicholson, Sarah	tract					437 A 53 P	131.20
Aitkin, Robert, Jr. unoccupied B5 E5	South Mountain Aitkin, Robert & VanHolt, Valentine	tract					436 A 109 P	131.00
Albright, Henry D3		house & lot stable	23 x 26 16 x 20	wood wood			30.5 P	350.00
Alexander, Emy D12 E2	State Road Duncan, Daniel, heirs & McCune, Robert	house & lot	20 x 18	wood	1		1 A 79 A	120.00 948.00
Anderson, Seth Peel, Jacob B1 D1 E1	Shippensburg, King Street Beamer, John	house & lot barn hatter shop	17 x 17 50 x 17 18 x 18	wood wood log	2	3 36	61 P 30.5 P	550.00 80.00
Anthony, Avis unoccupied B6 E6	South Mountain Clippinger, Anthony & Krehl, Nicholas						437 A 11 P	131.12
Atherton, Thomas D2		house & lot kitchen	30 x 24 16 x 12	wood wood	2	9 105	122 P	320.00

163

Southampton Township

Owner / Occupant	Ref.	Location / Adjoining Owner	Structure	Size	Descr.	Stories	Windows	Lights	Area	Value
Auld, David		Hiland, William & Hunter, William	house & lot barn	25 x 22 40 x 20	wood log	1	6	63	1 A 149 A	140.00 954.00
	B3 D6 E3									
Auld, David Claudy, Martin	D4		house & lot	40 x 16	wood	1	3	36	61 P	120.00
Auld, David Spielman, John	D5		house & lot	30 x 16	wood	1	3	36	61 P	140.00
Baird, William		King St. Fleming, Archibald	house & lot stable storehouse wagonmaker shop smith shop	34 x 24 18 x 13 28 x 18 20 x 24 28 x 19	wood wood log wood	2	9	108	61 P 30.5 P	600.00 80.00
	B7 D13 E7									
Barr, William		King St. Heap, John, Esq. & Albright, Henry	barn storehouse	64 x 20 28 x 18	log				61 P	200.00
	B8 E8									
Barr, William		King St. McKnight, D. & Plunket's heirs	house & lot kitchen store	29 x 34 24 x 16 32 x 20	stone stone wood	2	7	168	61 P 30.5 P	1200.00 40.00
	B9 D23 E9									
Barr, William		on Bird's Run Shipen, E. & J. & Culbertson, Robert	tract						56 A	1120.00
	B10 E10									
Barr, William		York Co. Road Lowrey, James, Esq.	tract						145 A	2900.00
	B11 E11									
Barr, William Brown, Kennedy	D24		house & lot kitchen	30 x 26 16 x 16	stone wood	1	4	60	61 P	450.00
Barr, William Trexlo, Peter		Southampton Mahan, David & Duncan, Stephen, heirs	house barn	18 x 18 18 x 18	log log				 200 A	40.00 3250.00
	B13 E13									

Southampton Township

Owner / Occupant	Location / Adjoining Owner	Structure	Dimensions	Descr.	Stories	Lights Windows	Area	Value
Barr, William Weiser, Christy B12 D25 E12	Southampton Duncan, Daniel, heirs & Clark, John	house & lot	28 x 24	wood	1	3	30	1 A 196 A	200.00 2382.00
Baughman, Philip B17 E17	Pines Hunter, William & Norton, Thomas	house barn	20 x 18 30 x 16	log log				120 A	90.00 490.00
Bell, William D17		house & lot kitchen stable store potash house	22 x 18 12 x 14 12 x 14 25 x 18 28 x 34	wood & brick wood wood wood wood	1 1/2	6	72	61 P	800.00
Bell, William Sr. Elliott, Widow D18		house & lot stable	24 x 30 20 x 14	wood wood	2	8	105	61 P	550.00
Bell, William Sr. Smith, John D19		house & lot	22 x 20	wood	1	2	24	61 P	140.00
Beyman, John D14		house kitchen stable	20 x 20 15 x 15 15 x 15	wood wood wood	2	7	90	30.5 P	500.00
Bidleman, Abraham D21		house & lot stable	33 x 20 16 x 20	wood wood	1	3	26	61 P	450.00
Blackburn, Samuel D16		house & lot kitchen stable hatter shop	24 x 26 14 x 14 14 x 15 16 x 18	wood wood wood wood	2	7	93	61 P	800.00
Blythe, Benjamin, Jr. B20 E20	South Mountain Blythe, Benjamin, Sr. & Clippinger, Anthony	tract						170 A	2024.00
Blythe, Benjamin, Sr. B19 D30 E19	South Mountain Culbertson, Joseph & Blythe Benjamin, Jr.	house & lot kitchen barn	40 x 35 16 x 13 80 x 37	stone stone stone	2	16	360	1 A 194 A 80 P	1000.00 4340.00

Southampton Township

Owner Occupant	Ref.	Location Adjoining Owner	Structure	Size	Descr.	Stories	Lights Windows		Area	Value
Boher, John	D15		house & lot	20 x 16	wood	1	2	15	30.5 P	160.00
Brittain, John	B16 D28 E16	Mahan, David & Culbertson, Robert	house & lot barn note: name also Britton	35 x 18 30 x 20	wood log	1	4	25	1 A 69 A	200.00 1065.00
Brookens, William	D20		house & lot stable	23 x 26 14 x 14	wood wood	2	8	114	61 P	420.00
Brookens & Wall Johnston, Alexander	B18 D29 E18	Pines McLean, John & McLean, Allen	house & lot powder mill	22 x 18 28 x 20	wood frame	1	3	27	1 A 3 A	120.00 98.00
Broomfield, John, heirs Kerr, Thomas	B15 D27 E15	Barrens Clark, Robert & Duncan, Stephen, heirs	house & lot kitchen barn	25 x 20 14 x 14 60 x 20	wood wood log	1	3	36	1 A 149 A	200.00 1530.00
Brymer, Frederick	D14		house & lot kitchen stable smith shop	16 x 20 12 x 15 16 x 16 16 x 20	wood wood wood wood	2	6	52	30.5 P	550.00
Burkholder, John	B14 D26 E14	Middle Spring Colwell, James & Longnecker, Michael	house & lot spring house barn	30 x 28 22 x 10 68 x 30	wood stone stone	2	14	168	1 A 139 A	400.00 3012.00
Burns, James	D22		house & lot	18 x 20	wood	1	3	14	61 P	120.00
Campbell, Ebenezer	B31 D34 E31	Middle Spring Campbell, Francis & Colwill, James	house & lot kitchen	22 x 22 20 x 14	wood stone	2	6	72	1 A 120 A	350.00 2160.00
Campbell, Francis	D33		house & lot kitchen stable	38 x 20 22 x 25 12 x 16	wood wood wood	1	11	100	61 P	500.00
Campbell, Francis Campbell, Ebenezer	B32 E32	Middle Spring Peebles, Robert & Campbell, Ebenezer	barn spring house	40 x 20 18 x 16	log log				120 A	2260.00

Southampton Township

Owner Occupant	Ref.	Location Adjoining Owner	Structure	Size	Descr.	Stories	Windows Lights		Area	Value
Campbell, John	D32		house & lot	38 x 20	wood	2	6	58	61 P	300.00
Cannon, Samuel	B28 D45 E28	Penn St.	house & lot kitchen stable	24 x 28 14 x 14 14 x 18	wood wood wood	2	9	108	61 P 61 P	500.00 40.00
Chesnut, Samuel	B39 D58 E39	Quigley, John & Duncan, Thomas	house & lot kitchen barn malt house	22 x 20 15 x 15 45 x 18 18 x 18	wood wood log log	1	2	24	1 A 299 A	200.00 3678.00
Cissna, James	B24 E24	King St. Simpson, John	lot						61 P	50.00
Cissna, James	B25 D38 E25	Southampton Tate, Samuel & McKnight, William	house & lot kitchen stable	22 x 24 16 x 16 18 x 20	wood wood wood	2	9	123	61 P 176 A	850.00 2112.00
Cissna, James Miller, Widow	D39		house & lot	18 x 20	wood	1	2	18	61 P	120.00
Clark, George	B37 E37	Barrens Clark, Robert & Brown, John, heirs	house barn	20 x 18 50 x 24	log & stone log				150 A	50.00 1600.00
Clark, John Graham, William	B38 D57 E38	Barrens Clark, George & McCollum, John	house & lot barn	26 x 22 50 x 24	wood log	1			1 A 149 A	140.00 1540.00
Clark, Robert	B35 D55 E35	Barrens Broomfield, John, heirs & Clark, George	house & lot [addition ?] barn house 2 kitchen	20 x 20 20 x 20 50 x 20 40 x 30 18 x 18	wood wood log stone, unfinished stone, unfinished	1 2	4	32	1 A 499 A	200.00 5630.00
Clark, Robert Sterrett, James	B36 D56 E36	Creamer, Peter & Simpson, John	house & lot barn	20 x 20 40 x 18	wood log	1	3	25	1 A 259 A	160.00 4702.00
Clever, Barnabas	B40 E40	Walter, Christopher & Cress, John	house barn	25 x 20 45 x 20	log log	1			200 A	20.00 460.00

Southampton Township

Owner Occupant	Ref.	Location Adjoining Owner	Structure	Size	Descr.	Stories	Lights Windows		Area	Value
Clippinger, Anthony			house 1 & lot	24 x 28		2	10	165	1 A	1000.00
		Blythe,	[addition ?]	20 x 26	stone					
		Benjamin, Jr.	barn	60 x 30	stone				799 A	5982.00
		& Clippinger	house 2	18 x 20						30.00
		Frederick	house 3	18 x 20						60.00
			saw mill							
	B46 D63 E46		note: Muterspaugh, Robert & Pickens, John, occupants of houses 2 & 3							
Clippinger, Frederick			house 1 & lot	22 x 22	wood	1	4	42	1 A	300.00
		Clippinger,	kitchen	22 x 15	wood					
		Anthony & Krehl,	barn	60 x 30	frame				748 A	7169.00
		Nicholas	saw mill							
			house 2	16 x 16	log					80.00
	B45 D61 E45		note: Cresler [?], George, occupant of house 2							
Clippinger, Frederick Fught, Matthias	D62		house & lot	22 x 18	wood	1	2	10	1 A	120.00
Clopper, Abraham	D36		house & lot	25 x 21	wood	1	3	28	30.5 P	300.00
Cochran, Patrick		Earl St.	house & lot	39 x 20	wood	1 1/2	11	90	61 P	1500.00
		Rahm, Jacob	[addition ?]	18 x 26	stone					
			kitchen	18 x 20	wood					
			stable 1	40 x 37	stone					
	B21 D35 E21		stable 2	18 x 18	wood					
Cochran, Patrick		Earl St. Kern, Jacob,	lot						61 P	40.00
	B22 E22									
Coffee, Robert King, George		Pines Coffee, Thomas & McLean, John	house tract	20 x 24	log	1			89 A 80 P	80.00 259.00
	B43 E43									
Coffee, Thomas		Pines Coffee, Robert & Cisna, James	house & lot	30 x 26	wood	1	4	28	1 A 88 A 80 P	180.00 265.50
	B44 D60 E44									
Coffman, John			house & lot	22 x 22	wood	2	6	84	61 P	450.00
			kitchen	12 x 12	wood					
			stable	18 x 16	wood					
	D40		smith shop	22 x 22	wood					

Southampton Township

Owner Occupant	Ref.	Location Adjoining Owner	Structure	Size	Descr.	Stories	Windows Lights	Area	Value
Colwell, James		Middle Spring Burkholder, John & Culbertson, Robert	house 1 & lot [addition ?] barn house 2	24 x 20 20 x 22 70 x 30 16 x 18	wood wood stone log	2 1	4 42	1 A 152 A	400.00 3276.00 40.00
	B47 D64 E47								
Colwell, John		Middle Spring Colwell, James & Campbell, Ebenezer	grist mill	40 x 42	stone			10 A	2180.00
	B48 E48								
Colwell, John		Barr, William & Mahan, David	tract					137 A	1644.00
	B49 E49								
Coney, Peter		Earl St. Shoemaker, John & Snyder, John	smith shop	20 x 20	log			61 P	80.00
	B23 E23								
Copely, William, heirs McBeth, James	D31		house & lot kitchen stable	24 x 26 10 x 18 14 x 18	wood wood wood	2	6 72	61 P	550.00
Copenhauer, Benjamin	D47		house & lot stable	21 x 21 15 x 15	wood wood	2	3 57	61 P	200.00
Corbet, Hannah	D43		house & lot kitchen	30 x 16 18 x 14	wood wood	1	2 27	61 P	180.00
Cowan, William		King St. Hickman, Widow	house 1 & lot stable barn house 2	23 x 24 15 x 18 27 x 18 27 x 18	stone wood log log, unfinished	1	3 36	61 P 61 P	450.00 250.00
	B29 D46 E29								
Cowan, William		Walnut Bottom Road Lowry, James & McCandless, George	tract					26 A	468.00
	B30 E30								
Cox, Samuel Henderson, David	D37		house & lot	22 x 20	wood	1	3 36	61 P	140.00
Coyler, Conrad		Pines Cress, John & Hippensteel, Joseph	still house saw mill	20 x 20	log			149 A	378.00
	B42 E42								

169

Southampton Township

Owner Occupant	Ref.	Location Adjoining Owner	Structure	Size	Descr.	Stories	Lights Windows		Area	Value
Coyler, Leonard unoccupied	B27 E27	King St. Thrush, Daniel	house	20 x 24	log, unfinished	2			61 P	90.00
Creamer, Peter	B34 D54 E34	Barrens Clark, Robert & Duncan, Stephen heirs	house & lot barn still house	26 x 24 60 x 22 20 x 18	wood log log	2	3	30	1 A 269 A	160.00 2930.00
Cress, John	B41 E41	Pines Clever, Barnabas & Coyler, Conrad	house tract	24 x 20	log	1			150 A	60.00 360.00
Croft, George	D44		house & lot [addition ?] stable	12 x 24 20 x 22 22 x 20	stone wood wood	2	5	62	61 P	600.00
Culbertson, Andrew	B26 D41 E26	Prince St. German School House lot	house & lot [addition ?] kitchen stable	18 x 18 39 x 18 15 x 20 30 x 18	wood wood wood wood	2 1	13	131	122 P	1000.00
Culbertson, Andrew Myers, Adam	D42		house & lot stable	30 x 20 12 x 15	wood wood	1	6	65	61 P	250.00
Culbertson, Joseph Culbertson, Joseph & Arbuckle, William	B33 D48 E33	Reynolds, John, heirs & Blythe, Benjamin, Sr.	house 1 & lot kitchen barn house 2	22 x 18 22 x 20 40 x 20 18 x 18	wood wood log log	2 1	2	24	1 A 199 A	300.00 4060.00 40.00
Culbertson, Robert	B50 D49 E50	Barr, William & Colwell, James	house & lot stable barn 1 barn 2 smith shop	44 x 34 15 x 14 96 x 34 50 x 16 20 x 20	stone log stone log log	2	15	240	1 A 495 A	1200.00 9464.00
Culbertson, Robert	B51 E51	Pines Kline, George & Clever, Barnabas	tract						50 A	100.00
Culbertson, Robert Campbell, Samuel	D52		house & lot	25 x 24	wood	1	2	24	1 A	200.00

Southampton Township

Owner / Occupant	Ref.	Location / Adjoining Owner	Structure	Size	Descr.	Stories	Windows	Lights	Area	Value
Culbertson, Robert Cowen, William	D53		house & lot	20 x 18	wood	1	2	18	1 A	120.00
Culbertson, Robert Irwin, Andrew	D51		house & lot	20 x 18	wood	1	1	12	1 A	110.00
Culbertson, Robert Parks, Joseph	D50		house & lot	22 x 22	stone	1	3	45	1 A	400.00
Dunbar, John	B52 E52	Tate, Samuel & Barr, William	tract						64 A	768.00
Duncan, Arnold	D65		house & lot kitchen stable 1 stable 2	40 x 45 40 x 18 20 x 22 20 x 22	stone stone wood wood	2	13	228	51 P	1600.00
Duncan, Daniel, heirs	B53 E53	King and Washington Streets	barn	22 x 20	log				30.5 P	60.00
Duncan, Daniel, heirs	B54 E54	King and Washington Streets	lot						30.5 P	40.00
Duncan, Daniel, heirs McKinney, Patrick	B56 E56	near Walnut Bottom Road Maxwell, William & McElroy, John	house barn	12 x 14 40 x 20	log log				400 A	10.00 2830.00
Duncan, Daniel, heirs Peoples, John	D69		house & lot kitchen stable	26 x 28 19 x 15 20 x 18	stone stone wood	2	10	198	61 P	800.00
Duncan, Daniel, heirs Smith, William	B55 D70 E55	State Road Rippey, Samuel & Alexander, Emy	house & lot barn	24 x 22 50 x 20	wood log	2	8	93	1 A 229 A	300.00 3286.00

Southampton Township

Owner	Location		Structure	Size	Descr.	Stories	Lights Windows	Area	Value
Occupant	Ref.	Adjoining Owner							
Duncan, David			house 1 & lot	25 x 18	wood	2	5 60	1 A	300.00
		Foglesanger,	kitchen	16 x 16	wood				
		David & Duncan,	barn	70 x 16	log			169 A	2784.00
		Stephen, heirs	house 2	16 x 18	log				50.00
	B58 D72 E58		note: Claudy, Martin occupant of house 2						
Duncan, Joseph			house & lot	33 x 35	brick	2		107 P	800.00
	D66		kitchen	34 x 17	brick				
Duncan, Joseph			house & lot	16 x 16	wood	1	2 18	61 P	160.00
Green, Christy			smith shop	18 x 25	wood				
	D67								
Duncan, Joseph			house & lot	22 x 22	wood	1	4 42	30.5 P	160.00
Keller, Jacob									
	D68								
Duncan, Stephen, heirs			house	20 x 18	log				40.00
Dine, John			barn	45 x 16	log				
	B57b E57b		note: on 1500 acre tract with four others; E gives barn as 24 x 20						
Duncan, Stephen, heirs			house	24 x 20	log				80.00
Fry, Peter			barn	20 x 18	log				
	B57c E57c		note: on 1500 acre tract with four others						
Duncan, Stephen, heirs			house	18 x 22	log				50.00
McCaunahy, James			barn	50 x 18	log				
	B57d E57d		note: on 1500 acre tract with four others						
Duncan, Stephen, heirs		Barrens	house	18 x 16	log				50.00
		Bass, William &							
Long, Henry		Duncan, David	note: on 1500 acre tract with four others						
	B57e E57e								
Duncan, Stephen, heirs			house & lot	30 x 18	wood	2	8 51	1 A	300.00
Swanger, Christian			barn	50 x 20	frame			1500 A	15,500.00
			note: D gives Swanger, Jacob as occupant [Five persons are listed as						
	B57a D71 E57a		being occupants on this tract, each with a separate house.]						
Duncan, Thomas			house	15 x 18	log				50.00
Wright, John		Chesnut, Samuel	barn	20 x 25	log			300 A	4560.00
		& Peoples, Robert							
	B59 E59								
Elnode, Peter			house & lot	17 x 26	wood	1	5 60	61 P	300.00
	D75		shop	30 x 17	wood				

Southampton Township

Owner Occupant	Ref.	Location Adjoining Owner	Structure	Size	Descr.	Stories	Windows	Lights	Area	Value
Ely, Andrew		Leiper, William & McKnight, William	house & lot barn	40 x 18 30 x 25	wood log	1	2	18	1 A 163 A	140.00 1344.00
	B60 D74 E60									
Ely, George heirs Heck, John			house & lot kitchen barn	35 x 30 18 x 20 40 x 16	wood wood wood	2	8	120	61 P	1000.00
	D73									
Farmer, Lewis		mountain Nicholson, Samuel & Aitkin, Robert	tract						438 A 105 P	131.60
	B64 E64									
Findley, James			house & lot kitchen smoke house stable	22 x 26 12 x 12 9 x 9 34 x 28	brick brick stone wood	1	4	60	61 P	500.00
	D76									
Fleming, Archibald			house & lot [addition ?]	24 x 18 10 x 15	wood & stone wood & stone	1	3	30	30.5 P	160.00
	D77									
Foglesonger, David		Cunningham, Adam & Duncan, David	house still house barn	20 x 20 40 x 20 55 x 25	log log log				125 A	60.00 1560.00
	B62 E62									
Foglesonger, Michael Foglesonger, John		Duncan, David & Colwell, James	house 1 stable house 2	18 x 20 18 x 16 15 x 18	log log log				200 A	60.00 2550.00 80.00
	B63 E63		note: Unger, Peter, occupant of house 2							
Fry, Jacob		Shippensburg, on road to McAllister's gap	house	15 x 15	log				61 P	60.00
	B61 E61									
Gladstone, William		Penn St.	house 1 & lot stable house 2	18 x 18 18 x 18 24 x 24	wood wood log unfinished	1 2	4	27	61 P 61 P	180.00 100.00
	B65 D78 E65		note: value varies; may not be a single property; name also Gladson							
Glen, Moses heirs Glen, Widow		State Road McCollum, John	house 1 house 2 tract	16 x 16 16 x 18	log log				100 A	30.00 30.00 1260.00
	B66 E66		note: Thrush, David, occupant of house 2							

Southampton Township

Owner / Occupant	Ref.	Location / Adjoining Owner	Structure	Dimensions	Descr.	Stories	Lights Windows	Area	Value
Griffen, Josiah			house & lot	28 x 28	wood	2	5	57	61 P	200.00
			kitchen	16 x 16	wood					
	D79		stable	20 x 18	wood					
Hamil, Robert			house & lot	34 x 32	wood	2	5	87	122 P	450.00
			kitchen	16 x 16	wood					
	D87		stable	30 x 30	wood					
Hamilton, James		Queen St.	house & lot	25 x 25	stone	2	10	207	122 P	800.00
McCandless, George		Wingler, Jacob	kitchen	15 x 15	stone					
	B70 D88 E70		stable	20 x 20	wood					
Haney, John			house	16 x 16	wood	1	2	18	30.5 P	150.00
	D85									
Heap, John			house & lot	30 x 26	stone	2	9	216	140 P	1600.00
			kitchen	14 x 14	stone					
	D81		store	30 x 28	wood					
Heap, John			house & lot	22 x 24	brick	1	6	94	61 P	400.00
Kutesner, Michael			stable	16 x 16	wood					
	D82									
Heckman, Widow			house & lot	18 x 16	wood	1	3	36	61 P	140.00
	D89									
Helms, Jacob		Pines	house	24 x 18	log					60.00
		McCollum, John &	barn	40 x 18	log				50 A	180.00
		Lamberton, James								
	B74 E74									
Henderson, Margaret			house & lot	30 x 28	wood	2	10	135	122 P	460.00
		Shipping, E. & J.	kitchen	18 x 15	wood					
		& Barr, William	barn	24 x 18	log				22 A	456.00
	B67 D86 E67									
Henderson, Margaret		York Co. Road	tract						12 A	168.00
		Reynolds, John &								
		Culbertson, Joseph,								
		heirs								
	B68 E68									
Henderson, Margaret			tract						9 A 40 P	166.50
		Barr, William &								
		Shippen, E. & J.								
	B69 E69									

Southampton Township

Owner Occupant	Ref.	Location Adjoining Owner	Structure	Dimensions	Descr.	Stories	Windows	Lights	Area	Value
Highlands, John		Pines Coyler, Conrad & Highlands, William	house 1 barn saw mill house 2	20 x 24 18 x 17 16 x 16	log log				376 A	50.00 902.00 20.00
	B75 E75		note: name also Hiland							
Highlands, William		Pelce, John & Auld, David	house & lot barn	22 x 22 25 x 22	wood log	2	5	51	1 A 199 A	200.00 1218.50
	B72 D91 E72									
Hippensteel, Joseph		Pines Coyler, Conrad & McLean, John	house stable	35 x 18 18 x 16	log log				109 A	80.00 288.00
	B76 E76									
Holt, Elizabeth	D80		house & lot stable	24 x 20 16 x 14	wood wood	1	3	39	61 P	190.00
Hooper, Jacob	D83		house & lot kitchen	18 x 20 14 x 12	wood wood	2	5	51	61 P	160.00
Hoover, Christian		Middle Spring Longnecker, Michael	house 1 & lot [addition ?] barn saw mill fulling mill house 2	25 x 21 16 x 18 45 x 18 19 x 21 18 x 16	wood wood log log log	1	2	21	1 A 107 A	200.00 2052.00 40.00
	B71 D90 E71		note: Green, Luke, occupant of house 2							
Hunter, William		Auld, David & Maxwell, William	house 1 & lot barn still house house 2	22 x 18 40 x 18 18 x 18 20 x 20	wood log log log	1	2	18	1 A 199 A	160.00 1423.00 40.00
	B73 D92 E73		note: Alpiner, Ralph [?], occupant of house 2							
Hutton, John	D84		house & lot stable	30 x 15 15 x 15	wood wood	1	3	27	61 P	160.00
Jameson, David		King St. Miller, Michael	house kitchen stable apothecary shop	24 x 24 18 x 14 20 x 16 24 x 24	wood wood wood log	1	4	45	61 P 61 P	350.00 200.00
	B77 D94 E77									
Jameson, William	D93		house & lot kitchen stable	34 x 30 40 x 18 20 x 20	wood wood wood	2	13	168	61 P	600.00

Southampton Township

Owner / Occupant	Ref.	Location / Adjoining Owner	Structure	Dimensions	Descr.	Stories	Windows Lights	Area	Value
Johnston, Ann		Barr, William & Mahan, David	house & lot kitchen barn	18 x 20 14 x 10 40 x 16	wood wood log	1	2 18	1 A 49 A	140.00 746.00
	B78 D95 E78								
Jones, Owen		mountain Spring, Marshall & Farmer, Lewis	tract					438 A 105 P	131.60
	B79 E79								
Kearlsey, Jane	D98		house & lot stable	40 x 18 18 x 20	wood wood	1	5 54	61 P	200.00
Kelso, James	D101		house & lot kitchen stable	24 x 24 14 x 14 16 x 16	wood wood wood	2	5 51	61 P	300.00
Kerns, Jacob	D97		house & lot kitchen	22 x 20 30 x 14	wood wood	1	4 51	122 P	250.00
Kerr, Thomas Jones, Nicholas	D99		house & lot	18 x 18		2	4 48	61 P	150.00
Kline, George Buchanan, John	B81 D102 E81	Pines Walter, Christopher & McColouch, John	house & lot barn grist mill paper mill saw mill	24 x 24 40 x 22 28 x 22 30 x 20 40 x 22	wood log log frame	2	6 48	1 A 159 A	250.00 1418.00
Kline, Matthias	D100		house & lot [addition ?] smith shop	20 x 20 12 x 17 18 x 18	wood wood	2	5 51	61 P	200.00
Krehl, Nicholas Kelsbower, Jacob	B80 D96 E80	Pines Reynolds, John & Clippinger, Frederick	house 1 & lot kitchen stable powder mill house 2 note: Kutlner, Michael, another occupant.	35 x 25 20 x 20 25 x 25 20 x 20 18 x 18	wood wood wood frame log	2	8 84	91.5 P	800.00 40.00
Lamberton, James Russel, Thomas	B85 E85	Big Pond, Pines Helms, Jacob & Norton, Thomas	house 1 stable saw mill house 2 note: Hawthorn, Adam, occupant of house 2	20 x 15 16 x 15 20 x 18	log log log			600 A	40.00 1335.00 30.00

Southampton Township

Owner / Occupant	Ref.	Location / Adjoining Owner	Structure	Dimensions	Descr.	Stories	Lights Windows	Area	Value
Latshaw, Joseph			house & lot	24 x 25	wood	1	4 48	61 P	400.00
			kitchen	15 x 15	wood				
			stable	20 x 15	wood				
	D104		still house	15 x 12	wood				
Lear, Henry			house & lot	26 x 30	stone	2	12 161	61 P	800.00
Quigley, Samuel			[addition ?]	20 x 16	stone	1			
			kitchen	16 x 16	wood				
	D103		stable	14 x 15	wood				
Leeper, William			house & lot	24 x 26	wood	2	7 75	106.5 P	500.00
Vance, William			kitchen	14 x 14	wood				
	D107		stable	18 x 20	wood				
Leiper, William		Walnut Bottom Road	house	44 x 20	stone, unfinished	2			
		Shippen, E. & J. & Tate, Samuel	stable	18 x 20	log			223 A	4900.00
	B86 E86								
Lightner, Jacob			house & lot	23 x 23	wood	2	3 44	61 P	350.00
	D105								
Longnecker, Michael		Middle Spring	house 1 & lot	28 x 21	wood	1	3 36	1 A	250.00
		Burkholder, John	barn	50 x 30	stone			70 A	3880.00
		& Hoover,	grist mill & distillery	55 x 27	burned				
		Christopher	cooper shop	20 x 15	log				
			house 2	18 x 20	log				80.00
	B84 D108 E84		note: Kerey, Adam, occupant of house 2						
Lourey, James		King St.	house & lot	34 x 18	wood	2	12 138	61 P	500.00
		Duncan, Daniel,	kitchen	20 x 15	wood				
		heirs	barn	54 x 22				61 P	130.00
			shop	20 x 20	wood				
	B82 D106 E82		note: last name is Lowry in D						
Lourey, James		Walnut Bottom Road	tract					50 A	1000.00
		McCandless, George & Cowen, William							
	B83 E83								
Magee, Alexander			house & lot	28 x 24	wood	2	8 96	61 P	300.00
	D109		stable	20 x 20	wood				
Mahan, Archibald		on branch	house & lot	22 x 16	wood	1	2 18	61 P	160.00
			stable	16 x 22	log				
			currying shop	30 x 22	log			46 P	400.00
			bark house	30 x 22	log				
	B91 D116 E91		note: name also Mahon						

Southampton Township

Owner Occupant	Ref.	Location Adjoining Owner	Structure	Dimensions	Descr.	Stories	Lights Windows		Area	Value
Mahan, David		Barr, William & Culbertson, Robert	tract						184 A	2944.00
	B99 E99									
Mahan, David		State Road Barr, William	house 1 & lot	28 x 19	wood	1	2	24	1 A	350.00
			kitchen	19 x 17	wood	2				
			spring house	12 x 12	stone					
			barn	50 x 19	log				314 A	7538.00
			still house	26 x 24	log					
			malt house	11 x 11	log					
			house 2	50 x 30	brick, unfinished	2				
	B98 D130 E98		note: house 2 49 x 48 in E							
Martin, Thomas		King St. his other lots	house & lot	25 x 25	wood	2	5	60	61 P	500.00
			kitchen	14 x 14	wood				61 P	60.00
	B93 D122 E93		stable	20 x 20	wood					
Martin, Thomas Bayle, John			house	22 x 25	wood	2	7	90	61 P	300.00
	D123									
Maxwell, William		Walnut Bottom Road Duncan, Daniel, heirs & Hunter, William	house & lot	40 x 16	wood	1	2	11	1 A	140.00
			barn	40 x 16	wood				107 A	866.00
	B107 D138 E107									
McCall, James Scott, James			house & lot	33 x 28	stone	2	13	262	61 P	700.00
			kitchen	15 x 15	stone					
	D128		stable	20 x 20	wood					
McCall, Robert, heirs McCall, Sarah		Barr, William & Reynolds, John	house & lot	30 x 35	stone	2	10	222	91.5 P	1100.00
			stable	16 x 18	wood				4 A	40.00
	B100 D131 E100									
McCall, Robert, heirs Noble, William			house & lot	18 x 18	wood	1	1	4	61 P	105.00
	D132									
McCandless, George		King & Queen Sts.	stable	20 x 20	log				61 P	100.00
	B94 E94									
McCandless, George		York Co. Road Barr, William	tract						31 A	558.00
	B95 E95									

Southampton Township

Owner Occupant	Ref.	Location Adjoining Owner	Structure	Dimensions	Descr.	Stories	Lights Windows		Area	Value
McCandless, George	B96 D96	State Road Lourey, James	tract						41 A	820.00
McCarrol, John			house & lot	28 x 20	wood	2	6	69	61 P	600.00
			[addition ?]	26 x 29	stone					
			kitchen	14 x 14	wood					
	D115		stable	16 x 16	wood					
McClean, Cornelius	D120		house & lot	20 x 18	wood	1	3	27	30.5 P	140.00
McClean, Cornelius Adams, John	D121		house & lot	32 x 20		1	4	37	30.5 P	160.00
McClure, Samuel			house & lot	24 x 22	wood	2	9	109	61 P	700.00
			stable	18 x 14	wood					
	D118		warehouse	14 x 22	wood					
McCollum, John McIntire, Robert		State Road Glen, Moses, heirs & Quigley, John	house & lot barn	22 x 20 45 x 18	wood log	1	2	18	1 A 99 A	200.00 1228.00
	B106 D137 E106		note: owner also McColm; occupant McKibben in D							
McColouch, John	B108 E108	Pines Kline, George & Helm, Jacob	tract						150 A	300.00
McConnel, William	D119		house & lot stable	24 x 28 18 x 20	wood wood	2	7	84	30.5 P	450.00
McCune, John		Middle Spring Haney, John & Fishburn, Conrad	house 1 & lot barn grist mill	40 x 24 75 x 34 45 x 30	wood stone stone	1 1/2	6	54	1 A 499 A	350.00 11,322.00
	B103 D134 E103		house 2	16 x 18	log					40.00
McCune, Robert		near State Road Clark, John & Coyler, Conrad	house & lot barn still house	21 x 30 60 x 24 18 x 20	stone log log	1	3	39	1 A 199 A	400.00 2518.00
	B105 D136 E105									
McElhear, Archibald			house & lot	20 x 18	wood	2	7	75	40 P	500.00
			stable	30 x 16	wood					
	D124		smith shop	18 x 26	wood					
McKnight, David		King & Washington Streets	house & lot kitchen	24 x 28 24 x 16	wood	2	8	170	61 P 30.5 P	800.00 40.00
	B97 D129 E97		stable	18 x 18						

Southampton Township

Owner / Occupant	Ref.	Location / Adjoining Owner	Structure	Dimensions	Descr.	Stories	Lights	Windows	Area	Value
McKnight, William		Tate, Samuel	house & lot	36 x 20	wood	2	13	156	1 A	400.00
		Ely, Andrew	kitchen	15 x 15	wood					
			barn	40 x 20	log				306 A	3140.00
	B109 D139 E109									
McLean, Allen			house	20 x 20	log					60.00
		McLean, John &							120 A	420.00
		Clippinger, Frederick								
	B111 E111									
McLean, John		Pines	house 1 & lot	18 x 18	wood	1	2	18	1 A	130.00
		McLean, Allen &	kitchen	14 x 12	wood					
		Myer, Adam	house 2	20 x 20	log, unoccupied					
			house 3	22 x 18	log					60.00
			saw mill						224 A	842.00
	B110 D140 E110		note: Hendrick, James, occupant of house 3							
Means, James		Shippensburg	house & lot	24 x 30	stone	2	13	252	36 P	800.00
		Means, John	kitchen	19 x 13	wood					
			bark house &	56 x 22	log				80 P	400.00
	B88 D114 E88		currying shop							
Means, James		State Road	tract						4 A 20 P	74.25
		Shippen, E. & J.								
	B89 E89									
Means, John			house & lot	22 x 16	wood	1	4	31	45.75 P	200.00
		Means, James	[addition ?]	12 x 10	wood					
			currying shop	63 x 20	log				61 P	400.00
	B101 D133 E101		& bark house							
Means, John		Pines	house 1	20 x 18	log					60.00
Ingle, Henry		Means, John, Sr.	barn	30 x 20	log				280 A	940.00
		& Stumbaugh, Peter								
	B102 E102									
Megurk, Stephen			house & lot	24 x 26	wood	2			61 P	200.00
	D110		kitchen	16 x 14	wood					
Megurk, Stephen			house & lot	16 x 16	wood	1	3	17	30.5 P	140.00
Noble, John			stable	12 x 12	wood					
	D111									
Megurk, Stephen			house & lot	16 x 16	wood	1	3	20	91.5 P	140.00
Yates, Robert										
	D112									

Southampton Township

Owner / Occupant	Ref.	Location / Adjoining Owner	Structure	Dimensions	Descr.	Stories	Lights	Windows	Area	Value
Miller, French		Pines	house	22 x 18	log					80.00
		Clippinger, Frederick &	barn	40 x 20	log				100 A	440.00
		Coffee Robert								
	B112 E112									
Miller, Michael			house & lot	25 x 22	wood	2	10	120	61 P	700.00
			kitchen	14 x 14	wood					
			stable	18 x 18	wood					
	D125		shop	14 x 14	wood					
Mitchel, Samuel			house & lot	23 x 23	wood	2	5	54	61 P	300.00
			kitchen	12 x 14	wood					
	D126		stable	16 x 16	wood					
Moore, James			house & lot	16 x 16	wood	1			61 P	120.00
	D127									
Moore, Solomon		King St.	stable	18 x 18	log				61 P	80.00
		Perch, Andrew &								
		Means, John								
	B90 E90									
Moore, Thomas		State Road	house & lot	22 x 22	wood	2	6	72	61 P	500.00
		Shippen, E. & J.	kitchen	15 x 15	wood				80 A	1280.00
		& Peoples,	stable	25 x 20	wood					
		Robert	shop	20 x 20	wood					
	B87 D113 E87									
Mull, John		Earl St.	house & lot	36 x 20		1	6	72	61 P	700.00
		Reynolds, John	kitchen	13 x 13	wood					
		heirs	stable	20 x 14	wood				61 P	40.00
	B92 D117 E92		shop	8 x 15	wood					
Myer, Adam		Pines	house	20 x 18	log					80.00
		McKnight, William	barn	35 x 16	log				148 A	574.00
		& Nichols, Thomas								
	B113 E113									
Myer, Jacob			house & lot	25 x 20	wood	1	2	24	1 A	200.00
		Creamer, Peter &	barn	40 x 16	log				99 A	1228.00
		Duncan, Stephen,									
		heirs								
	B104 D135 E104									
Nichols, Thomas		Pines	tract						130 A	390.00
		Myer, Adam &								
		Highlands, John								
	B115 E115									

Southampton Township

Owner / Occupant	Ref.	Location / Adjoining Owner	Structure	Dimensions	Descr.	Stories	Windows / Lights	Area	Value

Norton, Thomas
  McIntire, John
	B114 D141 E114	Pines
		  Hunter, William
			house & lot	36 x 18	wood	1		1 A
								147 A
									160.00
									588.00

Nugent, Peter	B116 E116	Pines
		  Hippensteel, Joseph
		  Reynolds, John, heirs
			house	30 x 20	log			100 A	60.00
									260.00

Page, John	D145		house & lot shop	29 x 26 19 x 16	wood wood	2	5 66	61 P	500.00

Pelce, John	B121 D152 E121	Walnut Bottom Road
		  Peoples,
		  Alexander &
		  Highlands, William
			house & lot
			barn
			weaver shop
				24 x 28
				24 x 24
				12 x 12
					wood
					log
					log
						1	3 33	1 A
								153 A
									250.00
									1603.00

Peoples, Alexander	B119 D151 E119	Duncan, Daniel
		  heirs, &
		  Shippen, E. & J.
			house & lot
			kitchen
			barn
			smith shop
				36 x 21
				16 x 18
				60 x 20
				16 x 16
					stone
					wood
					log
					log
						2	9 124	1 A
								216 A
									600.00
									3360.00

Peoples, Robert	B120 E120	Peoples, Alexander & Duncan, Thomas	tract					50 A	750.00
Piper, Lucinda	D142		house & lot kitchen	24 x 28 16 x 16	wood wood	2	9 96	61 P	300.00
Piper, Robert	D147		house & lot stable	22 x 22 15 x 15	wood wood	2	7 90	122 P	500.00
Pisel, Andrew Pisel, Christopher	D150		house & lot kitchen building	26 x 22 16 x 18 22 x 22	wood wood wood	2	4 36	61 P	400.00
Plum, Adam Trump, Philip	D148		house & lot stable shop	24 x 24 18 x 20 18 x 18	wood wood wood	2	6 60	61 P	500.00

Plunket, Dr., heirs
  Barr, William
	B118 E118	King St.
		  Barr, William
			stable	18 x 16	wood			61 P	80.00

Porter, Robert	B117 D149 E117	York Co. Road
		  McCandless,
		  George
			house & lot
			kitchen
			stable
			note: innkeeper
				30 x 28
				18 x 18
				24 x 46
					stone
					stone
					wood
						2	11 240	122 P
								12 A
									1200.00
									168.00

Southampton Township

Owner / Occupant	Location / Adjoining Owner	Structure	Dimensions	Material	Stories	Lights Windows	Area	Value
Porter, Robert		house & lot	25 x 27	stone	2	6 144	44 P	800.00
		kitchen	14 x 14	wood				
	D143	shop	14 x 14	wood				
Porter, Robert		house & lot	21 x 17	wood	2	5 50	61 P	250.00
		kitchen	13 x 16	wood				
		stable	14 x 15	wood				
	D146	note: saddle maker						
Porter, Robert Oniel [?]	D144	house & lot	1- x 24	wood	2	6 72	17 P	200.00
Quigley, John	State Road McCollum, John Chesnut, Samuel B123 D153 E123	house & lot barn house 2 note: Mullen, James, occupant of house 2	28 x 25 60 x 20	wood log	1	3 27	1 A 199 A	200.00 2502.00
Quigley, Samuel	King St. Mahan, Archibald & Kott, Jacob B122 E122	house barn	24 x 21	frame, unfinished	2		61 P	400.00
Rahm, Jacob	Earl St. his other lot B130 D161 E130	house & lot barn kitchen & bark building stable 1 stable 2	39 x 20 30 x 30 51 x 30 30 x 24 12 x 15	wood log & frame wood wood wood	2	14 244	61 P 61 P	2000.00 120.00
Raum, Jacob Altick, Daniel	D163	house & lot	21 x 21	wood	1	3 36	122 P	140.00
Raum, Jacob Keady, John	D162	house & lot kitchen	20 x 15 12 x 19	wood wood	1	2 22	61 P	150.00
Raum, Jacob Reily, Patrick	D164	house & lot	22 x 20	wood	1	3 36	61 P	140.00
Redat, John Patterson, Robert	D158	house & lot stable	20 x 16 15 x 15	wood wood	1	3 7	61 P	140.00

Southampton Township

Owner Occupant	Ref.	Location Adjoining Owner	Structure	Dimensions	Material	Stories	Lights Windows	Area	Value
Redatt, John		King St. Rotts, Jacob & Baker, John	house & lot kitchen stable bark & mill house currying shop	28 x 32 18 x 16 20 x 26 60 x 20 28 x 20	stone wood wood log	2	8	180	61 P	1200.00
	B126 D157 E126								
Reynolds, John, heirs		Pines Clippinger, Frederick & Krehl, Nicholas	tract					182 A	364.00
	B132 E132								
Reynolds, John, heirs Know, Joseph	D168		house & lot smith shop	30 x 26 22 x 20	wood wood	2	11	146	61 P	800.00
Reynolds, John heirs Leeper, William		Middle Spring Peoples, Robert & Shippen, E. & J.	house 1 & lot [addition ?] kitchen barn grist mill still house house 2	25 x 28 12 x 25 16 x 18 45 x 20 40 x 30 28 x 30 20 x 18	wood wood wood frame & log stone stone log	2	11	144	1 A 99 A	450.00 4580.00 80.00
	B131 D169 E131		note: Henderson, William, occupant of house 2.						
Rice, Simon	D165		house & lot	16 x 20	wood	1	2	20	30.5 P	150.00
Richards, Alexander	D167		house & lot	30 x 17	wood	1	4	39	61 P	150.00
Richart, John	D155		house [addition ?] stable shop	22 x 20 18 x 15 15 x 12 15 x 20	wood wood wood wood	2 1	7	93	61 P	700.00
Rippey, Samuel	B128 E128	Branch	stable bark house currying shop	15 x 18 55 x 20 40 x 15	log stone log					
Rippey, Samuel	B127 D159 E127	King St. Bell, William	house 1 & lot kitchen house 2	40 x 30 19 x 20 20 x 20	brick stone log, unoccupied	2	11	264	30.5 P 61 P	2000.00 160.00
Rippey, Samuel Rippey, Widow	D160		house & lot spring house	20 x 20 18 x 18	wood stone	1	2	24	30.5 P	180.00

Southampton Township

Owner / Occupant	Ref.	Location / Adjoining Owner	Structure	Dimensions	Material	Stories	Windows / Lights	Area	Value
Rippey, Samuel		State Road	house	15 x 16	log				90.00
Thrush, Richard		Mahan, David & Duncan, Daniel, heirs	barn	20 x 20	log			140 A	1810.00
	B129 E129								
Rippey, William		on Branch	house & lot	44 x 34	stone	2	18 366	124 P	2600.00
		his other lots	[addition ?]	21 x 18	stone				
			kitchen	22 x 18	stone				
	B124 D154 E124		stable	24 x 46	wood			1 A 40 P	30.00
Rotts, Jacob		King St.	house & lot	24 x 24	wood	2	3 45	30.5 P	500.00
		Redat, John &	kitchen	16 x 18	wood				
		Quigley, Samuel	stable	18 x 20	log				
			bark & mill house	35 x 20	frame			30.5 P	350.00
	B125 D156 E125		note: name Rolls in D						
Russel, James			house & lot	20 x 18	wood	1	3 36	61 P	140.00
	D166		stable	14 x 16	wood				
Sadler, Matthias		mountain Spring, Mary & Jones, Owen	tract					438 A 105 P	131.60
	B140 E140								
Salskeever, Gasper			house & lot	32 x 15	wood	1	2 16	61 P	120.00
	D185								
Scott, Elizabeth			house & lot	30 x 16	stone	2	6 123	61 P	400.00
	D179								
Shepley, Frederick			house & lot	18 x 16	wood	1	11 125	61 P	400.00
			[addition ?]	19 x 16	wood				
	D186		stable	16 x 12	wood				
Shippen, Edward & Joseph		around Shippensburg	tract					214 A	4708.00
	B136 E136								
Shippen, Edward & Joseph		Leeper, William & Peoples, Alexander	tract					350 A	7000.00
	B137 E137								
Shoemaker, John			house & lot	20 x 15	wood	1	6 66	61 P	200.00
	D171		[addition ?]	15 x 20	wood				
Shriver, Daniel			house & lot	24 x 26	wood	2	6 72	61 P	250.00
	D184		smith shop	16 x 14	wood				

Southampton Township

Owner / Occupant	Ref.	Location / Adjoining Owner	Structure	Dimensions	Material	Stories	Lights Windows	Area	Value
Shutley, Jacob	B134 E134	Earl St. Shutley, John	lot					61 P	40.00
Shutley, John	B133 D174 E133	Earl St. Shutley, John	house & lot	30 x 24	wood	2	4 57	61 P	450.00
Shutley, John	B133b E133b	Earl St. his other lot	lot					61 P	40.00
Shutley, Mary	D173		house & lot kitchen stable	24 x 18 24 x 12 16 x 16	wood wood wood	2	6 78	61 P	400.00
Simpson, John	D180		house & lot stable shop	27 x 27 24 x 15 18 x 18	stone wood wood	1	5 106	61 P	450.00
Snyder, John	D172		house & lot stable shop	24 x 27 16 x 16 24 x 20	wood wood wood	2	11 135	61 P	450.00
Spear, William	D177		house & lot stable smith shop	20 x 18 12 x 12 40 x 20	wood wood wood	1	3 28	61 P	500.00
Speelman, George	D181		house & lot stable	30 x 18 20 x 18	wood wood	1	3 27	61 P	160.00
Speelman, Jacob	D182		house & lot shop	20 x 20 20 x 24	wood wood	1	3 20	61 P	200.00
Speelman, Jacob Atherton, Caleb	D183		house & lot	30 x 20	wood	1	2 13	61 P	140.00
Spencer, John	D170		house & lot stable	25 x 28 16 x 16	wood wood	2	9 117	61 P	400.00
Spring, Marshall	B138 E138	mountain Jones, Owen & Vanolt, Valentine	tract					432 A 58 P	129.70
Spring, Mary	B139 E139	mountain Anthony, Avis & Spring, Marshall	tract					438 A	131.40

Southampton Township

Owner / Occupant	Ref.	Location / Adjoining Owner	Structure	Dimensions	Material	Stories	Windows	Lights	Area	Value
Stewart, John	D178		house & lot	18 x 20	wood	1	3	36	61 P	150.00
Stumpaugh, Peter		Means, John & Clippinger, Anthony	house & lot	28 x 24	wood	2	6	81	61 P	500.00
			kitchen	12 x 12	wood					
			stable	20 x 18	wood					
	B135 D175 E135		barn	40 x 15	log				199 A	1443.00
Stumbaugh, Peter Roup, Michael	D176		house & lot	20 x 20	wood	1	2	12	1 A	140.00
Tate, Samuel			house & lot	24 x 22	wood	2	7	68	61 P	400.00
			kitchen	11 x 22	wood					
			stable	14 x 18	wood					
	D188		barn	18 x 18	wood					
Tate, Samuel Derr, Nicholas		Leeper, William & McKnight, William	house & lot	18 x 18	wood	1	3	27	1 A	120.00
	D141 D190 E141		barn	30 x 15	log				149 A	1540.00
Tate, Samuel Trimble, John			house & lot	18 x 18	wood	1	3	27	61 P	150.00
	D189		stable	15 x 15	wood					
Tetrick, John	D187		house & lot	28 x 24	wood	1	3	28	1 A 23 P	450.00
			shop	18 x 14	wood					
Usher, Baltzer	D191		house & lot	20 x 20	wood	2	1	12	61 P	140.00
Vanhold, Valentine		mountain Reynolds, John, heirs	tract						404 A	121.90
	B143 E143									
Vernor, Conrad		State Road McCune, Robert & Duncan, Thomas	house & lot	24 x 20	wood	1	1	9	1 A	150.00
	B142 D192 E142		barn	40 x 16	log				99 A	1238.00
Wall, John	D194		house & lot	22 x 22	wood	1	3	33	61 P	150.00
			stable	14 x 14	wood					
Walter, Christopher		Pines Kline, George & Clever, Barnabas	house & lot	30 x 24	wood	1			1 A	120.00
	B145 D197 E145		stable	18 x 18	log					

Southampton Township

Owner Occupant	Ref.	Location Adjoining Owner	Structure	Dimensions	Material	Stories	Lights Windows		Area	Value
Whitmer, Jacob	B144 D196 E144	Brittain, John & Mahan, David	house & lot barn	24 x 18 20 x 20	wood log	1	1	12	1 A 39 A	160.00 556.00
Wingler, Jacob	D195		house & lot	16 x 14	wood	1			61 P	110.00
Wolf, Adam	D193		house & lot [addition ?]	18 x 16 18 x 16	wood wood	1	3	33	30.5 P	160.00
Yates, George	D198		house & lot	15 x 18	wood	2	5	48	30.5 P	160.00
Yates, Thomas	D198		house & lot kitchen	17 x 16 14 x 14	wood wood	2	4	42	30.5 P	180.00

CHAPTER XI WEST PENNSBORO TOWNSHIP

Owner Occupant	Ref.	Location Adjoining Owner	Structure	Dimensions	Descr.	Stories	Windows	Lights	Area	Value
Abraham, Enoch			house & lot	23 x 19	wood	2	7	80	2 A	300.00
		McCaskey, Samuel	kitchen	21 x 20	stone	1				
			barn	69 x 16					148 A	1974.00
	A2 D2 E2		note: illegible remark follows entry.							
Adair, James		Spring Field	house & lot	18 x 12	wood	1 1/2	2	16	2 A	110.00
			room	18 x 12	stone	1				
	A3 D3 E4		barn	30 x 16					190 A	190.00
Alter, Jacob			house & lot	22 x 18	wood	1 1/2	3	28	2 A	140.00
		Whitmore, Joseph	stable	16 x 16					4 A	1960.00
			grist mill	50 x 47	stone					
	A1 D1 E1		sawmill							
Atchison, James			house	20 x 18						
		McKeehan, John							100 A	860.00
	E3									
Bear, Widow			house & lot	36 x 18	wood	1 1/2	7	32	2 A	160.00
		Snider, David	barn	78 x 30					193 A	3554.00
	A4 D4 E5									
Beaty, William			house & lot	22 x 18	wood	1 1/2	7	52	2 A	105.00
		McKeehan, John	kitchen	14 x 12	wood	1	1	9		
	A7 D7 E8		barn						150 A	1510.00
Bell, William			house & lot	26 x 26	stone	2	7	120	80 P	800.00
			work shop	15 x 10	stone	1	1	8		
	A11 D11		tan house	16 x 18	wood					
Bitchel, Jacob			house & lot	21 x 20	wood	1 1/2	3	12	2 A	170.00
		Peirce, Joseph	barn	58 x 22					61 A	893.00
	A10 D10 E13									
Black, Peter			house & lot	22 x 18	wood	1 1/2	3	27	2 A	110.00
		Miller, John	kitchen	18 x 20	wood	1	1	6		
	A9 D9 E12		barn	62 x 20					218 A	3766.00
Blain, David			house & lot	30 x 27	stone	2	9	120	2 A	500.00
		McBeth, Alexander	kitchen	16 x 13	stone					
	A5 D5 E6		barn	50 x 20					201 A	2462.00
Blaine, Ephraim			tract						50 A	400.00
		Clever, Martin								
	E11									

West Pennsboro Township

Owner Occupant	Ref.	Location Adjoining Owner	Structure	Dimensions	Material	Stories	Windows	Lights	Area	Value
Blair, Rummel	A8 D8 E9	McKeehan, George	house & lot kitchen barn	18 x 16 22 x 18 61 x 24	wood wood	1 1/2	4	42	2 A 194 A	250.00 2448.00
Blair, Rummel Blair, John	E10	Graham, Jerred	house barn	17 x 19					42 A	346.00
Brown, John	A6 D6 E7	Trett, Peter	house & lot kitchen	30 x 28 16 x 16	stone stone	2 1	8 1	105 9	2 A 178 A	350.00 1793.00
Campbell, Thomas Atchison, James	E14	McKeehan, John	tract						100 A	800.00
Carothers, Andrew	A16 D16 E21	McCallister, Andrew	house & lot kitchen barn	22 x 22 14 x 22 58 x 22	wood wood	1 1/2 1	3 1	14 4	2 A 298 A	105.00 3596.00
Carothers, Armstrong	A15 D15 E20	Carothers, Martin	house & lot room barn	23 x 20 23 x 16 56 x 20	wood wood	2 1	4	36	2 A 198 A	160.00 2030.00
Carothers, James	A13 D14 E16	Davidson, John	house & lot barn saw mill	40 x 30	stone	2	18	270	2 A 248 A	800.00 4914.00
Carothers, James Pence, Peter	E17	Carothers, A.	house	21 x 18					250 A	3050.00
Carothers, John	A14 D13 E18	Dunbar, John	house & lot barn	26 x 24 50 x 20	wood	2	8	96	2 A 248 A	300.00 3502.00
Carothers, John	A19 D19 E22		house & lot kitchen barn	25 x 27 16 x 32 54 x 19	wood wood	2 1 1/2	8	96	2 A 328 A	180.00 3330.00
Carothers, Martin	E19	Carothers, A.	tract						200 A	2000.00
Clever, Martin	A12 D12 E15	Graham, Jerred	house & lot stable barn house 2	35 x 30 16 x 18	stone	2	25	268	2 A 95 A	268.00 1222.00

West Pennsboro Township

Owner Occupant	Location Ref. Adjoining Owner	Structure	Dimensions	Material	Stories	Windows	Lights	Area	Value
Clinbagh, John	A18 D18	house & lot	23 x 21	wood	1 1/2	5	45	40 P	150.00
Crever, Jacob Holsaple, Adam	Carothers, John A17 D17 E23	house & lot kitchen barn	20 x 18 20 x 10 26 x 22	wood wood stone	1 1/2 1	1 1	8 6	2 A 98 A	101.00 1472.00
Davidson, George	Davidson, Matthew A28 D28 E31	house & lot kitchen room barn	19 x 24 22 x 18 11 x 24 86 x 20	wood wood wood	2 1 1/2 1	5 2 1	51 15 9	2 A 176 A	150.00 2504.00
Davidson, George	E32 Young, Eleanor	tract						176 A	2464.00
Davidson, George Jr.	A20 D20	house & lot	40 x 28	stone, unfinished	2			2 A	130.00
Davidson, John	Young, Eleanor A31 D31 E33	house & lot kitchen barn still house	24 x 34 18 x 33	wood wood	2 1	12 2	128 16	2 A 198 A	400.00 2262.00
Davidson, Matthew	Foster, Thomas A27 D27 E30	house 1 & lot kitchen barn house 2	31 x 20 20 x 20 70 x 26 18 x 16	stone wood	2 1 1/2	5 2	54 13	2 A 198 A	500.00 2862.00
Diller, Abraham	Abraham, James A22 D22 E25	house & lot barn	45 x 20 80 x 22	wood	2	3	30	2 A 186 A	200.00 3418.00
Diller, Francis	Peirce, Joseph A23 D23 E26	house & lot barn store house	45 x 25 80 x 30 12 x 12	wood wood	1 1/2	5	50	2 A 158 A	200.00 3274.00
Diller, Peter	Diller, Abraham A21 D21 E24	house & lot barn	23 x 20 90 x 35	wood	2	3	24	2 A 298 A	130.00 5764.00
Dunbar, John	A29 D29	house & lot kitchen	43 x 20 13 x 13	wood wood	2 1	11	108	2 A	400.00
Dunbar, William	A30 D30	house & lot kitchen	27 x 21 16 x 16	wood wood	2 1	5	42	2 A	120.00
Duncan, William	Scroggs, Alexander A24 D24 E27	house & lot barn	28 x 24 60 x 22	wood	1 1/2	3	22	2 A 211 A	120.00 2600.00

West Pennsboro Township

Owner Occupant	Ref.	Location Adjoining Owner	Structure	Dimensions	Material	Stories	Windows	Lights	Area	Value
Dunlap, Mary Haroff, Jacob	A25 D25 E28	Glenn, David	house & lot	34 x 17	wood	1 1/2	2	18	2 A 126 A	102.00 1028.00
Dunlap, William	A26 D26 E29	Dunlap, Mary	house & lot stable	20 x 20	wood	1 1/2	1	9	2 A	101.00
Ferguson, William	A32 D32 E34	Black, Peter	house & lot kitchen	22 x 19 22 x 19	wood wood	2 1 1/2	2 3	20 36	2 A 40 A	120.00 884.00
Fishburn, Peter	A35 D35 E37	Myers, Abraham	house & lot kitchen barn 1 barn 2	24 x 20 16 x 20	wood wood	2 1 1/2	4 1	48 9	2 A 184 A	350.00 2868.00
Forbes, John	A34 D34 E36	Musselman, Jacob	house & lot room barn	26 x 17 18 x 12 50 x 22	wood wood	1 1/2 1	3 1	20 12	2 A 184 A	101.00 2984.00
Foster, Thomas	A33 D33 E35	Black, Peter	house 1 & lot kitchen barn house 2	30 x 20 19 x 17 70 x 22 18 x 17	wood wood	2	5	44	2 A 256 A	250.00 3384.00
Glenn, David	A41 D41 E42	Dunlap, Widow	house & lot	22 x 20	wood	1 1/2	1	9	2 A 42 A	105.00 336.00
Glenn, Jane	A37 D37 E39	Laughlin, Atchison	house 1 & lot barn grist mill house 2	40 x 23 60 x 25 26 x 22	wood stone	2	4	40	2 A 351 A	250.00 6654.00
Good, Peter	A36 D36 E38	Wasmood, Martin	house & lot kitchen barn	20 x 18 16 x 14 45 x 20	wood wood	2	5	55	2 A 71 A 80 P	120.00 1051.00
Gourley, Samuel	A42 D42		house & lot	28 x 24	wood	2	10	128	40 P	250.00
Graham, James	A39 D39		house & lot	26 x 24	wood	2	9	96	2 A	250.00
Graham, James Graham, Isiah	A38 D38 E40	Diller, Abraham	house & lot barn tan house & vats	26 x 16 50 x 20	wood	1 1/2	4	21	2 A 198 A	160.00 3579.00

West Pennsboro Township

Owner Occupant	Ref.	Location Adjoining Owner	Structure	Dimensions	Material	Stories	Windows	Lights	Area	Value
Graham, Jerred		Clever, Martin	house 1 & lot kitchen barn	22 x 20 13 x 15 64 x 24	wood stone	2 1	5 1	46 6	2 A 113 A	200.00 1365.00
	A40 D40 E41		house 2	16 x 20						
Hay, Henry		Diller, Francis	house & lot barn	24 x 24 54 x 22	wood	2	4	39	2 A 112 A	150.00 2066.00
	A44 D44 E44									
Hickes, Andrew		Carothers, James	house 1 & lot kitchen stable barn smith shop	30 x 20 18 x 16	wood wood	2 1	10	176	2 A 221 A	400.00 4299.00
			house 2	24 x 22	wood	2	3	36		
	A46 D46 E46		note: house 2 listed in A and D, but no value given							
Houts, Henry Mell, Adam		Hickes, Andrew	house & lot kitchen spring house barn still house	18 x 16 18 x 15 15 x 12	stone wood stone	1 1/2	1	6	2 A 210 A	200.00 3830.00
	A45 D45 E45									
Huston, James		Beatty, William	house & lot kitchen barn shop	20 x 18 18 x 12	wood wood	1 1	4 1	36 6	2 A 160 A	110.00 1510.00
	A43 D43 E43									
Irvine, Samuel Lewis, John [?]		Big Spring	house & lot grist mill	20 x 16	wood	2	5	48	10 P 50 A	120.00 1756.00
	A47 D47 E47		note: name also Irwin							
Jumper, Conrad McDonald, Daniel		Dunbar, John	house & lot stable	35 x 15 18 x 17	wood	1 1/2	3	24	2 A 78 A	110.00 1034.00
	A49 D49 E49									
Junkin, Joseph McIntire, John		McCulloch, John	house & lot	23 x 20	wood	2	3	36	2 A 248 A	110.00 1944.00
	A48 D48 E48									
Kean, Percival			house & lot kitchen stable	24 x 26 12 x 13 14 x 16	wood wood wood	2	7	72	80 P	300.00
	A51 D51									
Kinslo, Jacob		Lefevre, Lawrence	tract smith shop						23 A	150.00
	E50									

West Pennsboro Township

Owner / Occupant	Ref.	Location / Adjoining Owner	Structure	Dimensions	Material	Stories	Windows / Lights		Area	Value
Kirkpatrick, James	A50 D50 E51	Patton, John	house & lot stable barn	24 x 20 18 x 17 40 x 18	wood	1 1/2	3	29	2 A 18 A	200.00 168.00
Lackey, Alexander Rell, John	A58 D58 E59	Myers, Jacob	house & lot barn	28 x 20 50 x 30	wood	1 1/2	3	27	2 A 160 A 120 P	120.00 1640.00
Laughlin, Atchison	A53 D53 E52	Laughlin, Mary	house & lot	40 x 18	wood	1 1/2	3	32	2 A 148 A	150.00 1776.00
Laughlin, Mary	A52 D52 E53	Laughlin, Atchison	house & lot grist mill	30 x 27	wood	2	4	42	2 A 193 A	200.00 4126.00
Lefever, George Lefever, Isaac	A55 D55 E55	Laughlin, Atchison	house & lot barn	28 x 19 55 x 19	wood	2	4	36	2 A 131 A 80 P	200.00 2150.00
Lefever, George Lefever, Lawrence	A54 D54 E54	Laughlin, Atchison	house & lot barn	30 x 20 85 x 30	wood	1 1/2	3	22	2 A 131 A 80 P	110.00 2696.00
Lefever, Lawrence	A56 E56 [omitted in D]	Patton, John	house & lot stable	24 x 20 25 x 20	wood	1 1/2	2	20	2 A	102.00
Love, James	E58	Love, John	tract						63 A	1070.00
Love, John	A57 D57 E57	Love, James	house & lot room barn	20 x 12 26 x 14 56 x 22	wood wood	1 1/2 1	1 2	9 18	2 A 104 A	110.00 1882.00
Mathers, John	E54	Springfield	house lot	18 x 18					40 P	70.00
Mathers, Samuel	A62 D62 E63	McClure, Charles	house & lot kitchen barn	22 x 18 18 x 16 50 x 20	wood wood	2 1 1/2	5 1	57 8	2 A 149 A	200.00 1565.00
McAlister, Andrew	A68 D68 E70	Carothers, Andrew	house 1 & lot room kitchen barn house 2	33 x 22 16 x 11 24 x 22 75 x 22 18 x 18	wood wood wood	1 1/2 1	2 2	18 18	2 A 235 A	250.00 3400.00

West Pennsboro Township

Owner Occupant	Location Ref.	Adjoining Owner	Structure	Dimensions	Material	Stories	Windows	Lights	Area	Value
McBeth, Alexander	E84	Duncan, William	barn smith shop						150 A	2000.00
McCaskry, Samuel Hiskey, Adam	A78 D78 E82	McCallister, Andrew	house & lot barn	24 x 21 58 x 18	wood	1 1/2	3	24	2 A 147 A	110.00 1961.00
McClure, Charles Cope, John	A77 D77 E81	Mathers, Samuel	house 1 & lot kitchen barn house 2	26 x 20 16 x 18 50 x 16 18 x 20	wood wood	2 1	3 1	36 4	2 A 528 A	120.00 5320.00
McCracken, William	A80 D80		house & lot	18 x 20	wood	2	4	42	40 P	200.00
McCullough, John	A66 D66	Myers, Jacob	house & lot kitchen stable barn	28 x 28 22 x 21	stone stone	2 1	11 1	148 9	2 A 288 A	600.00 3198.00
McFarland, James	A60 D60 E61	Peirce, Joseph	house & lot kitchen barn	23 x 23 22 x 22 62 x 20	stone, unfinished wood	2	8	60	2 A 161 A	300.00 2951.00
McFarlane. Robert Shaw, Alexander	A61 D61 E62	McFarlane, James	house & lot barn	25 x 23 65 x 28	wood	2	8	60	2 A 133 A	250.00 2499.00
McFarlane, William	E83	Big Spring	house stable cooper shop	18 x 20					1 A	60.00
McKee, David	A79 D79		house & lot	28 x 28	wood	2	7	90	40 P	230.00
McKeehan, Benjamin	E78	Kinslo, Jacob	house	12 x 16					50 A	406.00
McKeehan, Benjamin	A74 D74 E77	McKeehan, John	house & lot barn	24 x 24 58 x 20	wood	2	4	39	2 A 278 A	120.00 3078.00
McKeehan, George Hoon, Felty	A75 D75 E76	McKeehan, Sr, George	house 1 & lot house 2	21 x 21 16 x 15	wood	1 1/2	3	18	2 A 110 A	105.00 1180.00

West Pennsboro Township

Owner Occupant	Ref.	Location Adjoining Owner	Structure	Dimensions	Material	Stories	Windows	Lights	Area	Value
McKeehan, George, Sr.	E79	Woods, Richard	barn note: [middle diget in acreage is uncertain]	60 x 21					560 A	5550.00
McKeehan, James	A72 D72 E74	Myers, Jacob	house & lot barn	30 x 20 60 x 20	wood	1 1/2	4	44	2 A 198 A	120.00 2678.00
McKeehan, James McKeehan, John	A73 D73 E75	McKeehan, Benjamin	house & lot barn	20 x 20 60 x 2-	wood	2	3	32	2 A 198 A	110.00 2426.00
McKeehan, John	A76 D76 E80	Beatty, William	house & lot room barn	24 x 20 20 x 11	wood wood	1 1/2 1	4 1	21 9	2 A 183 A	130.00 1880.00
Miller, John	A65 D65 E67	Mt. Rock	house & lot kitchen store room bar room smith shop & stable	22 x 30 18 x 16 26 x 22 18 x 9	stone wood wood wood	2 1 1/2 2	6 1 2	132 12 18	2 A 423 A	1000.00 8500.00
Miller, William	A64 D64 E66	Foster, Thomas	house 1 & lot kitchen house 2	17 x 19 16 x 13 23 x 17	wood wood	1 1/2 1 1/2	2 1	24 4	2 A 158 A	120.00 2054.00
Mitchel, Andrew	A63 D63 E65	Wilt, John	house & lot barn	25 x 22 40 x 18	wood	1 1/2	3	33	2 A 134 A	150.00 1350.00
Moore, William Crocket, Thomas	A67 D67 E69	Rhodes, John	house & lot barn	22 x 18 60 x 18	wood	1 1/2	2	24	2 A 272 A	104.00 3314.00
Mussleman, George	A71 D71 E73	Mussleman, Jacob	house & lot barn still house	26 x 20 54 x 26 26 x 8	wood stone	1 1/2 1	5	60	2 A 58 A	200.00 1260.00
Mussleman, Jacob	A70 D70 E72	Forbes, John	house & lot kitchen barn	30 x 22 20 x 20 80 x 36	wood wood stone	2	21	145	2 A 220 A	400.00 4580.00
Myers, Abraham	A69 D69 E71	Fishburn, Peter	house 1 & lot kitchen barn weaver shop smith shop house 2 house 3	28 x 20 15 x 15 80 x 36 15 x 18 18 x 20 18 x 20 15 x 20	wood wood wood wood	2 1 1 1	8 1 1	84 6 6	2 A 211 A	300.00 4444.00

West Pennsboro Township

Owner / Occupant	Ref.	Location / Adjoining Owner	Structure	Dimensions	Material	Stories	Windows	Lights	Area	Value
Myers, Jacob		McKeehan, James	house & lot	32 x 32	stone	2	10	150	2 A	900.00
			kitchen	16 x 14	stone	1	1	9		
			barn	50 x 30					263 A	3176.00
	A59 D59 E60		workshop	16 x 13	wood	1				
Nailor, George			house & lot	25 x 19	wood	1 1/2	4	40	2 A	150.00
Nailor, Jacob		Rhode, Philip	kitchen	16 x 12	stone	1 1/2	1	4		
	A81 D81 E85		stable	16 x 16					24 A	384.00
Negro, Catharine	E86	Schooners Road	house	16 x 12					1 A 80 P	30.00
Parker, Alexander, heirs			house & lot	27 x 25	wood	1 1/2	5	45	2 A	150.00
Blackwood, William		Fishburn, Peter	barn						158 A	2716.00
	A87 D87 E92									
Patton, John			house 1 & lot	20 x 16	wood	1 1/2	1	4	2 A	101.00
		Lefever,	house 2	18 x 16						
		Lawrence	house 3	20 x 17						
	A82 D82 E87								151 A	2416.00
Peebles, Robert			house & lot	30 x 28	stone	2	12	60	40 P	500.00
Wallace, Thomas	A86 D86									
Peirce, Hannah			house & lot	27 x 25	wood	2	10	120	2 A	250.00
			kitchen	16 x 16	wood	1	1	4		
	A85 D85		lumber house	18 x 20	wood					
Peirce, Joseph		Whitmore, Joseph	house & lot	52 x 25	wood	1 1/2	7	68	2 A	300.00
			barn	60 x 22					101 A	1656.00
	A84 D84 E89									
Peirce, Joseph		Summers, Andrew	tract						28 A	280.00
	E91									
Peirce, Joseph		Diller, Francis	barn	66 x 25					328 A	5954.00
Peirce, Hannah	E90									
Piper, Jane		Wilson, Samuel	house & lot	20 x 20	wood	1 1/2	3	18	2 A	110.00
			barn		old				92 A	1430.00
	A83 D83 E88		grist mill							
Ralston, David		Showalter, Joseph	house	20 x 36	wood	1 1/2	4	36	2 A	130.00
			kitchen	20 x 20	wood	1				
	A88 D88 E93		barn	56 x 20					198 A	2426.00

West Pennsboro Township

Owner Occupant	Ref.	Location Adjoining Owner	Structure	Dimensions	Descr.	Stories	Lights Windows		Area	Value
Ramsey, Hugh	E99	State Road	house barn	18 x 16					3 A	46.00
Rippet, John	A89 D89 E94	Mathers, Samuel	house & lot kitchen barn	22 x 20 18 x 16 40 x 15	wood wood	1 1/2	4	42	2 A 186 A	120.00 1308.00
Ristlers, Thomas, heirs Rhine, Henry	A91 D91 E98	Waswood, Martin	house & lot kitchen barn	24 x 19 14 x 19	wood wood	2 1	9 1	108 9	2 A 98 A	180.00 1000.00
Roadacre [?], Philip Road, Philip	E95	Carothers, Armstrong, J.	lot						1 A 40 P	50.00
Roads, John	A92 D92 E98	Moore, William	house & lot kitchen barn	30 x 25 16 x 16 46 x 30	wood, unfinished wood	2	2	24	2 A 148 A	200.00 1748.00
Rodair, Philip	A90 D90		house & lot kitchen	22 x 18 15 x 12	wood wood	1 1/2 1	3	32	2 A	150.00
Rodman, William	E97	Springfield	house lot	26 x 20					40 P	60.00
Scroggs, Alexander	A100 D100 E108	Duncan, William	house 1 & lot kitchen barn still house house 2	25 x 25 16 x 13 16 x 16	wood wood	2 1	6	53	2 A 244 A	200.00 2988.00
Shants, Henry	A96 D96 E103	Blair, John	house & lot stable	20 x 18 29 x 21	wood	2	8	86	2 A 105 A	150.00 1070.00
Showalter, Joseph	A93 D93 E100	Ralston, David	house 1 & lot barn house 2	28 x 30 18 x 15	stone	1 1/2	4	60	2 A 201 A	120.00 2472.00
Shuler, Christian	A97 D97 E104	Brown, John	house & lot barn	40 x 20 60 x 20	wood	1 1/2	2	12	2 A 98 A	130.00 911.00
Smith, John	A101 D101 E110	Springfield	house 1 & lot house 2	27 x 15 16 x 20	wood	1 1/2	4	28	1 A 3 P [?] 40 A	140.00 60.00

West Pennsboro Township

Owner Occupant	Ref.	Location Adjoining Owner	Structure	Dimensions	Material	Stories	Windows	Lights	Area	Value
Snider, David		Conodoguinet Creek	house 1 & lot	30 x 24	wood	2	12	144	2 A	600.00
			kitchen	16 x 12	stone	1	1	9		
			barn						67 A	3426.00
			grist mill	30 x 35	stone					
			saw mill							
	A94 D94 E101		house 2	18 x 16						
Snider, David		Conodoguinet Creek	house 1 & lot	26 x 23	wood	1 1/2	1	4	2 A	120.00
Snider, Baltzer			barn		old				151 A	2452.00
	A95 D95 E102		house 2	16 x 14						
Spear, William			house & lot	20 x 18	wood	2	4	42	2 A	130.00
		Striker, Arnold	stable							
	A99 D99 E107		barn						121 A	978.00
Striker, Arnold			house & lot	22 x 20	wood	2			2 A	110.00
		Spear, William			unfinished					
	A98 D98 E105		barn						114 A 120 P	917.00
Striker, Arnold			tract						51 A	408.00
		Spear, William								
	E106									
Summers, Andrew			house & lot	28 x 25	stone	2	6	72	2 A	500.00
		Shank, Henry	kitchen	26 x 25	wood	1	1	9		
	A102 D102 E109		barn	50 x 22					98 A	1286.00
Tritt, Peter			house & lot	30 x 22	stone	2	10	120	2 A	400.00
		Brown, John	barn	70 x 24					118 A	1398.00
	A104 D104 E112									
Turner, James		State Road	house & lot	24 x 30	stone	2	7	127	2 A	800.00
			kitchen	18 x 16	wood	1 1/2	1	9		
			stable							
	A103 D103 E111		barn						48 A	1215.00
Walker, John			house & lot	29 x 21	wood	2	8	81	40 P	250.00
Hay, Samuel			smith shop	14 x 16	wood	1				
	A111 D111									
Warnor, Henry			house & lot	20 x 20	wood	1 1/2	2	12	2 A	110.00
		Ristler heirs	kitchen	16 x 16	wood	1				
	A109 D109 E119		barn	100 x 20					118 A	1536.00
Wasmood, Martin			house & lot	24 x 20	wood	1 1/2	3	19	2 A	110.00
		Good, Peter	barn	60 x 30					88 A	1130.00
	A110 D110 E120									

West Pennsboro Township

Owner Occupant	Ref.	Location Adjoining Owner	Structure	Dimensions	Material	Stories	Lights	Windows	Area	Value
Whitmore, Joseph Alter, David	A108 D108 E118	Peirce, Joseph	house & lot barn work shop	31 x 25 61 x 26 12 x 12	wood wood	1 1/2 1	7 1	67 4	2 A 121 A	300.00 1673.00
Wike, Christopher	A105 D105 E114	Blain, David	house & lot barn	31 x 23 43 x 18	wood	2	7	51	2 A 153 A	200.00 1876.00
Will, John	E115	Mitchel, Andrew	house	20 x 18					190 A	2010.00
Wilson, Samuel, deceased Nettle, Samuel	A106 D106 E116	Piper, Jane	house & lot barn	23 x 23 56 x 22	wood	2	4	38	2 A 153 A	120.00 1570.00
Wilson, Widow	E113	Bankers Hill	cabin lot						1 A 80 P	20.00
Woods, Richard	A107 D107 E117	McKeehan, George	house & lot barn	28 x 30 60 x 20	stone	2	7	90	2 A 400 A	400.00 4020.00
Young, Eleanor	A112 D112 E121	Davidson, John	house 1 & lot kitchen barn house 2 house 3	25 x 25 16 x 17 60 x 26	wood wood	2	16	120	2 A 228 A	350.00 3362.00

APPENDIX

INTRODUCTION TO THE MICROFILM EDITION
OF THE PENNSYLVANIA TAX LISTS

CIRCULAR OF THE SECRETARY OF THE TREASURY

SAMPLE PAGES OF FORMS A, B, 1, AND 2

At the beginning of Roll 1 appear an introduction to the microfilm edition of the Pennsylvania tax lists, and a Circular of the Secretary of the Treasury, dated September 8, 1798. These documents provide an outline of the procedures followed in producing the original tax lists, and some idea of the subsequent history of those documents.

Both the Introduction and the Circular refer to lists that do not appear, for various reasons, in the Pennsylvania material. There are, of course, no lists of slaves (Lists C and F). The designations for the General Lists are, in both documents, denominated Lists D and E. No lists so designated appear in the Pennsylvania material; instead, the content of Lists 1 and 2 provide the information that should appear in Lists D and E. Why the list designations so vary is not explained.

It should also be pointed out that for the Pennsylvania lists, the General Lists 1 and 2 (but here C and D) seem very often to be a duplication rather than a summary of the Particular Lists (A and B).

The initials at the end of the Circular from the Secretary of the Treasury are an "O" followed by a letter which bears no particular resemblance to any letter in the English language. Since Oliver Wolcott was the Secretary at the time, that letter has been interpreted as a "W".

The final paragraph of the Introduction to the Pennsylvania microfilms is a reminder of the singular good fortune of the Pennsylvania records. Apparently only Massachusetts and Maryland records are extant in reasonably complete form, most of the records for other States have fallen into oblivion. The few records missing from those of Pennsylvania make that State an excellent source of information on housing and land ownership in the early days of the Republic.

Appendix--Introduction to the Microfilm Publication

INTRODUCTION TO THE MICROFILM EDITION

On the 24 rolls of this microfilm publication are reproduced 717 volumes containing tax lists and related summary abstracts for Pennsylvania created under an act of July 14, 1798 (1 Stat. 597), the first direct tax law of the U. S. Government, and under certain related acts. The related acts include the one of July 9, 1798 (1 Stat. 580), which provided for the valuation of lands and dwelling houses and the enumeration of slaves. Other acts which amended or affected the basic acts and which pertained to all the States include those enacted on February 18, 1799; January 2, May 10, and May 13, 1800; February 27 and March 3, 1801; March 16, 1802; and March 3, 1804.

The tax lists show names of persons who owned real property or slaves subject to the direct taxes levied by the act of July 14, 1798. Many lists also show valuations of the properties, amounts of taxes assessed, and some show the amounts of taxes collected. Initial assessments were made "with reference to" October 1, 1798. Among types of lists created after the initial assessment and included in this microfilm publication are lists of property omitted from or dwelling houses built after the assessment, lists of property sold or transferred, lists of uncollected taxes, lists of property sold because of unpaid taxes, and lists of receipts by the U. S. marshal from property sales.

The 1798 acts established nine divisions in Pennsylvania and provided for the appointment of a commissioner at the head of each. A division was composed of from two to five counties (except the First Division, which was composed of only Philadelphia County and city). The commissioners, acting as a board, divided the State into 38 assessment districts, each consisting of a county or part of a county. Boundaries of some counties were changed during the period covered by the records; Centre County, for example, was formed in 1800 partly from Northumberland County. The 1798 acts specified the duties of the commissioners and other officials who, under the direction of the Secretary of the Treasury, were charged with assessing and collecting the direct tax. Pennsylvania's apportioned share of the $2,000,000 tax levy was $237,177.727 [sic].

The National Archives arranged the volumes by divisions and thereunder by district, county, township, or other subdivision, and assigned a number to each volume. The number is filmed immediately before each volume. Five books are comprised of lists for locations within more than one division. Each of these lists has been filmed with the lists for the pertinent assessment district. The assigned volume numbers begin with the First Division, First District, and continue through the Ninth Division, Fifth District. The explanatory note microfilmed at the beginning of each roll gives the volume numbers and the division, district, county, and township or other subdivision for the lists on the roll.

The tax lists that constitute the main body of the records are of several types. The principal ones are described in a circular from the Secretary of the Treasury, dated September 8, 1798, which is reproduced after the alphabetical listing of place names on Roll 1. They comprise "Particular Lists" (Forms A, B, and C) and "General Lists" (Forms D, E, and F) of dwelling houses and other buildings, lands, lots, wharves, and slaves; and Summary Abstracts (Forms G, H, I and K) compiled from the General Lists.

The Particular Lists for Dwelling Houses (Form A) give information generally on locations, dimensions, number of stories, number and dimensions of windows, materials of which built, description of outhouses, and names of owners or occupants. (The so-called "window tax" provision of the July 9, 1798, act was repealed by an act approved February 28, 1799.) The Particular Lists of Lands, Lots, Buildings, and Wharves (Form B) show in general the size of each tract or lot, and the claimed exemptions; the number, description, and dimension of wharves and buildings except dwellings over $100 in value; and the names of owners or occupants. The Particular Lists for Slaves (Form C) usually gives the names of superintendents or owners, the total number owned, the number exempt from taxation because of State laws or disability, and the number between the ages of 12 and 50 subject to the tax.

The General Lists (Forms D, E, and F) are consolidations of the Particular Lists; and the Summary Abstracts

Appendix--Introduction to the Microfilm Publication

(Forms G, H, I, and K) are the "results or footings" of the General Lists presented on a township and district basis.

Reproduced on Roll 1, after the circular from the Secretary of the Treasury, is a printed table "showing the amount of TAX payable upon lands in Pennsylvania." (The conditions under which lands were taxed are set forth in the act of July 14, 1798.)

All tax lists for the Third District of the Second Division (part of Chester County) and for the First District of the Fourth Division (part of Berks County) are known to be missing. Only one entry (in volume 172) is known to be for the Second District of the Second Division (part of Lancaster County) and a few entries (in volumes 372 and 373) are the only entries for the Third District of the Fifth Division (part of Northampton County). Summary Abstracts for all these areas, however, are in volume 717. Many of the various types of lists once extant are now missing. Also, some volumes that have been filmed consist only of covers. Efforts of the National Archives to locate missing volumes have been unsuccessful.

As a rule, each volume pertains to only one township, but some pertain to two or more and may include names of smaller civil divisions. Usually a volume contains only one type of list, but some volumes contain several types. Also, some volumes may include a list or lists having no apparent relation to the cover title or to other lists in the same volume. Pages or parts of pages are missing from some volumes and others are badly discolored. Some entries are faded and others are illegible. A few volumes contain loose documents that have been identified and placed after the related list.

There is no general index to the records, but entries in some volumes are alphabetical by the first letter of the person's surname. An alphabetical list of place names that appear in the records was prepared by the National Archives as a finding aid and is included in this microfilm publication immediately after these introductory remarks. In preparing the list and the roll notes, the National Archives, as necessary, used the spelling of place names as they appear in the U. S. Bureau of the Census, Census of Population, 1950, Number of Inhabitants, Volume I (Washington, 1952), or Census of 1790, Heads of Families (Washington, 1908).

These tax lists are one of the few known collections of records relating to the first direct tax program of the U. S. Government. Most of the information in them is not available in other Federal records and the related Federal Government publications chiefly contain only statistical data on the direct tax program and not information on persons or items referred to in the records.

The records reproduced in this microcopy are a part of the Department of the Treasury records in the National Archives designated as Record Group 58, Records of the Internal Revenue Service. They were received in the National Archives from the U. S. District Court for the Eastern District of Pennsylvania.

Additional records received from the U. S. District Court for the Eastern District of Pennsylvania and placed in Record Group 58 include correspondence, account books, and other documents relating to the 1798 direct tax in Pennsylvania. The correspondence includes a copy of the table reproduced on Roll 1 of this microcopy and of a table of tax rates on dwellings. In the same record group are letters sent by the Commissioners of the Revenue and the Revenue Office, 1792-1807, that contain letters pertaining to the 1798 tax. They have been reproduced as Microcopy 414.

The circular reproduced on Roll 1 and later circulars relating to the 1798 direct tax are in a volume identified as Circulars from the Secretary of the Treasury, T Series, 1795-1818, Volume No. 0, in Record Group 56, General Records of the Department of the Treasury. Also in this record group is a volume containing correspondence 1807-1829, which pertains in part to 1798 direct tax matters.

Other records relating to the 1798 direct tax program are the accounts of accountable officers, which are in Record Group 217, Records of the U. S. General Accounting Office. Record Group 60, General Records of the Department of Justice, contains an opinion of the Attorney General concerning the power of a marshall to execute

Appendix--Introduction to the Microfilm Publication

deeds for land sold by a predecessor under the direct tax law. This opinion, dated December 29, 1817, is No. 6 in Opinions of the Attorney General's Office, Volume A, November 17, 1817 - June 19, 1821.

Government publications relating to the first direct tax include the American State Papers, Finance (volumes 1 and 2) and the annual Receipts and Expenditures of the United States for the period of the collection of the tax. Other published contemporary sources of information include street directories for the City of Philadelphia and a ward genealogy of the city and county of Philadelphia compiled by the Department of Records, Philadelphia, and published in 1959.

Miss Martha Simonetti and Mr. William H. Work from the Pennsylvania Historical and Museum Commission, Harrisburg, aided in identification and arrangement of the volumes reproduced in this microfilm publication, and in the preparation of the introduction, when they were enrolled in the Institute in the Preservation and Administration of Archives given by the American University, Washington, D. C.

The New England Historic Genealogical Society, Boston, has custody of 1798 direct tax records for the State of Massachusetts. Those for the State of Maryland are in the custody of the Maryland Historical Society, Baltimore. A few lists and contemporary copies of lists for Georgia are in the custody of the Department of Archives and History, Atlanta. The National Archives has no information on 1798 Federal tax lists for other States.

Appendix--Circular of the Secretary of the Treasury

CIRCULAR OF THE SECRETARY OF THE TREASURY

Treasury Department
Trenton, September 8th, 1798

(Circular)
To the Commissioners of
Direct Tax

Sir,

Agreeably to what was promised in my letter of August 7th, I have now the honour to transmit certain forms, which I request may be observed, in the execution of the Act "to provide for the valuation of Land and Dwelling Houses, and the enumeration of Slaves, within the United States."

The ninth section of the aforesaid act authorizes the assessors to require all persons "owning or possessing any Dwelling Houses, Lands, or Slaves, or having the care or management thereof," to deliver separate written lists, specifying and describing in one list the Dwelling Houses, in another the Lands and in a third the Slaves owned, possessed, or superintended in each Assessment District of the same State or any other of the United States.

As the accuracy of every part of the details, contemplated by the forms now transmitted will depend on the manner in which the Lists of Individuals are exhibited, it will be proper that the Assessors should be particularly instructed respecting this part of their duty.

The circumstances or information which ought to be exhibited in the Lists, as rendered by individuals, are indicated or specified in the columns marked 1, 2, 3, 4, and 5 of the form marked A; in the columns marked 1, 2, 3, 4, 5, & 6 of the form marked B; and in the columns marked 1, 2, 3, 4, 5, and 6 of the form marked C. If all the Lists of Individuals could be obtained according to the prescribed forms, much trouble would be saved to the assessors. Those above mentioned appear to be proper--in one or more of the States some of the columns will be found useless and may be suppressed; perhaps the Commissioners will judge that several columns ought to be substituted in lieu of those marked 3 in the forms A and B; they will, of course, decide on this point, having regard only to the principles of the system now communicated. The promulgation of the forms, as established, for the information of the people, appears to be expeditious.

In many instances, however, individuals will not be prepared to exhibit written Lists, and in such cases, it will be the duty of the Assessors, under the tenth section, to form the lists according to the information which may be disclosed. To enable the Assessors to perform this duty with facility, they ought to be provided with convenient Books, ruled according to prescribed forms, and of sufficient size to contain all the lists in each sub-division of an Assessment District. The pages of these books may be alphabetically marked and thus the lists of individuals entered in proper order at the time when they are originally taken.

It is, however, hardly to be expected that Individuals will, in rendering Lists, precisely comply with the forms marked A, B, and C, or such as may be established by the Commissioners. When the information required by Law is substantially given, the Lists must be received; when they are defective, erroneous, or fraudulent they must be corrected by the Assessors, according to the powers vested by Law, and the whole abstracted into the books before mentioned; the valuations are then to be made in the column marked 6 of the form A and in the column marked 7 of the form B. The numbers of Slaves, returned by individuals, are also to be classed according to the form C.

The Assessors ought to be instructed punctually to execute the direction contained in the twelfth section of the Act, by transmitting to the Commissioners of their respective divisions all particular lists of Dwelling Houses, Lands, or Slaves taken with reference to any other Assessment District, than that in which the owners or possessors reside; these lists will be separately taken and the Commissioners of Divisions will, of course,

Appendix--Circular of the Secretary of the Treasury

transmit them to the principal Assessors of the proper Assessment Districts; when the Principal Assessors are not known such lists may be transmitted to the Commissioners superintending the Divisions.

Particular caution will be necessary on the part of the Assessors in discharging the duty enjoined by the fifteenth section, so as, on one hand, to include in the lists all Dwelling Houses, Lands, and Slaves, belonging to persons not residing in their Assessment District, and on the other, to prevent double lists and valuations of the same property.

It will be useful to state, when practicable, in the descriptions of Dwelling Houses and Lands, the names of adjacent possessors or proprietors, thereby to facilitate the detection and correction of errors in the Particular Lists,

When the Particular Lists, A, B, and C, have been completed, except the column marked 7 in the form A, and the column marked 8, in the form B, which are to be filled up by the principal assessors under the authority vested in them by the 19th and 20th sections of the Act, they are to be abstracted by the Assessors into the General Lists marked D, E, and F; the columns marked 1 and 2 in the forms D and E are, however, to be left blank until the decision of the Commissioners shall have been communicated to the Principal Assessors, pursuant to the 22nd and 23^{d} sections of the Act; in forming the General Lists D, E, and F, the particular lists, taken with reference to each Township, or other civil division of the State, ought to constitute a distinct alphabetical series.

As Dwelling Houses with their Land and Appurtenances, are subject to taxation at different rates, in distinct classes, care must be taken to define separately, in the General Lists, agreeably to the form E, the valuation of each Dwelling House with the appurtenances; for the description, required by Law, a reference to the number of the particular list, which is to be inserted in the first column, must suffice.

The results or footings of the General Lists, marked D, E, and F, are, by the Assessors to be stated in Summary Abstracts, agreeably to the forms marked G, H, and I, which are to be transmitted to the Commissioners [one word undecipherable] these abstracts, and such copies of the General or Particular Lists as the Commissioners may direct to be transmitted to them, the Commissioners will proceed to revise, adjust, and vary the proceedings of the Assessors in the mode prescribed by the 22nd Section. The rate of addition or deduction, which may be determined on in relation to the valuations of the Dwelling Houses and Lands, will be inserted in the columns marked 1 of the forms marked G and H; the amounts extended into the succeeding column marked 2; and the Principal Assessors direction pursuant to the 23rd section to make the necessary calculations upon the Lists of Lands and Dwelling Houses which are to be inserted in the columns marked 2 of the forms D and E.

When the General List of Dwelling Houses according to the form D has been fully completed, the Principal Assessors are, pursuant to instructions from the Commissioners, to abstract therefrom a summary statement, according to the form K, exhibiting the gross valuation of Dwelling Houses with the number and value falling within each of the nine classes mentioned in the second section of the Act, "to lay and collect a Direct Tax within the United States."

The results of the proceedings of the Commissioners which are to be transmitted to my office in pursuance of the 22nd section of the Act "to provide for the valuation of Lands, &c" will be as follows:

1st A Statement of the Dwelling Houses and appurtenances within the State, according to the form K with the names or numbers of the Assessment Districts. This Statement will comprize all the returns of the Principal Assessors, agreeably to the said form; and the footings of the several columns will exhibit the whole valuation of Dwelling Houses &c, and the number and value of those referred to each class.

2nd A Statement of the Lands and valuations thereof in each Assessment District, to be collected from the Summary Abstracts completed agreeably to the form H.

Appendix--Circular of the Secretary of the Treasury

3rd A Statement of the number of Slaves in each Assessment District and in the State, to be collected from the summary Abstracts to be rendered agreeably to the form marked I.

I think it not superfluous or improper to mention, that instructions to the Assessors to be careful in arranging and numbering the Particular Lists, and to cause the General Lists to be fairly recorded on durable paper, would probably save expense and prevent errors.

The transmission of these forms has been delayed somewhat longer that was expected, in consequence of the interruptions occasioned by the removal of the public offices from Philadelphia.

I have the honor, &

O. W.

Appendix--Forms

Typical pages from each of the four lists are reproduced on pages 210-213. Because these pages are difficult to read the Titles of the Lists and the column headings in each are provided. The Form descriptions and the column headings are printed. Information to be added in longhand is here printed in italics.

TITLES AND COLUMN HEADINGS OF THE FORMS USED IN THE CUMBERLAND COUNTY, PENNSYLVANIA

Form A Particular List or Description of each Dwelling-house, which with Outhouses appurtenant thereto, and the Lot on which the same are erected, not exceeding two Acres in any case, and exceeding in Value the sum of One Hundred Dollars, which were owned, possessed, or occupied on the first day of October, 1798, in *[name of Twp.]* Cumberland County in the 3rd Assessment District and 6th Division.

　　[Entries are numbered in the space to the left of the first ruled column.]
　　Column 1　　Name of Occupant or Possessor
　　Column 2　　Name of Owner
　　Column 3　　[no overall heading--7 sub-headings]
　　　　Dwelling Houses [number of such structures]
　　　　Outhouses Appurtenant [number of such structures]
　　　　Dimensions or Area
　　　　Materials of which built
　　　　Number of stories
　　　　Windows
　　　　Lights
　　Column 4　　Number of Houses, &c, claimed to be exempted from valuation [overall heading--three sub-headings]
　　　　Dwelling Houses
　　　　Outhouses
　　　　Quantity of Land in the Lot [three subheadings: Acres, Perches, Square Feet
　　Column 5　　Number of Houses, &c admitted to be subject to valuation [three sub-headings]
　　　　Dwelling Houses
　　　　Outhouses
　　　　Quantity of Land in the Lot [sub-headings: Acres, Perches, Square Feet]
　　Column 6　Valuation of each Dwelling House with the Lot and Outhouses appurtenant thereto, by the Assistant Assessor (sub-headings for Dollars and Cents)
　　Column 7　Valuation of each Dwelling House with the Lot and Outhouses appurtenant thereto, by the Principal Assessor (sub-headings for Dollars and Cents)

Form B Particular List or Description of all Lands, Lots, Buildings and Wharves, owned possessed or occupied on the First Day of October, 1798 in *[Township and County]* being within and 6th Division, *[Assessment District]* in the State of Pennsylvania excepting only such Dwelling Houses as with Outhouses appurtenant thereto, and the lots on which they are erected, not exceeding two Acres in any Case, are above the Value of One Hundred Dollars.

　　[Entries are numbered in the space to the left of the first ruled column.]
　　Column 1　　Name of Occupant or Possessor
　　Column 2　　Name of Owner
　　Column 3　　REMARKS　　Number, Description, and Dimensions of Buildings and Wharves, situation, boundaries, or names of the adjacent Proprietors; also the circumstances under which an exemption from Valuation is claimed.

Appendix--Forms

Column 4   Dwelling Houses and Outhouses of a value not exceeding 100 Dollars [two sub-headings]
   Number of Dwelling Houses
   Value [sub-headings for Dollars and Cents]
Column 5   Quantities of Land and Lots to be exempted from Valuation (sub-headings for Acres, Perches, and Square Feet)
Column 6   Quantities of Land and Lots admitted to be subject to Valuation (sub-headings for Acres, Perches, and Square Feet)
Column 7   Valuation of each tract, lot, wharf, &c. by the Assistant Assessor (sub-headings for Dollars and Cents)
Column 8   Valuation of each tract, lot, wharf, &c. by the Principal Assessor (sub-headings for Dollars and Cents)

Form No. 1   A List or Description of each Dwelling-House, with the Out-houses appurtenant thereto, and the Lot on which the same are erected, not exceeding two acres in any case, and exceeding in Value the Sum of One Hundred Dollars, which were owned, possessed, or occupied on the first day of October 1798 in [name of township]. Cumberland County in the 3rd Assessment District and the 6th Division in the STATE of PENNSYLVANIA [Columns are not numbered on the Form.]

   Column [1]   Number of Returns
   Column [2]   Name of the Occupant
   Column [3]   Name of the Owner
   Column [4]   Dwelling House [number]
   Column [5]   Out-houses apurtenant [number and type]
   Column [6]   Dimensions or Area
   Column [7]   Materials of which built
   Column [8]   Number of Stories
   Column [9]   Number of Windows
   Column [10]   Number of Lights
   Column [11]   Quantity of Land in each Lot (sub-headings for Acres, Perches, and Square Feet)
   Column [12]   Situation and Adjoining Proprietors
   Column [13]   Valuation of the Assistant Assessor
   Column [14]   Claims of Exemption (if any) and Circumstances Thereof

Form No. 2   A List of All Lands, Lots, Buildings, and Wharves, owned, and possessed or occupied, on the first day of October, 1798, [Township and County] in the [District and Division] in the STATE of PENNSYLVANIA, excepting only such dwelling-houses as, with out-houses appurtenant thereto, and the lots on which the same are erected, not exceeding two Acres in any case, are above the Value of One Hundred Dollars. [Columns are not numbered on the Form.]

   Column [1]   Number of Returns
   Column [2]   Name of the Occupant
   Column [3]   Name of the Owner
   Column [4]   Number of Dwelling-Houses of a Value not exceeding One Hundred Dollars
   Column [5]   Dimensions of Dwelling-Houses & Out-Houses
   Column [6]   Number and description of all other BUILDINGS
   Column [7]   Quantity of Land in each Lot (sub-headings for Acres, Perches, and Square Feet)
   Column [8]   Situation and Adjoining PROPRIETORS
   Column [9]   Valuation of the Assistant Assessor
   Column [10]   Claims of Exemption (if any) and Circumstances Thereof and any other REMARKS on PROPERTY

Form A

A.

PARTICULAR List or Description of each Dwelling-house, which, with the Outhouses appurtenant thereto, and the Lot on which the same are erected, not exceeding two Acres in any Case, were owned, possessed, or occupied, on the First Day of October, 1798, in the Borough of Carlisle, in the County of Cumberland, being within the Sixth Division, of the Assessment District in the State of Pennsylvania, and exceeding in Value the Sum of One Hundred Dollars.

	Name of Occupant or Possessor	Name of Owner	Dwelling House	Outhouses Appurtenant	Dimensions or Area	Materials of which made	Number of Stories	Windows		Number of Houses, &c. claimed to be exempted from Valuation		Quantity of Land in the Lots			Number of Houses, &c. admitted to be subject to Valuation		Quantity of Land in the Lots			Valuation of each Dwelling-house with lot	Valuation
										Dwelling House	Out Houses	Acres	Perches	Square feet	Dwelling House	Out Houses	Acres	Perches	Square feet	Dollars	Cents
88	John Pope	Given James	1		26by31	Stone	2	9	145						1	2	—	26	121½	600	600
				Kitchen	15by17	Stone	1	2	24												
				Stable	11by18	Wood															
89	George Stuart	The Same	1		23by19	Wood	1	4	36						1	1	—	26	121½	200	200
				Kitchen	19by11½	Wood	1	2	10												
90	John Greenwood	Greenwood Jr.	1		18by18	Wood	1	7	54						1	3	—	52	243	300	300
				Kitchen	15by10	Wood	1	2	10												
				Corn Crib	15by15	Wood	1	3	14												
				Stable	9by9	Wood															
91	George Couse	Gray Widow	1		24by24	Wood	2	9	80						1	1	—	52	243	400	400
				Out House	15by13	Wood															
92	James Elliott	Gregg James Heirs	1		22by22	Wood	2	2	16						1	1	—	52	243	200	200
				Stable	18by12	Wood															
93	Thomas Clark	Gamble Widow	1		21by24	Wood	1	2	18						1	—	—	52	243	110	110
94	John Oliver	Holt Elizabeth Heirs	1		27by25	Stone	2	11	252						✓	3	—	52	243	1700	1700
				Kitchen	18by12	Stone	1	1	12												
				Smoke house	21by20	Wood	1	4	48												
				Stable	16by15	Wood															
95	James Hamilton Esqr	Hamilton Js. Esqr	1		30by36	Brick	3	20	198						1	5	—	52	243	3500	3500
				Kitchen		Brick	2	7	80												
				Office		Brick	2	8	192												
				Stable	28by36	Stone															
				2 Carriage Houses																		
96	John Hughes Esqr	Hughes John Esquire	1		30by38	Stone	2	6	130						1	2	—	22	10½	1300	1300
				Kitchen	28by18	Stone	1½	4	36												
				Stable	18by16	Wood															

Form B

PARTICULAR List or Description of all Lands, Lots, Buildings and Wharves, owned, possessed or occupied on the First Day of October, 1798, in Frankford Township _____ being within the Sixth Division, and the _____ _____ in the State of Pennsylvania, excepting only such Dwelling Houses as with the Outhouses appurtenant thereto, and the Lots on which they are erected, not exceeding two Acres in any Case, are above the Value of One Hundred Dollars.

No.	Name of Occupant or Possessor	Name of Owner	REMARKS — Number, Description, and Dimensions of Buildings and Wharves, &c.	Dwelling Houses and Out-houses Value not exceeding 100 Dollars	Value Dollars	Cts	Acres	Perches	Square feet	Acres	Perches	Square feet	Valuation of each Tract, Lot, Wharf, &c.		Valuation of each Principal &c.	
89	Officer, Alex.	Officer, Alex.	1 Log Barn 20 feet by 18; 1 Log Stable 20 by 18; Adjoining John Bell and the Mountain Land Very Stony				243						1379	50	1379	50
90	Jophen Myers G.	Jophen Myers Jacob	1 Log Barn 54 feet by 20; 1 Log Stable 20 by 16; Adjoining William Manna				178						1646	50	1646	30
91	Henery Horner	Potters Heirs	1 Log Dwelling House 30 feet by 20; Barn Logs 48 feet by 22; Adjoining Mathew Wilson	1	75		155						1715 75 1790		1790	
92	Parker, William	Parker, William	Fulling Mill the House of Logs 22 feet by 20 So more than half the Year an old Log Barn 30 feet by 18 Adjoining Jacob				98						784 790		790	
"	Charles Cohan	Do	Small Cabin House	1	6											
93	Painter Martin	Painter Martin	Barn under part Stone 60 feet by 30; Shop of Logs 18 feet by 16 an old Log Stable				128						1344 75			
"	George Varns	Do	1 Log Dwelling House 20 feet by 18; Adjoining Thomas Bilsel Esq	1	75								1419		1419	

No. 1.

A List or Description of each Dwelling-house, with the Out-houses appurtenant thereto, and the Lot on which the same are erected, not exceeding two Acres in any case, and exceeding in Value the Sum of One Hundred Dollars, which were owned, possessed, or occupied on the first day of October, 1798, by or in Eastpennsborough Township, Cumb. County, in the 3rd Assessment District, 6th Division, in the STATE of PENNSYLVANIA.

Number of Returns	NAME of the OCCUPANT	NAME of the OWNER	Dwelling House	Out-houses appurtenant	Dimensions or Area		Materials of which built	Number of Stories	Number of Windows	Number of Lights	Quantity of Land in each Lot			Situation and adjoining PROPRIETORS	Valuation of the assistant Assessor	Claims of Exemption (if any) and Circumstances thereof
											Acres	Perches	Square feet			
14		Bowman John	1	2	41 by	30	wood & stone	2	24	234	2				2350	
15		Berou Daniel	1		28 by	24	wood	1	5	60	2				400	
16	Michael Brein	Ditto	1	1	28	24	"	1	2	12	2				400	
17		Bladon Christly	1		25	24	"	1	2	12	2				400	
18		Byers Stephen	1	1	40	18	"	1	4	36	2				400	
19		Berlin John	1		30	20	"	1	6	48	2				400	
20		Bell Rice	1		40	22	"	1	4	36	2				400	
21		Bell James	1	1	28	22	"	2	7	61	2				450	
22		Butner Jacob	1	1	42	24	"	1	8	66	2				600	
23		Butner Jacob Jun	1		29	18	"	1	3	25	2				200	
24		Budorf Leonard	1		20	23	"	1	5	20	2				450	
25		Bour William	1	1	28	26	"	2	12		2				600	
26		Benage George	1		20	18	"		2	8	2				300	
27		Bell James	1	3	43	34	Stone	2	22	283	2				2200	
28		Bartholdi William	1	2	28	25	wood & stone	1	6	48	2				700	
29		Cath Jacob	1	2	26 by	24	wood	2	10	120	72				600	
30	Rudy Mulhelm	Caigther Thomas	1	2	22	16	"	2	5	60	2				520	
31	Robert Timson	Ditto	1		24	16	"	1	2	18	1				200	
32	Shail McElwain	Ditto			24	20	"	1	3	24	1				110	
33		Culbertson Sam'l	1	2	32	20	Stone	2	18	166	2				1400	
34		Culbertson Agnes	1	1	30	26	"	2	10	129	2				1400	
								1	4	36	2				500	

Form 2

No. 2.

A List of all Lands, Lots, Buildings, and Wharves, owned, and possessed, or occupied, on the first day of October, 1798, in Middleton Township, Cumb'd County — in the 3rd Assessment District 16th Division in the STATE OF PENNSYLVANIA, excepting only such Dwelling-houses as, with the Out-houses appurtenant thereto, and the Lots on which the same are erected, not exceeding two Acres in any case, are above the Value of One Hundred Dollars.

Number of Return	NAME of the OCCUPANT	NAME of the OWNER	Number of Dwelling Houses of a value not exceeding One Hundred Dollars	Dimensions of Dwelling-Houses & Out-Houses	Number and description of all other BUILDINGS	Quantity of Land in each Lot			Situation and adjoining PROPRIETORS	Valuations of the assistant Assessor	Claims of Exemption (if any) and Circumstances thereof, and any other REMARKS on PROPERTY
						Acres	Perches	Square Feet			
		Wise Jacob			Barn 62.26	295			James Hamilton	3610	
		Ditto Jun'r			"	98			David Stewart	1176	
		Wolf John			Stone Barn 60.30	228			Gibson Craighead	3000	
		Wolf And'w			Barn 20.20	148			John Lowe	230	
		Walliman Ludl.			"	98			And'w Ralston	490	
		Wolf Henry			"	48			Ritchy Thomas	96	
		White David			Barn 75.40 Grist & Sawmill	248			Gibson Craighead	1320	
	Alex'r Carothers	Ditto			"	100			James Smith	1240	
		Wolf Henry			"	25			Rob't Miller	336	
		Ffrang Silas			Barn 50 by 20	157			Thomas Duncan	1924	
		Higho And'w			Barn 48.20	295			Patrick Davidson	2484	

Indexes

INDEXES

Separate indexes are provided for property owners, and for occupants other than owners. The very few other persons who are mentioned are indexed in the Occupant Index

1 Index of Property Owners

The Index of Property Owners lists each owner in alphabetical order. When two owners are listed for a single property, the names are separately indexed. If on a single page the same name appears more than once the number of appearances is given in parenthesis. This listing does not imply that the listings are for the same person since it is usually necessary to use other sources of information to determine if a given person owns more than one piece of property or if there are two or more persons with identical names.

For the convenience of the reader the township or borough in which the property lies is given with each entry.

2 Index of Occupants and Other Persons

Occupants, other than owners, appear in this index, along with a few other persons (agents, surveyors, and others). Here too the township or borough is given with each entry.

Owner Index

INDEX TO LAND OWNERS

Owner	Twp.	Page	Owner	Twp.	Page	Owner	Twp.	Page
Abraham, Enoch	WPEN	189	Atchison, James	WPEN	189	Binder, Peter	NEWT	145
Achison, Thomas	SHTN	163	Atchley, Thomas	EPEN	63	Bishop, Adam	ALLN	1
Adair, James	CARL	18	Atherton, Thomas	SHTN	163	Bitchel, Jacob	WPEN	189
Adair, James	WPEN	189	Aukerman, Paul	EPEN	63	Bitner, John	ALLN	1
Adams, Abraham (2)	EPEN	63	Auld, David (3)	SHTN	164	Black, Andrew	ALLN	1
Addams, Matthew (2)	SHTN	163	Baird, William	SHTN	164	Black, John	ALLN	1
Admiston, Elizabeth	SHTN	163	Baker, Catharine, Widow (2)	MIDD	105	Black, Peter	WPEN	189
Aikey, Alexander	SHTN	163				Black, William	CARL	19
Aikman, John	NEWT	145	Baker, John	MIDD	105	Blackburn, Samuel	SHTN	165
Aitken, Robert	SHTN	163	Barber, John	CARL	18	Blain, Alexander	CARL	19
Aitkin, Robert, Jr.	SHTN	163	Barkley, Robert	CARL	19	Blain, David	WPEN	189
Albert, Henry	FRAN	82	Barnett, John (2)	MIFF	131	Blaine, Alexander (2)	MIDD	105
Albright, Henry	SHTN	163	Barnhart, John	EPEN	63	Blaine, Ephraim (3)	CARL	19
Alexander, Emy	SHTN	163	Barr, Robert	MIFF	131	Blaine, Ephraim	WPEN	189
Alexander, John	DICK	49	Barr, William (7)	SHTN	164	Blaine, Ephraim, Colonel	MIDD	105
Alexander, William	DICK	49	Barr, William	SHTN	165			
Alexander, William	MIDD	105	Bartholomy, Peter	CARL	19	Blaine, Ephraim, Colonel (4)	MIDD	106
Alexander, William, Esq.	CARL	18	Barton, William (2)	CARL	19			
Allen, Hugh, heirs	MIFF	131	Bashore, Daniel (2)	EPEN	63	Blaine, James	CARL	20
Alter, Jacob	FRAN	82	Baughman, Philip	SHTN	165	Blaine, James (3)	MIDD	106
Alter, Jacob	WPEN	189	Bear, Samuel	MIFF	132	Blaine, Robert (2)	CARL	20
Alter, John	FRAN	82	Bear, Widow	WPEN	189	Blaine, Robert (5)	MIDD	106
Anderson, Benjamin	ALLN	1	Beatty, James	NEWT	145	Blaine, Robert	MIDD	107
Anderson, James	EPEN	63	Beaty, William	WPEN	189	Blair, Isaiah, Dr.	CARL	20
Anderson, James	NEWT	160	Beelman, Christopher	ALLN	1	Blair, Rummel (2)	WPEN	190
Anderson, John	CARL	18	Beelman, Jacob	ALLN	1	Blair, William	CARL	20
Anderson, Joseph	CARL	18	Beelman, Peter	ALLN	1	Bloser, Christley	EPEN	64
Anderson, Seth	SHTN	163	Beigle, William Henry	CARL	19	Blythe, Benjamin, Jr.	SHTN	165
Andrew, Lodewick	NEWT	145	Bell, Andrew	MIFF	131	Blythe, Benjamin, Sr.	SHTN	165
Ansberger, Henry	EPEN	63	Bell, James	EPEN	63	Boar, William	EPEN	64
Anthony, Avis	SHTN	163	Bell, James	EPEN	64	Boher, John	SHTN	166
Apley, John	ALLN	1	Bell, John	FRAN	82	Bollinger, Abraham	ALLN	1
Apple, John	MIDD	105	Bell, John	MIFF	131	Bonner, John	CARL	20
Armor, Feby	CARL	18	Bell, Robert	EPEN	64	Bosler, John	EPEN	64
Armor, John	CARL	18	Bell, Walter (3)	MIFF	131	Bower, Elizabeth	EPEN	64
Armor, William	CARL	18	Bell, William	SHTN	189	Bower, George	EPEN	64
Armpister, Jacob	MIDD	105	Bell, William	WPEN	189	Bower, Martin	MIDD	107
Armstrong, Andrew	EPEN	63	Bell, William, Sr. (2)	SHTN	165	Bowman, Christopher	ALLN	2
Armstrong, James	DICK	49	Belsover, George	ALLN	1	Bowman, Jacob	FRAN	93
Armstrong, James, Dr.	CARL	18	Benage, George	EPEN	64	Bowman, Jacob	MIFF	131
Armstrong, James, Dr.	MIDD	105	Benedum, George	FRAN	82	Bowman, John	EPEN	64
Armstrong, James, heirs	FRAN	82	Beyman, John	SHTN	165	Bowman, Joseph	MIFF	132
Armstrong, John	EPEN	63	Bidleman, Abraham	SHTN	165	Bowman, Samuel	EPEN	64
Armstrong, John	MIDD	105	Bigler, John	CARL	19	Boyd, Abraham	HOPE	95
Arthur, John (3)	DICK	49	Bigler, William Henry	FRAN	82	Boyd, Adam	HOPE	95

Owner Index

Owner	Twp.	Page	Owner	Twp.	Page	Owner	Twp.	Page
Boyd, Elizabeth	NEWT	145	Bullock, Moses	CARL	21	Carver, Christopher	ALLN	3
Boyd, James	HOPE	95	Burkholder, Abram	FRAN	83	Carver, John	ALLN	3
Boyd, Simon	CARL	20	Burkholder, Christopher	MIDD	107	Cashler, David	ALLN	3
Boyd, William	NEWT	145	Burkholder, John	MIDD	107	Casper, Nicholas	MIFF	132
Brady, Joseph	HOPE	95	Burkholder, John	SHTN	166	Caul, John	MIDD	107
Brand, Adam	ALLN	2	Burkholder, Wilbrick	EPEN	65	Caupher, George	DICK	50
Brand, Jacob	ALLN	2	Burns, James	SHTN	166	Cerfass, Daniel	DICK	50
Brand, John	ALLN	2	Burns, Mary	CARL	21	Chain, Martha	EPEN	65
Brand, Ludwick	ALLN	2	Butler, Richard, Gen. heirs	CARL	21	Chambers, Robert	CARL	22
Brand, Martin	ALLN	2				Chambers, Robert (2)	MIDD	107
Bricker, Jacob	ALLN	2	Butler, Thomas, Colonel (3),	FRAN	83	Chambers, William (2)	MIDD	108
Bricker, Jacob, Jr.	ALLN	2				Chapman, James	NEWT	147
Bricker, John (2)	MIDD	107	Butner, Jacob	EPEN	65	Chapman, John	CARL	22
Bricker, Peter	ALLN	2	Butner, Jacob, Jr.	EPEN	65	Chesnut, Samuel	SHTN	167
Bricker, George	ALLN	2	Byerly, Andrew	NEWT	146	Chrislip, Charles	MIFF	132
Brindle, Adam	ALLN	2	Byers, Jacob	MIDD	107	Christian, Ludwig	MIFF	132
Briniser, Adam	ALLN	3	Byres, Stephen	EPEN	65	Cisna, James (3)	SHTN	167
Briniser, John	ALLN	3	Byremaster, Chri----	ALLN	3	Clark, George	FRAN	83
Brinizer, John	EPEN	64	Calbreath, Duncan	NEWT	146	Clark, George	HOPE	95
Brison, James	ALLN	3	Calhoun, Robert, heirs	CARL	21	Clark, George	SHTN	167
Brison, William	ALLN	3	Calpatrick, James	CARL	22	Clark, James	ALLN	3
Brittain, Adam	MIFF	132	Calvert, James	DICK	49	Clark, John	ALLN	3
Brittain, John	SHTN	166	Camp, Christopher	DICK	49	Clark, John	DICK	50
Brookens (& Wall)	SHTN	166	Camp, Stophel	DICK	50	Clark, John	SHTN	167
Brookens, William	SHTN	166	Campbell, Ebenezer	SHTN	184	Clark, Robert (2)	SHTN	167
Brooks, Joseph	ALLN	3	Campbell, Elizabeth	CARL	22	Clark, Thomas	NEWT	147
Brooks, William	ALLN	3	Campbell, Francis (2)	SHTN	166	Clark, Thomas, Sr.	NEWT	147
Broomfield, John, heirs	SHTN	166	Campbell, John	FRAN	83	Clark, William	ALLN	4
Brotherton, Samuel	HOPE	95	Campbell, John	SHTN	167	Clark, William	MIDD	108
Brown, Ephraim	ALLN	3	Campbell, Robert	MIDD	107	Clendennon, Samuel	EPEN	66
Brown, Henry	CARL	20	Campbell, Thomas	WPEN	190	Clendenon, John, Esquire (3)	EPEN	66
Brown, Henry	MIDD	107	Cannon, Samuel	SHTN	167			
Brown, James	ALLN	3	Carnahan, Adam, heirs	NEWT	146	Clever, Barnabas	SHTN	167
Bown, James (3)	NEWT	145	Carnahan, Robert	MIFF	132	Clever, Martin	WPEN	190
Brown, James	NEWT	146	Carnes, Richard	EPEN	65	Clinbagh, John	WPEN	191
Brown, John	CARL	20	Carothers, Andrew	EPEN	65	Clippinger, Anthony	SHTN	168
Brown, John	FRAN	82	Carothers, Andrew	WPEN	190	Clippinger, Frederick (2)	SHTN	168
Brown, John	WPEN	190	Carothers, Armstrong	WPEN	190			
Brown, Joseph	DICK	49	Carothers, James	EPEN	65	Clopper, Abraham	SHTN	168
Brown, William (2)	CARL	21	Carothers, James (2)	WPEN	190	Clopper, John	DICK	50
Brown, William	NEWT	146	Carothers, John	FRAN	83	Clouser, John	MIDD	108
Brown, William, Jr.	CARL	21	Carothers, John (2)	WPEN	190	Clouser, Margaret	MIDD	108
Brymer, Frederick	SHTN	166	Carothers, Martin	WPEN	190	Cochran, Patrick (2)	SHTN	168
Bryson, Hugh	NEWT	146	Carothers, Thomas (3)	EPEN	65	Cochran, Robert	DICK	50
Bryson, Samuel	MIFF	132	Carothers, William	EPEN	65	Cockley, Jacob	ALLN	4
Buchanan, Thomas (2)	NEWT	146	Carruthers, Sarah	DICK	50	Cockley, John	ALLN	4
Buchanan, Thomas	DICK	49	Carson, John (2)	NEWT	146	Coffee, Robert	SHTN	168
Buchanan, William (2)	CARL	21	Cart, Jacob	CARL	22	Coffee, Thomas	SHTN	168
Buck, George	MIFF	132	Cart, Jacob, heirs (2)	CARL	22	Coffman, Christley (2)	EPEN	66
Buddorff, Leonard	EPEN	65	Carter, Andrew, heirs	CARL	22	Collier, Hannah	CARL	22

Owner Index

Owner	Twp.	Page	Owner	Twp.	Page	Owner	Twp.	Page
Coffman, John	SHTN	168	Criswell, Samuel	CARL	24	Dicky, Margaret	MIDD	110
Colwell, James	SHTN	169	Crocket, Andrew, heirs	ALLN	5	Dill, John, Jr.	CARL	25
Colwell, John (2)	SHTN	169	Crocket, James	ALLN	5	Dill, Michael	EPEN	67
Coney, Peter	SHTN	169	Crocket, George	ALLN	5	Diller, Abraham	WPEN	191
Connelly, Joseph	FRAN	83	Croft, George	SHTN	170	Diller, Benjamin	MIDD	123
Contz, George	EPEN	66	Crone, John	NEWT	147	Diller, Casper	ALLN	5
Cooper, Adam (2)	MIDD	108	Croph, Casper	CARL	24	Diller, David	MIDD	124
Cooper, Charles (2)	CARL	22	Crous, Nicholas	CARL	24	Diller, Francis	WPEN	191
Cooper, John	NEWT	147	Crowel, Samuel (4)	NEWT	147	Diller, Martin	ALLN	5
Cooper, Robert, Dr.	HOPE	95	Crum, Dolly	EPEN	66	Diller, Martin	MIDD	124
Coover, Frederick	ALLN	4	Culbertson, Agness	EPEN	66	Diller, Peter	WPEN	191
Cope, Adam	CARL	22	Culbertson, Andrew (2)	SHTN	170	Dixon, Barnabas	FRAN	83
Copely, William, heirs	SHTN	169	Culbertson, Joseph	SHTN	170	Dixon, John	DICK	50
Copenhauer, Benjamin	SHTN	169	Culbertson, Robert	SHTN	170	Dodds, Joseph	ALLN	5
Corbet, Hannah	SHTN	169	Culbertson, Robert	SHTN	171	Dodds, Mary	EPEN	67
Cornman, John	MIDD	108	Culbertson, Samuel	EPEN	66	Donaldson, Andrew	DICK	50
Cornman, Valentine	MIDD	108	Culp, Jacob	EPEN	66	Donaldson, Thomas (2)	EPEN	67
Cort, Jacob	MIDD	108	Cunningham, Adam	HOPE	95	Donally, Barney	NEWT	148
Cory, Henry	MIDD	108	Cunningham, James	ALLN	5	Donnell, Francis	MIFF	133
Cosh, Philip	FRAN	83	Cunningham, John	HOPE	95	Douglass, James	ALLN	5
Cover, George (2)	ALLN	4	Dagon, Jacob	MIFF	132	Douglass, John	EPEN	67
Cover, Gideon	ALLN	4	Dale, George	MIDD	110	Douglass, John	MIDD	111
Cowan, William (3)	SHTN	169	Daugherty, Sarah	CARL	24	Douglass, William (2)	FRAN	84
Cox, Samuel	SHTN	169	Davidson, George (2)	WPEN	191	Duck, George	NEWT	148
Cox, William	ALLN	4	Davidson, George, Jr.	WPEN	191	Duck, William	NEWT	148
Coyler, Conrad	SHTN	169	Davidson, John	MIFF	132	Dull, Conrad	DICK	50
Coyler, Leonard	SHTN	170	Davidson, John	NEWT	147	Dunbar, John	FRAN	84
Craig, David	CARL	23	Davidson, John	NEWT	148	Dunbar, John (3)	NEWT	148
Craighead, Gilson	MIDD	108	Davidson, John	WPEN	191	Dunbar, John	SHTN	171
Craighead, Gilson	MIDD	109	Davidson, Matthew	WPEN	191	Dunbar, John	WPEN	191
Craighead, James	CARL	23	Davidson, Patrick	MIDD	110	Dunbar, William	WPEN	191
Craighead, John	MIDD	109	Davidson, Robt., Rev.(2)	CARL	24	Duncan, Arnold	SHTN	171
Craighead, Richard	MIDD	109	Davidson, Robert, Rev.	MIDD	110	Duncan, Daniel, heirs (5)	SHTN	171
Craighead, Thomas (2)	MIDD	109	Davis, Adam	NEWT	148	Duncan, David	SHTN	172
Craighead, Thomas, Jr.	MIDD	109	Davis, Elijah	MIDD	110	Duncan, James, Esq. (2)	CARL	25
Craighead, Thomas, Sr.	MIDD	109	Dearmin, Henry	NEWT	148	Duncan, James, Esq. (2)	MIDD	111
Craine, Richard (2)	MIDD	109	Deddo, John	ALLN	5	Duncan, John	HOPE	95
Crane (& Fought)	MIDD	109	Dedwiler, Jacob	NEWT	148	Duncan, John	HOPE	96
Crawl, Abraham	ALLN	4	Delaney, John (2)	CARL	24	Duncan, John, heirs (3)	CARL	25
Crawl, Mathias	ALLN	4	Delaney, John	CARL	25	Duncan, Joseph (3)	SHTN	172
Creamer, Peter	SHTN	170	Delap, John	ALLN	5	Duncan, Stephen	CARL	25
Creigh, John (4)	CARL	23	Denny, Daniel	MIDD	110	Duncan, Stephen, Esq.(2)	CARL	25
Creigh, John	MIDD	109	Denny, Ebenezer	CARL	25	Duncan, Stephen, Esq.(3)	CARL	26
Cress, Henry	EPEN	66	Denny, Jane	EPEN	67	Duncan, Stephen, heirs (2)	SHTN	172
Cress, John	SHTN	170	Denny, William	MIDD	110	Duncan, Thomas, Esq.	CARL	26
Crever, Jacob	WPEN	191	Devalt, John	MIFF	133	Duncan, Thomas (2)	MIDD	111
Crever, Jacob, Esq. (2)	CARL	23	Dibbs, Abraham	MIFF	133	Duncan, Thomas	NEWT	172
Crever, John	CARL	24	Dickey, George	MIDD	123	Duncan, Thomas	SHTN	191
Crisor, Jacob	ALLN	5	Dickson, Thomas (2)	CARL	25			
Criswell, Robert	DICK	50	Dicky, George	MIDD	110			
			Dicky, James	EPEN	67			

Owner Index

Owner	Twp.	Page	Owner	Twp.	Page	Owner	Twp.	Page
Duncan, William	WPEN	191	Esrig, Simon	NEWT	149	Frank, Adam	CARL	27
Dunlap, Mary	WPEN	192	Everly, Henry	ALLN	6	Frank, Jacob	CARL	27
Dunlap, William	WPEN	192	Everly, John	EPEN	68	Frederick, Peter	EPEN	68
Dunn, Jacob	MIDD	111	Evers, Philip	EPEN	68	Free, Henry	ALLN	6
Dunn, Nicholas	FRAN	84	Eversole, Jacob	MIDD	112	Freelin, Mary	CARL	27
Dysert, Benjamin	HOPE	96	Eversole, John	MIDD	112	Frenkelbarger, George	ALLN	6
Dysert, James	HOPE	96	Ewing, John	DICK	52	Fridley, George	ALLN	6
Eagy, Michael	ALLN	5	Ewing, William	DICK	52	Fry, Jacob	SHTN	173
Eagy, Michael	ALLN	6	Eylor, Jacob (tailor)	CARL	27	Fulton, Francis	DICK	52
Early, Hugh	NEWT	149	Farmer, Lewis	SHTN	173	Funk, Daniel	DICK	52
Ebright, Philip	FRAN	84	Feeman, Adam	ALLN	6	Galbraith, Alexander	CARL	27
Eby, Henry	CARL	26	Felair, Andrew	MIFF	133	Galbraith, Andrew, Esq.	EPEN	68
Eby, Moses	CARL	26	Felair, Christopher	MIFF	133	Galbreath, John	EPEN	68
Echelbarger, Christopher	ALLN	6	Felair, Jacob	MIFF	133	Galbreath, Joseph	DICK	52
			Felter, Jacob	CARL	29	Galbreath, Samuel (3)	DICK	52
Echelberger, Stophel	EPEN	67	Fenner, Godfrey	DICK	52	Galbreath, William	FRAN	85
Eckart, Jonas	MIDD	111	Fenton, Samuel	MIFF	133	Gamble, Widow	CARL	28
Eckles, Nathaniel	DICK	50	Ferguson, Andrew	EPEN	68	Gammel, Benjamin	NEWT	149
Ediburn, Jacob	MIDD	111	Ferguson, William	NEWT	149	Gander, Peter	MIFF	134
Ege, Michael (3)	DICK	51	Ferguson, William	WPEN	192	Garvin, Henry	MIDD	113
Ege, Michael (3)	MIDD	111	Filson, Samuel (2)	DICK	52	Gatshall, Philip	ALLN	6
Ege, Michael	MIDD	112	Findley, James	SHTN	173	Gault, Alexander	MIFF	134
Ege, Thornburgh & Aitkin (4)	DICK	51	Findley, Samuel	MIFF	133	Gault, James	MIFF	134
			Findley, Samuel	MIFF	134	Gaw, John	CARL	28
Egolf, Michael	CARL	26	Fireovid, John	MIDD	112	Geddes, John, Esq.	NEWT	149
Eiley, Phillip	FRAN	84	Fishburn, Peter	WPEN	192	Geddis, James (2)	FRAN	85
Ekhart, Conrad	MIDD	112	Fisher, James	EPEN	68	Geddis, Samuel, heirs	EPEN	69
Eliot, Joseph	ALLN	6	Fisher, Leonard (2)	EPEN	68	Gees, Christopher	MIFF	134
Elliot, David	MIDD	112	Fisher, Samuel	EPEN	68	Gees, Conrad (2)	MIFF	134
Elliot, James	MIDD	112	Fisher, Thomas	EPEN	68	Gees, John	ALLN	7
Elliott, Alexander	MIFF	133	Fite, Jacob	MIFF	134	Gees, Peter	FRAN	85
Elliott, James	CARL	26	Fleming, Archibald	SHTN	173	Gees, Samuel	ALLN	7
Elliott, John	CARL	26	Fleming, James	MIDD	112	George, David	MIDD	113
Elnode, Peter	SHTN	172	Fleming, John	MIDD	112	George, Jacob	MIFF	134
Elter, Samuel	MIDD	112	Fleming, John	MIDD	113	George, Martin	ALLN	7
Ely, Andrew	SHTN	173	Foglesonger, Jacob	HOPE	96	George, Martin (2)	FRAN	85
Ely, George, heirs	SHTN	173	Foglesonger, David	SHTN	173	Gerish, Hanicle	FRAN	85
Ely, Jacob	EPEN	67	Foglesonger, Michael	SHTN	173	Gibb, John	HOPE	96
Emminger, Andrew	EPEN	67	Forbes, John	WPEN	192	Gibson, John	DICK	53
Emminger, Conrad (2)	EPEN	67	Forney, Jacob	EPEN	68	Giffen, James (2)	MIDD	113
Emminger, Susannah	EPEN	67	Fosler, George (2)	MIDD	113	Giffen, Samuel	MIDD	113
Ensminger, Jacob	MIFF	133	Fossett, Robert	CARL	29	Gilbert, George	HOPE	96
Ernest, John	FRAN	84	Foster, Thomas	CARL	29	Gilbreath, Hannah	HOPE	96
Ertford, Dewalt (2)	EPEN	68	Foster, Thomas	WPEN	192	Gillespie (or Syke)	FRAN	85
Erwin, Samuel	HOPE	96	Fought (& Crane)	MIDD	122	Gillespie, George	FRAN	85
Erwin, Samuel, Esq.	ALLN	6	Fought, Frederick	MIDD	113	Gillespie, Nathaniel	MIFF	134
Espy, Thomas (2)	FRAN	84	Fought, Jacob	MIDD	113	Gillespie, Robert	MIFF	134
Espy, Widow	FRAN	84	Foulk, Stephen (2)	CARL	30	Gillespie, Widow	FRAN	86
Espy, William	FRAN	85	Foulk, Stephen (2)	MIDD	113	Gilson, Richard	EPEN	69
Esrig, Jacob	MIFF	133	Fox, John	NEWT	149	Ginger, Ludwick	EPEN	69

Owner Index

Owner	Twp.	Page	Owner	Twp.	Pg.	Owner	Twp.	Page
Given, James (4)	CARL	28	Hafson, Jonathan (2)	MIDD	114	Hefflefinger, Martin	HOPE	97
Gladstone, William	SHTN	173	Haft, John	DICK	53	Hefflefinger, Philip	HOPE	97
Glen, Moses, heirs	SHTN	173	Hair, Daniel	ALLN	8	Heger, John	MIDD	114
Glenn, Alexander	DICK	53	Hamil, Robert	SHTN	174	Helms, Jacob	SHTN	174
Glenn, David	WPEN	192	Hamilton, Jams	CARL	29	Hemphill, James (2)	HOPE	97
Glenn, Elizabeth	DICK	53	Hamilton, James	MIFF	135	Henderson, Benjamin	MIDD	114
Glenn, Jane	WPEN	192	Hamilton, James	SHTN	174	Henderson, James (2)	HOPE	97
Glenn, John	MIDD	114	Hamilton, James, Esq.	CARL	29	Henderson, Matthew (2)	MIDD	115
Glenn, Thomas	DICK	53	Hamilton, James, Esq.(2)	MIDD	114	Henderson, Margaret (3)	SHTN	174
Good, Peter	WPEN	192	Handle, Jacob	CARL	29	Hendricks, John	MIFF	149
Goodour, Peter	ALLN	7	Hannah, Ezekiel	HOPE	96	Henry, Master [?]	ALLN	8
Goorly, John	DICK	53	Hannah, Samuel	HOPE	96	Hess, John	HOPE	97
Goosewelder, John	ALLN	7	Hannah, Samuel	HOPE	97	Hesson, Jack	DICK	54
Gourd, Joseph	DICK	53	Hannah, William	FRAN	86	Hewit, Michael	ALLN	8
Gourley, Samuel	WPEN	192	Hare, Abraham	ALLN	8	Hickes, Andrew	WPEN	193
Graham, Arthur	FRAN	86	Hare, Abraham (2)	CARL	29	Hickrenel, Abraham	ALLN	8
Graham, Isaiah	FRAN	86	Harkness, William	ALLN	8	Hickrenel, David	ALLN	9
Graham, James	ALLN	7	Harman, Christly	EPEN	69	Hickrennel, Frederick	ALLN	9
Graham, James (2)	WPEN	192	Harman, Martin, Jr.	EPEN	69	Hide, Abraham	ALLN	9
Graham, Jerred	WPEN	193	Harman, Martin, Sr.	EPEN	69	Highlands, John	SHTN	175
Graham, John, heirs	ALLN	7	Harper, James	MIFF	135	Highlands, William	SHTN	175
Gray, James	CARL	28	Harper, James	NEWT	149	Hill, Henry	HOPE	97
Gray, Widow	CARL	28	Harper, John	DICK	54	Hinkle, Philip	MIDD	115
Greenwood, John (2)	CARL	28	Harper, John, Jr.	DICK	54	Hiry, Christopher	HOPE	97
Greer, Samuel	CARL	28	Harper, John, Sr. (2)	DICK	54	Hock, Henry	MIDD	115
Greer, Samuel	CARL	29	Harper, William	MIFF	149	Hoge, David, Esq.	EPEN	70
Greer, Thomas	DICK	53	Harps, John, Rev.	CARL	29	Hoge, John, Rev.	EPEN	70
Greger, Abraham	MIFF	135	Harshbarger, Ann	EPEN	70	Hoge, Jonathan,	EPEN	70
Gregg, Andrew	MIDD	114	Hartman, Henry	DICK	54	Esq. (2)		
Gregg, James, heirs	CARL	29	Harvey, Andrew	FRAN	86	Hoge, Jonathan, Jr.	EPEN	70
Gregg, John	MIDD	114	Haslett, Samuel	CARL	30	Hogg, James (2)	MIDD	115
Gregor, John	ALLN	7	Haun, Jacob	MIFF	149	Hollar, Peter	NEWT	149
Gregory, James	ALLN	7	Hauser, John	MIFF	149	Holler, Henry	HOPE	98
Gregory, Widow	FRAN	86	Hawk, George	EPEN	70	Hollinger, Jacob	ALLN	9
Greson, William (2)	EPEN	69	Hawk, John	EPEN	70	Holmes, Andrew	CARL	30
Grice, John	EPEN	69	Hawk, Michael (2)	EPEN	70	Holmes, Andrew	MIDD	149
Griffen, Josiah	SHTN	174	Hawker, John	EPEN	70	Holmes, Hugh	NEWT	149
Griger, John	DICK	53	Hawthorn, James	NEWT	149	Holmes, John	CARL	33
Grouse, Jacob	MIFF	135	Hay, Henry	WPEN	193	Holmes, John	MIDD	115
Grouse, John	ALLN	8	Hays, John	DICK	54	Holmes, Jonathan	MIDD	115
Grouse, John	EPEN	69	Hays, Joseph	CARL	30	Holmes, William	MIDD	115
Grouse, Simon	EPEN	69	Hazleton, Hamilton	NEWT	149	Holt, Elizabeth	SHTN	175
Grumbley, Adam	ALLN	8	Heap, John (2)	SHTN	174	Holt, Elizabeth, heirs	CARL	30
Grumley, Frederick	EPEN	69	Heap, John, Esq.	CARL	30	Hoon, Stophel	NEWT	150
Grumley, Stophel	ALLN	8	Heck, Jacob	ALLN	8	Hooper, Jacob	SHTN	175
Grupe, Philip (2)	DICK	53	Heck, John	ALLN	8	Hoopstater, Jacob	FRAN	86
Gunkle, Michael	EPEN	69	Heckman, Widow	SHTN	174	Hoosenight [?], Barbara	CARL	30
Gustine, Lemuel	CARL	31	Hedrick, George	MIDD	114	Hoover, Christian	SHTN	175
Gustine, Lemuel, Dr.	CARL	31	Hedrick, John	MIDD	114	Hoover, Frederick	MIFF	135
Gustine, Lemuel, Dr.	FRAN	86	Hefflefinger, Frederick	HOPE	97	Hoover, Michael	ALLN	9
Guy, Thomas	MIDD	114	Haney, John	SHTN	174	Hippensteel, Joseph	SHTN	175

Owner Index

Owner	Twp.	Page	Owner	Twp.	Page	Owner	Twp.	Page
Houk, Adam	DICK	54	Johnston, James	FRAN	87	Kitch, John	ALLN	10
Houk, Adam, Sr.	DICK	54	Johnston, William	MIDD	116	Kitch, Martin	MIDD	117
Houke, Adam	DICK	54	Jones, Owen	SHTN	176	Kittera, John W. (2)	MIDD	117
Houser, John	NEWT	150	Jones, Thomas	CARL	31	Kitters [?], John	DICK	55
Houser, Martin	ALLN	9	Jones, William	ALLN	9	Klay, John	FRAN	88
Houser, Martin	EPEN	70	Jumper, Conrad (2)	FRAN	87	Klay, Mathias	FRAN	88
Houts, Henry	WPEN	193	Jumper, Conrad	WPEN	193	Kline, George	CARL	23
Houts, Henry, heirs	MIFF	135	Jumper, Jacob	FRAN	99	Kline, George (2)	CARL	32
Hover, David	ALLN	9	Junken, Benjamin (2)	EPEN	71	Kline, George	SHTN	176
How, Henry	HOPE	98	Junken, Joseph	EPEN	71	Kline, John	MIDD	117
Howard, Nicholas	NEWT	156	Junkin, Joseph	WPEN	193	Kline, Matthias	SHTN	176
Hudley, Samuel	MIFF	135	Kean, Percival	WPEN	193	Knettle, George	MIFF	136
Hughs, John	CARL	30	Kearlsey, Jane	SHTN	176	Knisley, Samuel	ALLN	10
Hughs, John, Esq.	CARL	30	Kearn, Henry	FRAN	87	Kosh, Michael	MIDD	117
Humes, James	EPEN	71	Keith, William	CARL	31	Kraft, Ralph	FRAN	88
Hunter, John	CARL	30	Keller, Henry	EPEN	72	Krehl, Nicholas	SHTN	176
Hunter, John	MIDD	116	Keller, Leonard	CARL	31	Kreishner, John	CARL	32
Hunter, Joseph	HOPE	98	Kelly, Francis	MIDD	116	Krips, Joseph	MIDD	117
Hunter, Joseph	NEWT	150	Kelso, James	SHTN	176	Kritzer, Nicholas	EPEN	72
Hunter, William	ALLN	9	Kelso, William	EPEN	72	Krutzer, Adam	EPEN	72
Hunter, William	MIFF	136	Kennedy, Hugh	CARL	31	Kulp, Simon	FRAN	88
Hunter, William	SHTN	175	Kennedy, Joseph	MIDD	116	Lackey, Alexander (2)	FRAN	88
Hursh, Jacob	EPEN	71	Kennedy, Thomas	MIFF	136	Lackey, Alexander	WPEN	194
Huston, James	WPEN	193	Kennedy, Thomas (2)	NEWT	150	Laird, Hugh	ALLN	10
Huston, John	DICK	54	Kennedy, Thos., Esq.(3)	FRAN	87	Laird, James	FRAN	88
Huston, John (2)	EPEN	71	Kennedy, Thos., Esq.(3)	FRAN	88	Laird, James	FRAN	89
Huston, Jonathan	EPEN	71	Kenny, Robert (3)	MIDD	116	Laird, Matthew	MIDD	117
Huston, William (2)	DICK	55	Kerns, Jacob	SHTN	176	Laird, Samuel	MIDD	117
Hutton, James	CARL	30	Kerr, Andrew	CARL	31	Laird, Samuel, Esq. (2)	CARL	32
Hutton, John	DICK	55	Kerr, Thomas	SHTN	176			
Hutton, John	SHTN	175	Keys, James, Jr.	EPEN	72	Lamb, John	ALLN	10
Hutton, Solomon	ALLN	9	Kibler, George	MIDD	117	Lamberton, James	MIDD	118
Hyser, Rudolph	FRAN	86	Kiehl, Francis	MIDD	117	Lamberton, James	SHTN	176
Irvin, Armstrong	EPEN	71	Kilgore, Jesse	NEWT	150	Lamberton, Simon	MIDD	118
Irvin, James	EPEN	71	Kilgore, Robert	NEWT	150	Lambuton, James (2)	CARL	32
Irvin, John	EPEN	71	Kilgore, William	NEWT	150	Lambuton, John (2)	CARL	32
Irvin, William	EPEN	71	Kimble, Samuel	EPEN	72	Lamerson, Joshua [?]	DICK	55
Irvine, Samuel	WPEN	193	Kincaid, John	MIDD	117	Lammond, James	NEWT	151
Irvine, William, Gen.	CARL	31	Kincaide, John	CARL	32	Lane, Widow (2)	MIDD	118
Irwin, James	MIDD	116	King, David (2)	DICK	55	Lantz, Philip	EPEN	72
Irwin, Samuel, Esq.	MIDD	116	King, John	FRAN	88	Latshaw, Joseph	SHTN	177
Irwin, William, Gen.(2)	MIDD	116	Kinour, Jacob	ALLN	9	Laughlin, Alexander	MIFF	136
Iselt [?], John	CARL	31	Kinsemore, John	FRAN	88	Laughlin, Atchison	WPEN	194
Jackson, Samuel	CARL	31	Kinsey, Jacob	EPEN	72	Laughlin, Hugh	MIFF	136
Jacob, Thomas	MIFF	136	Kinslo, Jacob	WPEN	193	Laughlin, John	HOPE	98
Jameson, David	SHTN	175	Kipford, Abram	NEWT	151	Laughlin, Mary	WPEN	194
Jameson, William	SHTN	175	Kirkpatrick, James	WPEN	194	Layman, Abram	FRAN	89
Jamison, John	NEWT	150	Kish heirs	MIFF	136	Lear, Henry	SHTN	177
Johnston, Adam	CARL	31	Kissel, Jacob, Jr.	EPEN	72	Lechler, Henry	CARL	33
Johnston, Ann	SHTN	176	Kissel, Jacob, Sr.	EPEN	72	Lee, John	DICK	55
Johnston, James	FRAN	86	Kisshecker, Nicholas	ALLN	9			

Owner Index

Owner	Twp.	Page	Owner	Twp.	Page	Owner	Twp.	Page
Lee, Richard, heirs (2)	CARL	33	Longstorff, Martin	EPEN	73	Maxwell, Robert	DICK	56
Lee, Thomas	DICK	55	Lootz, George	EPEN	73	Maxwell, William	NEWT	151
Lee, Timothy	ALLN	10	Lose, Jacob (2)	MIDD	118	Maxwell, William	SHTN	178
Leeper, William	MIFF	136	Louchridge, Abraham (2)	CARL	34	McAlister, Andrew	WPEN	194
Leeper, William	SHTN	177	Louchridge, Abraham (3)	CARL	35	McAvoy, John	NEWT	151
Lefever, George	CARL	33	Loudon, Archibald	CARL	35	McBeath, Alexander	MIDD	119
Lefever, George	WPEN	194	Loudon, Archibald	EPEN	73	McBeath, Alexander	MIDD	120
Lefever, Lawrence	WPEN	194	Loudon, Matthew	EPEN	73	McBeth, Alexander	WPEN	195
Lefferry, David	CARL	33	Loughridge, Abraham (3)	CARL	38	McBride, Alexander, Jr.	DICK	56
Legget, Patrick	CARL	33	Lourey, James (2)	SHTN	177	McBride, Alexander, Sr.	DICK	56
Leiper, William	SHTN	177	Love, James	MIDD	118	McCalister, Archibald	EPEN	73
Leirston, Jacob (2)	EPEN	72	Love, James	WPEN	194	McCall, James	SHTN	178
Lemmon, Adam	FRAN	89	Love, John	MIDD	118	McCall, Robert, heirs, (2)	SHTN	179
Lemmon, Jacob	FRAN	89	Love, John	WPEN	194			
Leonard, Jane, Widow	MIDD	118	Lusk, Robert	MIFF	136	McCandless, George (2)	SHTN	178
Leonard, Philip	MIDD	118	Lusk, Robert	NEWT	151	McCandless, George	SHTN	179
Lepard, Henry	FRAN	89	Lusk, William (2)	DICK	56	McCann, Robert	NEWT	151
Lepard, John	FRAN	89	Lusk, William, Esq.	DICK	56	McCarrol, John	SHTN	179
Lesher, Gasper	HOPE	98	Lutz, Balser	MIDD	119	McCartney, Patrick	CARL	35
Levy, William	CARL	33	Lyon, Samuel (2)	MIDD	119	McCaskry, Samuel	WPEN	194
Levy, William, Esq.	CARL	33	Lyon, William (2)	MIDD	119	McCauley, John	CARL	35
Leyburn, Robert	CARL	33	Lyon, William, Esq. (3)	CARL	35	McClean, Cornelius	SHTN	179
Lidack, Adam	ALLN	10	Magaw, Robert, heirs	CARL	35	McClelland, Thomas	HOPE	98
Lightcap, Solomon, Jr. (2)	NEWT	151	Magee, Alexander	SHTN	177	McClintock, Alexander, heirs (2)	MIFF	137
			Mahaffey, Andrew	MIDD	119			
Lightcap, Solomon, Sr.	NEWT	151	Mahaffey, John	MIDD	119	McClintock, John	MIDD	120
Lightner, Jacob	SHTN	177	Mahaffey, Margaret (2)	MIDD	119	McClintock, Sarah	MIFF	137
Limes, Michael	FRAN	89	Mahan, Archibald	SHTN	177	McClure, Charles (3)	CARL	36
Lindsay, Robert	FRAN	89	Mahan, David (2)	SHTN	178	McClure, Charles (7)	MIDD	120
Lindsay, Widow	FRAN	89	Malter, Jacob (2)	MIDD	119	McClure, Charles	WPEN	194
Lindsay, William	FRAN	89	Mann, George	EPEN	73	McClure, Robert, heirs	FRAN	90
Lindsey, David (3)	CARL	33	Mark, Henry	ALLN	10	McClure, Samuel	SHTN	179
Lindsey, Sidney	CARL	34	Markley, John	ALLN	10	McClure, Thomas	EPEN	73
Line, Abraham	DICK	55	Marlin, Joshua	DICK	56	McCollum, John	NEWT	151
Line, John	DICK	55	Marshall, John	MIFF	136	McCullum, John	SHTN	179
Line, William (2)	DICK	56	Marshall, William	MIFF	136	McColouch, John	SHTN	179
Loffman, Philip	CARL	34	Martin, Edward (3)	EPEN	73	McConnel, Mathew	EPEN	73
Logan, Alexander	FRAN	90	Martin, Paul, Jr.	MIFF	137	McConnel, William	SHTN	179
Logan, Henry	FRAN	90	Martin, Paul, Sr.	MIFF	137	McCormack, Elizabeth	HOPE	98
Logan, John	FRAN	90	Martin, Samuel	ALLN	11	McCormack, Hugh	MIDD	120
Loghridge, Abraham	MIDD	118	Martin, Thomas	NEWT	151	McCormack, Sarah, Widow	MIDD	120
Logue, Adam	CARL	34	Martin, Thomas (2)	SHTN	178	McCormick, James, Esq.	CARL	36
Logue, George, Esq. (5)	CARL	34	Marvet, Hartman	ALLN	11	McCormick, Joseph	MIFF	137
Logue, George, Esq. (2)	MIDD	118	Mason, Isaac	HOPE	98	McCormick, Robert	EPEN	73
Long, Benjamin	ALLN	10	Masoner, Jacob	DICK	56	McCormick, Robert	NEWT	152
Long, Frederick	ALLN	10	Mather, Jacob	CARL	35	McCormick, Samuel	MIFF	137
Long, John	ALLN	10	Mathers, James	DICK	56	McCormick, Thomas	MIFF	137
Longnecker, Abraham	EPEN	72	Mathers, John	WPEN	194	McCormick, William	EPEN	83
Longnecker, Joseph	EPEN	73	Mathers, Samuel	WPEN	194	McCoskey, Samuel A. (2)	CARL	36
Longnecker, Michael	SHTN	177	Mathers, Thomas	MIFF	137	McCoy, Archibald	MIFF	137
Longsdorff, Adam	EPEN	73						

Owner Index

Owner	Twp.	Page	Owner	Twp.	Page	Owner	Twp.	Page
McCoy, Archibald	NEWT	152	McFeely, John	MIDD	121	Micky, Robert	NEWT	171
McCoy, James	NEWT	152	McGinnis, John	CARL	37	Miller, Abraham	ALLN	12
McCoy, John	CARL	36	McGrew, Archibald	ALLN	11	Miller, French	SNTN	181
McCracken, William	NEWT	152	McGuffin, James	NEWT	153	Miller, George	NEWT	154
McCracken, William	WPEN	195	McGuffin, Joseph, heirs	NEWT	153	Miller, Henry	ALLN	14
McCue, John	ALLN	11	McGuire, James	EPEN	74	Miller, Jacob	EPEN	74
McCue, Widow	ALLN	11	McKain, William	NEWT	154	Miller, Jeremiah (2)	CARL	37
McCulloch, James	NEWT	152	McKee, David	WPEN	195	Miller, John, heirs	CARL	37
McCullogh, John (2)	DICK	57	McKee, Jane, Widow (2)	MIDD	121	Miller, John, (2)	EPEN	74
McCullough, Hugh	CARL	36	McKee, John	HOPE	99	Miller, John (2)	MIDD	121
McCullough, John	WPEN	195	McKeehan, Benjamin (2)	WPEN	195	Miller, John	WPEN	196
McCune, Esq., heirs	CARL	36	McKeehan, George	NEWT	154	Miller, Ludwick (2)	HOPE	99
McCune, Hugh	NEWT	152	McKeehan, George	WPEN	195	Miller, Matthew (4)	MIDD	121
McCune, John	NEWT	152	McKeehan, George, Sr.	WPEN	196	Miller, Michael (2)	CARL	38
McCune, John	SHTN	179	McKeehan, James (2)	WPEN	196	Miller, Michael	SHTN	181
McCune, Mary (2)	NEWT	152	McKeehan, John	WPEN	196	Miller, Peter	EPEN	74
McCune, Robert	SHTN	179	McKibben, Jeremiah (2)	NEWT	154	Miller, Philip	CARL	38
McCune, Samuel	NEWT	152	McKinley, Daniel	CARL	37	Miller, Philip	MIFF	139
McCune, William	CARL	36	McKinley, Henry	CARL	37	Miller, Rinehart	ALLN	12
McCurdy, John	CARL	36	McKinney, David	HOPE	99	Miller, Robert (2)	MIDD	121
McDanel, James	ALLN	11	McKinney, Joseph (2)	HOPE	99	Miller, Robert, Esq.(4)	CARL	38
McDanel, John	ALLN	11	McKinsey, John	ALLN	11	Miller, Thomas	ALLN	12
McDanel, John	FRAN	90	McKinstry, James	DICK	57	Miller, William	CARL	38
McDaniel, Daniel	MIFF	137	McKnight, David	SHTN	179	Miller, William	DICK	57
McDaniel, Daniel	MIFF	138	McKnight, William	SHTN	180	Miller, William	EPEN	74
McDannell, Joseph	MIFF	138	McLaughlin, Daniel	MIFF	139	Miller, William	WPEN	196
McDonald, John	CARL	37	McLean, Allen	SHTN	180	Minor, Michel	MIFF	139
McDonald, Margaret	CARL	37	McLean, John	SHTN	180	Mish, John	ALLN	12
McDonald, Rebecca	HOPE	98	McManis, Charles	CARL	37	Mitchel, Andrew	WPEN	196
McDonald, William	DICK	57	McMean, John	ALLN	11	Mitchel, Samuel	SHTN	181
McDowell, John (2)	FRAN	90	McMean, William	ALLN	11	Mitchel, James, heirs	CARL	38
McDowell, Samuel	FRAN	90	McMeekin, William	NEWT	154	Mitchell, John	HOPE	99
McElhear, Archibald	SHTN	179	McMonagle, William (2)	NEWT	154	Mitchell, John (2)	MIFF	139
McElheny, Hugh	MIFF	138	McMurry, Thomas	CARL	37	Mitchell, Ross	MIDD	121
McElheny, Samuel	MIFF	138	McMurry, William	CARL	37	Mitchell, Samuel	MIFF	139
McElheny, Samuel, heirs	MIFF	138	McNeal, Daniel	ALLN	11	Mitchell, Samuel	NEWT	155
McElroy, John	NEWT	152	McNickle, Alexander	MIFF	139	Moffett, William	MIFF	139
McElwain, Andrew	MIFF	138	McPherson, William	CARL	37	Montgomery, James	NEWT	155
McElwain, Andrew, heirs	MIFF	138	McTaggart, Hugh	DICK	57	Montgomery, John	MIDD	122
McElwain, James	MIFF	138	McTeer, James	ALLN	12	Montgomery, John, Esq.	CARL	38
McElwain, Joseph	MIFF	138	McTeer, James	CARL	37	Montgomery, John, Esq.(2)	MIDD	122
McEntire, Robert	HOPE	98	McTeer, James, Jr.	ALLN	12	Montgomery, William	HOPE	99
McEntire, William	HOPE	99	McTeer, Samuel	ALLN	12	Montgomery, William	MIFF	139
McFarland, James	WPEN	195	McTeer, William	ALLN	12	Moor, Andrew (2)	EPEN	74
McFarlane, James	MIFF	138	Means, James (2)	SHTN	180	Moor, Howard (2)	EPEN	74
McFarlane. John	MIFF	138	Means, John (2)	SHTN	180	Moor, James (3)	DICK	57
McFarlane, Robert	WPEN	195	Megaugh, Anthony	EPEN	74	Moore, James	SHTN	181
McFarlane, Widow	FRAN	90	Megurk, Stephen (3)	SHTN	180	Moore, John	DICK	57
McFarlane, William	DICK	57	Mickey, David	NEWT	154	Moore, John (4)	DICK	58
McFarlane, William (6)	NEWT	153	Micky, James	NEWT	154	Moore, Solomon	SHTN	181
McFarlane, William	WPEN	195						

Owner Index

Owner	Twp.	Page	Owner	Twp.	Page	Owner	Twp.	Page
Moore, Thomas	SHTN	181	Nisbit, Charles, Rev.	CARL	39	Peebles, Robert (2)	NEWT	156
Moore, William (5)	CARL	39	Noar, Frederick	MIDD	123	Peebles, Robert	WPEN	197
Moore, William (blacksmith)	CARL	39	Noble, James	EPEN	74	Peirce, Hannah	WPEN	197
			Noble, John	CARL	39	Peirce, Joseph (3)	WPEN	197
Moore, William (5)	MIDD	122	Noble, John	CARL	40	Pelce, John	SHTN	182
Moore, William	WPEN	196	North, Jacob	MIFF	140	Pendergrass, Margaret	CARL	40
Moore, William, Sr.	DICK	59	Norton, Thomas	DICK	58	Penney, Jacob	MIFF	140
Moorhead, James	CARL	39	Norton, Thomas	NEWT	155	Peoples, Alexander	SHTN	182
Moreland, James	MIDD	122	Norton, Thomas	SHTN	182	Peoples, Robert	SHTN	182
Morrette, Nicholas	HOPE	100	not known	NEWT	171	Pepper, Philip	DICK	59
Morrison, Josesph	ALLN	12	Nugent, Peter	SHTN	182	Peters, Richard, Esq.	MIDD	123
Morrison, Robert (2)	MIDD	122	Ober, John	EPEN	75	Philip, John	EPEN	75
Morrison, Robert	MIDD	123	Officer, Alexander (2)	FRAN	91	Philips, Robert, heirs	CARL	40
Morrow, John	MIFF	139	Officer, John	CARL	40	Phisick, Edmund	EPEN	75
Morrow, John	NEWT	155	Oliver, John	EPEN	75	Pile, Laurance	EPEN	75
Morrow, Samuel (2)	MIFF	139	Orr, John (2)	EPEN	75	Piper, James	HOPE	100
Mull, John	SHTN	181	Orr, Widow (4)	EPEN	75	Piper, Jane	WPEN	197
Murray, Thomas	MIFF	140	Orwan, John	CARL	40	Piper, Lucinda	SHTN	182
Musselman, Jacob	CARL	39	Over, David	NEWT	155	Piper, Robert	SHTN	182
Musselman, Jacob	FRAN	90	Over, John	HOPE	100	Piper, Samuel	NEWT	156
Mussleman, George	WPEN	196	Overline, Adam	HOPE	100	Piper, William	HOPE	100
Mussleman, Jacob	WPEN	196	Paddow, Peter	CARL	40	Pisel, Andrew	SHTN	182
Mustard, Archibald	HOPE	100	Page, John	SHTN	182	Plum, Adam	SHTN	182
Myer, Adam	SHTN	181	Painter, John	FRAN	91	Plunket, Doctor, heirs	SHTN	182
Myer, Jacob	SHTN	181	Painter, Martin	FRAN	91	Pollinger, Abraham	MIDD	123
Myers, Abraham	WPEN	196	Parcel, John	DICK	58	Pollock, James	CARL	40
Myers, Bostain	FRAN	91	Parker, Alexander, hrs.	WPEN	197	Pollock, John	CARL	41
Myers, George	ALLN	13	Parker, Andrew	EPEN	75	Pollock, Oliver (3)	EPEN	75
Myers, George	DICK	58	Parker, William	FRAN	91	Pollock, Oliver	EPEN	76
Myers, Jacob	ALLN	13	Parkison, Richard	MIDD	123	Poorman, Christopher	ALLN	13
Myers, Jacob	WPEN	197	Patterson, Andrew	MIFF	140	Poorman, Stophel	ALLN	13
Myers, John	HOPE	100	Patterson, James (2)	NEWT	155	Pope, John, heirs	DICK	59
Myers, Joshua	ALLN	13	Patterson, Josiah	DICK	59	Pope, Nicholas	EPEN	76
Myre, George	EPEN	74	Patterson, Obediah	DICK	59	Popenmyre, Gabriel	FRAN	91
Myres, John	MIFF	140	Patterson, Robert (2)	DICK	59	Porter heirs	FRAN	91
Nailor, George	WPEN	197	Patterson, Robert, Jr.	DICK	59	Porter, Robert	SHTN	182
Nailor, Thomas, heirs	CARL	39	Patterson, Robert, Sr.	DICK	59	Porter, Robert (3)	SHTN	183
Narns, John	DICK	58	Patterson, Thomas	DICK	59	Postlethwait, Samuel Esq.	CARL	123
Neel, Sarah	DICK	58	Patterson, William	MIDD	123	Postlethwaite, Samuel	MIDD	123
Negley, Eliab	ALLN	13	Pattison, Charles	CARL	40	Prats, Simeon	EPEN	76
Negro, Catharine	WPEN	197	Pattison, George	CARL	40	Purdy, James	MIFF	140
Nelson, Nancy	CARL	39	Patton, John	MIFF	140	Purdy, John	MIFF	140
Nesbet, Francis	HOPE	100	Patton, John	WPEN	197	Quigley, Christopher, Esq.	ALLN	14
Nesland, Daniel	ALLN	13	Patton, Robert	FRAN	91	Quigley, Henry	ALLN	14
Nettle, Henry	NEWT	155	Patton, Robert (2)	MIDD	123	Quigley, James	ALLN	14
Newton, Conrad	MIFF	140	Paxton, Samuel	EPEN	75	Quigley, James	EPEN	76
Nichols, Thomas	SHTN	181	Peck, George	NEWT	155	Quigley, John. deceased	EPEN	76
Nicholson, James (2)	MIFF	140	Peck, Philip (2)	NEWT	155	Quigley, John	NEWT	156
Nickey, George	FRAN	91	Peebles, Philip	NEWT	156	Quigley, John	SHTN	183
Nidigh, Abraham (2)	EPEN	74	Peebles, John F.	NEWT	156	Quigley, Mary	EPEN	76
			Peebles, Robert	HOPE	100	Quigley, Michael	CARL	41

Owner Index

Owner	Twp.	Page	Owner	Twp.	Page	Owner	Twp.	Page
Quigley, Robert	HOPE	101	Rippey, Samuel (3)	SHTN	184	Sanderson, William	MIDD	125
Quigley, Samuel	SHTN	183	Rippey, Samuel	SHTN	185	Sands, George	ALLN	14
Quigley, William	EPEN	76	Rippey, William	NEWT	157	Sands, John	ALLN	14
Rahm, Jacob (4)	SHTN	183	Rippey, William	SHTN	185	Sansebaugh, Christy	FRAN	92
Rainey, William (3)	CARL	41	Ristlers, Thomas, heirs	WPEN	198	Scandinger heirs	CARL	43
Rainy, William	DICK	59	Ritchey, Thomas	MIDD	124	Scoular, John	MIFF	141
Rainy, William	MIDD	123	Ritner, Michael	CARL	42	Scoby, James	CARL	43
Ralston, Andrew	DICK	59	Roadacre [?], Philip	WPEN	198	Scoot, William	ALLN	15
Ralston, Andrew	MIDD	123	Roads, John	WPEN	198	Scott, Andrew	MIDD	125
Ralston, David	WPEN	197	Roberts, John	MIFF	141	Scott, Elizabeth	SHTN	185
Ramsey, Archibald	CARL	41	Roberts, John	NEWT	157	Scroggs, Alexander	WPEN	198
Ramsey, Hugh	WPEN	198	Robinson, Andrew	NEWT	157	Scrogs, Alexander (3)	NEWT	157
Ramsey, James, heirs (3)	CARL	41	Robison, Elizabeth	CARL	42	Scrogs, James (2)	NEWT	157
Ramsey, Nathan	DICK	59	Robison, John	HOPE	101	Scrogs, James	NEWT	158
Ramsey, Nathan	DICK	60	Rodair, Philip	WPEN	198	Searight, Gilbert (2)	MIDD	125
Ramsey, Samuel	MIDD	123	Rodman, William	WPEN	198	Seerer, George	EPEN	77
Randle, Agness	CARL	42	Rogers, Richard	HOPE	101	Seewright, Gilbert (2)	CARL	43
Randolph, Ichabod	MIDD	124	Roop, Jonas, Jr.	EPEN	76	Sensebaugh, John	MIFF	141
Randolph, Jacob	MIDD	124	Roop, Jonas, Sr.	EPEN	76	Shaffer, Rudolph (2)	MIDD	125
Randolph, Paul	MIDD	124	Roop, Martin	EPEN	77	Shambaugh, George	FRAN	92
Rannels, Ruth	CARL	42	Roopley, Conrad	EPEN	77	Shambaugh, Philip	FRAN	92
Ratchford, Hugh	FRAN	92	Roopley, John (2)	EPEN	77	Shannon, John	MIFF	141
Raum, Jacob (3)	SHTN	202	Rooply, Frederick	EPEN	77	Shants, Henry	WPEN	198
Realing, Joseph	MIFF	141	Rooply, Jacob	EPEN	77	Sharp, Alexander (4)	NEWT	158
Redat, John	SHTN	183	Rooply, Michael	EPEN	77	Sharp, James	HOPE	101
Redatt, John	SHTN	184	Rose, William	CARL	42	Sharp, John	FRAN	92
Redsecker, Nicholas (2)	EPEN	76	Roseborough, Elenor	ALLN	14	Sharp, Robert (3)	NEWT	158
Reed, John	EPEN	76	Ross, James	NEWT	157	Sheely, Andrew	EPEN	77
Reed, John	MIFF	141	Ross, Simon	NEWT	157	Sheffer, John (2)	EPEN	77
Reese, Jeremiah	EPEN	76	Rotts, Jacob	SHTN	185	Shelley, Jacob	ALLN	15
Reese, Solomon	EPEN	76	Roush, Henry	MIDD	124	Shelley, Jacob, Jr.	ALLN	15
Reid, James	CARL	42	Rowan, David	CARL	42	Shelly, Michael	EPEN	77
Reighter, George	MIDD	124	Rowan, David	CARL	43	Shenenberger, Jacob	MIFF	141
Reighter, John	CARL	42	Rowan, David	MIDD	124	Shepley, Frederick	SHTN	185
Reisinger, Adam	CARL	42	Rowan, William	DICK	60	Shippen, Edward (2)	SHTN	185
Renard, John	MIFF	141	Rowney, James	CARL	43	Shippen, Joseph	EPEN	77
Renix, John	EPEN	76	Rufner, Conrod	FRAN	92	Shippen, Joseph (2)	SHTN	185
Renninger, Conrad	ALLN	14	Rupard, John	MIDD	124	Shoemaker, John	SHTN	185
Reynolds, John, hrs.(3)	SHTN	184	Russel, James	SHTN	185	Shoop, Jacob	EPEN	78
Rheem, Abram	NEWT	156	Sadler, Matthias	SHTN	185	Shoop, John	EPEN	78
Rhine, Henry	CARL	42	Sailor, Mathias	EPEN	77	Showalter, Joseph	WPEN	198
Rhine, Henry	FRAN	92	Salsburg heirs	MIFF	141	Shram, Joseph (2)	CARL	43
Rhine, John	CARL	42	Salskeever, Gasper	SHTN	185	Shram, Philip, heirs	CARL	43
Rhine, Stephen	NEWT	156	Sample, Charles	EPEN	77	Shriver, Daniel	SHTN	185
Rhodes, Jacob	NEWT	156	Sample, John	EPEN	77	Shuler, Christian	WPEN	198
Rice, Simon	SHTN	184	Sample, Joseph	MIDD	124	Shumaker, John	HOPE	101
Richards, Alexander	SHTN	184	Sanders, Frederick	MIFF	141	Shutley, Jacob	SHTN	186
Richart, John	SHTN	184	Sanderson, John, Jr.(2)	MIDD	124	Shutley, John (2)	SHTN	186
Rightmire, Lewis	NEWT	157	Sanderson, John, Sr.	MIDD	124	Shutley, Mary	SHTN	186
Rippet, John	WPEN	198	Sanderson, Robert	MIDD	125			

Owner Index

Owner	Twp.	Page	Owner	Twp.	Page	Owner	Twp.	Page
Simmeral, John	HOPE	101	Springer, Jacob	ALLN	15	Thomas, Martin	ALLN	16
Simmeral, Martha	HOPE	101	Sprout, John	DICK	60	Thompson heirs	HOPE	102
Simpson, John	SHTN	185	Stakemiller, Valentine	EPEN	78	Thompson, Abraham	MIDD	126
Singer, Henry	MIDD	125	Starr, John	ALLN	15	Thompson, Alexander	CARL	45
Slonaker, William	MIDD	125	Stayman, John (2)	EPEN	78	Thompson, Andrew	MIFF	142
Slusher, Philip (2)	HOPE	102	Stayman, Joseph (2)	EPEN	78	Thompson, Matthew	MIFF	142
Smith, David (2)	MIDD	125	Steel, Ephraim (3)	CARL	44	Thompson, Samuel	NEWT	176
Smith, Esther	MIDD	125	Steel, Ephraim	EPEN	78	Thompson, William	HOPE	102
Smith, Esther	MIDD	126	Steel, John, Esq. (2)	CARL	44	Thomson, Alexander	NEWT	159
Smith, George	ALLN	15	Steel, John, Esq. (2)	MIDD	126	Thomson, Ann	NEWT	159
Smith, Hugh	HOPE	102	Steel, Joseph	CARL	44	Thomson, Matthew (2)	NEWT	159
Smith, Hugh	MIDD	126	Steep, Jacob (2)	DICK	60	Thomson, Samuel	NEWT	159
Smith, James (cooper)	CARL	43	Sterrett, David	MIFF	142	Thomson, Samuel	NEWT	160
Smith, James	MIDD	126	Sterrett, James (2)	NEWT	159	Thomson, William	NEWT	160
Smith, John	ALLN	15	Sterrett, Robert	HOPE	102	Thrush, Barney	NEWT	160
Smith, John	CARL	43	Sterrett, Thomas (2)	NEWT	159	Thrush, Leonard	NEWT	160
(blacksmith) (2)		44	Sterritt, David	MIFF	142	Titler, Balsor	EPEN	79
Smith, John (tailor)	CARL	44	Stevenson, George, Dr.	CARL	44	Trimble, George	EPEN	79
Smith, John	DICK	60	Stevenson, James	MIFF	142	Trimble, John	EPEN	79
Smith, John	NEWT	158	Stevenson, William	MIFF	142	Trimble, William (2)	HOPE	103
Smith, John	WPEN	198	Stewart, James, heirs	MIFF	142	Tritt, Peter	WPEN	199
Smith, Samuel (2)	HOPE	102	Stewart, John	SHTN	187	Turner, James	WPEN	199
Snider, Christy (2)	FRAN	92	Stewart, Samuel	DICK	60	Turner, Joseph	DICK	60
Snider, David	MIFF	142	Stier, John, dec. (2)	EPEN	78	Uhler, Frederick	CARL	45
Snider, David (2)	WPEN	199	Stier, John, deceased	EPEN	79	Uhler, Frederick	CARL	46
Snider, George	CARL	44	Stinespring, Henry	ALLN	15	Umbarger, David	ALLN	16
Snider, George (2)	FRAN	92	Stoke, Rev. (2)	MIFF	142	Unanks, Henry	MIFF	143
Snider, Philip	EPEN	78	Striker, Arnold (2)	WPEN	199	Underwood, John	CARL	46
Snider, Philip	FRAN	93	Strock, Joseph	ALLN	16	Urie, Thomas	MIDD	127
Snively, Henry	EPEN	78	Strome, Samuel	EPEN	79	Usher, Baltzer	SHTN	187
Snively, Jacob	EPEN	78	Stuart, Elizabeth	MIDD	126	Vanderau, Adam	EPEN	79
Snively, John	EPEN	78	Stuart, James	CARL	44	Vanderbelt, Cornelius	NEWT	160
Snody, John	HOPE	102	Stuart, James, heirs	CARL	44	Vanderbelt, Jacob	NEWT	160
Snyder, George	FRAN	105	Stuart, James, heirs	CARL	45	Vanhold, Valentine	SHTN	187
Snyder, John	SHTN	186	Stuart, Samuel (3)	CARL	45	Vanlier, Christopher,	CARL	46
Sollenberger, John	ALLN	15	Stumbaugh, Peter (2)	SHTN	187	heirs (2)		
Souther, Jacob	FRAN	93	Sturm, George	CARL	45	Varner, George	FRAN	93
Sowers, Barnhart	HOPE	102	Summers, Andrew	WPEN	199	Varnes, Jacob (2)	DICK	60
Sowers, John	DICK	60	Swanger, Paul (2)	MIDD	126	Vernor, Conrad	SHTN	187
Spear, William	SHTN	186	Swarts, John	EPEN	79	Waggoner, Jacob	FRAN	93
Spear, William	WPEN	199	Swarts, Leonard	EPEN	79	Waggoner, Jacob	MIDD	127
Speck	FRAN	93	Swats, George	EPEN	79	Waggoner, Michael	ALLN	16
Speck, Bernard	NEWT	159	Swetser, Frederick	ALLN	16	Waggoner, Philip	NEWT	160
Speck, Frederick	MIDD	126	Swiler, Christley	EPEN	79	Walker, David (2)	EPEN	79
Speelman, George	SHTN	186	Syke (or Gillespie)	FRAN	97	Walker, James	MIFF	143
Speelman, Jacob (2)	SHTN	186	Tate, Samuel (3)	SHTN	187	Walker, John (2)	EPEN	79
Spencer, John	SHTN	186	Taylor, John	MIDD	126	Walker, John, Esq.	EPEN	80
Sponsler, Charles	ALLN	15	Templeton, John (2)	CARL	45	Walker, John	NEWT	160
Spring, Marshall	SHTN	186	Templeton, John	MIDD	126	Walker, John	WPEN	199
Spring, Mary	SHTN	186	Tetrick, John	SHTN	187	Walker, Joseph, heirs	NEWT	160
			Thomas, John (2)	CARL	45			

Owner Index

Owner	Twp.	Page	Owner	Twp.	Page	Owner	Twp.	Page
Walker, William	NEWT	161	Widle, Martin	EPEN	80	Wolf, Jacob, Jr.	MIDD	128
Wall (& Brookens)	SHTN	184	Wike, Christopher	WPEN	200	Wolf, Jacob, Sr.	MIDD	128
Wall, John	SHTN	187	Wiley, Robert (2)	EPEN	80	Wolf, John (4)	MIDD	129
Wallace, Hugh	NEWT	161	Will, John	WPEN	200	Wolf, Joseph	MIFF	144
Wallace, James	HOPE	103	Williams, John	ALLN	16	Wolf, Michel	MIFF	144
Wallace, John	FRAN	93	Williamson, David (2)	MIDD	127	Wolf, Philip	MIDD	129
Wallace, John	MIFF	143	Williamson, David	MIFF	143	Wolf, Sophia	NEWT	161
Wallace, Joseph	ALLN	16	Williamson, John	ALLN	17	Womeldorff, Eve	EPEN	81
Wallace, Moses	ALLN	16	Williamson, Thomas	EPEN	80	Wonderlich, Daniel (2)	MIDD	129
Wallace, Patrick (2)	FRAN	93	Wills, David	HOPE	103	Wonderlich, David	MIDD	129
Wallace, Samuel	ALLN	16	Wills, John	HOPE	103	Wonderlich, Frederick	MIDD	129
Wallace, William	CARL	46	Wilson heirs	FRAN	93	Wonderlich, John (3)	MIDD	129
Walter, Christopher	SHTN	187	Wilson, Archibald	MIDD	127	Wood, Alexander, heirs	CARL	47
Walters, Joseph	EPEN	80	Wilson, Hugh	CARL	47	Wood, Margaret	CARL	47
Waltimire, Ludwick	MIDD	127	Wilson, Isabella	EPEN	80	Woodburn, James (4)	NEWT	162
Waltimyer, Ludwick	DICK	60	Wilson, James	ALLN	17	Woodburn, John	DICK	61
Warnor, Henry	WPEN	199	Wilson, Joseph, dec.	EPEN	81	Woodburn, Matthew	NEWT	162
Warton, Thomas	EPEN	80	Wilson, Joseph	FRAN	94	Woodburn, Samuel	DICK	61
Wasmood, Martin	WPEN	199	Wilson, Joseph	MIDD	127	Woods, Jane	DICK	62
Watson, Allen	CARL	46	Wilson, Matthew (2)	FRAN	94	Woods, John, Esq.	HOPE	104
Watts, David, Esq.	NEWT	161	Wilson, Nathaniel (2)	HOPE	103	Woods, Richard	WPEN	200
Waugh, James	EPEN	80	Wilson, Richard	MIDD	128	Woods, Samuel, Jr. (2)	DICK	62
Waugh, John	EPEN	80	Wilson, Samuel	FRAN	94	Woods, Samuel, Sr. (2)	DICK	62
Waugh, Samuel	EPEN	80	Wilson, Samuel, dec.	WPEN	200	Woods, Thomas, heirs	DICK	62
Waugh, Samuel, Rev. (2)	EPEN	80	Wilson, Samuel, Rev.	MIFF	143	Work, James, heirs	NEWT	162
Waugh, William (4)	CARL	46	Wilson, Samuel, Rev. (2)	NEWT	161	Work, John	ALLN	17
Wax, Peter (2)	FRAN	93	Wilson, Widow	ALLN	17	Work, William	ALLN	17
Weakly, Edward (3)	DICK	61	Wilson, Widow	MIDD	128	Wormley, Hartley	EPEN	81
Weakly, James	DICK	61	Wilson, Widow	WPEN	200	Wormley, Jacob	EPEN	81
Weakly, Robert	DICK	61	Wilson, William (2)	NEWT	161	Wormley, John (4)	EPEN	81
Weakly, Samuel (2)	DICK	61	Wingler, Jacob	SHTN	188	Wormly, George	EPEN	81
Weaver, Conrad	ALLN	16	Wise, Adam	ALLN	17	Worst, Jacob	FRAN	94
Weaver, Henry	ALLN	16	Wise, Jacob	ALLN	17	Wray, John (2)	CARL	47
Weaver, Jacob	CARL	47	Wise, Jacob (2)	MIDD	128	Wright, Robert	CARL	48
Weaver, John	NEWT	161	Wise, Philip	MIFF	143	Wyncoop, Jacob	MIDD	129
Weaver, Martin	MIFF	143	Wiser, Jacob (3)	CARL	47	Yaley, John	CARL	48
Weaver, Philip	MIFF	143	Wishong, Conrad	CARL	47	Yates, George	SHTN	188
Weaver, Vandel (2)	MIFF	143	Witmer, Jacob (2)	MIDD	128	Yates, Thomas	SHTN	188
Weaver, William	MIDD	127	Witsel, Jacob	MIDD	143	Yecovah, Peter	MIFF	144
Weber, George	ALLN	16	Witt, Nicholas	EPEN	81	Yecovah, Philip	MIFF	144
Weir, George, heirs	NEWT	161	Wizer, Jacob	DICK	61	Young, Alexander	EPEN	81
Wetmire, Jacob	MIDD	127	Wolf, Abraham (2)	EPEN	81	Young, Eleanor	WPEN	200
Wherry, Samuel	HOPE	103	Wolf, Adam	SHTN	188	Young, Joseph	CARL	48
Whisner, John	HOPE	103	Wolf, Andrew	MIDD	128	Young, Peter	MIDD	130
White, David	HOPE	103	Wolf, Conrad	MIFF	143	Zeigler, Mark	CARL	48
White, David (2)	MIDD	127	Wolf, Henry (2)	MIDD	128	Zigler, Andrew	MIDD	130
Whitehill, Robert	EPEN	80	Wolf, Henry	MIFF	144	Zigler, Henry	MIFF	144
Whitmer, Jacob	SHTN	188	Wolf, Jacob	ALLN	17	Zigler, Jacob	MIDD	130
Whitmore, Baltzer	DICK	61	Wolf, Jacob	MIDD	128	Zigler, John	MIFF	144
Whitmore, Joseph	WPEN	200	Wolf, Jacob	MIDD	128			

Occupant Index

Index to Occupants and Other Persons

Name	Twp.	Page	Name	Twp.	Page	Name	Twp.	Page
Adams, John	SHTN	179	Bolinger, Peter	CARL	23	Claudy, Martin	SHTN	164
Aitken, William	DICK	57	Bollinger, John	ALLN	1	Claudy, Martin	SHTN	172
Alexander, John	DICK	49	Bone, Betsey	CARL	43	Clemens, James	FRAN	84
Allen, John	MIFF	131	Boring, Nathaniel	MIDD	121	Clemons, Benjamin	FRAN	87
Allen, Robert	NEWT	148	Bouvard, Charles	CARL	43	Close, Samuel	MIDD	123
Allen, William	MIFF	142	Bower, Daniel (note)	NEWT	157	Cloyd, John	HOPE	103
Allspaugh, George	CARL	39	Bower, Henry	FRAN	88	Cloyd, Solomon	HOPE	99
Alpiner [?], Ralph	SHTN	175	Bowers, John	HOPE	97	Cockins, Vincent	CARL	25
Alter, David	WPEN	199	Bradley, Robert	FRAN	90	Coffman, Andrew	EPEN	81
Altick, Daniel	SHTN	183	Bradley, Thomas	DICK	56	Cohan, Charles	FRAN	91
Anderson, Joseph	CARL	46	Brandt, Jacob	CARL	47	Colpt, Simon	MIFF	131
Anderson, John	FRAN	90	Brats, John	MIDD	119	Comfort, Andrew	MIDD	108
Anderson, John	NEWT	151	Brattan, John	NEWT	147	Conway, George	FRAN	84
Angeny, Isaac	MIDD	127	Brawley, Daniel	ALLN	14	Cook, John	FRAN	83
Arbuckle, William	SHTN	170	Brewkirk, David	EPEN	79	Cooper, David	NEWT	149
Armstrong, James	EPEN	73	Briggs, David	EPEN	76	Cooper, Henry	NEWT	146
Armstrong, John	EPEN	73	Briggs, Robert	MIDD	106	Coover, -----	EPEN	78
Atchison, James	WPEN	190	Brindle, Peter	ALLN	15	Cope, John	WPEN	195
Atherton, Caleb	SHTN	186	Brown, Hugh	HOPE	103	Cough, George	DICK	51
Baird, James	CARL	46	Brown, John (%)	FRAN	82	Cough, Joseph	EPEN	78
Barnes, John	CARL	34	Brown, Kathrine	FRAN	82	Cowan, Robert	FRAN	90
Barr, John	DICK	49	Brown, Kennedy	SHTN	164	Cowen, William	SHTN	171
Barr, William	SHTN	182	Brown, Robert	CARL	34	Cowper, Frederick	CARL	45
Barret, Richard	CARL	24	Brown, Robert	CARL	38	Cox, William	FRAN	87
Bashore, Michael	EPEN	63	Bryson (and Shannon)	NEWT	146	Craig, John	MIDD	106
Baughman, John	ALLN	14	Buchanan, James	EPEN	75	Craighead, Thomas	MIDD	109
Bayer, Frederick	CARL	23	Buchanan, Thomas	NEWT	161	Craine, George	MIDD	109
Bayle, John	SHTN	178	Buchanan, John	SHTN	176	Crane, Benjamin	MIDD	113
Beacom, John	CARL	46	Butler, James	NEWT	155	Crane, Richard	FRAN	91
Beam, Fish	ALLN	5	Byres, John	HOPE	101	Crawford, James	NEWT	153
Beaty, James	HOPE	97	Caldwell, Samuel	CARL	25	Crawl, Joseph	ALLN	2
Beigle, John	CARL	19	Campbell, Ebenezer	SHTN	166	Cresler, George	SHTN	168
Beigle, William	CARL	45	Campbell, Ennis	EPEN	69	Cress, Henry	EPEN	78
Beigle, William J.	CARL	45	Campbell, Robert	FRAN	83	Crocket, Thomas	WPEN	196
Bell, James	MIDD	114	Campbell, Samuel	SHTN	170	Croney, Thomas	MIDD	122
Bellow, Cornelius	MIDD	105	Carlisle, Daniel	MIDD	106	Crosby, William	DICK	58
Bidleman, Adam	MIDD	114	Carnahan, James	MIFF	142	Crouse, George	CARL	28
Bigler	DICK	56	Carothers, John, Esq.	CARL	29	Crouse, Jacob	CARL	28
Bigler, John	CARL	41	Carothers, Alexander	MIDD	127	Crow	FRAN	87
Black, William	EPEN	74	Carothers, Thomas	EPEN	80	Cryser, Sebastian	MIDD	106
Blackford, Benjamin	DICK	51	Carson [?], James	MIDD	110	Culbertson, Joseph	SHTN	170
Blackwood, William	WPEN	197	Carson, Elisha	NEWT	146	Davis, Francis	NEWT	153
Blaine, James	MIDD	121	Carson, Samuel	DICK	60	Davis, James	CARL	36
Blaine, Lue [?]	CARL	44	Cart, Christianna	CARL	22	Dawson, George	CARL	35
Blair, John	WPEN	190	Carten, John	CARL	27	Dawson, Richard	DICK	52
Bloser, Peter (2)	FRAN	83	Carter, Margaret	CARL	22	Day, John	MIDD	111
Bockley [?], David	DICK	55	Carter, Samuel	NEWT	153	Day, John	MIDD	118
Boden, Hugh	CARL	37	Chapman, William	NEWT	147	Deirdorf, Isaac	MIDD	116
Boggs, Francis	MIDD	121	Clark, Thomas	CARL	28	Denny, Agness	CARL	25
Boggs, Francis	MIDD	123	Clark, Thomas	NEWT	151	Denny, John	MIDD	110

Occupant Index

Name	Twp.	Page	Name	Twp.	Page	Name	Twp.	Page
Derr, Nicholas	SHTN	187	Frederick, Peter	EPEN	66	Haslet, Robert	CARL	23
Dice, Conrad	MIDD	124	Fry, Peter	SHTN	172	Hawthorn, Adam	SHTN	176
Dice, Martin	MIDD	117	Fught, Matthias	SHTN	168	Hay, Samuel	WPEN	199
Dimsey, George	CARL	43	Fulton, Francis (2)	DICK	52	Haynes, Godfrey	CARL	45
Dine, John	SHTN	172	Fulton, William	NEWT	155	Hays, John	NEWT	155
Dixon, Andrew	MIDD	109	Fury, John	MIDD	106	Hays, Samuel	CARL	33
Donnall, Thomas	MIFF	136	Galbreath	FRAN	85	Hearst, George	CARL	25
Dooey, Peter	DICK	53	Galbreath, Samuel	HOPE	101	Heck, John	SHTN	173
Doud, James	NEWT	146	Geerhart, Peter	MIDD	118	Hefflefinger, Frederick	HOPE	97
Douglass, John	CARL	32	George, Mary	MIDD	129	Heigle, William	CARL	27
Drayer, Peter	MIDD	108	Gibson, Ann	CARL	21	Hemming, Richard	CARL	28
Duffy, John	HOPE	100	Gibson, John	MIDD	125	Hemphill, John	ALLN	6
Dumon, Christy	NEWT	153	Gibson, Widow	CARL	44	Henderson (surveyor)	MIFF	138
Duncan, James, Esq.	CARL	26	Giffen, Widow	MIDD	113	Henderson, David	SHTN	169
Duncan, James, Esq.	CARL	46	Girling, William	CARL	46	Henderson, Samuel	HOPE	97
Duncan, Joseph	DICK	52	Glen, Widow	SHTN	173	Henderson, William	SHTN	184
Dunlap, Daniel	CARL	41	Glenn, John	CARL	39	Hendrick, James	SHTN	180
Dunn, Andrew	MIDD	109	Goebell, Henry	CARL	39	Hendricks, John	MIDD	107
Dunning, Agnes	NEWT	148	Goodshal, Goodley	EPEN	73	Henry, James	EPEN	77
Early, Robert	HOPE	101	Gormin, Archibald	HOPE	99	Henry, John	CARL	43
East, Stophel	HOPE	98	Gormley, Thomas	FRAN	84	Herman, Daniel	DICK	49
Eckles, Francis	CARL	44	Gould, Stophel	CARL	48	Herron, David	CARL	27
Egolf, Henry	MIDD	120	Graham, Andrew	ALLN	14	Herwick, Jacob	CARL	23
Elliot, Ann	CARL	30	Graham, Isiah	WPEN	192	Herwick, Mrs.	MIDD	120
Elliot, James	CARL	29	Graham, William	MIDD	122	Hiskey, Adam	WPEN	195
Elliott, James	DICK	52	Graham, William	SHTN	167	Hoffer, Isaac	CARL	44
Elliott, Widow	SHTN	165	Gray, Alexander	MIDD	119	Hoffer, Melchor	MIDD	106
Ensminger, Chris.	MIDD	116	Gray, Catharine	CARL	19	Holmes	MIFF	131
Erwin, Agnes	DICK	61	Greason [?], Robert	CARL	39	Holmes, George	HOPE	99
Erwin, William	ALLN	14	Green, Christy	SHTN	172	Holmes, Thomas	ALLN	11
Evers, John	EPEN	71	Green, Luke	SHTN	175	Holsaple, Adam	WPEN	191
Fass, Peter	CARL	46	Greenfield, Richard	CARL	26	Holts, John	EPEN	74
Faughner, John	SHTN	163	Greer, James	DICK	53	Hoon, Felty	WPEN	195
Fentonbinder, Martin	MIDD	141	Greer, Samuel	ALLN	6	Hopple, Christopher	MIDD	120
Ferguson, Col.	CARL	19	Greger, Adam	ALLN	7	Horner, Henry	FRAN	91
Fields, John	NEWT	158	Grogin, Charles	HOPE	103	Houke, Adam, Jr.	DICK	54
Filson, James	DICK	52	Grosscoat, Jacob	MIDD	117	Hover, Charles	ALLN	13
Fishbaugh, Catharine	CARL	35	Grove, Philip (sold)	CARL	20	How, Catharine	CARL	21
Fisher, James	MIDD	127	Guthrie, Robert D.	CARL	38	Hull, Henry	ALLN	15
Fisher, Thomas	EPEN	71	Hadden, Thomas	MIFF	131	Humes, Thomas	MIDD	110
Fleming, John	CARL	35	Hamilton, George	MIFF	135	Hunter, Elizabeth	CARL	47
Foglesonger, John	SHTN	173	Hamute [?], John	MIDD	123	Hunter, James	MIDD	106
Forsyth, John	CARL	27	Hannah, Samuel	HOPE	96	Hunter, John	MIDD	119
Fortney, Melchor	FRAN	86	Haroff, Jacob	WPEN	192	Huston, Samuel	MIDD	123
Fossett, Robert	CARL	42	Harper, Ebenezer	FRAN	89	Ingle, Henry	SHTN	180
Foster [?], Jonathan	CARL	33	Hart, Anthony, Rev.	CARL	20	Irvin, James	NEWT	156
Foster, Joseph	MIDD	126	Hart, David	MIDD	122	Irvine, Mrs.	CARL	32
Foster, Thomas	MIDD	111	Hartman, Adam	DICK	50	Irwin, Andrew	SHTN	171
Fostler, Peter	EPEN	81	Harvey, Andrew	FRAN	86	Isett, John	CARL	32
Frank, Daniel	MIDD	113	Harvey, William	FRAN	86	Jackson, William	HOPE	99

Occupant Index

Name	Twp.	Page	Name	Twp.	Page	Name	Twp.	Page
Jamison, Robert	FRAN	88	Lightcap, William	MIFF	138	McCrae, William	FRAN	94
Johnston, Hugh	CARL	25	Lipe, Peter	MIDD	111	McCreary, James	NEWT	158
Johnston, John	EPEN	75	List, George	EPEN	63	McCullough, Francis	CARL	36
Johnston, Alexander	SHTN	166	Lodorus, Joseph	FRAN	85	McCune, Samuel	MIFF	139
Jones, Joshua	CARL	41	Long, Benedict	MIDD	111	McDannel, John (note)	FRAN	82
Jones, Nicholas	SHTN	176	Long, Henry	SHTN	172	McDannell (surveyor)	MIFF	138
Jordan, Agness	CARL	46	Long, John	HOPE	97	McDonald, Daniel	WPEN	193
Jumper, Abram	FRAN	87	Longsdorf, Ann	EPEN	70	McElheny, Mable	MIFF	138
Junkin, Benjamin	EPEN	80	Lootz, George	EPEN	81	McElwain, Gail [?]	EPEN	65
Karlin, George	ALLN	14	Lose, George	MIDD	114	McGinnis, John	CARL	35
Keady, John	SHTN	183	Loudon, Anthony	EPEN	77	McGowan, Robert	MIDD	112
Keigley, Jacob	CARL	39	Louther, Joseph	HOPE	95	McGunnegle [?], Patrick	CARL	43
Keller, Jacob	SHTN	172	Love, Elijah	MIDD	118	McIntire, Andrew	DICK	57
Kelly, Patrick	CARL	25	Love, George	NEWT	147	McIntire, John	SHTN	182
Kelsbower, Jacob	SHTN	176	Loyd, Jacob	ALLN	11	McIntire, John	WPEN	193
Kenned, Archibald	MIDD	113	Lukes, Daniel	MIDD	111	McIntire, Robert	SHTN	179
Kennedy, Gilbert	HOPE	102	Lutz, Jacob	MIDD	119	McKee, William	MIDD	121
Kerey, Adam	SHTN	177	Lutz, John	FRAN	86	McKeehan, John	WPEN	196
Kernan, John	MIDD	105	Magauran [?], Edward	CARL	46	McKinley, John	MIDD	106
Kerr, Thomas	SHTN	166	Magaw, Robert (owner ?)	CARL	38	McKinney, Patrick	SHTN	171
Kincaid, James	DICK	58	Mark, Christian	MIDD	118	McKinzie, Mrs.	CARL	25
King, George	SHTN	168	Markel, Mathias	ALLN	8	McMacken, James	CARL	29
King, Nicholas	NEWT	157	Martin, George	FRAN	85	McManus, Charles	CARL	30
Kingler, Henry	MIFF	135	Martin, George, Jr.	FRAN	85	McMullen, Robert	NEWT	153
Kitch, David	MIDD	118	Martin, James	CARL	32	McTeer, James	ALLN	12
Kline, George	FRAN	83	Martin, Thomas	EPEN	81	Mell, Adam	WPEN	193
Knisely, Jacob	ALLN	9	Martin, Thomas	NEWT	159	Mercer, Henry	MIDD	119
Know, Joseph	SHTN	184	Mason, Isaac	HOPE	98	Mikesell, Andrew	NEWT	152
Koogan, John	MIFF	142	Mather, Robert	MIFF	134	Mill, William	DICK	61
Koonts, David	MIDD	126	Mathew, Agness	MIDD	122	Miller	FRAN	87
Kutesner, Michael	SHTN	174	Mathews, Adam	CARL	24	Miller, Jacob	EPEN	69
Kutlner, Michael	SHTN	176	Matthews, James	MIDD	118	Miller, Jeremiah, Sr.	CARL	38
Laird, James	FRAN	90	Maxwell, John	HOPE	95	Miller, Jeremiah	CARL	38
Laird, Samuel	ALLN	10	Maxwell, William	CARL	41	Miller, John	CARL	37
Lancaster, John	NEWT	146	May, Frederick	EPEN	79	Miller, Melchor	EPEN	79
Latshaw, Peter	MIDD	122	McAlreavy, John	CARL	20	Miller, Robert	FRAN	82
Lay [?], Mary	CARL	30	McAvoy, Margaret	NEWT	151	Miller, Widow	SHTN	167
Lechter, Casper	MIDD	124	McBeth, James	SHTN	169	Mish, Henry	ALLN	12
Leeper, William	SHTN	184	McBride, Robert	CARL	36	Mitchell, James	CARL	22
Lefever, Isaac	WPEN	194	McCall, Sarah	SHTN	178	Monosmith, Isaac	EPEN	74
Lefever, Lawrence	WPEN	194	McCally, Patrick	NEWT	145	Monosmith, Peter	EPEN	70
Lemon, Daniel	ALLN	8	McCalmont, Alexander	HOPE	99	Montgomery, Mary	CARL	25
Lemon, John	FRAN	86	McCandless, George	SHTN	174	Moore, Ralph	CARL	42
Lepard	FRAN	85	McCartney, Patrick	CARL	44	Moore, Robert	MIDD	122
Levinger, Mrs.	CARL	41	McCauley, John	CARL	35	Moore, William	DICK	58
Lewis, John [?]	WPEN	193	McCauley, William	FRAN	85	Morrison, James	HOPE	103
Leyburn, James	CARL	37	McCaunahy, James	SHTN	172	Morrison, James	MIDD	127
Lightcap, Samuel	NEWT	151	McClure, James	HOPE	98	Mower, George	MIDD	121
Lightcap, Solomon	NEWT	151	McClure, William	FRAN	90	Mulholm, Rudy	PENN	65
			McCoskey, Samuel	CARL	42	Mullen, James	SHTN	183
			McCoy, Archibald	NEWT	151			

Occupant Index

Name	Twp.	Page	Name	Twp.	Page	Name	Twp.	Page
Murry, Andrew	CARL	19	Reily, Patrick	SHTN	183	Smith, Henry	HOPE	101
Musselman, David	CARL	47	Rell, John	WPEN	194	Smith, Henry	MIDD	122
Mutchman, Man [?]	ALLN	7	Ress, Hugh	MIFF	142	Smith, James	ALLN	2
Muterspaugh, Robert	SHTN	168	Rhine, Henry	WPEN	198	Smith, John	CARL	19
Myers, Adam	SHTN	170	Rhine, Samuel	MIDD	129	Smith, John (shoemaker)	CARL	44
Nagle, John	MIDD	115	Rhinehart, Frederick	CARL	22	Smith, John	SHTN	165
Nailor, Jacob	WPEN	197	Rhode, Frederick	NEWT	148	Smith, Margaret	CARL	21
Neal, Thomas	DICK	54	Richardson, William	CARL	28	Smith, Peter	ALLN	13
Neil, Lawrence	NEWT	155	Richwine, Christopher	MIDD	107	Smith, Samuel	FRAN	91
Nettle, Samuel	WPEN	200	Righter, John	DICK	61	Smith, William	SHTN	171
Nimans, George	MIDD	111	Rinegar, Martin	EPEN	81	Snider, Baltzer	WPEN	199
Nisbet, Charles, Rev.	CARL	35	Rippey, Widow	SHTN	184	Snider, George, Jr.	FRAN	92
Nixon, John	CARL	18	Road, Philip	WPEN	198	Snyder, Conrad	ALLN	7
Noble, John	SHTN	180	Ross, John	ALLN	9	Snyder, Henry	ALLN	15
Noble, William	SHTN	178	Roup, Michael	SHTN	187	Speice, John	EPEN	67
O'Bryan, Margery	CARL	39	Rouse, Martin	CARL	37	Spielman, John	SHTN	164
Ohenbaugh, Henry	MIFF	140	Ruff [?], Catherine	CARL	45	Spiker, Ebenezer	MIDD	126
Oliver, John	CARL	30	Runion, Richard	MIDD	129	Sponsler, Nicholas	MIDD	106
Oniel [?]	SHTN	183	Russel, Thomas	SHTN	176	Spotwood, James	CARL	23
Orbison, Adam	HOPE	97	Ryan, Timothy	NEWT	156	Steel, John	FRAN	86
Orr, Widow	NEWT	158	Salander, Christopher	MIDD	121	Steel, John	NEWT	162
Orres, Jacob	ALLN	13	Sample, John	CARL	34	Stephens, John	MIDD	106
Osburn, Robert	CARL	45	Sample, Robert	DICK	49	Sterrett, James	SHTN	167
Palsley, John	DICK	60	Sample, Robert (5)	FRAN	83	Stevens, Evan	MIDD	120
Parks, Joseph	SHTN	171	Schell, Henry	CARL	19	Stewick, Joseph	MIDD	129
Patterson, Robert	SHTN	183	Scoot, Widow	ALLN	15	Stinicke, Charles	CARL	39
Patton, Andrew	NEWT	151	Scott, James	SHTN	178	Stone, Hugh	FRAN	92
Patton, Mary	CARL	35	Scranton, Hannah	CARL	18	Strong, Francis	EPEN	77
Patton William	FRAN	91	Shaffer, John	MIDD	125	Stuart, George	CARL	28
Peel, Jacob	SHTN	163	Shaffer, Peter	MIDD	123	Stuart, William	MIDD	123
Peetry, George	NEWT	152	Shannon and Bryson	NEWT	146	Stukey, John	MIDD	116
Peirce, Hannah	WPEN	197	Shannon, James	MIFF	134	Sturm, George	CARL	31
Pence, Peter	WPEN	190	Shannon, James	MIFF	136	Summers, Andrew	MIFF	132
Peoples, John	SHTN	171	Shannon, Leonard	NEWT	160	Surhots [?], Lar- [?]	MIDD	107
Peterson, Israel	DICK	51	Sharp, John	FRAN	93	Swalbridge, William	CARL	34
Pettigrew, James	NEWT	150	Shaw, Alexander	WPEN	195	Swanger, Christopher	MIDD	120
Philips, Daniel	MIDD	121	Sheaver, Samuel	ALLN	17	Swanger, Christian	SHTN	172
Philips, Widow	ALLN	7	Sheffer, John	ALLN	2	Swanger, Jacob	MIDD	120
Pickens, John	SHTN	168	Shimp, Widow	MIDD	116	Swanger, Jacob	SHTN	172
Pilgrim, Henry	FRAN	85	Shoop, Abraham	EPEN	66	Swanger, Michael	MIDD	115
Piper, James	DICK	55	Shoop, Christian	NEWT	157	Sweny, Hugh	MIDD	115
Pisel, Christopher	SHTN	182	Shoop, Jacob	EPEN	76	Swigard, Joseph	NEWT	148
Plunket, Isaac	FRAN	85	Shoutz, Nicholas	CARL	37	Switzer, Frederick	EPEN	66
Pope, John	CARL	28	Sipe, John	ALLN	14	Swoap, Mary	CARL	29
Prats, Samuel	EPEN	78	Skinner, Robert	CARL	28	Syphir [?]	MIFF	131
Quigley, Samuel	SHTN	177	Slone, William	EPEN	76	Taylor, William	MIDD	116
Ramsey, David	MIDD	122	Smiley, Thomas	CARL	32	Templeton, William	FRAN	86
Reed, David	DICK	55	Smith, Benjamin	DICK	62	Thomas, George	CARL	37
Reid, Francis	CARL	26	Smith, Eliphet	CARL	35	Thomas, John	FRAN	94
Reighter, Henry	CARL	42	Smith, Henry	EPEN	78	Thompson, Robert	EPEN	65
						Thompson, Robert	HOPE	99

Occupant Index

Name	Twp.	Page	Name	Twp.	Page
Thompson, William	CARL	25	Wolf, Philip	MIDD	105
Thrush, David	SHTN	173	Wolf, Valentine	MIDD	114
Thrush, Richard	SHTN	185	Womer, Henry	FRAN	91
Trexlo, Peter	SHTN	164	Wood, Joseph	MIDD	129
Trimble, John	SHTN	187	Woods, Jane	DICK	62
Trotter, Richard	NEWT	161	Woods, Nathan	DICK	62
Trump, Philip	SHTN	182	Woods, Robert	FRAN	88
Turner, James	WPEN	190	Woods, Samuel Jr.	DICK	62
Turner, William	DICK	58	Work, Peter	ALLN	5
Underwood, James	CARL	45	Wright, John	SHTN	172
Unger, Peter	SHTN	173	Wright, Joshua	CARL	43
Vance, William	SHTN	177	Yates, Robert	SHTN	180
Vanlier, Elizabeth	CARL	46	Yeints, Henry	ALLN	10
Waddle, James	HOPE	96	Yells, John	MIDD	118
Walker, Frank	HOPE	97	Yengst, Jacob	EPEN	72
Walker, James	MIFF	142	Yengst, John	EPEN	72
Walker, John	CARL	20	Yengst, William	MIDD	109
Walker, William	EPEN	79	Young, James	ALLN	1
Wallace, Jonathan	CARL	30	Young, John	NEWT	157
Wallace, Thomas	WPEN	197	Young, Robert	CARL	47
Ward, Philip	FRAN	90	Zigler, Jacob	MIDD	110
Warsham, Philip	MIDD	107	Zoniser, Robert	EPEN	65
Watt, David, Esq.	CARL	20			
Weakley, Nathaniel	CARL	36			
Weaver, John	ALLN	11			
Weaver, Peter	MIFF	143			
Weaver, Philip	MIDD	125			
Weaver, Vandal	MIFF	135			
Webber, Mrs.	CARL	34			
Weebley, George	DICK	57			
Weir, Margaret	NEWT	161			
Weiser, Christy	SHTN	165			
Wendle, Michael	CARL	21			
Wesley, John	HOPE	104			
White, John	DICK	60			
Whitmire, Jacob	MIDD	112			
Wibley, Jacob	MIDD	120			
Wickline	FRAN	85			
Wiley, Robert	HOPE	102			
Williams, Charles	CARL	45			
Williams, Isaac	CARL	44			
Williams, Samuel	CARL	41			
Willis, Abraham	EPEN	68			
Wilson, Henry	FRAN	90			
Wilson, John	HOPE	101			
Wise, George	CARL	29			
Wise, Jacob, Jr.	MIDD	128			
Witmer, John	MIDD	128			
Wolf, David	EPEN	63			
Wolf, John	EPEN	69			

www.ingramcontent.com/pod-product-compliance
Lightning Source LLC
Chambersburg PA
CBHW060249240426

43673CB00047B/1893